GREENLAND AT WAR

The United States, Germany and the
Struggle for the Arctic, 1939–45

PETER HARMSEN

CASEMATE

Pennsylvania & Yorkshire

First published in the United States of America and Great Britain in 2024 under the title *Fury and Ice*. This edition published in 2025 by
CASEMATE PUBLISHERS
1950 Lawrence Road, Havertown, PA 19083
and
47 Church Street, Barnsley, S70 2AS, UK

Paperback Edition: ISBN 978-1-63624-613-0
Digital Edition: ISBN 978-1-63624-372-6

A CIP record for this book is available from the British Library

Printed and bound in the United Kingdom by CPI Group (UK) Ltd, Croydon, CR0 4YY

Typeset in India by Lapiz Digital Services, Chennai.

For a complete list of Casemate titles, please contact:

CASEMATE PUBLISHERS (US)
Telephone (610) 853-9131
Fax (610) 853-9146
Email: casemate@casematepublishers.com
www.casematepublishers.com

CASEMATE PUBLISHERS (UK)
Telephone (0)1226 734350
Email: casemate@casemateuk.com
www.casemateuk.com

The Publisher's authorised representative in the EU for product safety is Authorised Rep Compliance Ltd., Ground Floor, 71 Lower Baggot Street, Dublin D02 P593, Ireland.
http://www.arccompliance.com

Contents

Preface to the Paperback Edition   v
Preface   vii
Introduction: *The Battle, April 1944*   xi

1   "Greenland's Ice-girt Shore," *Until 1900*   1
2   *Terra Incognita* No Longer, *1900–1939*   11
3   War, *1939–1940*   21
4   Orphan Island, *Early Spring 1940*   33
5   Force X, *Spring 1940*   41
6   Standoff at Ivigtut, *Late Spring 1940*   49
7   The First German Mission, *Summer 1940*   57
8   The Norwegian Connection, *Early Fall 1940*   63
9   Preempting the Nazis, *Late Fall and Winter 1940*   75
10   The Yanks Are Coming, *Winter and Spring 1941*   81
11   Of Dogs and Men, *Summer and Fall 1941*   91
12   Amerika-Bomber, *Winter to Summer 1942*   105
13   The Reluctant Commander, *Fall and Winter 1942*   113
14   The Hunt, *Winter and Early Spring 1943*   123
15   The Escape, *Late Spring 1943*   133
16   Crossroads, *Summer 1943*   143
17   "Bassgeiger," *Fall 1943 to Spring 1944*   153
18   "Meteorology's Finest Hour," *Summer to Winter 1944*   165
19   The End, *1945*   173

Postscript   179
Appendix: *Inuit equivalents of geographical names appearing in this book*   183
Notes   185
Bibliography   221
Index   233

Preface to the Paperback Edition

Sometimes present-day developments intervene and force us to look at history in new ways. This is the case with the subject of this book which first appeared under the title *Fury and Ice: Greenland, the United States and Germany in World War II.* When I completed the manuscript in the spring of 2024, few could have predicted how rapidly Greenland, a territory of the Kingdom of Denmark, would creep up the current agenda. Yet, by the beginning of the following year newly elected US President Donald Trump had made clear that control of the world's biggest island was a strategic priority for America, not ruling out the use of military force to make it happen.

Although the concept of annexing land from a long-time ally has been questioned, and doubts have been voiced about the need for a direct takeover to accomplish long-term American objectives, the geopolitical rationale behind the changing tones from Washington is apparent: As seen from the continental United States, Greenland forms a vast protective barrier to the northeast just as Alaska is a barrier to the northwest. In addition, the Greenland underground abounds in rare earths and other minerals deemed essential for the economies of the 21st century.

Viewed in a broader perspective, the rapidly growing interest in Greenland reflects intensified strategic rivalry over the Arctic among the superpowers. Rising temperatures contributing to the melting of sea ice have resulted in the prospect of the introduction of new sea lanes and the shortening of transportation routes between the Atlantic and the Pacific, at the same time as they are making the region's natural riches more accessible to economic exploitation.

While these developments are of concern to large parts of the public due to their long-term impacts on environmentally fragile parts of the globe, they have also whetted the appetite of major actors old and new. With its huge Siberian coastline, Russia has been an Arctic player since Czarist times, but China, too, has now declared itself a "near-Arctic state" by virtue not of geography but national interests. The stage, in other words, is set for a new frozen Great Game that could become one of the defining aspects of the coming decades.

This book explains how it all started, and how Greenland and the surrounding Arctic region after centuries on the fringes of the known world—or rather, the world as known to the West—gradually was sucked into the vortex of great power politics.

As we will learn in the following pages, American aspirations in Greenland can be traced back to the 19th century and the years around the Alaskan Purchase, but these aspirations only grew from hypothetical to real with the advent of the technologies of the 20th century, opening the Arctic not just for the individual feats of intrepid explorers but also for the mass deployment of military force.

World War II, the subject of this book, was pivotal in this respect. American participation in the global conflict was the shock that within a short span of years catapulted the United States to global pre-eminence, making its presence felt throughout the world, including in Greenland. In 1941, the US Navy and Coast Guard only had imprecise data on its jagged coastline. By 1945, GIs were posted in a network of bases and harbors all around the island, and they were not about to leave: The Nazis had been defeated, but a new Soviet enemy loomed over the horizon.

The reader will be taken back to the world of our grandparents and great-grandparents but will nevertheless find much that is eerily reminiscent of the news of the 2020s. The factors underlying Greenland's importance today and eight decades ago can be boiled down to two major headlines: Location and resources. Greenland's position makes it valuable whether your weapon of choice is the battleship or the nuclear missile. And just as Greenland today is blessed, or cursed, with minerals coveted across the globe, that was the case, too, in the 1940s. Only then the name of the prized commodity was cryolite and it was essential for building airplanes.

These are the constants that make history more than a mere pastime and transforms it into something akin to an applied science. While we often read about the past for mere enjoyment, we may also on occasion delve into the experience of the generations that came before us to be inspired and to learn. It is my hope that this book will form a modest contribution towards this learning in order that we will approach with just a little more wisdom the challenges of a world that, for all its civilizational advances, is as dangerous as ever.

This book is a reprint of the hardback version published in 2024. Apart from the title, only minor changes have been made to the text.

Preface

I remember the first time I saw Greenland. After hours in the plane over the deep blue Atlantic, the narrow coastline turned up in the distance, adding various hues of yellow and brown to the color mix. And then, for a very long time, there was nothing but white. Viewed from an altitude of 30,000 feet, the icecap that covered the entire vast interior of the island seemed to stretch from one horizon to the other. The year was 1977, and my father had signed up for two years as a geography professor at the island's only teachers' training college located in the capital, which was then still known as Godthaab, but now officially, is called Nuuk. We, a family of six, knew an adventure awaited us, but it was a very different adventure from the one I had already started piecing together in my nine-year-old mind.

I had expected to come to a place where the Inuit still lived as they had hundreds of years earlier, hunting seals from kayaks and building igloos in winter. Instead, my initial impressions of Greenland after stepping off the plane from Europe in the mild August sun, very much belonged to the late 20th century: Sondrestrom Air Base, run by the United States Air Force. Although located north of the Polar Circle, it had all the amenities of modern life, including a movie theater that featured the most recent Hollywood blockbusters while serving popcorn and Coca-Cola. My father told me the history of the place. It had been built in 1941, when the Americans first came to Greenland. So, World War II had even played out this far up north, I thought. An interest in the subject had been kindled.

Once we arrived in Godthaab, there was not much to suggest that little more than three decades in the past, this had been a country at war. Except the fact that the entire town—for with a population of less than 10,000 it was hardly a city—was testimony to the war. The frequent sound of explosions when new roads were being built (and the workers had to blow their way through the rocks with dynamite), were a constant reminder that this was not a natural place to create a capital. Still, the signs of what we have come to see as progress were everywhere: buildings made of concrete rather than wood, helicopters in the air, the port filling with diesel-powered fishing vessels. This was the result of developments that were set in motion during the war.

Yet, there were few who had much to say about the conflict, even though you would have only had to be in your 40s to have a recollection of that period in history.

The Americans had usually stayed away from the Inuit population during the war due to an active policy of preventing fraternization. The Germans had been there, too, but far away on the other side of the island. The war had taken place behind the scenes, so to speak, or in distant parts of Greenland where almost no people lived. Even though I had already developed an interest in history, I left Godthaab with my family two years later, without being much the wiser about what had happened on the big island during the war.

***

This book is an attempt to fill the hole in the historiography that existed in the 1970s when I lived in Greenland with my parents and sisters, and has remained to this day. While there have been several attempts to write about individual aspects of the war, for example the German endeavors to set up weather stations on the east coast, this is the first one to address the topic in its totality. Several surprises have turned up along the way. Some were, in a sense, expected. For example, it has not widely been described that Ultra—the top-secret Allied operation to intercept and decipher a significant part of German wartime communications—played a role in fighting off German meteorological expeditions on the Greenland east coast, but it makes sense. Other surprises were more counterintuitive. For instance, few probably realize that in 1940, the US government was almost more at odds with the Canadians and the British over Greenland, than with the Germans. The fact that a Nazi movement emerged among Greenland's Inuit population in the midst of the war, small and short-lived though it might have been, is also not common knowledge.

I have aimed to avoid value judgments about the actions and statements described in this book, trusting that the reader is perfectly capable of doing this without help from others and might even be annoyed to be told what to think. For example, when a German sailor is quoted as saying that a prisoner could feasibly be shot if proving a burden on his captors, I consider it redundant to add a sentence of opprobrium. I believe it will emerge from the narrative when someone behaved in a manner that was in some way morally dubious or counterproductive. That being said, it is easy—perhaps too easy—with the benefit of hindsight to say what historical actors "should" have done, especially sitting in one's comfortably heated office, rather than in sub-zero-degree polar weather. Still, with eight decades having passed, it is time to move beyond the facile heroic tales of the early post-war years and assume a more objective view.

This book builds on extensive research in archives. None has proven more useful than the Bundeswehr Military History Museum in Dresden, whose archive holds the unique collection of documents assembled by German historian Franz Selinger. The sources are listed in the bibliography. Some readers may notice the absence of David Howarth's classic book, issued under various titles such as *A Footprint in the Snow* or *The Sledge Patrol*. This is deliberate. While Howarth's work serves as a wonderful introduction to the subject, it must be dismissed as largely fictional. It speaks for itself that one of the main characters in the book is surnamed Schmidt, even though no person of this name was present in Greenland at the time of the events described.

I have endeavored to make this book as easy to read as possible. This means, among other things, that there will be several instances of dialogue occurring. I decided to adopt this technique wherever it made sense for narrative purposes, and crucially where the words used were given verbatim in the sources, for example, stenographic records of meetings. In other words, no conversation is made up. Some historiographical discussions that are hinted at in the text are dealt with in a more comprehensive way in the note section. For example, this goes for alleged German plans to use Zeppelins to bomb the United States via Greenland at the end of World War I, as well as possible German plans to land airplanes on the Greenland icecap.

A quick note on vocabulary: the word "Eskimo," in widespread use until perhaps a generation ago, is now largely considered offensive and outdated, and in this book the terms "Inuit" and "Greenlanders" have been used instead. However, when original sources are quoted verbatim, the word "Eskimo" has been preserved. The Greenland placenames used in the 1940s are the ones also used in this book. Their current Inuit names—for example Nuuk for Godthaab—can be found in the appendix.

Finally a words of thanks to the many people who have readily offered their help as I worked on this book: Jürgen Bleibler, historian at the Zeppelin Museum Friedrichshafen; Charles Dusch, command historian emeritus, US Air Force Academy; Benjamin Haas, independent German researcher; Christian Elsässer, expert on the Forschungsanstalt Graf Zeppelin; as well as the staffs of the Bundeswehr Military History Museum, Dresden; the National Archives; and Foreign Affairs Oral History Collection. Also, thanks once again, to the staff at Casemate Publishers, including Ruth Sheppard, Tracey Mills, Lizzy Hammond and Declan Ingram, for advice and support. Finally, thanks to my wife Hui-tsung and our daughters Eva and Lisa for putting up with me and my erratic sleep patterns while working on this book.

The Battle

April 1944

"The Americans are here!"

The radio operator Heinz Schmidt, "Heini" among his friends, was running from one cave to the next, dug into the massive glacier in snow-covered northeast Greenland where he and his comrades, sailors of Hitler's Kriegsmarine, had lived concealed for months. They had been troglodytes encased in ice, hoping to stay undetected while they went about their actual business, which was to make accurate measurements of the weather and send detailed reports back to Germany several times a day. This Saturday morning, April 22, 1944, as the cold air filled with the sharp cracks of small arms fire, they all knew they had been unsuccessful. The enemy had located them, and now they were under attack.

In fact, their attackers were not Americans, as Heinz Schmidt believed, but Danes supported and equipped by the US military. How soldiers of the Axis and the Allies could meet in battle in the far north, thousands of miles from the main fronts in Russia and Italy, was the result of one of the most peculiar stories of the entire global conflict. It was the story of how one island, the world's largest, had been moved to near the top of the strategic agenda in both the Allied and the Axis camp, despite its location in the geographical periphery, where men could barely survive.

Technology had made that shift both possible and necessary. The emergence of arctic aviation enabled the belligerents to reach Greenland with greater ease than ever before. At the same time, the need to fly in order to win battles made access to the island a precondition for coming out victorious in the war. Meteorological data from Greenland were required to put together weather forecasts that enabled operations in the air over Europe to be planned. At an even more fundamental level, cryolite from the island's underground was a key ingredient in the production of aluminum, which in turn was needed for making modern aircraft.

There was enough to fight for, but Greenland as a combat zone was like no other. Whereas the battles in Europe involved tens of thousands or hundreds of thousands of soldiers, the war in Greenland was fought on a much smaller, if not intimate, scale. In some cases, the opponents knew each other's names. They moved in small groups, usually just of two or three, trying to outwit each other in a deadly cat-and-mouse game that was further complicated by the fact that the implacable forces of nature constituted a constant menace to all. This made the experience of fighting in Greenland more akin to the war waged in the jungles of Burma and elsewhere in Asia and the Pacific, with the crucial difference that often there was nowhere to hide in Greenland's vast, open spaces.

Indeed, if one was to look for a close equivalent to what really happened in Greenland in the early 1940s, one would perhaps have to resort to science fiction. A war taking place at some time in the future on the Moon, with a tiny number of soldiers opposing each other in a place completely empty of people, far from any logistical support from home, having to rely on themselves for immediate survival, and knowing that their protective gear was the only thing separating them from certain death—this Hollywood-style scenario would probably be the closest one could get.

What also made Greenland peculiar was the actors involved, and how they aligned among each other and against each other. Strange rivalries emerged. The United States and Germany were the main protagonists, but an entire range of secondary actors also emerged: Britain, Canada, Norway, Denmark. The struggle for Greenland was not just fought with lethal weapons, but also with diplomatic tools, meaning that nations that were on the same side against the Axis could still compete for access to the island and its resources: the United States against Canada and Britain, Norway against Denmark. Even Japan entered the fray due to an interest in Greenland as a source of cryolite and as a great power policy test case: if the Western Allies can invade Greenland, Tokyo asked, why can Japan not do the same time to territories in the Pacific?

Like most other things happening in World War II, events in Greenland had a long prehistory reaching back centuries. To understand the background of this story, and also ultimately to understand the battle that took place on April 22, 1944, on the east coast of Greenland, and appreciate how it ended, and what happened to "Heini" Schmidt and his comrades, one has first to dig into the island's deep past.

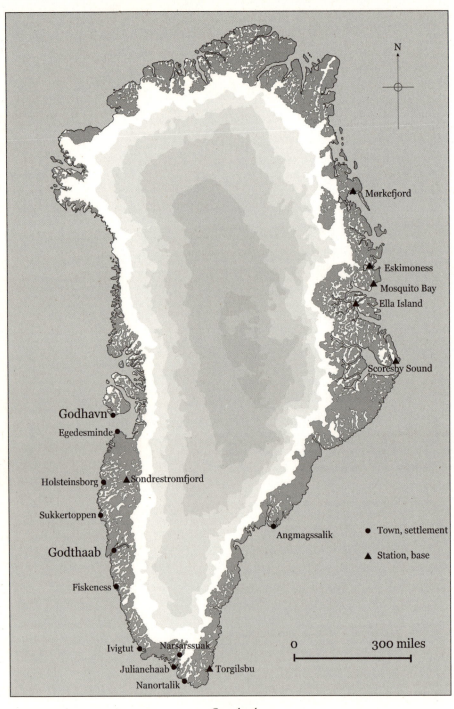

N

Mørkefjord

Eskimoness
Mosquito Bay
Ella Island

Scoresby Sound

Godhavn
Egedesminde

Holsteinsborg   Sondrestromfjord

Sukkertoppen

Godthaab   Angmagssalik   ● Town, settlement

Fiskeness   ▲ Station, base

Ivigtut   Narsarssuak
Julianehaab   Torgilsbu
Nanortalik

0   300 miles

Greenland.

CHAPTER I

"Greenland's Ice-girt Shore"

Until 1900

It was the contrasts that struck German ethnologist Paul Burkert when he visited Greenland as a member of a scientific expedition in 1937. The 43-year-old, who was also an *Untersturmführer* in the dreaded *Schutzstaffel* or SS, noted with appreciation the majestic beauty of the harsh polar country, but also its unforgiving, even cruel character. The ability of the Greenlanders to survive in some of the most inhospitable conditions in the world embodied the constant existential struggle that the Nazis believed to be the basic law of all life, while the natural splendor of the frozen expanses appealed to their sense of aesthetics. Perhaps more than any other place on Earth explored by the followers of Hitler's warped ideology in the ominous prewar years, Greenland represented to them the world they wanted to create over the bodies of millions of innocents. It was a world where man had put behind any concept of good and evil for a single-minded pursuit of triumph over his surroundings.

In a book published shortly after his return to Germany, Burkert extolled the Inuit hunter for his almost superhuman relish in a never-ending wrestling match with hostile elements: "He needs the boundless space, the frothing sea, the raging storm. He needs the struggle in the kayak, the danger of the ice." Burkert declared his unadulterated sympathy with a land where compassion and sorrow were alien notions, describing the spirit that it fostered instead in Nietzschean terms: "I love life because I have the strength to live it. Will I be dead tomorrow? Why not? That will happen to us all." But underlying the real or assumed death defiance was awe at the natural grandeur. "The sun breaks through the clouds. The ice shimmers in shades of blue, turquoise, golden silver and delicate red," Burkert wrote about a trip by boat along a strip of coastline that suddenly reveals itself in all its unconscious splendor. "From somewhere deep below, I come to understand the intense love that the Greenlander feels for his country."[1]

Burkert was very well acquainted with the basic geographical facts. Greenland was the world's largest island, three times the size of the second-largest, New Guinea, and by virtue of its sheer extent, it displayed all the extremes of an arctic climate. The far north was a vast, polar desert with minimal precipitation and average temperatures that rarely exceeded 40 degrees Fahrenheit even in July. In winter, it was shrouded in a five-month-long polar night when the Sun never appeared above the horizon. Further south, the island's deep fjords were warmed by Atlantic currents, allowing vegetation, even low trees, to turn a bright green in the summer.[2] But only along a thin brim near the rugged coastline was human habitation possible. Greenland's most dominant natural feature was its huge icesheet, reaching a thickness of up to 1.9 miles and covering four-fifths of the island's total area.

Like travelers both before and after him, Burkert read too much of his own personality into Greenland's otherworldly landscape. Still, the idea that beauty and struggle were fundamental to the island seemed coherent with the experience of those who had made it their home throughout history, or at least attempted to. They had settled down in successive waves, sometimes overlapping or even displacing each other, at other times finding the expanses completely empty. Greenland was among the last major territories to be populated by Homo sapiens in their expansion to the furthest corners of the world. It had been bypassed by the trickle of people that millennia earlier had led to the peopling of the Americas. It was not visited by humans until about 4,500 years ago when small groups of settlers who had come from Siberia across the Bering Straits arrived via present-day Canada and settled in Greenland's north. They may have initially been lured in by the absence of other people, but that absence had a reason, and several times, all these early immigrants managed was to make a tiny mark on the landscape, just enough for much later archeologists to detect that they had ever been there, before they disappeared again. Only three times during Greenland's prehistory, humans succeeded in making it all the way to the south of the huge island.[3]

The first people of Greenland, now known as Independence I, arrived at about the same time that the Great Pyramid of Giza was built. They constitute a ghostly presence in the island's historical record, leaving behind simple tools but no physical trace of themselves. There is no bone, not even a single tooth.[4] Other settlers followed in their footsteps. They have been given various names by posterity—Saqqaq, Dorset—but they tell the same basic story of man's struggle against the elements, and his eventual defeat. None of the early attempts at settling Greenland lasted, and the descendants of the pioneers either died out or retreated back into Canada. For over half a millennium at the beginning of the Common Era, it seemed as if the peopling of Greenland had been given up entirely. The island was completely deserted, but by AD 700, new groups again started settling down along the northwestern coast of Greenland, and from then on, there was a continuous history of human habitation.[5]

***

The first attempt to colonize Greenland from Europe was born out of violence. The Icelandic Viking Erik Thorvaldsson, later to be called Erik the Red because of the ginger color of his hair and beard, had been involved in a series of deadly clashes with rival clans and was banished from his home island for a three-year period in the 980s. With few other options left, he decided to sail west. Whether he had heard stories of a continent beyond the frothing, icy waves or simply headed out into the unknown is uncertain, but he chanced upon a huge landmass and spent the following years acquainting himself with its jagged coastline. With an explorer's desire to lay claim to newly discovered territory, he gave names to the places he came across, often after himself: "Erik's Fjord" or "Erik's Isles." The land as a whole he called Greenland. "Men will desire much the more to go there if the land has a good name," he is reported to have said with more than a little cunning.[6]

Erik's followers and their descendants settled along the west coast of Greenland, where the climate was generally milder, forming the first permanent European presence in the New World half a millennium before Columbus. The Norsemen reported scattered contacts, often violent, with strange people coming from the north, with darker skin and almost black hair. Most likely, they were members of the Dorset people, and they described them with an odd mixture of superstition and precise ethnographic detail. "When they are hurt by weapons their sores become white without bleeding," according to an 11th-century chronicler. "They have no iron at all; they use missiles made of walrus tusks and sharp stones for knives."[7] Neither party could know it at the time, but the encounter closed a chapter in world history. It was the end of a story that had begun tens of thousands of years before when small bands of humans had made their first forays out of Africa, some dispersing west towards Europe, others east towards Asia and the Americas. For the first time, descendants of these eastern and western offshoots met on the other side of the globe. Man's expansion around the world had come full circle.[8]

The Norsemen launched expeditions beyond Greenland, discovering a vast and remarkably fertile continent. There too, they encountered hostile strangers who were skilled in the art of archery and appeared in hide canoes so numerous that it seemed "as if the sea were strewn with pieces of charcoal."[9] Friction was inevitable, fighting erupted, and the Norsemen pulled back. "Though the land may be choice and good, there would be always war and terror overhanging them, from those who dwelt there before them," they reasoned as they abandoned any plans of establishing a new colony, according to *The Saga of Erik the Red*.[10] It would be centuries before European and American history again merged. Having withdrawn back to Greenland, the Norsemen settled into an existence that was always tenuous, with life never lived far from the edge of extinction. As one generation gave way to the next, their average number for all of the island is estimated to have hovered between 1,500 and 2,000.[11]

Eventually, a regular crisis set in. In the 13th century, a new, more vigorous people emerged from Canada. When they arrived, they replaced the Dorset people, perhaps by annihilating its last members. They were Inuit, descendants of immigrants from Siberia that had crossed the Bering Straits around the year AD 1000. Scattered evidence suggested hostility with the Norsemen, who described the newcomers derogatorily as "Skrælings," a word meaning "wretches." Still, the "wretches" were better adapted to the arctic conditions and often came out victorious in armed clashes with the Norsemen. Icelandic annals described a particularly bloody encounter taking place in a Norse settlement in 1379: "The Skrælings attacked the [Norsemen] and killed eighteen men and took two boys into slavery."[12]

For centuries after the events, the Inuit themselves passed down stories about conflict with the ever-dwindling group of pale-faced Norsemen. In one of the last confrontations, the Inuit covered their boats in white sealskins so that they looked like icefloes and managed to approach a Norse settlement in present-day Qaqortoq in southern Greenland without being discovered. At night, while the Norsemen were fast asleep, the Inuit placed piles of dry bushes around their houses, starting a fire which killed almost all of them before they could escape. Only one Norseman, their leader Ungertok, was able to run away, carrying his little son. One of the Inuit pursued Ungertok, and in the end he was forced to throw the boy into a lake to relieve himself of his burden. Ungertok did not survive in the long run, however. In the end, he was cornered by a group of Inuit but fought back so vigorously with his axe that none of them dared to get near him. Instead, he was felled with an arrow.[13]

While the Norse settlers came under pressure from the Inuit, the Black Death in Europe resulted in a radical reduction in the vital maritime communications with the old continent. It was too much for the fragile colony to survive. The body of the last Norseman, possibly the loneliest person in the world, was found by the crew of an Icelandic ship stopping by briefly in the 1540s. The clothes he was wearing were testimony to a civilization that despite its extreme isolation had maintained a certain level of material comfort but had still not been able to withstand the severe climate and was now gone forever. "He had a hood on his head, well sewn, and clothes from both homespun and sealskin," according to a contemporary account. "At his side lay a carving knife, which was bent and worn down by whetting. This knife they took with them for display."[14]

***

On June 24, 1721, the captain of the ship *Haabet* stepped down into the cabin allocated to his most important passenger, the 35-year-old Norwegian vicar Hans Egede, and told him and his family to make their peace with God and prepare for death. The crew on *Haabet*, which was accompanied by two other ships, had eyed the dark southern tip of Greenland almost three weeks earlier, but for the entire period since then they had been unable to reach the coastline due to dense pack ice. Now they were caught in a violent storm, and as *Haabet* was tossed among the waves amid impenetrable fog, they had no way of knowing what lay ahead. They had watched in horror as the ice smashed against one of the other ships, ripping open its bow, with disaster only averted because crew and passengers had frantically squeezed clothes and everything else that they could find into the gaping hole.[15]

Hans Egede was on a mission that now seemed likely to cost him his life even before it had properly begun. Acting on behalf of the king in Copenhagen as the sovereign of the Danish-Norwegian monarchy, he wanted to bring the Christian faith to Greenland. His primary target was the remnants of the Norse settlers, whom he believed to still be alive, but also the Inuit. Now he was praying for his life, hoping that he would be saved from the elements in the way that had miraculously happened to Saint Paul when he was shipwrecked in the Mediterranean on his way to spread the Gospel in Rome. Only after midnight did the storm weaken and the fog started lifting, and the icefloes surrounding *Haabet* were now more scattered than before. The ship and the people on board had been saved in a way that was "both unexpected and improbable," Egede wrote in his diary.[16]

Nine days later, the ship was finally able to make landfall. "Before we reached the shore, about two miles out, a few Greenlanders greeted us in their small boats, and for the first time, I had an opportunity to study the people for whose sake I had gone through so much hardship," Egede wrote in his diary July 3. "They looked miserable."[17] Later, his impression of the local Inuit population, who were curious rather than hostile towards the light-skinned visitors, improved somewhat. "Both men and women are well-shaped and well-proportioned people [...] and they have strong bodies," he wrote in a general introduction to Greenland for the lay reader back in Europe. "Even though they have no government and no common set of rules to discipline them, they are not lawless. Instead, their good nature is in itself a law to them."[18]

Egede's journey was historic and would change Greenland forever. For 300 years, since regular contact between Europe and the Norse settlements had ceased, the awareness of the lost colonies in the far north had never disappeared completely. In the early 1500s, shortly after Christopher Columbus' discovery of America, the Danish King Christian II had been involved in advanced planning to send ships to Greenland, perhaps in an attempt to reach East Asia by sailing west.[19] Had they ever managed to complete this journey, the seafarers might just have met the last survivors of the Norse colony. It never materialized, and Egede was the first white traveler to return to Greenland soil and to stay there for a lengthy period. Concerned with winning souls for the Christian faith, he set about spreading the Word of God from the moment he disembarked, initially founding a settlement which he called Haabets Koloni, the "Colony of Hope," before moving it to a new place, Godthaab, which was later to become the capital of Greenland.

Greenland had now been pulled firmly back into the orbit of world history, reestablishing the link with Europe that had been severed when the last Norseman died in the 16th century. Egede represented not only strategic interests, having been given permission to go to Greenland by the Danish king, but also mercenary agendas, as the journey itself had been financed by Norwegian firms hoping for new commerce through the establishment of a network of trading stations. In this fashion, missionizing zeal was matched by both political and economic ambition to claim the large island for the Danish-Norwegian kingdom. In the course of this endeavor, a model later used for Australia was pioneered: in a letter signed in April 1728, Frederick IV ordered the release of 12 convicts, all former soldiers, who were forcibly married to 12 women and shipped off to the distant polar possession with orders to help build the new colony. "They are to be provided with the necessary clothes, provisions and pay so that they can serve as soldiers in the fortification to be built in Greenland," the king said in his royal order.[20]

Life in the new land was harsh, and although he had some success winning converts for the Christian faith among the local population, Egede had to watch in agony how the link with Europe that he had helped establish also introduced new and unforeseen misery. A ship arriving from Denmark in May 1733 brought smallpox, and in the subsequent months, thousands died.[21] Egede's own wife did arduous work for the sick but was fatally weakened by the effort. Throughout most of 1735 she was ill, and three days before Christmas of that year, she died.[22] Egede seemed a broken man and saw no sense in staying. His last sermon in Greenland, on July 29, 1736, was a meditation over the intensely sad words from the *Book of Isaiah*, "I have labored in vain, I have spent my strength for nought, and in vain."[23] Eleven days later, when the wind was finally right, he boarded a ship bound for Copenhagen accompanied by his three children and his wife's coffin. "Thus, after 15 years of toil in Greenland, I left the poor Greenlanders," he wrote in his diary.[24]

While Egede ended up in a state of considerable doubt about the feasibility of the entire Greenland enterprise, the island was seen by others as a potential source of untold riches. Dutch whalers were frequent visitors in waters near the island and also undertook an intensive trade with the local Greenlanders. Tension with the Danes grew, and eventually it resulted in violence. In July 1739, a fleet of four Dutch ships was observed in a natural harbor near the trading post of Christianshaab. Sailors aboard three Danish ships approached the Dutch, issuing an order for them to leave Greenland, which they declined. Immediately afterwards, the Danish ships opened fire. "We decided to fire for as long as we had shots left," the Danish commanders wrote afterwards in an account. "We expected that they would not give up, and we resolved beforehand that in case they persevered we would retreat, as they were superior to us in both muskets and men."[25]

The shelling lasted for 75 minutes. All four Dutch vessels saw severe damage to their sails and rigging, and the one closest to the Danish guns suffered two hits to the side of its hull and one to its mainmast. At this point, the Dutch quickly hoisted a flag and lowered it again as a signal of surrender.[26] The Dutch commanders were rowed the short distance to the Danish fleet and disappeared under deck, entering the Danish captain's cabin to negotiate the terms that would allow them to leave Greenland. The four ships were taken as prize. The crews had to return to the Netherlands aboard other Dutch ships unless they agreed to enter into Danish service for the journey back to Europe. "When we were informed that everything in their cargo, with no exception, now belonged to us, a bottle of liquor was handed around more than once," a young Danish sailor wrote in his diary.[27]

In a bid to keep the Dutch and other foreign merchants at a distance, the Copenhagen-based General Trade Company was founded in 1747 and was gradually allowed to establish a monopoly on trade with Greenland. The flip side was that all other entities, whether Danish or foreign, faced a progressively tighter ban on commerce along the coast of Greenland. In a proclamation issued in 1758, King Frederick V extended the ban to the entire Greenland coastline, as well as the surrounding ocean within 20 miles. This applied to "whomever, whether our own subjects or aliens," the majesty emphasized. Foreign crews were allowed to set foot on Greenland soil only if they were shipwrecked or needed fresh water, and they were to depart again as soon as they could.[28] After the General Trade Company went bankrupt, its responsibilities were taken over by the Royal Greenland Trading Department, and the same restrictions applied. Greenland became forbidden territory. The Danish authorities did their best to keep the outside world at bay. Still, isolating Greenland completely was impossible, as the future would show.

***

On June 13, 1811, the British whaling ship *Trulove* appeared off the isolated Danish trading station of Tasiussaq in northwestern Greenland. The sight of the vessel immediately caused a stir among the spectators on land since Britain and Denmark were on different sides in the epic struggle kindled by Emperor Napoleon of France. The following day at 3am, five boats approached the coastline, unloading a party of whalers under the command of their captain, Thomas Forster. "All of them were armed with guns and sabers, as if they were up against a defensive force of a hundred men," the trading station's director, Madz Thomsen Lund, wrote in a report afterwards. *Trulove* doubled as a privateer, and the whalers immediately went about seizing everything they could in the name of the British Crown, painting the name of their ship in large letters on barrels and casks. They were delighted to also find "unicorn bone"—narwhal tusks.[29]

Forster, visibly inebriated, made no secret of what he was doing. "You must remember that a state of war exists between Denmark and Britain," he told Lund while his men were rolling down barrels filled with lard and sealskin to the shoreline. "I am a privateer and can take away everything here."[30] The Danes could do nothing but watch in frustrated impotence, not failing to notice that the British whalers were being helped by two eager Greenlanders. It was a sign, if they needed one, that the trading station was intensely unpopular with the local Inuit, taking up ancestral space without bringing any benefits to them. The looting continued for four days until June 18, when Forster departed with his men, self-confidently promising that he would visit some more Danish trading stations on his way home if he did not have any luck catching whales. "That way, I got rid of this self-invited guest," Lund wrote tersely in his report.[31]

Forster did not follow up on his pledge to continue his raids along the Greenland coastline, but the incident nevertheless had repercussions. It turned out that he had overstepped his boundaries. Since the war had interrupted normal commerce in the North Atlantic and brought great hardship to the people of Greenland, Inuit and Europeans alike, the British government had made an exception for the island, allowing peacetime shipping to continue despite the hostilities with Denmark. In other words, Forster's rights as a privateer had not applied in this case. The consequences were severe. Following an official complaint from Danish authorities in Greenland, a London court ruled that Forster be deprived of his letter of marque as well as his captain's commission. Reparations were even paid. This did nothing to change the fact that in Greenland, the Danish colonial authorities had suffered a blow to their prestige, showing that they could be bullied too. A distinct sense of *Schadenfreude* was palpable among the Greenlanders in the area where Forster had made landfall, and incidents of theft and vandalism against Danish property multiplied. "The Greenlanders are both insolent and gloating," an official wrote.[32]

Despite decades of Danish efforts since Egede's arrival, Greenland by the early 19th century remained thinly populated by settlers from Denmark, and they were barely enough to justify the territorial claims by the king in Copenhagen. Indeed, the Danish hold of the island may have been more tenuous by the time of the Napoleonic Wars than was commonly understood. It was far from a foregone conclusion that Denmark was to be allowed to keep Greenland when Nordic politics after the continent-wide conflict was settled in the British-brokered Treaty of Kiel in 1814. Indeed, in the same treaty, Denmark was forced to cede Norway to Sweden, and since Greenland had to a large extent been a Norwegian enterprise, few would have questioned it if Greenland had also been passed along to Sweden. The fact that it did not happen may primarily have been due to British preferences, including perhaps a wish to keep Sweden from becoming too powerful.[33]

However, at this very moment in history, the British empire was looking north, with a colorful range of colonial entrepreneurs seeing the huge island as a prize worth striving for. A medieval Norwegian text suggesting that Greenland's underground contained marble "of various colors red, blue, and green" attracted an interested British readership and was combined with speculation that its mineral wealth might also contain gold and silver.[34] At the same time, Greenland was seen as strategically valuable for its geographic location. Reviving the dream that had emerged in the 1500s when the Danish king had briefly considered a naval expedition, it was seen as a potential stopover linking Europe to the rich markets of East Asia, provided a viable route through the Arctic Ocean, the Northwest Passage, could be found.[35]

The prospect did not lack backers. The poet Archibald Johnston praised Britannia's "daring sons" who "wave their flag round Greenland's ice-girt shore."[36] The Irishman Bernard O'Reilly, who had observed Greenland from a whaling ship, sounded a similar note, arguing in a book addressed indirectly to the Admiralty that "the present wretched state of that colony renders it of little value to Denmark; but in the hands of Great Britain it would be rendered of great importance in many points of view."[37] Even so, the idea of the Union Jack flying over Greenland remained largely a mirage. No one in a position to take decisive action did so, and yet the idea would not die. As late as in the mid-1850s, the Lord Chief Justice John Campbell, when contemplating what to do with Britain's surplus prison population, echoed the visions of the long-dead Danish King Frederick when suggesting "that these convicts might be sent to the Falkland Island[s] or Greenland."[38] However, the plan was dismissed by critics as too expensive, and the suggestion of incorporating Greenland or parts of it into Britain's global empire did not reemerge in serious discourse.[39]

At the same time that Greenland was receding from British focus, it became a growing concern for the Americans. A first indication of a more activist US foreign policy which would much later pull Greenland inexorably into Washington's embrace, was the promulgation in 1823 by James Monroe, the fifth President of the United States, of the doctrine that was to bear his name, according to which "the American continents [...] are henceforth not to be considered as subjects for future colonization by any European powers." To the contemporaries, the Monroe Doctrine was primarily prepared with the Latin American countries in mind, reflected in the president's reference to his "southern brethren," and to some extent he was also inspired in his bold pronouncement by recent Russian moves to assert influence over the Pacific Northwest. Eventually, however, its logic would apply to Greenland as well, as it was undeniable that the island was geographically part of the Western Hemisphere.[40]

Still, despite Greenland's physical proximity to the Americans, it felt distant if not entirely beyond reach given the state of transportation technology at the time. For several decades, missionaries sent from North America to propagate the Gospel in Greenland were often the only source of information about the island, their writings appearing in publications such as *The United Brethren's Missionary Intelligencer*.[41] "The Greenlanders are very fond of music and singing, and many of the women have sweet voices," one of the preachers, the German-born Johan Conrad Kleinschmidt, reported from Frederiksdal on the southern tip of the island in 1829. "They are so easily taught their lessons. Many of them can read well."[42] However, more than a few of the new converts still stood with one foot in the pre-Christian culture, and in a telling incident, a missionary reported several defections during a period when he had fallen ill and had been unable to tend to his work. "A few indeed had suffered themselves to be seduced by their heathenish acquaintance," he wrote, but added that all of them "except one married pair, came and confessed their deviations with repentance."[43]

It is possible that the American interest in Greenland as a scene of missionary endeavor contributed to a sharpened awareness in the United States of the political significance of the island. Once the internal contradictions between North and South had been resolved in the devastating Civil War from 1861 to 1865, the young nation once again looked abroad with a keener eye, and new and grander visions for America's role in the world took shape. Greenland was sometimes part of these visions.

Former Treasury Secretary Robert J. Walker was a staunch early supporter of US acquisition of the island. "We should purchase Iceland and Greenland, but especially the latter," he argued in 1868 in a report commissioned by the State Department on the value of the North Atlantic islands. "The reasons are political and commercial."[44] Walker elaborated: Greenland had strategic heft, insofar as it could block a major European power—a polite way of saying Britain—from easy access to North America.[45] At the same time, the island also had economic significance, he noted in his report, pointing out the rich reserves of cryolite, which was believed to have potential as a key ingredient in the production of aluminum.[46]

It was, of course, no coincidence that the State Department had ordered the report. After the United States had consolidated its position in the Northern Pacific with the purchase of Alaska from Russia the year before, Secretary of State William H. Seward had ambitions to do the same in the North Atlantic with the acquisition of Greenland from Denmark.[47] However, Seward's enthusiastic promotion of the idea proved in vain, and he failed to gain sufficient followers, just as at the same time he failed to gain Congressional backing for a planned purchase of part of the Danish Virgin Islands in the Caribbean.[48] He was even derided as "insane" by a political rival for wanting to buy "ice-fields in Greenland."[49] He may not have realized it, but he was simply ahead of his time. Although the Americans now put their interest in Greenland on hold, the indifference was not going to last. Within a few decades, they were back in the game with renewed focus on the vast, isolated island.

CHAPTER 2

Terra Incognita No Longer

1900–1939

Greenland was an inescapable geographical fact for the Americans. Taking up almost as much space as the 26 states east of the Mississippi combined, it was impossible to ignore.[1] At the same time, Greenland's importance was not lost on a rapidly expanding nation on the verge of great power status which was beginning to think about foreign policy in global terms. As the 20th century dawned, the island's pivotal position in the North Atlantic, as a giant shield protecting the New World from the Old, was obvious to anyone with access to an atlas. Geologically a part of the Western Hemisphere, yet stretching further east than Iceland, its strategic location which could prove valuable in times of both war and peace, was remarked upon by a growing number of influential writers and thinkers.

Much of this renewed interest in Greenland was driven by technological advances, or even visions about where technology would be in the foreseeable future. In 1916, as much of the world was embroiled in a devastating conflict, the polar explorer Robert E. Peary, who was also an officer in the US Navy, noted that "with the rapid shrinking of distances in this age of speed and invention, Greenland may be of crucial importance to us in the future." In American hands, he argued, Greenland "may be a valuable piece in our defensive armor. In the hands of hostile interests it could be a serious menace."[2] Stranger things have happened, he added, than that an American-controlled Greenland "might furnish an important North Atlantic naval and aeronautical base."[3]

The idea of the island as a stopover not just for ocean-going vessels, but also for airplanes, was precocious at a time when no one had yet succeeded in crossing the Atlantic inside a cockpit, but it was not unique, as it was shared by far-sighted people in not just the United States, but also Canada. Just a few months after Peary committed his thoughts to paper, in April 1917, John Douglas Hazen, the Canadian minister of the naval service, remarked that "with the improvement in aviation [...] that will follow the war it is within the bounds of probability that before long airships may at regular intervals cross the Atlantic, in which case Greenland would prove a convenient and important location on a Trans-Atlantic aerial route."[4]

It was by no means coincidental that Peary was a prominent figure in the public American debate about what to do with Greenland. Waxing lyrical about the island as "the pendant brooch of the glittering necklace of snow and ice which circles the North Pole,"[5] he had led several expeditions across the largely unexplored northern part of the island. An important purpose of these missions had been to chart areas where no man had ever before set foot in the hope that by doing so, he could help bolster US claims to territory where Danish authority was tenuous. It was only natural, he argued, for "geographically Greenland belongs to North America."[6]

This took place against the backdrop of what, in American eyes, was general indifference among Danes towards the island. "[Denmark] gives very little attention to the development of the resources of Greenland, which is practically *terra incognita*," the US envoy to Copenhagen, Maurice Francis Egan, had written in a report to Washington in 1910.[7] It was, in the minds of most Danes, "waste territory," he added in another report.[8] Egan saw opportunity in this state of affairs, suggesting an imaginative if complicated deal, in which Denmark was to hand over Greenland to the United States in return for a number of southern Philippine islands. Denmark was then immediately to pass on its newly won Pacific possessions to Germany in exchange for territory in Schleswig lost in the German–Danish war of 1864. The proposal never got anywhere, as it involved too many moving parts, and would have given Germany a dangerous foothold in East Asia.[9]

While heading down a diplomatic cul-de-sac with his globe-spanning land deal, Egan was, on a more realistic level, deeply involved in negotiations over another Danish territory, the Virgin Islands in the Caribbean. This was a part of the world that was rapidly gaining strategic importance from a US perspective due to the Panama Canal, built between 1904 and 1914, and the cash-starved Danish government was becoming more inclined to sell. In an indirect manner, Greenland also became a topic in these talks. This was due to the government in Copenhagen, which made it a precondition for the sale of the Virgin Islands that the American government did not object to Denmark extending its political and economic interests to all of Greenland.[10] As a result, when the handover of the Caribbean islands was finally carried out in 1917, a side effect that was not much noted at the time, was a significant US concession: Greenland in its entirety was recognized as sovereign Danish territory.

While the dreams expressed by Peary and others of formal American control of Greenland or parts of it were thus crushed, the island's position within the US sphere of influence was nevertheless soon reinforced. This happened in May 1920, when the British government contacted its Danish counterpart, requesting that it be granted the right of first refusal if Denmark was ever to attempt to sell Greenland. "The geographical position of Greenland makes the question of ownership a matter of great importance to the British Empire as a whole and to Canada in particular," Lord Curzon, the British foreign secretary, told the Danish envoy to London.[11] The

US government reacted promptly, telling both London and Copenhagen that such a British privilege, or any similar privilege extended to any other third party, would be out of the question, owing to Greenland's proximity to the United States.[12]

Although the Monroe Doctrine was not mentioned explicitly in this communication, its principles were nevertheless the unspoken rationale underlying the American position, making this the first time that the US government signaled in unmistakable terms that Greenland was covered by this foundational document of American foreign policy, even though it happened with a significant delay, almost a century after it had been announced.[13] It was significant that in its messages to Britain and Denmark the US government ruled out prioritizing any "third government," not just a European one, when considering a sale of Greenland, as this also implied that a handover to Canada would be unacceptable.[14]

At the end of the same decade, in 1929, US Secretary of State Frank B. Kellogg stressed the US position further, making clear in a message to American envoys in capitals south of the Rio Grande that the Monroe Doctrine applied to the entire Western Hemisphere, not just Latin America.[15] In this way, three decades into the 20th century, the groundwork had been laid for future practical steps by the United States government to deny access to Greenland for any European powers and, just as importantly, to establish its own presence there.

While American diplomats were thus gradually consolidating Greenland's position as part of the territory protected by the Monroe Doctrine, the technological advances predicted in the 1910s were gradually becoming reality. In 1924, two US Army Air Force planes crossed southern Greenland as part of an adventurous bid to fly around the world with several stops in between, and in 1933, government circles in the United States again noticed Greenland's importance for international communications after pioneer aviator Charles Lindbergh overflew the island during a mission to test cross-Atlantic flight on behalf of Pan American Airways.[16]

This was just the beginning, according to observers. Vilhjalmur Stefansson, a Canadian-born explorer of Icelandic heritage and a visionary in the vein of Peary, argued in April 1939, that Greenland could play a "unique role" in the development of trans-Arctic aviation. "The practically level top of its ice cap […] forms a continuous and nearly perfect emergency landing field 1,500 miles long and up to 600 miles wide," he wrote in the influential periodical *Foreign Affairs*. "Coastal base stations can be selected which are not particularly windy. On the whole Greenland's climate seems suitable for flying."[17]

Even so, nothing really happened. Years passed without any decisive move by the US government to gain greater access to Greenland. Individual appeals pointing to its strategic significance collided with a military and political bureaucracy that considered it secondary to more pressing issues, including the distant but more feasible risk of invasion by a European power via Brazil, where the leap across the Atlantic was, after all, shorter.[18] As late as in May 1939, the War Plans Division still deemed it unnecessary to push for an American occupation of Greenland. "It is believed that strategic considerations offer no justification for the acquisition of Greenland. Informal conference with Naval War Plans supports this belief," the division said in a report.[19]

Adding to this cautious attitude, the feasibility of building air bases on Greenland was also questioned. Philip E. Mosely, a political scientist and government advisor, pointed out that careful study had demonstrated it was unsuitable for commercial aviation. "Its southern part is dangerous in summer because of fog, in winter because of ice, although ports on the west coast, such as Holstensborg [Holsteinsborg, *ed.*], are usable by hydroplanes during summer," he wrote in a piece in *Foreign Affairs* in July 1940. "While Greenland's ice cap and ice floes may serve as emergency landing fields for landplanes, they have no commercial value at present."[20]

***

On April 20, 1938, US President Franklin D. Roosevelt spoke to reporters in Washington DC, making the sinister point that modern technology had rendered North America less safe from outside attack than at any other time during the previous century. If the United States was ever to find itself at war again with a resurgent Germany, the home front could no longer be assured that it would not be made a direct target, he explained, pointing out that this had almost happened during the Great War that had raged two decades earlier. "We know today," he said, "that in 1918, before the war ended, the Germans were building a Zeppelin with the perfectly definite objective of sending her out in the spring of 1919 by way of the Great Circle Route, over Iceland, Greenland and down to New York, to drop a cargo of bombs on New York City. We have known that from the documents we picked up afterwards."[21]

It was not the first time this extraordinary claim was made. Fourteen years earlier, in January 1924, Rear Admiral William A. Moffett, chief of the United States Navy Department's Bureau of Aeronautics, described at a hearing in the House of Representatives alleged German plans to launch air raids against the US East Coast which might very well have come to fruition had it not been for the Armistice. Specifically, according to the high-ranking Naval officer, the Germans had built the Zeppelin *L-72* explicitly for the purpose of intercontinental flight, modeling it after the *L-59*, which had completed a voyage across the Mediterranean to German-held territory in Africa in November 1917. "She was intended to cross the Atlantic and bomb New York, and consequently everything was sacrificed to lightness," he told the lawmakers.[22]

There is good reason to be skeptical of the claims.[23] In all likelihood, the idea that the *L-72* was tailormade for cross-Atlantic bombing raids can be traced back to 1919, when US Army Colonel William N. Hensley traveled through Germany, inspecting the military facilities of the just-defeated foe. While being shown the airship, he was exposed to and persuaded by his guide's unsubstantiated boast that "she had been built to bomb New York."[24] Still, there was a kernel of truth to it. The *L-72* had indeed become the center of plans hatched immediately after the end of hostilities to cross the Atlantic and dock in the United States. On this mission, however, it would not be carrying bombs. Rather, the crew would be handing out leaflets, and the flight was meant as a gesture to gain goodwill for Germany with the American public. The senior command of the German armed forces, now involved in peace negotiations with the victorious Allies, vetoed the plans, deeming them too risky.[25]

On the one hand, therefore, Roosevelt's remarks in 1938 may have been primarily indicative of American fears about what a future war might bring, rather than describing any actual German war planning. On the other hand, the president's words reflected an underlying truth about an abiding German interest in flying to the Western Hemisphere. They were plans in which Greenland figured prominently. Indeed, the record suggests that during the interwar years, parts of the German military establishment exhibited growing interest in the strategic importance of Greenland. There is also ample evidence that German citizens carried out activities in and around the island which could be considered as intelligence gathering for use in a potential upcoming conflict with the United States in which the North Atlantic could become a major theater of not just naval but also aerial warfare.

To be sure, German expeditions to Greenland during the pre-war years may in many cases have been first and foremost scientific, a view also supported by some modern historians.[26] One example of a mission whose ultimate purpose can be hard to determine more than eight decades later was a voyage completed in the summer of 1938, aimed at catching gyrfalcons in order to bring them to the area around the Reich Hunting Lodge near the German city of Braunschweig. The head of the Luftwaffe, Hermann Göring, was also *Reichsjägermeister*, or "Reich hunt leader," and in that capacity was a frequent visitor to the lodge. It is therefore likely that Göring was involved in planning the expedition, possibly with a view to rearing hunting falcons in medieval style. Beyond that, the expedition yielded little intelligence that could be of any military benefit, according to a modern researcher.[27]

Their Danish hosts, however, were left somewhat apprehensive. "People talked a lot about that expedition in Greenland," said Knud Honoré Oldendow, a senior Danish official specializing in Greenland matters. "They caught some [gyrfalcons], but it was a widespread perception along the entire coastline that these people had a strange interest in acquainting themselves with the location of the Greenland colonies, the port conditions, and so on."[28] This and other German-funded missions during the interwar years could, with a modern expression, be termed dual-use. There was a civilian, mostly scientific component, but the knowledge gathered could easily be applied in times of war. This may also not have been lost on the participants of the expeditions, many of whom had fought in the Great War and were also often to fight in the coming war, for that matter.

In 1929, for example, the German geologist and climatologist Alfred Wegener, who had worked with military meteorology during the war, conducted research in the western part of Greenland in an expedition that also involved reconnoitering for feasible air routes to the interior of the island, according to a post-war account.[29] The following year, Wegener was back in Greenland, on what became his last expedition as he died while traveling across the island's central icecap. While no one doubted Wegener's basic scientific agenda, it was highly likely that many of the results he produced would also be of value to his country's armed forces. "The expedition had undoubtedly a military purpose," the Danish polar explorer Peter Freuchen wrote later in his memoirs. "The scientific data collected were of tremendous importance to European weather reporting, and thus to German aviation during the war."[30]

The year after Wegener's death, in 1931 the celebrity German aviator Wolfgang von Gronau overflew the Greenland icesheet in a seaplane. Gronau, the son of a Prussian general and also a veteran of the war, made no secret of his interest in understanding various aspects of Greenland aviation. "As the route was being prepared, a desire emerged to get to know Greenland better for the purpose of future air traffic," he wrote in a book on his expedition. "Therefore, it was decided to prepare for reconnaissance flights along the east and west coast."[31] Likewise, his expedition helped gain insights into whether aircraft could land on the icesheet in an emergency. "The innermost parts of the icesheet are the most suitable for emergency landings," said an article published two years later, based on findings from his mission. "However, one has to bear in mind that the loose snow can be rather deep in places, so that a landing aircraft may sink in."[32]

On board with Gronau on his seaplane was a meteorologist by the surname of Baumann from the German Traffic Pilot School, an institution that had been set up in the 1920s to allow Germany to build up a capability in military aviation despite the restrictions imposed by the Versailles Treaty.[33] Baumann stayed for an extended period in Greenland, accumulating detailed data about Greenland flying weather.[34] The German activities did not fail to trigger suspicion. Oldendow played host to Gronau during a lengthy stay in the capital Godthaab necessitated by engine problems. "I had long conversations with von Gronau, but never about the actual purpose of his flight missions," Oldendow wrote later. "It was understood that you were not supposed to talk about that. In this respect, von Gronau was not very talkative, unlike on any other subject."[35]

Those who read the published German sources with sufficient attention to detail could be in no doubt that the interest in meteorological observations in Greenland all had a simple explanation: they were key to predicting the weather in Europe. Paul Burkert, the ethnologist and SS officer, traveled to the island on an expedition in 1937 and described it as a "weather kitchen," or, in other words, a place where

European weather was made.[36] In a book published about the expedition, he recalled sitting in his outpost in the high north, listening to a German weather forecast over the wireless and noticing the frequent references to Greenland: "It clearly showed how dependent meteorologists are on Greenland and the extent to which they must take it into account."[37]

It was probably more than mere chance, therefore, that when a three-member delegation from the German civilian airline, Lufthansa, arrived in the Icelandic capital of Reykjavik in March 1939 to explore the possibility of North Atlantic air routes, they were accompanied by two meteorologists.[38] A decade earlier, Lufthansa had offered technical assistance to a partly German-owned domestic Icelandic airline in return for the right to land on Icelandic airfields. This was a potentially valuable arrangement that could benefit German aviation in organizing flights onwards to North America, possibly via Greenland, and when the Icelandic airline closed down in 1931, Lufthansa had secured a promise that during the years until 1940, it would be offered at least the same landing rights on Iceland as any other foreign airline company. It was in order to hold Iceland to this agreement that the Lufthansa delegation had arrived.[39]

The Germans most likely had hoped for discreet talks, but their visit caused significant domestic debate in Iceland, triggering criticism especially from the left side of the political spectrum, while it was covered intensely by papers in both Britain and the United States.[40] The uproar reflected general unease in Reykjavik about German intentions six years after Hitler's assumption of power, especially as his deviousness had been highlighted once again when a few days earlier, German forces occupied what had been left of Czechoslovakia after the 1938 Munich agreement. Besides, even though few might have known it at the time, it made absolute sense to be concerned about the consequences of a greater Lufthansa presence in the North Atlantic. Although it was ostensibly a civilian airline, it fulfilled paramilitary functions, and it was poised to hand over its planes, airports and maintenance facilities to the Luftwaffe if and when war started.[41]

Once it was obvious that the negotiations would lead nowhere, things moved fast in Reykjavik. Only three days after the German delegation's arrival, the Icelandic government declared in a public statement that there was nothing to talk about. No other foreign airline had been given the right to land in Iceland, and therefore, as per the terms of the agreement of 1931, Lufthansa had no right either. But that was only the legal justification. "Most importantly, the severe uncertainty and security around the world has been decisive for the government's position," the statement said, arguing why it would not be the one that granted Germany access by air to a large part of the North Atlantic. In addition, it added, "one must avoid any discrimination when it comes to the regular flights of foreign powers to Iceland."[42]

***

Early in the afternoon of June 26, 1931, Carl Marstrander, a professor of Celtic languages at the University of Oslo traveling under the assumed name of Reverend Jonas Dahl, dictated a cryptical message at the telegraph office in the Swedish city of Gothenburg: "The Gospel is spread across the city of Oslo. Rev. Dahl." There was a reason for the secrecy, and for traveling by plane in order to send the telegram from Sweden rather than from Norway. The message was code meant for Norwegian trappers in Greenland, signaling to them that they were to carry out a planned private occupation of the island's east coast between 71.3 and 75.4 degrees latitude north. It was a bold move in time of peace and bound to trigger the anger of the Danish government, which considered itself the sole authority over all of Greenland.[43]

The following day at 5pm local time, a group of Norwegians led by Hallvard Devold, a 32-year-old explorer, hoisted the Norwegian flag over Mosquito Bay in East Greenland, issuing a written statement in which they said that "in the name of King Haakon VII," they had claimed several hundred miles of coastline, calling it "Erik the Red's Land."[44] The Norwegian government was caught unprepared by the startling development, but after some debate decided on July 10 to back up the initiative by giving it the official stamp of approval. The Danish government promptly condemned the action and brought it before the Permanent Court of International Justice in The Hague.[45]

The Norwegian claims to Greenland or parts of it, had become louder in the period since 1905 when Norway emerged as an independent kingdom after little less than a century in the political union with Sweden forged in the Treaty of Kiel in 1814. To be sure, the Norwegian foreign minister had assured Danish representatives in an oral statement in 1919 that his country had no issue with Danish control of all of Greenland, but Norway had refrained from confirming this position in writing.[46] The signals coming out of Oslo had been mixed, and now it was up to the court in The Hague to pass judgment and put the matter to rest.[47]

The high-profile dispute came at a time when the Danish government's ability to hold onto Greenland seemed in doubt to many Europeans, just as it had done to the Americans. Denmark, never among the major European colonial powers, had in one way or the other let go of most of its overseas possessions in Africa, Asia and the Americas in the course of two centuries of rapid imperial decline, and the loss of its North Atlantic possessions, which also included a loose union with Iceland, would almost seem a logical next step. The German newspaper *Hamburgischer Correspondent* had recently made a stark prediction about the near future: "Denmark has so far not been able to learn anything from its history. It lost Norway and Schleswig-Holstein. It will probably lose Iceland soon, which will drag Greenland and the Faroe Islands with it."[48]

However, when The Hague court finally issued its verdict in the spring of 1933, its ruling was in favor of Denmark, while it declared the Norwegian occupation of part of the island illegal. The main argument was that the Treaty of Kiel had made it clear that Greenland was transferred from Norwegian to Danish control.[49] The ruling saved the Americans a diplomatic conundrum, as a Norwegian takeover of part of Greenland would have run counter to the US principles confirmed in 1920. Norway's political establishment largely accepted the outcome, but for a small number of activists, it remained a burning issue.[50] "You are sharing the fate of many brave and skilled generals who lost battles because of traitors in their own ranks," a friend wrote in a letter to one of the leading activists, venting what almost seemed like a stab-in-the-back theory: "The politicians have behaved stupidly."[51] This Norwegian sentiment of having been the victims of a great historical wrong was to have consequences less than a decade later.

CHAPTER 3

War

1939–1940

Christian Vibe, a 26-year-old Danish zoologist at the start of a career as a researcher of polar wildlife, was on an expedition in northern Greenland in early September of 1939, when he was confronted with startling news from home. Traveling through the empty expanse, hundreds of miles from the nearest major settlement, he had a chance encounter with a friend who had access to a radio. He asked if anything major had happened out in the world. Almost as an afterthought, the friend replied:

"Oh yes, that's right, war has broken out in Europe."

"War," Vibe burst out, in surprise. "How? With whom?"

"The Germans have invaded Poland, and Britain and France have declared war on Germany."[1]

Further south, news that the great powers of Europe had entered into their second conflict in a generation was received with less sangfroid. In the town of Egedesminde, the clerics of Greenland had been assembled for a convention during the last days of August. Many of the middle-aged men had children attending boarding school in Denmark, and the reports of the gathering clouds in Europe had caused them to discuss whether it was time to get them home to relative safety in Greenland. All of them had decided to do nothing, as there was no obvious way that the children could receive the same education in Greenland that they received in Denmark. Now it was perhaps too late for second thoughts. On September 1, at 7am, a 43-year-old minister approached his colleagues who were still asleep in their dormitory. "The war has begun," he said. His back was bent with worry like that of an old man.[2]

The thought of another great European war just decades after the end of the previous one was almost too much to bear. "Events come pouring out of the radio every day," Troels Brandt, a Danish artist, wrote in his diary in the northern town of Godhavn.[3] Modern communications had indeed brought the war closer compared with the previous global conflict a quarter century earlier. Back then, there had been no telegraph installed at Godhavn, and the only news was by ship from Denmark. This meant that during the entire winter of 1914 and 1915, when the ocean had been frozen and no one was able to sail to the town's harbor, the residents had been left guessing about the war. Was it still on? Who was winning?[4]

Now, by contrast, there was almost too much news. Poland fell with shocking ease, and the Soviet decision to attack it in the rear when it was most vulnerable added to a sense of doom. Then, however, a long period of comparative quiet set in, and with it hopes that war on a mass scale could be avoided. It was also a relief to many Danes in Greenland that Denmark had declared its neutrality, kindling wishful speculation that it might be able to stay out of the conflict the way it had done in the Great War. Or so they thought.[5] The outbreak of the Winter War between Finland and the Soviet Union shook that illusion and was replaced by concern that the Nordic region might in fact, find itself at the center of events.[6]

Reactions among the Greenlanders were mixed. Some seemed indifferent to the events in Europe. "They hardly have any inkling that terrible things are happening out in the world," wrote Brandt. When a local community leader was asked to sign a call for money to be collected to aid the Finns, his answer was confused: he could not understand why anyone would want to spend money on war.[7] Puzzlement at the strange logic of the Europeans was widespread. In the settlement of Angmagssalik in eastern Greenland, which had only established regular contact with the outside world in the late 19th century, the oldest members of the community remembered how the first Danes to arrive had impressed upon them the need for non-violence. "They clearly recalled one of the first requirements which was that no one was to reach for the harpoon or the knife if men got into quarrels over women," a contemporary observer wrote. "The East Greenlanders had accepted that, and therefore they had a hard time grasping why the Danes did not demand the same of the evil men in Europe who were now shooting at each other with big guns."[8]

The Danes might feel they were more clued in, but few at the time realized how profoundly life as they knew it, was going to be transformed. Perhaps they did not even want to realize it. In the late 1930s, Denmark's arctic colony shared one characteristic with other European possessions around the world: the people in charge believed that their rule was fundamentally safe, and that the routines they were used to were set in stone. Everything would remain roughly the same, unaltered and unalterable, for generations to come. There might be minor disturbances, even crises, but colonial government could not be challenged. "We have ruled here for 300 years with the whip and the club, and we shall still be doing it in another 300 years," declared B. C. de Jonge, governor general of the Dutch East Indies.[9]

The Danish rule in Greenland was mild compared with the often harsh regime imposed by the Dutch on the Indonesians, but the basic mood was the same. Among these Europeans in their imperial outposts scattered around the globe, there was no understanding that the world of yesterday was about to end. Instead, their minds were dulled by a strange complacency. In the words of a senior official in Copenhagen, "we have colonized, civilized and christened the people, who wish to stay with

Denmark, its mother."[10] A member of the Danish administration on the ground in Greenland voiced similar views, writing in retrospect about the atmosphere at the time: "The colonial relationship was something natural, we thought."[11]

The ultimate objective was to enable the people of Greenland to govern themselves, but it was a prospect pushed so far into the future that it almost had no meaning. "The basic principle of the system was to carefully and gradually guide the as yet far too underdeveloped Greenlanders towards greater maturity and autonomy," a Danish official said later, reflecting a patronizing mindset that was common at the time.[12] True independence, if it was ever to happen, would not be realized for centuries. Caution was the word, embodied in Jens Daugaard-Jensen, an old-school official at the top of the Greenland Board, a Copenhagen-based bureaucracy that tended to all matters related to the island. "He was capable of nurturing a fanatical conservatism in young people," according to an observer. "Change suggesting that the country moved with the times only happened because he was unable to prevent it."[13]

Two senior officials, with radically different personalities and approaches to their responsibilities, had been sent to Greenland to represent Denmark as governors. One of them, Aksel Svane, 41, oversaw the southern part of the island from his office in the capital of Godthaab. In the eyes of many who met him, he personified the factors that kept Greenland from evolving at a faster pace. He had arrived in 1932, and by the time war erupted, he was approaching the end of his tenure and was eager not to rock the boat, preparing for a new position back home. "All his actions, therefore," according to an observer, "are influenced by his understandable desire to avoid any act which would prejudice his chances of obtaining a desirable appointment in Denmark."[14] In other words, he was a good man for a colonial government determined to stay the same.

In northern Greenland, a new governor, 35-year-old Eske Brun, was preparing to assume office in Godhavn. In many ways, he was everything that Svane was not, although he was only six years his junior. By his mere actions, he suggested a novel style, more active and more open to change. "He has erected two large windmills, which are to provide his official residence with power, and he even plans an electric kitchen," a fellow Dane wrote with a whiff of envy, noting that he himself had to make do with paraffin lamps.[15] Brun could be rash, and according to one unfriendly assessment, he was "not young enough to comfortably seek guidance from others and not old enough to acknowledge that the wiser a man is, the more willing he is to seek other's opinions."[16] Still, these were minor flaws that did not detract from his youthful energy and initiative. Brun was to become, in the words of the future Canadian consul Maxwell John Dunbar, "the most important and necessary man in Greenland during the whole of the war."[17]

***

President Roosevelt was awakened from his sleep early on September 1, 1939, by an urgent telephone call from his ambassador to Paris, William Bullitt.[18] Nazi forces were streaming across the eastern German border into Poland. War in Europe was a fact, and the security of the Western Hemisphere was once again imperiled and had to be protected. This would become a key theme in Washington's foreign policy for the next 27 months, until Pearl Harbor tore the United States out of its isolationism. Two days later, as Britain and France declared war on Germany, Roosevelt directed a radio address at the American people. "We seek to keep war from our own firesides by keeping war from coming to the Americas," he said. "For that we have historic precedent that goes back to days of the Administration of George Washington."[19]

While the governments of the Western Hemisphere had taken no coordinated steps during the Great War from 1914 to 1918 to keep the European belligerents at a distance, this time was different. On the same day that Roosevelt's sonorous voice filled American living-rooms across the nation, Washington urged eight Latin American governments to join in an invitation for a meeting on the preservation of neutrality.[20] The conference opened less than three weeks later in Panama City, resulting within days in the promulgation of the Pan-American Safety Zone, stretching from the American coastline up to 1,000 nautical miles into the Atlantic. This area was to be kept "free from belligerent activities," according to a statement issued at the end of the conference, which also made clear that the decision was to be backed up by patrols.[21]

Significantly, the part of the Atlantic that was north of the United States border with Canada, including Greenland, was not covered by the zone. "Back there in 1939 the area of the patrol on the Atlantic was nearer, because there didn't seem to be any danger of an attack on places like Bermuda or Newfoundland, or Greenland, or Trinidad, or Brazil," Roosevelt explained later.[22] Still, the participants at Panama were keenly aware of the possibility that in the fluid situation brought about by the war, things could change fast. "Danger to the security of the American Continent" might arise if any region in the Americas controlled by a European power were to change hands, the representatives stated at the end of the talks in Panama, warning that such an outcome could very well warrant further action.[23]

There were several reasons why Greenland did not figure prominently in early deliberations in Washington DC about the proper reaction to the war. First and foremost, bureaucratic inertia played a role. Senior planners in the American capital had downplayed the island for years, and now they continued to do so. However, there were also other explanations. Transatlantic flight was still in its infancy, and the role that Greenland would later play as a refueling stop was not fully appreciated. As a source of valuable meteorological information, Greenland's worth was widely recognized, but Danish authorities had already established a network of weather stations which produced measurements of temperature, wind and precipitation several times a day, and as beneficiaries of these data, the Americans saw no compelling reason to change existing routines.[24]

Meteorological data was one important Greenland asset; its mineral wealth another. As had been established since the 1800s, Greenland was rich in one universally recognized resource: cryolite. Known among the Inuit as "the ice that will not melt in summer,"[25] it was an essential input in the production of aluminum. Aluminum, in turn, was invaluable for aircraft production, weighing only one-third as much as steel and other base metals.[26] The result was what had been termed an "aluminum revolution." The expatriate Jewish-German economist Siegfried Moos put it succinctly: "The extent and character of air forces are determined by the quantities of aluminum available."[27] To cite one telling example, 85 percent of the Consolidated B-24 Liberator bomber, about to enter into mass production in 1939, consisted of aluminum alloy.[28]

This made the small mining community of Ivigtut in southern Greenland one of the most important strategic spots in the world, since its oval pit located dangerously close to the water's edge was the only place in the world where cryolite was extracted in commercially viable amounts.[29] Just 400 feet long and 200 feet deep, this hole in the ground could help decide the outcome of the war, and yet it was a remarkably small operation. Run by a corporation in which the Danish government owned half the shares, it employed a total of 102 workers and 27 clerical staff and their families. It was, in the words of one author, "a state in the state," administratively sealed off from the rest of Greenland with minimal contact with the locals.[30] The employees lived in apartments with electrical lighting and modern plumbing, were treated at a modern hospital, and ate at a mess hall that served European food and Carlsberg beer. "The map, the climate, and the treeless barrenness proclaim Ivigtut in Greenland," a foreign visitor wrote, "but Ivigtut seems scarcely aware of it."[31]

It was not a direct concern for Germany, as its scientists had developed an efficient technique for making synthetic cryolite, and therefore it did not need access to Ivigtut. Yet, the fact that it was useful to potential enemies triggered Berlin's interest, and German intelligence had been active in the area from an early date, stretching back into the pre-Nazi era. In 1932, the year before Hitler came to power, a German Army officer by the name of Max Grünewald had attracted the attention of the Danish authorities while he was employed on a project to build a meteorological station close to the mine, as the inconsistent explanations he gave about his own background suggested he was a spy. In 1933, Paul Burkert, the ethnologist and SS officer, was also observed near Ivigtut and was shunned by the mine's management who suspected he was on an espionage mission.[32]

Paradoxically, the people to whom the mine mattered the most seemed to know the least about it. Apart from regular shipments of cryolite to the world market via Denmark, the mine supplied two main foreign customers directly, Aluminum

Company of Canada and Pennsylvania Salt Manufacturing Company of the United States, also known as Penn Salt. Up until the outbreak of the war, the stream of cryolite was sufficient and satisfied the demand of both companies with little reason to argue over distributions. It was not a political issue, and most decision makers in Washington DC were not even aware of the existence of Ivigtut. It was a mistake and an oversight, and they should have known. They were in for a rude awakening, as they would realize the following spring.[33]

***

If American planners put Greenland down their list of priorities, they were not alone. The island did play a role in the German Atlantic strategy in the winter of 1939 and 1940, but a marginal one. Like the Americans, the Germans took advantage of the Danish meteorological observations from the Greenland coast, having no immediate need to supplement with their own measurements. The German Navy's activities were also limited. When the campaign against Poland was being set in motion in late August, it ordered the heavy cruiser *Deutschland* and the supply ship *Westerwald* to positions east of Greenland.[34] Their task was "the disruption and destruction of enemy merchant shipping by all possible means."[35]

However, the role *Deutschland* and *Westerwald* could play was initially severely curtailed, partly because Hitler was hoping for a negotiated peace with Britain and France and therefore banned attacks on shipping from the two countries during most of September. The lack of overseas bases also meant that any battle damage sustained would require a return trip to Germany for repairs.[36] Finally, and most importantly, the German dictator was bent on avoiding any incidents that would involve the United States. The Americans were the ultimate foe, the final obstacle to German world domination, but that was for much later, and at this early stage, Hitler would go to great lengths to keep them in their pacifist slumber. Indeed, in mid-September he had pushed his generals to bring about an early end to the battle of Warsaw in order to achieve a decision in the Polish campaign before the opening of the American Congress.[37]

The upshot was that *Deutschland* and *Westerwald* had little to do, and before long they were ordered out of waters near Greenland. Germany had entered the war with a limited surface fleet, especially by comparison with its mighty British adversary, and it had to husband its resources. Adding to the German Navy's reluctance to maintain a presence near Greenland, it was maneuvering in the dark as it had little intelligence about the British Navy's movements. Instead, it had to rely on second-hand knowledge. In one instance, an unnamed Danish citizen acting as an informer for the Germans reported from a trip to the Faroe Islands rumors that the Royal Navy was appearing frequently in Greenland's waters, boarding neutral vessels to prevent essential war supplies from reaching German harbors. It was tenuous intelligence at best, but it was better than nothing, and it was good enough to make it into the German Naval Command's war diary.[38]

In this situation, with Greenland lingering in the periphery of German strategic thinking, a bid was made to place it near the top of priorities. The attempt originated with the chief Norwegian Nazi, Vidkun Quisling. He had been his country's defense minister during most of the East Greenland spat in the early 1930s, although back then he had been in an administration led by the Peasants' Party. He was known primarily for his passive and taciturn demeanor during Cabinet meetings and, according to the justice minister at the time, only really showed any passion when it came to two topics: the perceived threat of socialist revolution in Norway and the question of Norway's claim to Greenland.[39] Quisling left the government position in the spring of 1933, shortly afterwards founding *Nasjonal Samling*, or National Gathering, a Norwegian Nazi party.

He may have given up executive power, but he remained committed to the Greenland cause. He ensured that the call for Greenland's return to Norwegian rule was included in the platform of his Nazi party, both because he fervently believed in the cause himself, and because he assumed, more tactically, that it would be helpful in mobilizing support among the voters.[40] His zeal when it came to Greenland was so intense that he fell out over the issue with his counterpart in Denmark, the Danish Nazi leader Frits Clausen, as he believed there could be no cooperation between the two Scandinavian countries while the problem still festered.[41]

In December 1939, Quisling paid a visit to Berlin and was twice granted audiences with Hitler. A record of these meetings exists in the form of chief ideologue Alfred Rosenberg's diaries, revealing that at the second of these meetings, on December 17, Greenland was placed on the agenda by the Norwegian visitor. This happened within the context of a request by the Norwegian Nazi for German intervention in Scandinavia against what he perceived to be a British threat.

"Mr. State Councilor, are you aware when you ask me for help, that England will declare war on you?" Hitler asked.

"Yes, I know," Quisling replied, "and I expect that Norway's trade will take a temporary hit as a result."[42]

Quisling then handed over a memorandum to Hitler concerning the strategic importance of what the document termed "old Norwegian dependencies", the Faroe Islands, Iceland and Greenland. In order to get the strategic upper hand in its ongoing war with Britain, Germany should occupy these islands in cooperation with a nationalist government in Norway, the paper argued. Subsequently, the Norwegians should seek a permanent solution to the territorial disputes with Denmark, the paper said, assuming that the Danish government would in future be Nazi-dominated, presumably as a result of German occupation.[43]

"Hitler read it attentively but without commenting on it," Rosenberg wrote in his diary.

At the end of the meeting, Quisling was eager to ensure that he was on the same page as Hitler: "Mr. Reichskanzler, have I understood you correctly that you will help us?"

"*Jawohl*," Hitler replied. "I will."[44]

The German Führer's reaction to the memorandum, reading it but saying nothing, is open to interpretation. What went through the dictator's head when he got to the imaginative scheme for a strategic reordering of the North Atlantic is anyone's guess. It is likely, however, that the German leader quietly dismissed the Norwegian Nazi's document as an unwelcome distraction. A German occupation of Greenland would be a straightforward challenge to the United States, likely to bring about conflict with the world's strongest industrial power. If he was careful not to take his Atlantic campaign too far for fear of provoking the Americans, he was even less inclined to triggering their wrath in turn for control over Greenland, a strategic prize that at the time seemed of dubious value.

A secondary consideration on Hitler's mind might be the prospect of sowing disagreement between two fellow Aryan nations, Denmark and Norway, with no discernible gain to be had for Germany. Quisling might have left Berlin that winter believing he had got his admired German master's tacit promise not just to come to Norway's rescue, but also to assist it in recovering lost Greenland territory, but he was wrong. As events of the coming months would show, it would not be the last time that the Germans refrained from getting involved in the slumbering Danish–Norwegian dispute over the island.

***

With the ruling in The Hague six years earlier in the dispute between Oslo and Copenhagen, Greenland had been confirmed as the sole responsibility of Denmark. This was, however, a mixed blessing. Greenland was isolated, sparsely populated, and poverty-stricken. By the 1930s, Greenland had 19,000 indigenous inhabitants. There were no real towns or cities. The biggest settlement was Godthaab with 750 residents, including 50 Danes, "Looking at the few scattered houses one would never suspect [that there were even that many]," wrote a foreigner who passed through.[45] By population size, this was followed by Sukkertoppen and Julianehaab, with about 700 residents each. The rest of the population lived in communities that typically had less than 100 people.[46]

Godthaab, the colonial "capital", illustrated how primitive conditions really were, even by contemporary standards. A few wooden buildings greeted those arriving from the sea, including a red edifice "which might be farmer Jones' chicken coop, but which is actually the colony store," according to an American visitor. A cluster of other cabins contained the main symbols of colonial rule: the governor's residence, the doctor's home, the colony office, the post office, the hospital, and a teachers' training college. "Around and about these more pretentious buildings is scattered what seems like just a handful of small square wooden residences. That, plus the suburban radio station, ship's harbor, fox farm, sheep shelters and cemetery, is Greenland's capital."[47]

In fact, the few wooden buildings were reserved for the small group of Danes, built with timber ferried across the Atlantic. The Greenlanders, by contrast, had homes made from local materials. On three sides, the walls were made from layers of flat stones and peat, while the fourth side was a wooden wall with a door and windows. It looked basic and it was, but the result was an efficiently insulated building that could be easily heated, which was an advantage given the scarcity of fuel in the area.[48] All Greenland homes were lit with fish-oil lamps, as kerosene lamps were considered too much of a fire hazard and banned. Rather than actually lighting up houses in the long Arctic nights, the lamps "spread the dimness of an Egyptian sepulcher," a Dane remarked.[49] The only modern entertainment was once every two or three weeks, when the gymnasium at the teachers' training college was converted into a movie theater. "Anyone who has the necessary 3c to buy a ticket can see, for example, a French movie of a Russian war story with Danish subtitles," the American visitor said.[50]

Godthaab was not even representative of life as it was lived by most Greenlanders. For testimony to the conditions faced by the majority, one would have to go to a place such as Angmagssalik, a small settlement on the less developed east coast. There, all water had to be carried by hand from a brook for half a mile along a path that turned dangerously slippery when water inevitably spilled from the buckets and froze in the chilly temperatures. The job was carried out by boys and young men who saw it as a first step up the ladder towards the eventual fulfilment of the dream of getting a job in the colonial administration, and they braved all the attendant hazards, including the occasional polar bear that would turn up on the path. "It was tough to be a water carrier, and the heavy duty destroyed the health and broke the spirit of many boys, but it was the only way to carry water to the various houses," a Danish colonial official wrote.[51]

Greenland's material backwardness was to some extent a product of its isolation, and its isolation was largely by design. The Danish authorities had traditionally sealed the island off from the outside world in order to preserve a Danish monopoly on trade, but also to protect the population from epidemic diseases. This had been only somewhat successful. In the 1930s, there was a common saying among Greenlanders: "Every year, the first ship from Denmark brings the flu."[52] Most epidemics were harmless, but some were not. The many instances of venereal disease were evidence that the official policy of preventing interaction between outsiders and the locals could only be enforced to some extent.

During the years from 1934 to 1936, a flu epidemic raged through Greenland, killing more than three percent of the population.[53] A Danish nurse described the view at a particularly badly affected area, where entire communities were collapsing. "They were all about to starve to death," she later recalled. "No one was able to get food. The grown-ups had died already, and some children had tried to kill a dog to get a little to eat, but their strength had not sufficed."[54] Tuberculosis was, however, the main killer, and at any one time, 70 percent of the patients in hospitals suffered from the disease. In the estimate of medical professionals, no other society in the world was as badly affected as a percentage of the total population.[55]

Even in normal times, without devastating epidemics, death was a frequent visitor. Two groups especially were at risk. One consisted of young men starting out as trappers and exposing themselves to the kind of dangers that their more experienced elders knew how to avoid. The other group was made up of young children. Given the poor state of public health, child mortality was high. "If they lived to become a year old, the thinking was that they would probably survive," a Danish resident wrote. "Therefore, the one-year birthday was a big day in the life of all Greenland families."[56]

Those in charge were very well informed about all this, and mostly had to tell themselves that it could have been even worse. "Compared with Denmark, everything was primitive and insufficient," wrote Eske Brun, the "northern" governor, in his memoirs. "But compared with what happened elsewhere in the world with similar natural and geographic conditions and an equivalent economic foundation, it was much."[57] In other words, Greenland was not Africa. A global survey of literacy carried out by the US government in 1929 gave Greenland good marks for its educational system. "The illiteracy rate is low," it stated.[58] Schools in Greenland had been expanded to an extent where almost all young Greenlanders had the opportunity to get a basic education.

However, in some remote areas, where the Danish colonial administration had only been active for a few decades, many grownups were still unable to either read or write. Math was also not widespread among adults in some isolated communities. "They were not used to having money as all trade took place in the local shop, where they handed in skins and got products in return," wrote a Dane who lived in Greenland in the 1930s.[59] Besides, for all the efforts to make education available, most Greenlanders spoke only their Inuit language and were unable to communicate in Danish. Similarly, very few Danes spoke the Greenland language, erecting an invisible barrier between the two groups.[60] More advanced or specialized education was also only available in Denmark, and no more than a select few were ever given that chance. The effect was that virtually all senior positions within government and business were occupied by Danes.[61]

The inequality had a political dimension, too. For a country like Denmark, which prided itself with one of the world's oldest democracies, it was remarkable how little the Greenlanders were allowed to participate in their own politics. A form of limited democracy existed in Greenland in the late 1930s. All male residents were able to vote for members of local councils, which had some ability to make decisions for the community. Still, the most important power rested with the Danish colonial administration, headed by the two governors.

One group in particular was left behind. Women were facing the toughest odds and were often given the physically most demanding work by the male members of their families. There was no female suffrage, and there would not be one until 1948, nearly three decades after women in Denmark were allowed to vote.[62] The lack of political representation was matched by an inferior position in legal affairs, reflected in the outrageous decisions of some of the courts. In 1938, a judge made clear what he considered the proper distribution of power in the family, ruling in a case where a woman had married a man who had children from an earlier marriage: "When Greenland spouses don't see eye to eye, the opinion of the man in the house must be decisive [...] When the man beats his wife for the sake of the children, she must not let it out on her stepchildren."[63]

CHAPTER 4

Orphan Island

Early Spring 1940

The 30-year-old Danish artist Troels Brandt was sitting in his studio on the outskirts of the town of Godhavn on the morning of Tuesday, April 9, 1940. It was a beautiful day. The sun was shining from a bright, cloudless sky, its rays reflected in the stark, almost blinding white of the icefloes that were drifting by so slowly in the ocean outside that they seemed motionless. In the distance, Brandt eyed a lone figure approaching along a path that was carved out in the deep snow and connected his home to the town center. It was Hugo Holten-Møller, the operator of the telegraph station. He was the bearer of shocking news. Early on the same day, four time zones away, Denmark had been occupied by German forces. Scattered fighting had taken place along the border, but after a few hours, the government in Copenhagen had ordered a halt to all resistance.[1]

Brandt followed Holten-Møller the short way back. The news had already spread among the tiny cluster of houses that constituted downtown, and the small community of Danes were all in a daze. The first sparse information about the invasion, which was part of a larger German operation aimed at seizing control of Norway, had reached Greenland between 8 and 9am, but little else was known.[2] Members of the Wehrmacht had cut off radio communications from Denmark, and all that was left was silence. Brandt and others assembled in Holten-Møller's private home, listening to snippets of information from British and German broadcasts in the hope of somehow being able to piece together a more complete picture of the situation and what it might mean for them in Greenland and for their loved ones trapped in now-occupied Denmark. "It is so overwhelming that it is almost beyond one's grasp," Brandt wrote in his diary. "As of today, everything has changed."[3]

The top official in Godhavn, Eske Brun, the 35-year-old who had built a modern home powered by windmills, was nowhere to be found. He had departed by dawn on a dog sleigh to go hunting for narwhal with a small group of experienced trappers. He was finally located on a frozen fjord and informed about the radically changed situation. Rushing back, he whipped his dogs so mercilessly that he later felt bad about it.[4] To him too, the German attack came as a surprise. There had been worrying reports of German naval movements in the Baltic, but most residents of Greenland had been half expecting that it was a false alarm.[5] "We had hoped so strongly that it had almost turned into a belief that we would once again see our nation make it through without being pulled into the conflict," Brun said later.[6]

It would be weeks before the population of Greenland got the full account of what had happened on that history-changing morning of April 9, 1940. It was the end of the Phony War, the period of strange inactivity along the major frontlines in Europe that had set in after the completion of the German conquest of Poland the previous fall. Denmark was needed by the Nazi war machine mainly as a staging area for the invasion of Norway. Shortly after 4am local time, a German force consisting of the 170th and 198th divisions reinforced by a brigade, had crossed Denmark's southern border and disembarked in various harbors on islands in the eastern part of the country, including the port of Copenhagen. After scattered fighting, and under the threat of German bombing of the capital from the air, the Danish Army had been ordered to stand down. In a matter of just hours, Denmark in its entirety had come under the heels of a foreign power for the first time in its thousand-year history as an independent kingdom.[7]

Throughout Greenland, everything stopped, and some flew the flag at half-mast.[8] Others found other more unorthodox ways to cope with the feeling of powerlessness. Apollus Noassen, the head of the municipal council in the small settlement of Fiskeness, threw away the cigar he had just lit and vowed not to smoke again until Denmark had been liberated.[9] The Greenlanders were surprised to see Danes, who normally maintained a stiff upper lip in public, hug each other and weep uncontrollably.[10] "*Qavdlunait nunanguat*," they said, shaking hands with Danes they met. "Poor little Denmark!"[11] Some Greenlanders were contemptuous. "Those of us who have been to Denmark and have seen both soldiers and warships—those of us who are familiar with Danish history and have heard about defeats but also Danish victories—we don't understand that you couldn't offer more resistance," one of them said.[12]

Often, the Greenlanders tried to make sense of the events in their own words. Christian Vibe, the young zoologist who had heard about the outbreak of the war in Europe while traveling in the wilderness, was still far from any major human habitation, and only learned about the occupation of Denmark when reaching a depot and finding a can of pemmican, a mixture of tallow and dried meat, on which an ominous text had been engraved with a knife in Inuit language: "The Germans take all the meat away from the Danes. Only the King has not lost heart. There is no kerosene in the shop."[13]

Generally, the confusion among the Greenlanders was as deep as among the Danes. "Those who understood what it meant were in a sinister mood wondering what would now happen to them," an eyewitness reported.[14] Recognizing the need for better information, the principal of a school for teenage boys resolutely organized a lecture at the local assembly hall, pulling out a large map of Europe in order to explain the war through an interpreter.[15]

Memories of occasional scarcity during the previous World War were fresh for some, and tidy gardens were broken up and covered with rows of potato plants.[16] Some people panicked and started hoarding necessities,[17] prompting the authorities to threaten hefty fines for this kind of behavior,[18] while at the same time also reassuring the population there was no need to worry: following efforts to replenish stocks during the months since the outbreak of war in Europe, there would be enough to go around at least until early 1941.[19] Still, fuel consumption was reduced, and traffic with engine-powered boats, the most frequent way of connecting the isolated communities with each other, was curtailed. In some small communities, letters were now again being carried by kayak, as in the olden days.[20]

Aksel Svane, the governor of southern Greenland, moved swiftly to enforce order, calling on Greenlanders and Danes to pull through the hard times together. "Under the impression of these shocking events," he wrote in a proclamation from his office in the capital of Godthaab, "it is my duty in the name of the Danish government to encourage all Greenlanders and Danes to individually do their utmost to ensure that life here in Greenland can continue in its usual peaceful manner."[21] Still, what truly united all residents of Greenland, far more than any official exhortations could do, was a sense of intense isolation. "Everybody, both Greenlanders and Danes, felt cut off from the outside world at the news of the events on April 9," said Frederik Lynge, a merchant from Kutdligssat, a mining town on the west coast of Greenland.[22]

For several days after the news of the occupation, residents in Godthaab looked anxiously down the fjord that connected their town with the ocean, half-expecting German warships to appear over the horizon.[23] "All were looking with concern towards the future," said Gerhard Egede, a vicar. "Perhaps we were also condemned to turmoil and suppression."[24] Some were equally concerned about the prospect of a British occupation of Greenland, similar to what had happened to the Danish-controlled Faroe Islands north of Scotland, where forces sent from Britain had disembarked as early as April 11.[25]

In the absence of reliable news, speculation was rife. The German occupation of Denmark had been largely peaceful, but that did not prevent false rumors from circulating that a series of Danish cities had suffered heavily from air raids. "A very large number believe that whatever they hear from Denmark, whether through newspapers, radio, letters or telegrams, is a lie," a Danish resident reported. "Especially they believe that only letters offering a 'rosy' version of the situation slip through the censors and reach Greenland."[26]

For several weeks, the mood was depressed among the Danes. "It was easier to cope if you lived in a really small community and could forget about it rather than constantly running into other Danes and be reminded of what had happened," said a Danish woman from the town of Nanortalik.[27] One thing was certain. Life had taken an unexpected turn for the Danes in Greenland, many of whom had planned to stay on the island only for a limited period of time, perhaps a couple of years, but now had to face the fact that events in Europe meant a complete reorientation. "It may be that the future will mean that some Danes will never see their country again," Svane said. "As governor my view is that our endeavors are now tied to this place. This is what all our capabilities must be focused on."[28]

**

In Washington DC, there had been no forewarning about Germany's intention to invade Denmark. Henrik Kauffmann, the suave 51-year-old Danish envoy to the United States, had left his residence at 2343 Massachusetts Avenue and gone to Charleston, South Carolina with his wife to watch the azaleas bloom. Late on April 8, just before midnight, he received a call from Povl Bang-Jensen, his enthusiastically anti-Fascist right-hand man, informing him that Nazi troops were now standing on Danish soil. "I hardly had time to put on my clothes on top of my pyjamas before rushing to [a train bound for] Washington in a taxi," Kauffmann recalled later. "It all happened so fast that a friend who was assisting me broke a toe in the rush."[29]

Once back in Washington DC on the morning of April 9, Kauffmann returned to an office in disarray. Bang-Jensen and Agnar Klemens Jonsson, another member of Kauffmann's staff, had spent the entire night trying in vain to reach Copenhagen and get more information on what was happening on the ground while also fielding incessant phone calls from inquisitive journalists who had been alerted to the sensational news from Denmark. "Truth be told, my impression of the first days after the occupation of Denmark was that we, both I myself and the other members of the legation, felt that everything was like one big chaos," Jonsson recalled later. "We had no connection to the [Danish foreign] ministry, and we felt as if we had nothing to refer to, and it seemed quite meaningless to continue the daily work."[30]

Kauffmann, too, was unsure how to react. After briefly passing by the Danish legation,[31] Kauffmann went straight to see Adolf A. Berle, assistant secretary of state with a special interest in Scandinavian affairs, and also a friend of Kauffmann's. The Danish envoy wanted personal advice about his status now that the Danish government was no longer a free agent. Berle was reluctant to speak out but shared his perspective anyway. "I said I thought that there was such a thing as Denmark and would continue to be, even though its government was temporarily submerged; that I thought he might say so and continue to represent it, even if it was, for the time being, nothing more than an idea in the breasts of a few courageous Danes," Berle wrote in his diary. "Henrik clasped my hand and left, in tears."[32] The passion that Kauffmann demonstrated during the meeting on that fateful day would be decisive for Berle's future views of the Danish envoy.[33]

It seems that Berle's words of encouragement, even though they were accompanied by a remark that the present situation implied "tremendous danger to him and his family," were instrumental in swaying Kauffmann towards defiance. Shortly afterwards, the Danish diplomat met Jay Pierrepont Moffat, the head of the State Department's Westen European Division, and he now seemed significantly more determined. "He said that he assumed that his Government was incapable of independent action because it was in the hands of Germany," Moffat wrote in his diary. "That being the case he would not follow any instruction he might receive from it, as he, Henrik Kauffmann, would not serve Germany either directly or indirectly."[34]

Kauffmann was now ready to tell the public about his stance. Meeting with reporters, he stated that he was not prepared to take orders from the German government. "I represent Denmark and the King of Denmark here and nobody else. Denmark cannot be considered free as long as she is under the military control of a foreign power," he said.[35] The same evening, he spoke on national radio, striking some of the same notes but now being less direct about his refusal to take orders from Copenhagen: "I will work for one thing alone, the re-establishment of a free and independent Denmark. Many will work with me and I know we shall succeed."[36]

It was typical of Kauffmann, born in Frankfurt, Germany, to a Danish father and a German mother, to draw on his personal connections, in this case Berle, in the hour of crisis. A people person who liked to stay informed by working his network of acquaintances, he was the envy of the diplomatic corps, with connections stretching from the Soviet Foreign Ministry to the White House.[37] President Roosevelt was known to be very fond of him,[38] and in the words of Secretary of State Cordell Hull, he was "a dignified man of great courage and integrity"[39] Married to the daughter of US Rear Admiral William D. MacDougall,[40] he was helped in all his efforts by his good looks and his significant personal charm. "Not only the ladies of the diplomatic corps, but also its gentlemen acknowledged him as 'the best looking man in Washington'," according to an official who knew him well.[41]

***

The question of Greenland was lingering in the background the entire time in Washington DC, as news of the German aggression ticked in. The sources suggest that Kauffmann did not discuss the status of the island during April 9, but due to its geographical proximity, it was at the forefront of American minds right from the outset, although there was also a clear sentiment of having been caught on the wrong leg on a subject that should have been the subject of more attention. President Roosevelt was on the Presidential Special Train en route from the hamlet of Highland, upstate New York, to Washington DC, when at 2:15pm he agreed to an impromptu press conference with journalists traveling with him.

"If Germany has taken Denmark, does that extend Germany's domain into Greenland?" a journalist asked.

"You see, the trouble is this: We are all talking about things we don't know anything about. Nobody knows what has happened to Danish sovereignty at the present time," Roosevelt replied.[42]

The president was stalling for time, holding back any more consequential statements until after he had met with his closest advisors in Washington DC and been updated on the events in Europe. Luckily for Roosevelt, Cordell Hull had done his homework. "My associates at the State Department brought me maps showing that Greenland was wholly, and Iceland largely, in the Western Hemisphere," the secretary of state wrote in his memoirs. "Therefore the islands fell within the provisions of the Monroe Doctrine."[43] This interpretation of geography was duly shared with Kauffmann when he met Roosevelt the following day in the White House. "We agreed, of course, that Greenland belonged to the American continent," the Danish envoy told reporters as he left the Executive Mansion.[44]

The political ramifications of spelling this out were considerable. If Greenland was covered by the Monroe Doctrine, the US government was ultimately obliged to prevent German attempts at landing forces on the island or otherwise oppose German claims to the strategic territory, taking the United States a step further to active participation in the war. A memo hastily prepared by a junior State Department official on the day of the German invasion of Denmark said as much, concluding that the doctrine was clearly applicable "to the present possibility that Germany may absorb title of sovereignty to Greenland and Iceland."[45]

It is therefore no surprise that Roosevelt himself was careful about what he said in public, lest he alienate the large number of Americans who did not want their country to be involved in the European conflict. When meeting with the Press at the White House on April 12, he studiously skirted the issue of Greenland and the Monroe Doctrine, calling it "very, very premature."[46] In fact, the president had already made up his mind and did believe that the island was covered by the doctrine, but he thought the American public was not ready for the idea yet.[47] He chose instead to broach the subject of increased US engagement with the island in a less drastic manner, suggesting a humanitarian mission that would transport supplies to the isolated population now that shipments from Denmark had been cut off. "I think the American people will be glad to chip in and help those people go through the next winter," he said.[48]

On April 18, when once again talking to journalists, Roosevelt was more forthcoming, admitting that due to his concern about a negative reaction from the public, he had not been completely earnest when discussing Greenland with them less than a week earlier. "The American people are way out ahead of me," he said. "I think I am right in saying that most of the American people today, as most of you sense, would O.K. it if this Government said tomorrow that Greenland is inside the

Monroe Doctrine. They are ahead of their Government. Now, that is the actual fact."[49] In practical terms, he suggested that the United States might take responsibility for Greenland as long as Denmark was unable to shoulder this burden. "I am thinking a little bit at the present about trusteeship," he said.[50]

At least part of the American public was backing the idea of a more activist approach to Greenland. One day earlier, Edith Rogers, a Republican Congresswoman from Massachusetts, had called for a US protectorate of the island. "It is only six hours by air from New York," she had said in the House of Representatives on April 17. "Considering it as a naval base, an air base, a submarine base, this territory must not fall into the hands of any European country at the present time."[51] To emphasize her point, she also hung in the lobby of the House two maps showing "Greenland's relation to Europe, Greenland's relation to the Western Hemisphere, and its great importance to us."[52]

It was paving the way for a greater American presence in Greenland that the island's own government, cut off from Denmark, was actively looking to Washington for protection. At the very same time that Roosevelt was making his remarks about a trusteeship, the two governors, Svane and Brun, sent a telegram to Kauffmann, broaching the subject: "Given Greenland's current situation, the governors agree [...] to directly request political and maritime protection from the US government."[53] Two days later, on April 20, Kauffmann passed on the request to his good friend Berle, the assistant secretary of state, along with a suggestion that a Coast Guard ship would be a welcome gesture. Berle was positive, but cautious. "Any request they might make for consideration of their special situation would receive sympathetic consideration here," he said.[54]

To some members of Roosevelt's administration, the Monroe Doctrine was mainly an excuse for extending American power to Greenland at a time when the island was left dangerously exposed in the wake of the German occupation of Denmark. This became clear just after Berle's meeting with Kauffmann, when the assistant secretary of state was talking over the phone to Henry Morgenthau, the treasury secretary, who was involved in Greenland matters mainly because the US Coast Guard, whose ships would potentially be sent to waters around the island, was in the jurisdiction of his department in peacetime.

"Greenland, which is nothing but a chunk of ice, as you know, is a little closer to home [than Iceland] and an air base, for instance, on the southern tip of Greenland could make us a considerable lot of nuisance. So if anybody were going to rake it in, we'd prefer to rake it in ourselves," Berle said.

"What I don't understand is this, in the eyes of international law, and maybe you can explain it to me: On what basis have we got to act as protector for Greenland?" Morgenthau asked.

"We have none," Berle replied.

"I mean, I can understand why it's to our interest to do it, but what's the excuse we are going to give?" Morgenthau persisted.

"Well, the excuse is that President Monroe made that statement a few thousand years ago," Berle said, with deliberate exaggeration.[55]

Shortly afterwards, the Coast Guard was readying a ship to go to Greenland.[56] Thus, just days after the German strike north against Denmark and Norway, Greenland's fate had been set on a new path, for the first time in history veering towards the American sphere of influence. To be sure, weeks and months would pass before the United States would be ready to back this fact up with military power. Indeed, in April 1940, the US government maintained a "hands-off" policy towards Greenland and still did not have the right to place even one armed man on its soil, but a first step had been taken in that direction.

Yet, the situation was extremely complex and much more than just a simple matter of keeping Germany away from the Western Hemisphere. Necessitating a brand of American diplomacy that was both hard-hitting and subtle, the range of actors quickly turned out to be wider than most would have imagined at the outset. One of these actors was surprisingly close to home, just north of the American border. Canada was about the enter into the fray in an unexpected fashion.

CHAPTER 5

Force X

Spring 1940

On April 9, just hours after German troops crossed the border with Denmark, Fraser Bruce, the vice president of the Aluminum Company of Canada, or Alcan, penned a letter to Norman Robertson, a senior official with the Department of External Affairs in Ottawa.[1] The news from Europe was a source of great concern to the aluminum executive. It left open the fate of the Ivigtut mine, without which Alcan would be unable to keep up its annual production of 160,000 tons of aluminum. As Norway had also been invaded, and Great Britain and France had relied on Norwegian smelters for a sizeable tonnage of aluminum, the importance of Canadian aluminum production, and, consequently, Greenland cryolite, could not be stressed enough. "This matter, in fact, is so important to us, and to the Allied aluminum industry, that we urge the Canadian Government to see that immediate action is taken to protect the Greenland cryolite mines and ensure their production for the Allies," he wrote. Alcan, he pointed out, would be happy to play its part: "Should it be decided to occupy Ivigtut, we would be only too glad to place our extensive mining experience at your disposal."[2]

In fact, a transition to the new synthetic technologies that Germany relied on were within Alcan's grasp, but it was considered costly and time-consuming.[3] It was an important company, essential for the Canadian economy, and the government listened. Bruce's letter triggered a sense of alarm in Ottawa, where officials began laboring under the impression that Canada was in a race against Germany to get to Greenland first, and that Canada might lose this race. On the day of the invasion of Denmark, the Department of External Affairs reported ominously that "enemy ships" were heading in the direction of Southern Greenland, raising concern about possible interference with the cryolite production at Ivigtut.[4] Hugh Keenleyside, a senior advisor at the department, reiterated in a memo shortly after that "certain German vessels are reported to be heading for Greenland."[5] The concern was quickly shared with the prime minister, William Lyon Mackenzie King. "Found little comfort in new problem of enemy approach to our shores through Greenland, having the one mine which can supply cryolite for aluminum manufacture," the premier wrote in his diary on April 11.[6]

In fact, no German ships were on the way to Greenland, but the flawed intelligence that had led to this perception meant that the Canadian decision makers thought they had to act fast. Keenleyside suggested in his memo that two or three naval and air bases should be established on the Greenland coast. "At least one of these—that at Ivigtut, the site of the cryolite deposit—should be established at once," he stressed, referring to the need to preempt a German takeover. Oscar D. Skelton, undersecretary of external affairs, argued that Canada, a North American country, would face less American opposition on the grounds of the Monroe Doctrine if it were to occupy Greenland than if it was done by the British or the French.[7] Prime Minister Mackenzie King remained skeptical, however, and was not convinced either by the argument that a military occupation could be accompanied by a humanitarian mission. "The unemployed in Canada would criticize looking after Eskimos in Greenland's icy mountains [...] rather than Canadians at home," he said in a meeting on April 12.[8]

Despite the prime minister's hesitation, officers from the Canadian army and navy, under the direction of prominent lawmaker Charles Gavan Power, a World War I veteran and former ice hockey player, hastily drafted a plan for a possible military intervention in Greenland. As an initial step, the Canadian Department of Transport's Marine Service icebreaker *N. B. McLean* was to be sent to protect the Ivigtut mine. The vessel was to carry an advance party, Force X, numbering about 100 men from the army, navy, and Royal Canadian Mounted Police, to be followed in early June by an infantry company and supporting units.[9] Colonel Maurice Pope, the director of Military Operations and Intelligence at the National Defense Headquarters, was put in charge of preparing the expedition and ensuring that the *N. B. McLean* was properly equipped. "There was no end to the 'two by fours,' nails, stoves, corrugated iron, and goodness knows what else which the Engineers rightly insisted that a little self-contained force would require," he wrote in his memoirs. "Loaded beyond her marks as she would have been, this unfortunate vessel would have had the appearance of a Christmas tree floating."[10]

Britain also had an interest in Greenland's cryolite, and its government was targeted in separate lobbying efforts by Alcan,[11] but there were limits to what it could do and still remain on friendly terms with the United States. To be sure, within days of the German invasion of Denmark, British forces had been sent to occupy the Faroe Islands, and subsequently they had also landed in Iceland, which was independent but with some remnant political ties to the former colonial masters in Copenhagen. Both actions were accepted by Washington, as the territories were deemed to be wholly or partly in European waters, and thus outside of the Monroe Doctrine, although Iceland was considered a borderline case, halfway between the two hemispheres. With regards to Greenland, however, the American attitude to British interference was entirely different.

As early as on April 12, State Department officials had met and decided to "flash a red light against any Allied move in Greenland."[12] This was in line with Congresswoman Rogers of Massachusetts, who had a well-known interest in the island and declared a few days later that "this country should very definitely notify all European countries—and this includes England—that any attempt to occupy Greenland by any country will be considered an unfriendly act, and the United States will oppose any such action."[13] Pressure was building on Philip Kerr, the British ambassador to the United States, who in turn was keen to mitigate any American fears, stating in remarks to reporters that "if Britain decided that Greenland should be occupied to forestall a German move, the undertaking would be carried out by Canada in order to avoid complications involving the Monroe Doctrine."[14]

Britain thought it could afford to leave the matter to Canada, limiting itself to the contribution of the Royal Navy, which was, after all, significant as its ships offered a powerful screen in the North Atlantic that the German Navy would have difficulty penetrating. However, even Canadian moves on Greenland were anathema to Washington. On April 20, Berle received reports via the Federal Bureau of Investigation (FBI) that Canada was planning to send members of the Royal Canadian Mounted Police to Greenland. He was not amused. "I think the Royal Mounted should mind its own damned business, and let the governments settle high policy," he wrote in his diary.[15]

At this point, the matter was further complicated by the emergence of an unexpected player on the scene: Japan. Less than a week after the German invasion of Denmark and Norway, the Japanese government had expressed concern that the Netherlands would soon be dragged into the European conflict, with the Dutch East Indies being thrown into limbo.[16] This triggered concern that Japan, thirsty for energy to fuel its never-ending war in China, was planning a takeover of the oil-rich archipelago in case the Netherlands was occupied by Germany, and if the decision-makers in Tokyo needed an excuse for doing so, an Allied occupation of Greenland in the wake of the German occupation of Denmark would offer a precedent that they could point to as justification.

In other words, in one of the earliest instances of a direct linkage between the two parallel conflicts in Europe and Asia, American diplomats had to carefully consider their actions in the Atlantic with an eye to their repercussions for events in the Pacific. This was more than just speculation on the part of the Americans, and it appears that Japan was actually observing developments in Greenland with great interest. At a meeting with Cordell Hull on April 20, the Japanese ambassador Horinouchi Kensuke discreetly linked Japan's policy regarding the East Indies to the US approach to Greenland: at the end of a conversation mostly about Japan's position in the Pacific, the ambassador casually asked if there was any news about Greenland. "I replied that there were no new developments and no relations about which the slightest question could be raised," Hull wrote in his report of the meeting.[17]

The Japanese, too, were interested in the cryolite produced in Greenland, as a letter sent from the Danish mission in Tokyo to Kauffmann in Washington DC pointed out. "As you know, in recent years, Japan has bought large quantities of cryolite and will likely be interested in the continued ability to buy," the letter stated, asking Kauffmann to help make arrangements for future sales.[18] Thus, in a matter of just weeks after the German occupation of Denmark, several actors spread across different continents, both state and business, were involved. "The number of individuals and organizations with a direct and relevant interest in the island was as extensive as their relations were complicated," a Canadian official wrote in his memoirs.[19]

***

Despite the independent foreign policy reflected in the plans for Force X, for Canadian Prime Minister Mackenzie King, his nation's main mission in the world of diplomacy was to act as "an interpreter" between Britain and the United States, and therefore relations with Washington, and with Roosevelt personally, were paramount to him.[20] In fact, the American president was such a presence on his mind that he even turned up in his sleep while off work. "Before waking, dreamt that I was in what seemed to be New York and that I was called to the telephone," Mackenzie King wrote in his diary in late April as he was wrapping up a vacation in the United States. "It was long distance saying that the President wanted to speak to me from the White House."[21] He had actually met Roosevelt in person a few days earlier at Warm Springs and had been told in no uncertain terms that the United States did not appreciate the plans Canada had prepared for Greenland. "The Americans were anxious that Canada should not undertake anything in particular," Mackenzie King wrote in his diary, summarizing Roosevelt's message.[22]

Japan was the problem, as a senior advisor at the US State Department had made clear in a conversation with the Canadian envoy to Washington. "If Canada, United Kingdom or France were to send defense forces to Greenland, Japanese would claim on this analogy they were entitled, in the event of the Netherlands being involved in war, to send defense forces to Netherlands Indies," the Canadian envoy wrote, paraphrasing the American position.[23] Similarly, in talks with US officials, Mackenzie King was alerted to the fact that one of the chief causes of American concern was the conclusion Japan might draw from Allied activity in Greenland. Norman Davis of the American Red Cross told him that "Japan might take that as an excuse for protecting the Dutch East Indies, if any attempt was made by the U.S., Canada or Britain to 'protect' Greenland."[24] Cordell Hull also raised his concern over Japan with Mackenzie King.[25]

Apprehension about Japan observing events in the North Atlantic with a view to using them as a pretext for further aggression in the Pacific was probably genuine in Washington DC, and it was based in part on subtle hints from the Japanese themselves.[26] Still, mixed into this was a reluctance to let any other power, even an Allied one, gain a position in Greenland, combined with a gradually emerging desire to establish a foothold on the strategic island for itself. "Washington did not need, and quite clearly did not want, Canadian assistance," Keenleyside wrote in his memoirs.[27] It may have added impetus to these efforts—and reinforced the view of the decision-makers in Washington DC of themselves as champions of a just cause—that the Danish authorities on the island reportedly preferred an American presence to the alternative of involvement of an Allied nation actually at war with Germany. "They were apprehensive lest a British or a Canadian force be landed in Greenland, saying they considered the landing of any belligerent armed force undesirable," Cordell Hull wrote.[28]

Mackenzie King was swayed by his fundamental desire to stay on good terms with the United States. Still, there were plenty of misgivings in Canadian government circles, born out of fears that the actual US objective was economic and aimed at securing privileged access to the cryolite. The Danish envoy Kauffmann assured the Canadian envoy to the United States that he would "act to the satisfaction of the Canadian and British Governments" and guarantee continued supply of cryolite, but the Canadians were reluctant to take his word for it.[29] Likewise, the Canadians were not ready to accept it at face value when Davis, the Red Cross official, assured them that if German submarines or destroyers were suddenly to appear off the coast of Greenland, the United States "would immediately send some of her navy and blow them out of existence."[30]

Meanwhile, the US government took steps to increase its own Greenland presence, so far virtually non-existent, in a bid to forestall similar moves by other nations, friendly and hostile alike. One of these steps was to set up, for the first time ever, an American consulate in Greenland. "The Consulate, of course, will be a gesture suggesting that other people ought to keep out," Berle wrote in his diary on April 30. He had already started looking for candidates to take up the position of consul, but it was more difficult than expected. A candidate that had initially looked like a good match was abandoned as he was seen as not tough enough for what was likely to become a hardship posting: "When he got to the stage of wondering whether his wine would keep and a seven room knock-down house could be shipped up there, we called that one off and looked over some other candidates," Berle remarked.[31]

At the same time, Kauffmann appointed a so-called American–Danish Greenland Commission to ensure the wartime supply to the Greenland population and, crucially, assist the export of the island's products, including cryolite. The commission's members were all American citizens, including a representative of Penn Salt.[32] The establishment of the commission immediately sent jitters through Canadian government circles. "They, of course, are afraid that we are going to grab the territory—sublimely ignoring the fact that their own people have made several tentative attempts to grab it," Berle wrote in his diary.[33]

The lack of mutual trust between what was, on the surface, friendly nations was such that Canada was engaged in active espionage against both the Americans and the Danes, taking advantage of the fact that telegrams to Greenland had to go via Canadian territory. "Any further communications between the Danish Legation at Washington DC and Greenland should be stopped, and only forwarded after approval from this Department," J. E. Read, a government lawyer in the Department of External Affairs, wrote in a letter in mid-April. In the same letter, he urged that identical procedures should be applied to communications "between United States interests and the Kryolite [sic] Mines," reflecting suspicions that US policies on Greenland were primarily motivated by commercial concerns.[34] A senior official in the same department wrote five days later that "telegrams from [Kauffmann] and from Penn-Salt have been intercepted by our cable censor and in all cases have been sent on after being translated and examined."[35] Alcan was on the same page, and a senior executive suggested that sensitive mail sent from the United States to Greenland could be opened and read before being passed on.[36]

When he returned to Canada from an American holiday filled with official business and encounters with top-ranking decision-makers, Mackenzie King was eager to pass on the critical US view of Canadian adventures in Greenland. At a Cabinet meeting on May 2, he tried to explain the unwisdom of "giving an excuse to the Japanese for adopting toward the Dutch East Indies the kind of protection that Canada would have been exercising over Greenland."[37] It was an uphill battle. "It seemed impossible to bring home the picture of what the United States was doing to keep the Pacific quiet as against Japan," he complained in his diary. Power, the former ice hockey player, asked if this meant that Force X and the mission to seize the Ivigtut mine had to be scrapped. "Certainly, and at once," Mackenzie King replied curtly.[38]

Within minutes, a cable was sent to the Canadian Chiefs of Staff: "Force X is to be demobilized and all action in connection with it suspended."[39] Supplies that had already been stored in anticipation of the operation were dispersed, and mobilization orders were recalled.[40] Frustration and a sense of humiliation spread among the ranks. "The guillotine swiftly fell," Maurice Pope, the colonel responsible for preparing the *N. B. McLean* for the now-scuttled mission, wrote in his memoirs. "The State Department—or was it that Old Tennessean mountaineer Mr. Cordell Hull himself told us in no uncertain terms to stay the hell out of Greenland. A case of the Monroe Doctrine being applied against Canada!"[41]

The story could have ended here, but it did not. The May 2 meeting of the Canadian Cabinet in which Force X was abandoned ended at 7:30pm. At exactly the same time, a message ticked in from London. It was from Vincent Massey, Canada's top envoy to Britain, reporting that the British side was as interested in Greenland as ever.[42] "United Kingdom Government will be glad if the Canadian Government would consider the immediate dispatch of an expedition to Greenland with the purpose of taking over the mines," he wrote, adding: "In the opinion of the United Kingdom authorities, it would not be necessary to make a formal communication to United States Government before the expedition is dispatched."[43] The very moment that Force X was laid to rest, Canadian officials, under pressure from Britain, returned to the planning table, preparing a new foray into Greenland.

CHAPTER 6

Standoff at Ivigtut

Late Spring 1940

Should Canada go along with the telegrams from London and act on the Greenland issue without prior American approval? Not in the view of Oscar Skelton, the undersecretary of external affairs who had previously noted that a British occupation would be met with opposition from Washington. He was dismayed and said dismissively that the British suggestion reflected the mentality "of the genius who organized the campaign in Norway," which at the time, was shaping up to be a tragic waste of limited British resources.[1] Still he was persuaded that Canada could not afford to ignore Greenland, and he prepared a lengthy memo in cooperation with Keenleyside, the top advisor at the department of external affairs who had been among the first to sound the alarm about potential German designs for the island.[2] Canada was back as a player in the game over Greenland.

Still, Skelton and Keenleyside were aware of the potential for upsetting Washington. In their memo, they called for keeping the Americans in the loop, and now that *N. B. McLean's* mission had been abandoned, they suggested the dispatch of the vessel *Nascopie* to Greenland.[3] *Nascopie*, a 2,500-ton, 285.5-foot steamship named after the indigenous people of Quebec and Labrador, was a more palatable alternative. Built in 1911, it was best known in the public for having carried 550 reindeer from Norway to Baffin Island in 1921.[4] By 1940, it was the Hudson's Bay Company's mail ship and also carried out annual supply runs to Greenland, and altogether its mission would be less conspicuous and appear more a matter of routine than if the *N. B. McLean* had been sent.[5]

Meanwhile, the pressure coming out of London for Canadian action was building up. The Danish vessel *Julius Thomsen*, owned by the company running the cryolite mine at Ivigtut, had been on the way to Greenland when Denmark was occupied and was now being held back in the port of Kirkwall, in the Orkney Islands north of Scotland. This gave the British Director of Naval Intelligence the opportunity to question the ship's master, who had worrying news: the mine was located close to the shoreline, and most of it was below sea level. "A small amount of explosive would be enough to destroy the mines," the Danish sailor had said ominously, according to a dispatch sent by Massey, the Canadian envoy, to Ottawa on May 3.[6]

The warnings resonated in Canada, where officials argued that "the assurances so far given by the United States are practically valueless as it would probably take a German raider or submarine less than an hour to put the mine more or less permanently out of operation."[7] Despite the urgency, it was decided at an early stage that *Nascopie*'s mission was to have a less overtly military character than foreseen for *N. B. McLean*. Rather than a contingent of soldiers, it was to carry a detail of six Royal Canadian Mounted Police constables, of whom only two were to be uniformed. Still, the possibility of future military involvement in Greenland was left open, and the passenger list would also include Major G. L. W. MacDonald of the Royal Canadian Artillery. He was ordered to reconnoiter the area near the Ivigtut mine for a suitable location for two 4.7-inch coastal defense guns and searchlights with instructions to be "scrupulously careful that your actions do not disclose the purpose of your presence in Greenland."[8]

In the United States, the State Department had now found a suitable candidate for the position of consul in Greenland. James K. Penfield, a career diplomat who had spent nearly a decade in China and therefore was deemed sufficiently conditioned for the physical challenges of life in the Arctic, departed on board the US Coast Guard cutter *Comanche* on May 10, accompanied by his vice consul, George L. West.[9] Prior to their departure, West was sent by the State Department to an outlet of sporting outfitter Abercrombie & Fitch to buy what was needed for a lengthy stay in the far north, returning with skis, snow shoes and cashmere underwear.[10] Both diplomats, excited by reports of rich fishing opportunities in Greenland, also brought fishing tackle.[11] "Preparations were carried on with a speed disgracefully out of keeping with the traditional dignified tempo of the State Department, and with a thoroughness and efficiency which landed us in Greenland with a few overdoses—we found 18 rulers for the two of us, for instance—but only one lack, we were not given a single letter size envelope," Penfield wrote.[12]

After 10 days at sea, *Comanche* appeared off the Ivigtut mine on May 20. The mining town presented itself as "a large corrugated iron building, a considerable collection of crane-looking objects and a couple of dozen vari-colored houses straggling up the barren mountainside," according to Penfield.[13] It was the first time since the occupation of Denmark six weeks earlier that a ship had arrived from the outside. The miners came out onto the coastline, standing in clusters and watching the alien vessel with cheerless suspicion. Some feared it might be German. Only when the American vessel broke out the Danish flag on her foremast was the tension relieved. Members of the isolated mining community hoisted the Danish flag too, and one miner also brought out the only US flag in town.[14] Penfield met with the top Danish official at Ivigtut, Controller Albrecht Fischer, who explained that the mining operation was woefully underequipped to defend itself against enemy attack, with only a few rifles at its disposal. "Although he seems to regard a raid on Ivigtut as improbable he is somewhat concerned over the almost total lack of defense," Penfield reported to Washington DC.[15]

After the brief stop at the mine, *Comanche* continued on to Godthaab, where it arrived on May 22, before returning to Ivigtut.[16] Svane, the Danish governor, was determined to avoid any kind of incident when the Americans arrived and had issued strict orders to avoid overt expressions either for or against.[17] "We were greeted by His Excellency in formal attire (the best we could do in this respect being black homburg [hat] and gloves) and by a three gun salute—the limit of the Godthaab battery," Penfield wrote.[18] "Very few Greenlanders understood the significance of their arrival," a Danish sailor said later. "They were definitely seen as strangers, and people let them alone."[19]

Svane understood that the cryolite mine was essential for Greenland's ability to maintain a viable economy in times of war, and without being alarmist, he was somewhat more concerned than the mine management itself about the risk of a German strike. Therefore, he went straight down to business in one of his first meetings with the American consul, calling for an armed US unit to be stationed to protect the mine.[20] In reply, Secretary of State Hull informed Penfield that the United States was prepared to deliver an antiaircraft gun that could be used against both planes and surface vessels, as well as eight Lewis machine guns and 50 Springfield rifles. The stationing of US troops was out of the question for the time being, the secretary noted.[21]

While the US government remained cautious about any involvement in Greenland, events in Europe had taken an ominous turn. On May 10, German troops had invaded the Netherlands, Belgium, Luxembourg, and France, shocking the world with their rapid advances. The momentous developments in Europe immediately had repercussions in the Western Hemisphere, as French and British troops on May 11, launched a preemptive invasion of the Dutch-controlled islands of Aruba and Curaçao in the West Indies, setting a potential precedent for similar moves in Greenland.

Washington was also affected. In a statement to Congress on May 16, 1940, delivered under the impression of the initial German successes in western Europe, Roosevelt stated that "the American people must recast their thinking about national protection." Reminding his audience that the advent of aviation had made the United States drastically more vulnerable, he spelt out the strategic importance of Greenland. "From the fjords of Greenland, it is four hours by air to Newfoundland; five hours to Nova Scotia, New Brunswick and to the Province of Quebec; and only six hours to New England," he said, mirroring words uttered by Congresswoman Rogers one month earlier.[22]

It was against this backdrop that the US government was preparing a second Coast Guard cutter, *Campbell*, for dispatch to Greenland with the weapons cargo promised for the cryolite mine. It departed from the United States on May 30, with orders to pass by Godthaab to pick up Penfield and Svane before continuing on to Ivigtut, where it would be joining *Comanche*.[23] Berle knew that the arms for the mine marked a symbolic move with little practical significance. "This is designed primarily to keep the British quiet. Obviously, one coast gun and a few machine guns cannot defend Greenland," he wrote in his diary.[24] Altogether, it seemed at times that the British, not the Germans were the US government's main concern when it came to Greenland. Earlier that month, Roosevelt had instructed Berle to tell the British ambassador to Washington that he had no particular objection to the British occupation of Iceland. "But if they tried the same trick as to Greenland, he would be very angry," the president told Berle.[25]

Meanwhile, the Canadians had repeatedly called on the British to release the Danish ship *Julius Thomsen* owned by the Ivigtut mining company, as it carried spare parts needed for the operation of the mine. The British relented, but it was only allowed to leave Kirkwall after an armed guard consisting of nine servicemen, including three officers, was placed on board, mainly in an effort to prevent it from sailing back to a German-controlled port. "They thought all Danes were Nazis because they had allowed the Germans unhindered access to their country," the ship's captain Otto Nielsen recalled later.[26] Before departure, it received a new passenger: the Canadian diplomat Kenneth P. Kirkwood, who had been his country's representative in The Hague until the German invasion of the Netherlands and had now been assigned as Canada's first consul in Greenland.[27]

Nascopie left Louisburg, Nova Scotia, at 9pm on May 24.[28] On board was H. J. Hendra, a representative of Alcan sent with orders, according to a Canadian official, to "negotiate for the purchase of the total cryolite output or even the outright purchase of the Danish Government-owned Mine by the Canadian corporation."[29] When Alf Erling Porsild, the Danish-born Canadian vice consul, who was also on board, remarked casually that he was expecting mail from Penn Salt, he infuriated most of the other passengers and might even have lost his job as representative of the Canadian government if it had not been too late to find a replacement. "I understand we are working entirely in the interests of Canada and not the Pennsylvania Salt Company," Hendra said sternly.[30]

***

In the early hours of June 1, four ships were converging on Ivigtut, the tiny community on the southwestern tip of Greenland whose production of a vital raw material had suddenly catapulted it to unexpected global prominence. *Comanche* was on its way from Godthaab. *Nascopie* was approaching after a longer journey from Nova Scotia. *Julius Thomsen* was in the North Atlantic east of Greenland. And *Campbell* had the furthest distance to go, having only departed from its US harbor little more than 24 hours earlier.[31] None of the ships were Axis-controlled. In fact, all four represented countries that were in some loose sense allied against Germany. And still, in one of the great ironies of the ongoing war, they were headed for a standoff.

Comanche arrived at Ivigtut in the morning of June 1, and *Nascopie* appeared in waters off the mine just a few hours later on the same day,[32] followed by *Julius Thomsen* three days later.[33] In reaction to the presence of *Nascopie* and *Julius Thomsen* at the mine, the US Coast Guard ordered *Campbell* to increase its speed.[34] The Danish officials at Ivigtut, too, saw the appearance of *Nascopie* and *Julius Thomsen* as potentially bad news, and they were determined that no military personnel on either ship be allowed to disembark. "They are convinced that the Canadians would land a force on the slightest excuse (such as alleged inadequacy of a local Danish defense force) and would in fact already have done so had it not been for the presence of *Comanche*," Penfield wrote in a dispatch to Washington DC.[35]

Even though *Nascopie* carried only a limited complement of armed men, and all except one were police officers, this was not obvious to the Danes. Shortly after the Canadian ship's arrival, they ordered it to be sailed to an anchorage at some distance from the mine.[36] On June 3, Svane sent a cable to the mine at Ivigtut demanding an immediate investigation of the *Nascopie* and who was on board: "Request that you act without delay, demanding a response from the vice consul and the captain of the *Nascopie* if it is carrying military personnel," he wrote.[37] In a telegram on the following day, Svane emphasized that none of the prize crew, including officers, were allowed to leave the *Julius Thomsen*. "The ban on the combatants is absolutely categorical, and if they disobey, you must protest and then report to us," he said. "The motivation for the ban is the neutrality clauses under The Hague Convention. Besides, we owe the United States absolute and strict neutrality."[38]

Prior to the *Nascopie*'s departure, the Canadians had downplayed the significance of its mission in conversations with the Americans, telling them that the Royal Canadian Mounted Police was only represented by two constables on board, assisted by four civilians who happened to be capable of handling the machine guns. The fact that these four men were actually members of the mounted police but in mufti, seems to not have been disclosed.[39] This may have added to American anger once reports arrived from Greenland about the jitters that the *Nascopie* had caused. "It now develops that the Canadian boat going to Greenland has [...] a bunch of Royal Mounted Police," Berle wrote in his diary.[40] On June 3, he called in a group of Canadian and British officials, telling them that "Cecil Rhodes had been dead a long time and even if alive, Greenland was hardly a place for his talents." He capped his lecture with a stark warning: "This is plain grand imperialism, on a miniature scale. If there is any more monkey business, we are going to have a destroyer sent up there and stop it."[41]

This was the beginning of a lengthy standoff at Ivigtut. The Danish authorities relaxed somewhat in the days that followed, even allowing some civilians to tour the mine facilities.[42] However, the military and paramilitary passengers on board both *Nascopie* and *Julius Thomsen* were ordered to stay, triggering complaints about "forced confinement."[43] In reality, the Royal Mounted Police and the prize crew could easily have prevailed against the unarmed Danes. The fact that they waited patiently, pending the arrival of Svane from Godthaab, reflected a wish to avoid a diplomatic incident, but also the American military presence in Ivigtut port in the form of *Comanche*. At the same time, Svane and his colleague Brun moved to tighten control of the mine, issuing a proclamation that until further notice they would be in charge, as the Danish company was unable to exploit its concession due to the interruption of communications and shipping between Denmark and Greenland.[44]

Svane finally arrived at Ivigtut on June 13, aboard the *Campbell*, accompanied by Penfield.[45] By now, *Julius Thomsen* was making preparations to return to Britain when shortly before midnight, Svane stepped on board claiming the ship in the name of the government of Greenland. The six men and three officers of the prize crew were to be transferred to the *Nascopie* and repatriated via Canada. The Canadian vice consul and the officer commanding the prize crew both protested but acquiesced. Again, it was probably the presence of the two American Coast Guard cutters more than anything else that convinced the Canadians to cooperate. "I hope you can approve of my action, which was motivated by the need to act before it was too late," Svane wrote with barely disguised pride to his fellow governor Brun. "The successful outcome seems to have underlined the independence of Greenland."[46]

The Canadian government was highly dissatisfied with the incident, sending a telegram to its consul, who was still confined to *Julius Thomsen*. "Please inform Governor Svane that neither the United Kingdom Government nor ourselves are prepared to accept his unilateral action in taking possession of the *Julius Thomsen*," it said.[47] This was the core of the matter, and only after the British authorities had agreed after more than a week of hesitation to acquiesce in the Danish takeover of the *Julius Thomsen* was the small crisis resolved, and it was agreed that the prize crew would be carried to Canada on board the ship on its first trip to North America under Danish command.[48] Three weeks had passed since *Nascopie* arrived at Ivigtut. It was an unusually long period given that its root cause was a dispute among nations that were otherwise on friendly terms.

With all outstanding issues cleared, on June 22, the men on board *Nascopie* were invited to dinner in Ivigtut. Hendra, the combative Alcan executive, was seated next to Oscar Corp, the mine's manager, who had arrived on board *Julius Thomsen*, but all attempts at getting information out of him about the mine were in vain. "It was very evident that all questions regarding the mine at Ivigtut […] would not be discussed in a satisfactory matter by Mr. Corp," Hendra remarked.[49] In other words, suspicions about Canada's commercial ambitions lingered.

While at Ivigtut, Svane was reminded how vulnerable the mine was, and he repeated his call for an armed US force near the mine, arguing that an American ship in the harbor, while better than nothing, would not be adequate protection, as it would be unable to stay during the winter months.[50] Hull remained unfazed, but in late June, for the first time ever, signaled the possibility that a force of former American servicemen could be employed as mine guards.[51] At the same time, *Campbell* unloaded the weapons it had carried for the protection of the mine, including the antiaircraft gun. However, since it did not bring any personnel proficient in handling the weapon or even assembling it, it remained disassembled in its crates for months afterwards.[52] Essentially very little stood in the way of any foreign aggressor. And on the same day that the men from *Nascopie* had dinner with the mine's managers, France signed an armistice near Compiègne, acknowledging defeat after a six-week German campaign. The Nazis were now masters of all continental northwestern Europe. They would soon make themselves felt across the Atlantic, as far away as Greenland, with its almost non-existent defenses.

CHAPTER 7

The First German Mission

Summer 1940

Hans-Jürgen Stumpff, general of the Luftwaffe and commander of 5th Air Fleet with a geographical area of responsibility covering Norway and Denmark, was showing growing interest in aviation in arctic conditions in the summer of 1940. Accompanied by his staff, he inspected a glacier 6,000 feet above sea level near the town of Finse, in the mountains west of the capital of Oslo, where a 3,000-foot airstrip was being prepared directly on the ice. Soldiers had been busy working on the airfield since shortly after the German invasion, filling in cracks in the glacier surface with ice and snow. "They believed it was possible to land with airplanes. There were no stones or anything," said Robert Pötzl, then a 20-year-old soldier from the Bavarian city of Bamberg, who had been sent to work on the airfield.[1]

Deep secrecy surrounded the project on the glacier, and all letters sent home by the German soldiers were carefully censored on the spot. Pötzl and other soldiers at his level had no idea what purpose the airfield was to serve. Some have later speculated it could be in preparation of the evolving air war over Britain, where Luftwaffe operating from bases in Norway played an important role.[2] According to another rumor that surfaced in the German press in the early post-war years, the project had a longer-term objective of preparing for a future strategic air offensive against the United States, still neutral but believed bound to eventually enter the war, with Iceland and Greenland as necessary refueling stops for the German planes.[3]

Georg Madelung, an influential aeronautical engineer with experience as a pilot over the Western Front during the First World War,[4] had allegedly approached Hermann Göring, the commander in chief of the Luftwaffe, with a scheme to set up airbases in the middle of the Greenland icecap. Göring, the post-war report went on, had been enthusiastic about the idea but had decided to start out in a small way by ordering the high-altitude experimental airfield in Norway. Polar experts, meteorologists, and veterans from the war in the Alps from 1915 to 1918, were all sent to the test area to share their experience.[5] "When famous scientists said it could be done, we believed it," said Pötzl. "It wasn't crazy. I also thought it was possible. Well, maybe it was a little bit crazy."[6]

While the Luftwaffe was busy building its glacier airfield in Norway, possibly with a view to future operations in Greenland, the German Navy had separate plans aimed at securing an uninterrupted stream of weather reports from the island. Remarkably, Danish and Norwegian meteorological stations in Greenland were still transmitting daily measurements abroad, for use by both parties in the conflict, but the German commanders assumed, correctly, that it was only a matter of time before the British would put an end to this. Therefore, the German Naval Command issued an order in June 1940 for Rupert Holzapfel, a Luftwaffe meteorologist who had participated in one of Wegener's expeditions to Greenland and had been seconded temporarily to the navy, to prepare a manned weather station on the East Greenland coast. It was to be located between Scoresby Sound and Angmagssalik, roughly in the area near Kap Nansen, and its staff was to stay there during the entire upcoming winter season.[7]

Germany had a strange relationship with Denmark, the country it had just occupied, treating it as if it was still somewhat independent with a will of its own, and one of Holzapfel's first priorities was to visit Copenhagen and seek the Danish authorities' permission to travel to Greenland. He had high hopes for the kind of assistance he thought he could expect. Not only did he want the green light to go to Greenland, but he also hoped that Denmark would be able to equip him with a ship suitable for the purpose.[8] A maverick, he decided to avoid the usual bureaucratic procedures, bypassing the German mission in Copenhagen and going straight to the top of the Danish government, which was still functioning much as it had in peacetime.[9]

In his talks with local officials, Holzapfel claimed, disingenuously, to have Berlin's backing, and a meeting was duly arranged at the Danish foreign ministry. It was attended by Nils Svenningsen, the director of the ministry's political and legal department, and also Knud Oldendow, the head of the Greenland Board, the top state agency overseeing the island, who had been called in due to the nature of the German request. The conversation was carried out in German. As the official with the most precise knowledge about Greenland matters, Oldendow did most of the talking, but for help in finding the correct phrase, he often had to resort to Svenningsen, who was the more accomplished German speaker.[10]

Oldendow had bad news for the German visitor: "It's no use for you to contact the Greenland Board on this. We have no communication with the island, and we can't possibly place a ship at your disposal. Quite apart from the question of whether we approve of your scheme or not, it is not in our power to provide you with any assistance." He continued: "If you decide to go there, you must understand that the risk is all yours. I am convinced that it's a very risky thing to try and sail to the east coast of Greenland given the conditions, with America just next door, and the mood in Greenland for Denmark and 100 percent against Germany. I would advise against it."[11]

Holzapfel left the foreign ministry empty-handed, but he did not give up. He was married to a Danish woman, and he tried once again to approach the Greenland Board, using his father-in-law, a mid-level official, as a go-between. However, Oldendow would not be budged. "My reply was the same," he told an interviewer later.[12] The Germans, incredulous at the audacity of a subdued people, interpreted the Danish intransigency as concern that German boots on Greenland soil could cause the Americans to take over the island. "The Danes fear that such an expedition would give the Americans an excuse to realize their aspirations for Greenland," the head of the German mission in Copenhagen, Cecil von Renthe-Fink, wrote in a letter to the German foreign ministry, evidently vexed that Holzapfel had not consulted him before talking to the Danish officials.[13]

Still, the bottom line was that it was not up to the Danes to decide. It was clear that a Danish permission for Germans to go to Greenland was a mere formality as the Copenhagen government had lost effective control over the island. Therefore, Holzapfel left Copenhagen on July 27, heading for Berlin, where he hoped to get the go-ahead he had not received from the Danes. To his chagrin, he found that the German foreign ministry was equally hesitant, and for similar reasons. The diplomats in Berlin were concerned that the United States would use a German presence in the Western Hemisphere as a reason to enter the war.[14] This left the Germans with only one other available option. It was to get the Danes themselves to carry out the expedition, ostensibly acting as a neutral provider of weather information from Greenland but in fact providing the Germans with essential information.

***

In early August 1940, the Danish journalist and Arctic explorer Ebbe Munck was approached in occupied Copenhagen by a man in his mid-40s, Curt Carlis Hansen. Carlis Hansen introduced himself as a Danish patriot who wanted to pick Munck's brains about a project that he was trying to bring to fruition: the establishment of a Danish weather station on the east coast of Greenland, to serve mainly the purpose of signaling Denmark's continued sovereignty over the island despite the special circumstances brought about by the war. Carlis Hansen had already hired the members of the expedition, and funding was also secured. All he needed was Munck's suggestion about where exactly to set up the station. Munck listened with an air of intense interest, but it was all an act. As he wrote in his post-war memoirs: "I knew more about Carlis Hansen than I let on."[15]

Munck was aware that he was a hardcore Nazi and had no intention of helping him. In fact, Carlis Hansen was so well-known for his extreme political views that it was something of a mystery that he even expected his story to be believed. He had attained national notoriety in 1934 when he had been the main organizer of an unsuccessful attempt to kidnap an *émigré* German communist in broad daylight in Copenhagen, allegedly in order to hand him over to Danish authorities for undercover agitation. At the time, the Danish newspaper *Politiken* had described Carlis Hansen as "a relentless man of action."[16] Like some other Danish Nazis, he had been filled with somewhat contradictory emotions of shame at Denmark's hasty surrender to the Germans in April 1940, but he had quickly recovered and was now deeply involved in the Greenland mission.[17]

As Munck suspected, there were sinister designs behind the idea of sending an ostensibly Danish weather mission to Greenland. It was aimed exclusively at aiding the German war effort, now that the initial attempt to get Danish acquiescence in going to the island had failed. Intriguingly, it was a mission in which General Stumpff, the Luftwaffe commander conducting trials on the Norwegian glacier, had expressed great interest.[18] British intelligence officers able to read enemy communication after breaking the Enigma code, were alerted to the German plans, with hints that their origin came from even higher up in the Luftwaffe hierarchy. "The decrypts revealed their intentions and the fact that Göring attached great importance to them," recalled Edward Thomas, then a young Royal Navy intelligence officer stationed in Iceland.[19]

Carlis Hansen, who had recently been hired by Abwehr, the German military intelligence service, was charged with organizing the expedition under the guidance of his case officer Ulrich Graf von Finkenstein, and he had been spending the days prior to meeting Munck recruiting other Danish citizens for the journey.[20] The aim, he claimed when talking to candidates, would be to trap wild animals for their fur, but at the same time, and more importantly, it would be to demonstrate sovereignty in northeastern Greenland at a time when Norwegians were attempting to gain a foothold with a view to taking over the area completely after the war. His first choice was Jørgen Tvermose, who had spent two years in Greenland in the late 1930s and now ran a small trapping company but was unable to return to the island because of the war. Three other recruits had no arctic experience at all.[21]

Carlis Hansen also informed the four that transmitting meteorological data would be an additional purpose of the expedition. Since the Danish and Norwegian weather stations were already sending this kind of information on a regular basis, they did not see this as a cause of concern. There was one last thing: they all had to invest a limited sum of money in the expedition. "They accepted this without any second thoughts, partly because of the national task that they had been introduced to, partly because they wanted to leave Denmark as life under German occupation was unbearable," they said later in a report. Carlis Hansen promised them that escaping Denmark would not be a problem since he had excellent connections with the Germans and was able to get the necessary exit permits.[22] He was fooling the four crew members, but some of them were fooling him back: "My sole purpose for leaving Denmark in the summer of 1940 was to get over to the Allied forces," Tvermose claimed after the war. "There were persistent rumors in Denmark during the summer of 1940 that the USA had already occupied Greenland."[23]

On August 8, Carlis Hansen accompanied by his crew of four departed Denmark for Norway where the seal hunting ship *Furenak* had been chartered for the journey. It was now clear that Carlis Hansen would not stay in Greenland with the men but would return to Norway with *Furenak*. While in Oslo, an expedition member who was an amateur meteorologist was introduced to two Norwegian-speaking Germans, who gave him professional instruction in how to carry out the weather work in Greenland.[24] "We promised—we had to—to send weather reports back to Norway, to the German HQ," said Tvermose after the war. "We never for one moment intended to keep that promise."[25] The *Sicherheitsdienst*, the Nazi Party intelligence service, was also helpful in seconding two officers and a translator to assist in transporting equipment from Oslo to the port of Ålesund in western Norway, where *Furenak* was anchored.[26]

Before leaving on *Furenak*, the entire five-man crew had dinner at Hotel Bristol in Oslo with Munck, the journalist, who was in Norway on unrelated business. Two officials from the Hamburg-based Deutsche Seewarte, a prestigious center of maritime meteorology, were also present. The conversation was remarkably frank and touched on the need to gather intelligence about "long-term weather," in order to facilitate air operations over Europe.[27] Munck listened with polite attentiveness, and even though some of the expedition members found an opportunity to discreetly share their concerns with him about the strong German element, he advised them to stick to the plan and to contact colonial officials in Greenland if they had further concerns after they arrived.[28]

There was a good reason why Munck advised the Danes to follow through with the expedition even though by now it was abundantly clear that it was serving Nazi purposes. He did not want the mission to be aborted at the last minute now that he knew about it in detail and could pass his knowledge on. Shortly afterwards, he was on his way to Denmark. "On the return journey to Copenhagen via Stockholm," he wrote in his memoirs, "the British were informed."[29] This supplemented information that the British already had received of the impending expedition from decrypted German messages, passed on from MI5 to the Naval Staff via a newly established unit of the British Naval Intelligence Division. It was one of the early successes of what was later to be known as Ultra.[30] Essentially, therefore, *Furenak*'s fate was sealed even before it departed from Ålesund and entered open sea in the middle of August.

CHAPTER 8

The Norwegian Connection

Early Fall 1940

Events happening in Greenland at the time when *Furenak* was setting out on its lonely journey across the North Atlantic revealed the extent of naval activity already taking place around the island. The Norwegian vessel *Veslekari*, also a sealer, had been at sea for a fortnight, and on August 14, it landed a lone telegrapher at the Norwegian weather station Mosquito Bay in northeastern Greenland. *Veslekari*, under the command of the Norwegian trapper and explorer John Giæver, was visiting Norwegian outposts along the Greenland coast, replacing personnel and bringing coal, oil and other essential supplies for the upcoming winter. It was ostensibly a humanitarian effort, organized by the state-run Norwegian Svalbard and Arctic Ocean Research Survey to provide for the altogether 14 Norwegian nationals stranded in northeastern Greenland because of the war, and unlike *Furenak*, whose departure was shrouded in secrecy, no effort was made to cover up *Veslekari's* mission.[1]

Still, there was more to *Veslekari* than met the eye. Carl Sæther, a Norwegian national who had been British consul in the city of Tromsø in northern Norway until it was occupied by the Germans at the end of the Scandinavian campaign in June, was deeply involved in the preparations during the summer for its departure. Most importantly, he wrote a letter that Giæver, the expedition leader, was to show to British authorities once the ship was intercepted by the Royal Navy to the effect that most on board were anti-Nazi. It was understood that in case of interception, *Veslekari* would not return to Norway, and it was essential that it be made to look like it had been taken over by the British against the will of the crew lest the Germans decide to retaliate against their relatives left behind in Norway.[2]

Once word was out that *Veslekari* was about to leave for the free world, it was inundated with requests from people who hoped to join in order to escape from newly occupied Norway, most planning to enroll in the Allied forces.[3] When reports of the planned Norwegian expedition reached Copenhagen, the Danish government initially prepared plans for a separate Danish expedition, but abandoned the idea and instead pulled the strings so space was made on the *Veslekari* for a group of three Danes who were to reinforce the personnel at Danish stations along the East

Greenland coast.[4] Among them was 31-year-old Ib Poulsen, who had previously worked as a radio operator in Greenland. He was surprised at the speed with which the German authorities gave him permission to leave Denmark. "We supposed it was because the Germans were interested in continuous [...] weather reports," Poulsen recalled. "Therefore [we] resolved that I should stop the broadcasts of the weather reports as soon as I arrived."[5]

Understandably, the Germans wanted to keep tabs on *Veslekari*, initially proposing to place an observer on board, which Giæver declined. He also managed to stop a plan to have a German ship escort the Norwegian vessel part or all the way to Greenland. In the end, the Germans insisted on seconding a Norwegian by the name of Axel Coll as a precondition for letting the ship depart.[6] He was to take photos for a German-language publication, allegedly in order to get maximum propaganda mileage out of the attempt to extend help to Norwegians in a remote, isolated place.[7] "He was running around taking photos of all kinds of things," a member of the expedition later recalled.[8] In fact, Coll was an agent for Abwehr and had simply been handed a camera with orders to take photos from the journey, although, as he later claimed, he had no experience whatsoever as a professional photographer.[9]

Even so, the Germans were suspicious. In the port of Ålesund, where *Veslekari* was being made ready for the expedition, German inspectors stepped on board, on an unannounced visit, threatening to reveal that the entire journey was a cover for escaping to the Allied side. This forced Giæver to think quickly and hastily dispatch two of his crew members, young men who wanted to go to Canada to receive training as pilots, to sweep the cabin floor, thus keeping a low profile. Meanwhile, another of his crew members plied the Germans with generous amounts of whiskey, softening their alertness.[10] The trouble was not over, however. Some days later, in the northern city of Tromsø, which was *Veslekari*'s last stop before departing, the German port commander seemed to have sensed foul play, and made no effort to disguise his dislike of the idea of allowing the ship to leave Norway and enter into waters controlled by the Allies. "He promised that the Germans would 'take care' of the families of everyone on board if we did anything that would hurt the German military," Giæver wrote in his memoirs, confirming the fears of the crew that their actions might trigger retributions.[11]

Veslekari left Tromsø on August 2, heading initially for Spitsbergen, an island in the Norwegian-controlled Svalbard archipelago, to load coal. Four days later it moved on, arriving off Greenland on August 11. Ib Poulsen, the Danish radio operator, immediately proceeded as he had decided to beforehand.[12] "I [radioed] the Mørkefjord station and asked the station to stop the broadcasts," he said.[13] This was going according to plan, but other things were not. The crew was getting worried, since the *Veslekari* had managed to cross the entire North Atlantic without yet being met by a British ship, even though they revealed their position every day in both radio and telegraph form to the weather stations in Greenland, hoping that it would be picked up by the British.[14]

In fact, an Allied ship was on its way with a specific mission to intercept *Veslekari*. The Norwegian Coast Guard ship *Fridtjof Nansen*, which had escaped to the British Isles after the end of the Norwegian campaign, had departed from Reykjavik, Iceland, on August 13 and was approaching the Greenland coast fast, with 12 Royal Marines on board. "It is safe to assume that the German authorities have only allowed the [*Veslekari*] expedition on the condition that the stations [along the Greenland coastline] are equipped to work in their interest," read the instructions given to Ernst Ullring, the commander of *Fridtjof Nansen*. "If *Fridtjof Nansen* encounters the expedition from Norway, the vessel must be seized, and unless other orders are received, it must be taken to an Icelandic port for further instructions."[15]

Part of *Fridtjof Nansen's* mission was also to ensure that meteorological reports from the Norwegian outposts in Greenland could no longer reach the Germans, and its first stop once it reached the island on August 16, was the weather station in Mosquito Bay, where *Veslekari* had just dropped off a telegrapher. The telegrapher, who was still settling in when *Fridtjof Nansen* anchored offshore, was scared out of his wits when he saw the 12 Marines, armed to the teeth and ready to fight, approach the coastline in a boat, and as the soldiers swarmed the station and seized its radio transmitter, he fled into the hills. Only when he realized they had been brought by

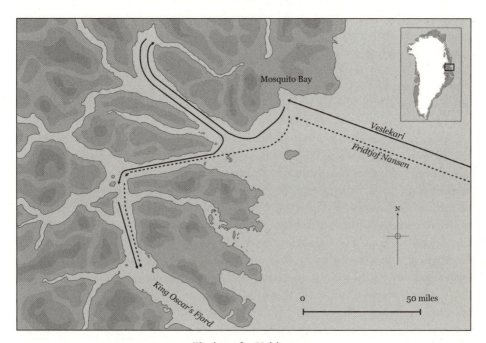

The hunt for *Veslekari*.

a Norwegian ship did he return.[16] He was taken on board *Fridtjof Nansen* where he told Ullring that *Veslekari* was still in the area, continuing its work replacing personnel and unloading supplies at the various Norwegian stations.[17]

Fridtjof Nansen's crew spotted *Veslekari* in King Oscar's Fjord in the afternoon of August 18, approaching it with their guns pointed at the civilian vessel. Sailing up alongside *Veslekari*, Ullring addressed its commanding officers by loudspeaker, ordering them on board for negotiations. Shortly afterwards, Ullring sat face-to-face on *Fridtjof Nansen* with Giæver and Coll, the Abwehr agent. Coll's real identity was not yet revealed, but the mere fact that *Veslekari* was carrying a photographer from a German magazine was taken as sufficient reason to dismiss any idea that it was a neutral vessel. Therefore, Ullring explained, *Veslekari* would be seized, any weapons in its hull would be captured, and it would be taken to Iceland with a prize crew on board. Giæver was furious at the treatment, which suggested he had the status of an enemy combatant, but there was nothing he could do.[18] Shortly afterwards, he and Coll were on their way to Iceland on board *Fridtjof Nansen*, while several of the other expedition members who had traveled with them on *Veslekari*, including Ib Poulsen and the two other Danes, were permitted to stay behind in Greenland.[19]

Upon arrival in the Iceland capital of Reykjavik, Ullring completed a report which characterized *Veslekari*'s voyage as an ordinary polar sea expedition, concluding in the recommendation that the vessel be released and its crew as well as the expedition members—all of them "good Norwegians," according to Ullring—be allowed to return to Norway.[20] Ullring's recommendation fell on deaf ears. A British prize crew boarded *Veslekari*, and it was sailed on to the port of Kirkwall in the Orkney Islands, where the Norwegians were given 20 minutes to leave the ship. Under guard they were taken to Pentonville Prison in London where lengthy interrogations began. Most of the crew were released after a short period of time, but Giæver and the telegrapher from Mosquito Bay, spent nine weeks in jail. Coll was not released until after the war.[21]

The British-Norwegian activities taking place in August—the seizure of *Veslekari*, the Royal Marines' occupation of the radio station, and, just before *Fridtjof Nansen*'s departure from Greenland, the forcible takeover of 35 barrels of aviation fuel from the Danish Navy's aviation arm over the vicious objections of a lone local representative of the Danish authorities[22]—were all minor, but clear challenges to the American policy of preventing the war in Europe from spreading to the Western Hemisphere. Remarkably, a US Coast Guard cutter, *Northland* commanded by Edward Hanson "Iceberg" Smith, was in adjacent waters at the time, partly to keep an eye on possible Axis activities, partly to make a preliminary survey of the east coast.[23] *Northland* could have interfered but did not, as the diplomatic fallout between two friendly nations, the United States and Britain, would have been intractable. "I assume Washington didn't want a meeting with *Nansen* to take place, and therefore they did like Nelson and turned a blind eye," Giæver wrote later.[24]

Giæver's instincts were right. The British had consulted with the Americans before *Fridtjof Nansen*'s mission, opting to go straight to Roosevelt, whom they had deemed to be in favor of a more proactive policy than the more cautious officials at the State Department.[25] When the United Kingdom's ambassador to the United States met with the president, the two had agreed that "the only important issue was that the British troops should arrive there ahead of forces of any inimical interest."[26] A few days later, Roosevelt gave an even more explicit approval of the activities in Greenland, stating that the Royal Marines' temporary occupation of the Mosquito Bay station was acceptable as long as "no publicity should be given to the landing."[27]

The fact that the United States had decided to pretend it did not see what was happening right under its nose became obvious a few days later. Further south along Greenland's east coast, another civilian Norwegian vessel, *Ringsel*, was on a mission similar to *Veslekari*, visiting a Norwegian weather station at Torgilsbu to take home the station chief, as his wife, who had accompanied him, was "hysterically homesick."[28] *Ringsel* escaped discovery by *Fridtjof Nansen*,[29] but it crossed paths with the Coast Guard's *Northland* not once, but twice, and on the second of these occasions, on August 31, the US commander, "Iceberg" Smith, even invited his Norwegian counterpart over for a drink and a chat. Shortly afterwards, *Ringsel* returned to occupied Norway, and *Northland* let it happen. Having tried to stop it would have involved all kinds of complications. The United States was not ready for that yet.[30]

***

The hunt for *Veslekari* had taken place while the Danish Nazi Carlis Hansen and his four-member team were still making their way slowly across the North Atlantic on *Furenak*. Ignorant of the events that were only now wrapping up in the area, they made landfall on Greenland's east coast on August 31, the very same day that the commanders of *Northland* and *Ringsel* had their friendly conversation, anchoring at Cape Biot, only a few miles from the point offshore where *Fridtjof Nansen* had seized *Veslekari*.[31] "Regarding our destination, Cape Biot, the decision was entirely mine, having been there before," Tvermose, Carlis Hansen's first recruit, recalled later. The explanation he gave the Germans was that it was necessary to be near the coast as it would facilitate radio transmissions. In reality, he argued later, it was in order to make it easier for the British to find them once they arrived.[32]

The suspicions that Tvermose shared with his fellow Danes about *Furenak*'s real mission were now confirmed. As they unloaded and unpacked the cargo they had carried from Norway, they were surprised to find, in addition to meteorological equipment, three machine guns, 20 rifles, 18,000 rounds, entrenchment tools, 20 pairs of skis, six dog sledges and 20 tons of coal.[33] "Only then did they realize that Carlis Hansen was probably a German agent, who had been able to fool them due

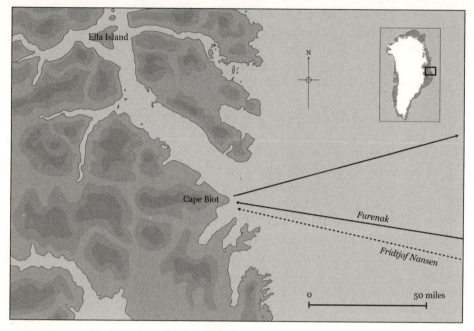

Furenak's mission.

to their own careless attitude," stated a report prepared shortly afterwards. "They had not been given any instruction in the use of the weapons, and in their view, either Hansen had the intention of persuading them now [to join him in the pro-German activities], or there were plans to ship over additional personnel."[34]

They protested against the landing of the equipment, but to no avail, and Carlis Hansen gave them a choice. They could decide to stay in Greenland, promising to send the weather forecasts as planned, or they could return to Denmark, where the German authorities might not look leniently on their failure to carry out their mission. It was even claimed later that Carlis Hansen had threatened them with being sent to a concentration camp upon their return, making a trip back even less inviting.[35] The upshot was that all four decided to stay behind at Cape Biot with their crates of equipment, while Carlis Hansen departed on September 1 after having spent just 24 hours in Greenland.[36] His last order to the four Danes was to immediately get the weather station into working order and then send weather reports three times a day, using a secret code which he handed to them.[37]

With Carlis Hansen gone, the four made no attempt to get either the meteorological equipment or the weapons ready for use, but they started building a cottage, as they had no idea how long they would be stranded on this isolated piece of coastline.[38] They did not have to wait long. The British were alerted to the *Furenak* expedition both from the Enigma intercepts and from Munck's message sent out of Stockholm, and as early as September 4, a ship was on its way to pick them up. Once again, it was *Fridtjof Nansen*. After spending nearly two days in a futile search of *Furenak*, crew on board the Norwegian Coast Guard ship caught sight of the half-finished cottage and four tents on land.[39]

Ullring, the commander of *Fridtjof Nansen*, led a small armed force which landed near the site in a lifeboat. They met the four Danes, who explained the situation, but nevertheless were placed under guard, while all the weapons and other pieces of equipment were also carried on board. Before departing, the Norwegians set fire to the cottage and the 20 tons of coal. Then the ship set course for Iceland, arriving on September 10.[40] "We protested against the capture by the Norwegians as we were Danes on Danish soil, but that was only pro forma, our purpose was to get in contact with the Allied Forces," Tvermose said.[41] "We were treated as friends, and were made to feel as comfortable as conditions permitted."[42]

Later, when the four Danes set foot on British territory, the attitude changed. "We were put in jail and treated as common prisoners, ending up among convicts," Tvermose complained in a letter to the Danish mission in London. "It is unbearable for us [...] as we have always been very pro-British and admired British culture and freedom, as well as Britain's struggle to assist smaller nations in preserving their independence."[43] After some months, Tvermose and two of the other Danes were released and subsequently entered Allied service as soldiers. One last member of the group of four stayed in jail as he was found to be a long-time Nazi, spending the rest of the war on the Isle of Man.[44]

Meanwhile, Carlis Hansen had returned to Denmark, telling his family that the journey to Greenland had been a success. He even showed his daughter a photo of a musk ox, which the expedition members had shot as they craved meat. "My father told me he was very sorry they had had to shoot this animal," his daughter wrote in a short biography of Carlis Hansen.[45] He probably was sorry for more than that. No reports arrived from the weather station which he had helped establish at great expense to his German masters and eventually intelligence confirmed that the enemy had destroyed the station.[46] Possibly in reaction to *Furenak*'s activities, all weather reporting from Greenland to occupied Europe soon stopped, as meteorological observations that had previously been transmitted uncoded to the benefit of anyone able to listen in were now encoded before being sent to Britain.[47] Copenhagen soon inquired about the missing weather reports, triggering a curt reply from the Greenland governors: "Interruption of reports has been necessitated by Greenland's exposed position as neutral territory."[48]

Shortly before 11am on November 10, the Danish police officer Aage de Lemos, who was keeping a lonely watch at a radio station on Ella Island, close to Cape Biot, was surprised to see a gray German airplane appear over the horizon. It flew a total of eight times over the radio station at an altitude of just a few feet before dropping a cigar tin containing a note: "The Administration takes this opportunity to ask whether you have seen or heard anything of the following trappers: Jørgen Tvermose, Starup, Børge Frank, Børresen." The note was signed "C. Hansen." de Lemos ignored the message and made no move to reply, and shortly afterwards, the airplane disappeared in north-northeasterly direction.[49]

Ultimately, Carlis Hansen's attempt to strengthen the weather service from Greenland ended in unadulterated failure, with the complete loss of all the men and equipment invested in the mission, while he possibly even contributed to the opposite outcome of what he had aimed for, by precipitating a decision to end transmission of weather reports to Europe. Still, it did not have any impact on his position with Abwehr. Quite to the contrary, shortly afterwards he joined an 11-man expedition on board the trawler *Heinrich Freese* sent to set up a weather station on Jan Mayen, an island halfway between Norway and Greenland. Shortly before reaching its target, *Heinrich Freese* was intercepted by the Royal Navy, and in the dramatic pursuit that followed, it was deliberately run aground. Two of the crew drowned, while the rest, including Carlis Hansen, were taken prisoner. On November 18, he reached Britain, now a captive like the other four members of the ill-fated *Furenak* expedition.[50]

***

On September 23, two weeks after *Fridtjof Nansen*'s second mission to Greenland, US Secretary of State Cordell Hull sent a sharply worded letter to Wilhelm Morgenstierne, the exiled Norwegian government's envoy to Washington, referring to "recent events on the East Coast of Greenland and in the waters adjacent thereto."[51] While Roosevelt had discreetly given a green light to British-led activities in Greenland and even permitted the temporary landing of Royal Marines, *Fridtjof Nansen*'s maneuvers had assumed an extent that caused the State Department to intervene. "In view of the geographical position of Greenland and the well-known policies of the United States with respect to the Western Hemisphere, my Government could not acquiesce in any political, military or naval steps which constituted a permanent occupation or change in the status of Greenland," Hull wrote.[52]

Hull stated, perhaps somewhat disingenuously, that he did not believe that Norway's government-in-exile, which had only recently established itself in London after the defeat at home, had "any thought of interfering with the present status of Greenland." Still, "having in mind the situation resulting from the War in Europe, and particularly as it relates to Denmark," he felt obliged to remind the Norwegians about the stance taken by the US government back in 1920 when it had made it clear to Britain, and everyone else in the Old World with possible designs for Greenland, that it would not accept transfer of the island or parts of it to any third power. Greenland would be in either Danish or American hands, and no third alternative was acceptable. "The position of the Government of the United States remains unchanged," Hull added drily.[53]

Even so, the reality on the ground seemed more complex. The maneuvers of four Norwegian ships—*Fridtjof Nansen*, *Veslekari*, *Ringsel* and *Furenak*—off eastern Greenland in the summer of 1940 were no coincidence. Neither was the fact that *Fridtjof Nansen*'s commander, Ullring, noted in his logbook that the Danish expedition led by Tvermose had been captured on "Norwegian" territory.[54] Nor the presence of several Norwegian trappers and weather observers in isolated posts up the island's long coastline. Or, for that matter, remarks by Halvdan Koht, foreign minister of the Norwegian government-in-exile in London, also made in September, warning against allowing "new powers to claim territory in the north," adding that he was specifically thinking about Greenland.[55]

Despite its defeat at the international court in The Hague in 1933, Norway remained an important factor when it came to Greenland. Scattered groups in Norwegian society maintained a strong interest in Greenland, mostly tolerated by the Danish government, as the political establishment in Oslo seemed to have given up any hopes of officially challenging Denmark's sovereignty over the island. However, as events in the early war years showed, some Norwegians saw the war, a period when all accepted arrangements were up for reevaluation, as an opportunity to reach out for Greenland once again.

Interestingly, these Norwegians were to be found on both sides, in the Axis as well as in the Allied camp.[56] During the exact same days that Hull sent the letter in a determined bid to rein in Norway's ambitions in Greenland once and for all, his German counterpart, Foreign Minister Joachim von Ribbentrop, was facing a similar situation in Berlin. The world-famous Norwegian writer Knut Hamsun, 81 years and by his own admission worn down by age in many ways, was visiting the German capital on urgent business. He wanted to meet with Ribbentrop in person to talk about Greenland and make his case for what he saw as Norway's historical claim to the island.[57]

Fundamentally, Hamsun's agenda was not all that different from the one quietly pursued by the Norwegian government in London. But while he had been considered a national treasure, especially after winning the Nobel Prize for Literature in 1920, he had placed himself in an awkward situation after the German attack on Norway, voicing the view that his young nation might benefit as a member of a new European order under Hitler's leadership. "Norwegians! Lay down your arms and go home," he had written in early May, while his countrymen were defending themselves desperately against the invading army. "The Germans are fighting for us all and are now breaking the British tyranny over us and all neutrals."[58]

Three months before his trip to Berlin, on June 8, 1940, Hamsun penned a letter to Josef Terboven, the newly appointed *Reichskommissar*—German governor—of Norway. Hamsun warned the high-ranking German that Denmark might use the war, when everyone's attention was directed elsewhere, as an opportunity to sell Greenland to the United States. "We Norwegians know our Danish brethren," he added. This would be completely wrong, Hamsun argued, as in his view Greenland was not for Denmark to sell: "Greenland is *Norwegian* land, from ancient times a Norwegian crown colony, where Norwegians have settled down and later had an income as trappers." The island, he added, had been "plundered" from Norway by Denmark in the Treaty of Kiel in 1814, and since then it had been impossible to wrench it from Denmark, Hamsun explained, with a clear reference to the 1933 ruling in The Hague.[59]

Hamsun had written his letter to Terboven at the prompting of Gustav Smedal, a high-profile activist campaigning for Norway's claim to Greenland. In a parallel effort, Smedal sent a document summarizing the Greenland issue to Terboven's temporary deputy in Norway, an official by the name of Hans Dellbrügge. It had the desired effect, he believed. Terboven seemed to have passed-on Hamsun's concern to Berlin, and his own appeal had apparently had an even bigger impact. "From a source I have heard that the written summary that I gave Dellbrügge has been forwarded to Hitler," Smedal wrote with a note of satisfaction in his diary in mid-June. "Any possibility that Denmark might sell Greenland during the war has been stopped."[60]

Having just sent off his letter to Terboven, Hamsun asked Smedal if the appeal should be taken further up the Nazi hierarchy, proposing yet another letter addressed to Foreign Minister Ribbentrop. "He has been positively inclined towards me in the past," Hamsun noted, obtaining Smedal's acquiescence.[61] In his letter to Ribbentrop, dated June 21,[62] Hamsun bemoaned the fact that the Greenland issue had "poisoned the relationship between Norwegians and Danes for four generations," and he was now more specific than he had been when writing to Terboven about what he thought should be done: Norway was to receive the lion's share, located to boot in the southern, more accessible part of the island, while Denmark had to make do with the distant and inhospitable north. "The Danish government must accede to a proposal from you that is beneficial and fair to both parties," Hamsun wrote.[63] To ensure that the letter had the desired impact, the author, who knew almost no German, asked Max Tau, a German *émigré* publisher, to help him translate it. Hamsun did not dwell on the fact that Max Tau was Jewish, and that he had left his country of birth for that very reason.[64]

The matter was clearly not a priority for Ribbentrop, and when he wrote back seven weeks later in August, he was nowhere near as enthusiastic as Hamsun had hoped, arguing that there were limits to what Germany could do given the American insistence on the Monroe Doctrine. Still, Hamsun was undeterred: "Ribbentrop's reply doesn't say much, but at least he doesn't say no," he wrote to Smedal.[65] It was over the following weeks that he hatched the idea of traveling to Berlin to meet face-to-face with Ribbentrop, believing that a personal appeal would help move the foreign minister into more action. "I must go to Berlin in late September," Hamsun wrote to his son Tore. "Greenland is at stake."[66]

Hamsun's other son Arild accompanied him when he arrived in Berlin at the end of the month. "I don't dare travel alone, I am old and have no energy, he knows Berlin well," the octogenarian said.[67] "I cannot *sprechen Deutsch*."[68] The old man was truly lost in the bustling German capital, and Ribbentrop had no time for him. It almost seemed a deliberate snub, even though Hamsun tried to explain it away and comforted himself with speculation that the Nazi foreign minister was probably too busy with more urgent political matters.[69] In early October, after long days of futile waiting, Hamsun left Berlin, having failed in his mission. "The trip has not been entirely successful," Smedal wrote in his diary. "He was not able to meet with Ribbentrop. He was told that Ribbentrop would only be able to see him in November."[70]

Smedal was dumbfounded. "Probably some intrigue has got in the way," he reasoned.[71] In fact, the explanation was probably much more straightforward. First of all, it was highly questionable that Germany was in a position to dictate a new international settlement for Greenland given its proximity with the United States. Besides, there was nothing to be gained for Germany in playing such a role, whereas it was bound to upset relations with Denmark, where the occupation had so far proceeded peacefully.[72] Most importantly, however, the real issue was the Monroe Doctrine, as Ribbentrop had revealed quite candidly in his earlier letter to Hamsun. In other words, he was moved by the exact same concerns that less than a year earlier had likely led Hitler to politely ignore Quisling's suggestion of a German occupation of Greenland. The Nazi leadership believed that conflict with the United States was inevitable in the long run, but for the time being, when Germany was still establishing itself as the dominant power in Europe and was secretly preparing a showdown with the Soviet Union, war or even tension with the world's strongest power was to be avoided at all costs.

Despite the failure of his Quixotic efforts, Hamsun was not about to abandon the hope of seeing the Norwegian flag flying over Greenland. It was a hope that united Norwegians on both sides of the chasm that had opened up because of the war. The followers of the government-in-exile in London and the supporters of a Nazified Norway under German tutelage might be mortal enemies, but some of them shared the aspiration of reversing the verdict from The Hague.[73] As events in the coming months would show, their Greenland dream had not been laid to rest and would come back again to complicate great power politics in the North Atlantic.

CHAPTER 9

Preempting the Nazis

Late Fall and Winter 1940

There was worsening concern in the United States about the risk of German attack and a growing conviction among decision makers that preemptive action was needed. Given the potential role of Greenland as a staging ground for Axis aggression, it was natural that the American focus on the island sharpened. "With the evolution of military technology, especially in aviation, Greenland has attained decisive strategic significance in the eyes of both the United States and Canada, not just as a base for attacks on shipping across the North Atlantic but also as a base for attacks on this continent," Kauffmann, the Danish envoy to Washington, wrote in a confidential report to Copenhagen in September 1940. "The many surprises that the war has had in store so far means that they would rather anticipate events than run an unnecessary risk."[1]

The anxieties in Washington DC had been exacerbated by the German-backed activities along the Greenland east coast during the summer. Berle at the State Department, for one, was concerned that the *Veslekari* incident reflected a pattern of German interest in the Western Hemisphere more generally and might be seen in an even broader light in connection with intensified German propaganda in Latin America and Spanish and Italian activities in Africa as part of a coordinated campaign to challenge the existing world order. "All of this might very easily be the advance flank of preparations for operations against this hemisphere based on the thesis of a German conquest of Great Britain—which of course has not happened yet and may never happen at all," he wrote in his diary.[2]

Reports of German espionage activities further fueled suspicions about Berlin's intentions. On December 7, 1940, Hugh Cumming, an official with the State Department's European Division, warned Einar Blechingberg, a senior diplomat at the Danish mission, that the New York-based photo agency "Black Star Publishing Co." might be connected to the German government. "Furthermore," Blechingberg wrote in a report to the Danish foreign ministry immediately after the conversation, "he had received information that the company was planning to approach people in Greenland, or possibly [a delegation sent from the Greenland government currently in the United States] to acquire intelligence about conditions on the east coast of Greenland, probably in connection with the '*Veslekari*' case." State Department had already seen to it that the two consuls in Greenland were informed, and Cumming asked that Kauffmann told the delegation, but in a discreet manner so that the photo agency was not made aware that it had aroused suspicion.[3]

"Black Star" had been suspected since the late 1930s of conducting espionage and spreading propaganda on behalf of the Nazi government in Berlin, ironically so, since it had been founded by German-Jewish *émigrés*. Some industry insiders believed that the suspicions were the result of malicious rumors spread by envious competitors, and the FBI, which kept an eye on the agency for years, never managed to come up with any solid evidence. One of the objects of investigation was German-born Paul Schulte, a priest with an interest in the polar regions, who carried out missionary work among the Inuit and documented his activities in photos on behalf of "Black Star." An FBI agent who reviewed the case amassed against Schulte, concluded that his photos only showed "churches and religious practices among the Eskimos."[4]

The fact was that most fears of immediate German offensive operations against Greenland on a significant scale, beyond attempts to improve weather reporting from the island, were overblown. On November 14, Hitler met with Admiral Erich Raeder, chief of the Germany Navy High Command, briefly discussing ways to attack the United States. The northern route across the Atlantic and Greenland was not a priority for the dictator, who maintained an advance across the ocean further south held more promise. "The Führer believes that the Azores give him the only option in case of American entry into the war of attacking the United States with a Messerschmitt-type airplane [...] thus forcing it to build up its still insufficient air defense rather than aiding Britain," according to a report written up after the meeting.[5] The German Naval Command was aware of the American concerns and, in its war diary, had even marveled at what it considered unwarranted paranoia: "Following press reports, precautionary measures 'against a German attack on Greenland' (!?) are being considered," it had written as early as August 9, adding exclamation and questions marks to underline its own surprise at the notion.[6]

Still, for some naval officers in Berlin, Greenland was indeed an objective, albeit for the long term. During the summer of 1940, in the afterglow of the lightening victories in the West, General Admiral Rolf Carls wrote a memorandum to the naval command, providing a vision of what the post-war world ought to look like in order for Germany to be able to defend its position as a global power with colonies in Africa and likely further afield. In that case, he argued, "Germany's strategic situation on the oceans would be fundamentally changed," and even if it respected the American sphere of influence, it would need to be the dominant power in the Atlantic to protect its maritime links with the components of its sprawling empire. "In the north, [Germany] will control a space including Norway with Spitsbergen [part of the Svalbard archipelago], the Faroe Islands Iceland, and Greenland."[7]

***

In August 1940, "Iceberg" Smith of the *Northland* met an old acquaintance on the east coast of Greenland, the American polar explorer Willie Knutsen, who had been able to hitch a ride out of occupied Norway on board *Ringsel*, the Norwegian ship that was allowed to go both to Greenland and back. Smith suggested that the hands-off attitude that the United States maintained in Greenland, including the decision to let *Ringsel* off the hook, was not going to last. "Look Willie," Smith said, "you are an American. I am going to tell you unofficially that America is not going to stay out of the war forever. President Roosevelt himself has activated plans to protect Greenland from being used by the Nazis."[8]

The same month, while *Northland* was surveying the east coast, another cutter from the US Coast Guard, *Duane*, was busy on the west coast of Greenland, reconnoitering for suitable locations for future airfields. In neither area did the Americans have adequate charts, and they often had to undertake the work from scratch, sailing up one side of a fjord and down the other while making soundings.[9] Captain Julius Lacey, a meteorological officer on loan from the Army Air Force, took part in the *Duane* expedition, taking photos from the air in a Curtiss SOC-4 biplane. There were no active plans to establish bases, but the military did what it was supposed to do and made ready for any eventuality, including an occupation of Greenland.[10] While stopping at Godthaab, Lacey also met Aksel Svane, the governor of southern Greenland. They had a revealing conversation.

"How would you react if Canadian or British troops occupied Greenland?" Lacey asked him.

"I would launch a formal protest, but I would make arrangements for positive and close cooperation as far as Danish interests and the welfare of the Greenland people allowed it," Svane replied.

"Would you protest if American forces occupied the island?" Lacey continued.

"No," Svane replied.[11]

In this way, officers in the field were discussing openly what was only hinted at further up the ranks in the US government: that an American military presence in Greenland was probably going to happen sooner or later. Those with political responsibility could not state this in a straightforward manner, as they feared being dragged into the war in Europe, but those who would be called on to implement an occupation of Greenland started making contingency plans. The American Army was also quietly getting ready for deployment on the island. In September, George C. Marshall, the army chief of staff, told one of his subordinate officers confidentially that ski training for a number of units was needed, partly due to "the possibility of some duty in Greenland."[12]

Meanwhile at Ivigtut, armed Americans were already deployed. Following repeated requests from the Greenland authorities for assistance in guarding the mine, Washington had relented and allowed a team of 13 former Coast Guard members to depart in August.[13] Once they had arrived, they were issued a special blue uniform with a star, on which was written "Ivigtut Cryolite Mine."[14] A small police force would probably not be able to do much against a German landing attempt or even a commando raid, and upon arrival, it did not even unpack the gun that had been brought earlier that summer by *Comanche*.[15] Although it was not said so openly at the time, the truth was that the 13 American guards were responsible as much for internal as for external security. "Guards were posted at the mine, also when no one was at work there, even during the lunch break," said Christian Sørensen, a sailor. "The reason was allegedly fear of sabotage. Rumors had circulated in Ivigtut that a Dane had spied on the mine two years earlier."[16]

While caution was the name of the game for the US government, decision-makers were gradually being pushed towards acceptance of bases in Greenland. In August, the State Department was disturbed by British and Canadian plans to set up a landing field in southern Greenland, permitting airplanes to make refueling stops while flying from Labrador via Iceland to Britian. Berle was not happy. "The difficulty of this is that if planes can go East that way they can likewise come West; and I am not enthusiastic about developing an air route which might be used by an enemy to make trouble for us," he wrote in his diary. "The moment it becomes an air ferry station, we would have to contemplate the possibility that the Germans might try to interrupt the place."[17] Berle asked the army if it objected to the Canadian plans and was surprised when it said it did not.[18] "My own feeling," Berle commented in his diary, "is that if anybody has a base in Greenland I prefer that we do."[19]

It all led up to a meeting at the State Department on November 12, which turned out to be crucial. Present on the Danish side were Kauffmann and Svane, the latter visiting from Greenland, while the United States was represented by Berle and Penfield, the US consul in Godthaab. At the start of the talks, Svane mentioned the incident just two days earlier when a German plane had dropped a message at Ella Island, inquiring about the fate of the four Danes in the Nazi-funded weather operation. Against this background, in a somber demonstration that Greenland was within striking distance of Hitler's war machine, Svane raised the issue of how to defend Ivigtut, essential both to American and Allied armaments and to the Greenland economy.[20]

"A more adequate defense of the mine is needed as the cryolite income is vital to the well-being of Greenland and capture or destruction of the mine would be catastrophic," Svane said.

He suggested that one more gun, along with the necessary crew to handle it, would be a welcome strengthening of the mine's ability to defend itself.

"Two three-inch guns would probably be sufficient to repel any casual small raider of the type which operated on the east coast this summer, but against any craft mounting six-inch guns they would hardly be able to provide any defense worthy of the name," Berle replied.

Perhaps what was needed was more robust defense beyond what the Greenland authorities themselves could mobilize, the American official said, adding:

"I have not considered exactly what form this might take but presume that it might be in the nature of some sort of base which would permit the conduct of adequate patrols."

The import of Berle's words was clear to those present. American bases were just a question of time, awaiting the official decision from the very top. As Svane recalled later: "The entire winter of 1940 and 1941, we were waiting for the Americans, who had of course announced their arrival in the meeting in Washington DC on November 12, 1940."[21]

***

By late 1940, the American presence in Greenland was still modest and characterized by makeshift arrangements. The small consular staffs of both the United States and Canada in Godthaab were initially housed in the home of the local Danish doctor. Their offices attracted quite a lot of attention among the population, as they were equipped "with all manners of American comfort," according to a Danish resident.[22] "After we'd been there awhile, we'd had a Sears Roebuck house shipped up, that is, all the parts, and it was constructed by a Greenland carpenter. We also had put in batteries and a wind charger," American diplomat George L. West recalled.[23]

On the surface, the encounter between Americans, Greenlanders and Danes was a friendly one. Brun, the northern governor, wrote to Roosevelt in October 1940 that it had been "impossible for the Danes in Greenland to carry on their social and cultural work for the education of the Greenlanders, which we always have found it our duty to carry on, but [for] the kind and humanitarian help from the United States." At the same time, however, Brun also expressed the hope that "we shall be able to get through these hard times without interruption of our work."[24] He had expressed similar sentiments a few months earlier when talking to *The New York Times*: "For the present at any rate, Greenland does not need any other assistance than good advice from experts in connection with her trade."[25]

There were signs of emerging friction between the Danes and the Americans in Greenland. In particular, Svane, the southern governor, was a cause of concern, according to the American consul, Penfield. Svane was "unable to grasp the 'feel' of the situations in his dealings with people, a fault which many times leads to unnecessary and unconscious tactlessness on his part," Penfield wrote in a dispatch to Washington DC.[26] This had severe consequences in one crucial respect: Unbeknownst to much of the outside world, the supply of Greenland cryolite, and by extension the fate of military aviation in the Allied camp, was held hostage to the whims of a fickle workforce at the Ivigtut mine. There was a tense relationship between the island's authorities and the mine workers, and it could be argued that Svane's conduct only worsened matters.

The workers were furious that the governor, who traveled up and down the coast visiting small communities during much of 1940, waited months to come to see them. It did not help that Svane also closed down a small newspaper that the miners published for internal distribution, carrying news from around the world. In this tense atmosphere, even the slightest faux pas could be interpreted as a deliberate slight and trigger an angry reaction from the workers. Representatives of the miners had visited the United States, and on the way back, their ship sailed straight to Godthaab before dropping them off at Ivigtut. The consequence was a two-day strike.[27]

Significantly, when Brun visited the United States in late 1940 with plans to stay until early the next year, he was encouraged to return to Greenland. "To leave the other Sub-Governor Svane all alone with many difficult local problems, such as the mines, the labor troubles, distribution and shipping, etc., would normally be unwise, but it is the more unfortunate in times like these," an influential New York-based Danish-American businessman wrote.[28] Berle issued a direct order to the Danish governor: "I told Brun bluntly he had to go back to Greenland."[29]

In fact, the governors were pressured from two sides. On the one hand, the Americans were constantly on their case, watching their every step, and on the other, the Danish envoy to Washington, Kauffmann, saw them as a challenge to his authority as Washington's main negotiating partner on Greenland issues. During the crucial winter months of 1940 and 1941, when the American decision about setting up bases in Greenland matured, Kauffmann took pains to ensure that both of the governors were far from the US capital where they could have left their footprint on the decision-making.[30]

The two Greenland governors entered 1941 in a weakened position. While Brun was still valued by the Americans for his vigor, Svane was increasingly seen as an obstacle to progress. "He was rather nervous," recalled American vice consul George West. "He was worried about his retirement when the Germans had won the war."[31] The impression of an official whose net contribution was negative also spread among the Danes. "It was the general impression," said a member of the Danish community in Greenland, "that Svane did not want to delegate responsibility, and as he did not avail himself of assistance from others, things didn't move as fast as they could. Many also felt that he seemed under too much strain."[32]

CHAPTER 10

The Yanks Are Coming

Winter and Spring 1941

At a press conference on January 7, 1941, President Roosevelt was asked to react to a report from Reuters out of Stockholm saying that the United States was in the process of occupying Greenland or had already done so. "New one on me! I must have been asleep," Roosevelt said, triggering laughter among the reporters.[1] That may have been true in a strict sense, but it is unlikely that the American president was unaware of the intense deliberations taking place on the subject in senior government circles. The dilemma that the Americans were in remained unaltered. Ideally, as long as the US government was aiming for neutrality in the conflict in Europe, it would prefer that Greenland stayed isolated from hostilities, fearing that if the island became a battleground, it would increase the risk that the United States would be dragged into the war. On the other hand, if any of the belligerents were to make a move on the island, the United States would rather get there first.

This was also true in case the belligerents making that move were the British or the Canadians. That scenario, which had already been discussed at length the previous year, moved up the agenda again in early 1941. The day before Roosevelt's remark, on January 6, a member of the Canadian mission in Washington DC had told Cumming at the State Department that Britain wanted Canada to explore the possibilities of setting up an airbase in Greenland. The airbase would be needed in order to transfer a total of 12,000 airplanes which the United States had agreed the previous fall to deliver to Britain.[2] At the same time, the Canadian diplomat opened up the possibility of direct American participation. "The Greenland authorities themselves could, with the assistance of the United States, undertake the construction of such facilities," he said.[3]

The Canadian approach, and other similar approaches by Britain, forced Washington to act. Over the next few weeks, the State Department prepared an appeal to the Greenland governors, explaining the Canadian ambitions and suggesting instead the dispatch of a group of American experts that were to survey the southern part of the island for proper locations for "civil aerodromes and additional radio and meteorological facilities." Crucially, these facilities were to be built by the Greenland authorities themselves.[4] The American consul in Greenland, Penfield, introduced the proposal in a meeting with Svane on January 31, and received a positive reply from Svane the following day: "The Greenland authorities will be pleased to receive a group of American Experts."[5]

There was not much time, for the Canadians were impatient. On February 6, Berle noted in his diary that a Canadian battalion had been lined up, ready to be sent to Greenland. "Either the Canadians or the British or we will be moving pretty soon," he noted.[6] On the same day, he met with representatives of the army, the navy and the Coast Guard, arguing that if the United States did not act on Greenland, others would, and the result could be war on America's doorstep. It seemed, Berle said, "obvious that the utilization of an aerodrome in neutral Greenland by Canadian or British military planes would open Greenland to the possibility of an attack by German forces."[7]

One week later, on February 13, Secretary of State Hull met with Roosevelt and got his approval to go ahead with the Greenland base plan.[8] The same day, Berle again met with Canadian diplomats, and now, armed with full political support, told them directly that "they couldn't grab an air base there." Instead, he informed the Canadians that the Greenland government would build one with American help, which seemed to satisfy them. To Berle, there was no question that a crucial turning point in American diplomacy had been reached. This was "a case where we are forced into a move primarily lest a military enemy should grab it first and make trouble for us," he wrote in his diary. "It is, I think, a distinct new step in the American position. For the first time, the Monroe Doctrine has to be implemented militarily on a frontier."[9]

***

On February 18, Kauffmann visited Berle in his office at the State Department. In the course of the conversation, it became clear to the Danish envoy how far the American plans for building bases in Greenland had progressed, including the imminent dispatch of American experts, and how deeply involved the two governors on the island had become. Kauffmann put up a brave front even though he was confronted with the possibility that he was being sidelined in the most important issue on the Danish-American agenda since the German occupation the year before. He offered his assistance in communicating with the governors, but Berle turned him down, saying it was not needed for the time being. Kauffmann tried again:

"I rather hope, however, that it will be taken up through me," he said.

"We can discuss that later," Berle replied, somewhat coolly. "I merely wanted to let you know how our minds are running."

While preparations for the dispatch of the American experts to Greenland were still under way, on March 5, a gathering in Berle's office of army, navy and Coast

Guard officials—"an impressive meeting" in Berle's own words—decided to change one key precondition for the entire mission. "Considerations of defense, jurisdiction, operation and maintenance" meant that it was no longer considered practicable to trust the Danish authorities in Greenland with building the landing fields, and the officials present agreed to hand the job to the United States Army.[10] With this altered brief, the team of experts, consisting of representatives from the State, Treasury, Navy and War Departments, left the United States on board the US Coast Guard cutter *Cayuga* on March 17.[11]

From this moment onwards, the role of the Greenland governors became more peripheral. To put it simply, they were outmaneuvered by Kauffmann, who mobilized his entire diplomatic skillset and his personal charm to persuade the Americans that he was the one they ought to deal with when it came to Greenland matters, not the governors. The fact that the State Department decided to listen to him, even though it was free to stick to the governors, may also have been caused by practical concerns, related to the decision by the Americans to build the bases themselves rather than entrust the Greenland authorities with the task. The governors, with their detailed legal and economic knowledge, would be harder to push around than Kauffmann, who was not to the same extent intimately involved in Greenland affairs.[12]

The stage was now set for detailed negotiations between the State Department and the Danish mission in Washington DC headed by Kauffmann. The resulting treaty, which was signed by Hull and Kauffmann on the symbolic day of April 9, 1941, one year after the German occupation of Denmark, gave the United States contractual rights to establish bases in Greenland. Article 2 of the agreement read that "it is agreed that the Government of the United States shall have the right to construct, maintain and operate such landing fields, seaplane facilities and radio and meteorological installations as may be necessary" to keep Greenland's existing status. The following article gave the Americans the right to deepen harbors, construct roads and build houses, in short "any and all things necessary to ensure the efficient operation, maintenance and protection of such defense facilities as may be established."[13]

The announcement was a shock to the Danish government. As late as on March 17, the *charge d'affaires* of the US Embassy in Copenhagen had visited the Danish foreign ministry, reassuring the officials there that no plans existed for American air bases in Greenland.[14] The governors in Greenland had also been kept out of the loop until the very last moment before it was made public. Only on April 5, it was presented to them in the form of a fait accompli. Svane was furious. "He appeared to appreciate the position of the United States but was much more agitated and concerned than I have ever seen him," Penfield wrote in a dispatch from Godthaab. The governor initially wanted it to be put on record that he concurred to the treaty "only under protest," but after having been talked down by Penfield, he agreed to a more moderate wording, concurring "under the extreme force of circumstances."[15]

Kauffmann had won, and the two governors were forced to see themselves rendered without influence on one of the most important Danish diplomatic agreements in decades. This turn of events had been facilitated by a sense in Washington DC that Svane was not to be trusted. "He will have to make a choice," Cumming of the State Department wrote in his diary about Svane shortly afterwards, "either play ball with the US which is trying to restore Denmark, or line up on the other side."[16] Soon, he realized he had been too harsh on Svane. When Cumming met with the governor in Godthaab in May, he described the way that the agreement had been imposed on the governors as a "diktat" and "a black page on the records."[17] At the same time, he moderated his views further in his diary: "I find that I like Svane more and more. He is slow but very honest in his thinking and rigidly devoted to his duty. He is certainly no pro-Nazi."[18]

***

At 6:25am on March 31, 1941, Rudolf Schütze, an experienced arctic pilot, took off from the Luftwaffe airfield at Trondheim, Norway. His objective was Greenland. His aircraft, a two-engine Heinkel He 111, carried 5,400 liters of fuel, enough for the long flight. After having flown for several hours across the North Atlantic, the dark gray monotony of the ocean surface started being broken up by icebergs, appearing as scattered specks of white. Then the jagged east coast of Greenland could be seen. He reached the town of Scoresby Sound and was taken aback by how small it was, with no more than twenty wooden houses. "We see clearly how a group of people run from one of the biggest houses towards a tall flagpole. There they hoist the Danish flag as fast as they can," Schütze wrote later. "Obviously they have noticed the German markings, and they want to show us that they are pro-German, or at least not loyal to Britain or the United States."[19]

Schütze's flight served no immediate purpose and was perhaps the closest he came to undertaking a regular sightseeing trip during his military career, as he had always wanted to view Greenland from the air and was granted permission to undertake the somewhat unusual flight because it was his 100th mission.[20] Unwittingly, however, he and Bernhard Jope, another German pilot who also flew to Greenland in late March, helped precipitate the signing of the Greenland treaty. The two German flights were reported immediately to Washington DC, which shared the information with London.[21] A few days later, Secretary of State Hull cited "the flights of German planes over Scoresby Sound" as one of the reasons why the agreement on bases in Greenland could not be delayed.[22]

Overall, the record on German air force plans for Greenland is scarce, as reflected in the scattered evidence about the Luftwaffe's experimental airfield on the glacier in Norway less than a year earlier. Still, there are tantalizing clues that the construction of air bases on the island were being discussed among German officers. When he drafted his war memoirs years later, British Prime Minister Winston S. Churchill described the American establishment of an air base in Greenland in the spring of 1941, then adding: "It was known that the Germans intended similar action."[23] Reports of this nature also reached the US government at about the same time. "Loyal Norwegians sent us the disquieting news that Germany was preparing to base an air squadron on the East Coast [of Greenland], and service it with U-boats," according to Samuel Eliot Morison, the official historian of the US Navy in World War II.[24] The State Department also noted that the Germans had purchased detailed maps of Greenland in occupied Denmark, while it was considered suspicious that some Danish individuals had been allowed to travel to Godthaab and Ivigtut with the German authorities' tacit approval.[25]

At the same time, both British and American intelligence received reports about German weather stations actually being established in Greenland. "It was known that the Germans had already installed weather-reporting stations on the east coast," Churchill wrote in his war memoirs.[26] Similarly, Secretary of War Henry L. Stimson noted in his diary about a Cabinet meeting on April 25, 1941: "The President mentioned the rumor that had come up to the effect that the Germans already had a force landed on the east coast of Greenland. He said that the British Admiralty and the Navy were not inclined to believe the rumor but the War Department did believe it and that he was inclined to believe the War Department."[27]

In fact, the War Department was wrong, and at this particular time, the spring of 1941, no such plans were actually in the works, mostly because of Hitler's reluctance to provoke the United States. Indeed, German propaganda tried to make light of these American concerns. This was reflected in the censored Danish media, which cited claims by Roosevelt that Axis troops had landed in Greenland. "In Berlin, they reject any reports of an occupation of Greenland as hallucinations and declare that Germany has never had any intention whatsoever of getting near the Danish colony," according to a report in *Nationaltidende*, one of the major Danish dailies.[28]

Behind the scenes, however, the Nazi leaders found nothing to laugh about. "Berlin showed a great deal of interest in the Greenland question," Cecil von Renthe-Fink, the German envoy to Denmark, said in post-war interrogations. "Kauffmann's conclusion of the agreement with the United States caused great consternation in Berlin." The German government was left with the impression that the Danish king had tacitly approved of Kauffmann's actions, and a crisis was only averted when the monarch made a public protest over the Danish diplomat's behavior.[29] Likewise, Foreign Minister Joachim von Ribbentrop confirmed during the Nuremberg Trial after the war, that it was an issue of great concern. "The occupation of Greenland, Iceland, on the African Continent, et cetera; the aid given to Soviet Russia after the outbreak of this war," he said. "All these measures strengthened the Führer's conviction that sooner or later he would certainly have to reckon with a war against America."[30]

***

The United States stumbled into the position of protector of Greenland, with only vague knowledge of the vast territory. In a conference in Washington DC in April, Assistant Secretary of War for Air Robert A. Lovett poured over a map of Greenland, saying in half-despair: "There is only one name in this I can pronounce."[31] The American giant, which had been tucked up in isolationist slumber, was waking up to global responsibilities. Secretary of Labor Frances Perkins later described how shockingly new it was. "I remember that at the May 1, 1941, cabinet meeting, Roosevelt said that we were going to use Greenland for patrols. I remember being so startled at the thought of Greenland's icy mountains coming to be an airbase," she recalled. "All of a sudden the world shrank. Greenland was something you went to and did things with, not just a place where Eskimos lived."[32]

In its public statements, the United States also ensured that its new position was known to friend and foe alike. In April 1941, Admiral Ernest J. King, commander of the Atlantic Fleet, drew a more comprehensive demarcation of the Western Hemisphere than the one made public after the Panama conference, now also including Greenland. He also made clear the consequences of entering into the area: "Entrance into the Western Hemisphere by naval ships or aircraft of belligerents other than those powers having sovereignty over territory in the Western Hemisphere is to be viewed as possibly actuated by an unfriendly interest toward shipping or territory in the Western Hemisphere."[33] Roosevelt declared an unlimited national emergency in a public address on May 27, 1941, describing the defense of the Western Hemisphere as beginning well into the Atlantic, including Greenland: "It is stupid to wait until a probable enemy has gained a foothold from which to attack," he said. "Old-fashioned common sense calls for the use of a strategy that will prevent such an enemy from gaining a foothold in the first place."[34]

The change brought about by the April 9 treaty also meant American forces began trickling into Greenland and its surrounding waters. Before the end of the month, the navy had established Task Force 11, consisting of the Coast Guard cutters *Northland* and *North Star* as well as the ageing USS *Bear*, a dual steam-powered and sailing ship. The force was ordered to patrol the northeastern coastline and "prevent establishment of military, naval and air bases, or landing of European nationals except as authorized by the Government of Greenland."[35] In a parallel effort, the US Army assembled a Greenland force consisting of 469 officers and men—engineers, artillery and infantry—and prepared it for shipment to the southern part of the island on board the two transports USS *Munargo* and USS *Chateau Thierry*.[36]

Despite the intensified activity, doubts were expressed from various parties. The Canadian government continued to voice concerns about the US ability to defend Greenland, especially the mine at Ivigtut, and as late as May, Ottawa's idea of sending a garrison to the island was not completely off the table, triggering a strongly worded message from Roosevelt to Mackenzie King: "The President would deprecate [a] Canadian garrison being sent to Greenland," the Canadian prime minister told London. "He has plans prepared for the protection of Greenland which he thinks would be effective in case of trouble."[37] More surprisingly perhaps, US General Marshall also openly vented worries that Greenland's geography might pose an insurmountable obstacle to the establishment of the airfields needed to ferry airplanes to Britain. "In fact it is rather probable that this route may be found impracticable," he wrote in a memorandum to Admiral Harold Stark, chief of naval operations.[38]

The initial attempts by the army force sent to Greenland to build the first base were not encouraging. It was at Narsarssuak, on the west coast, at a place that would be widely known as Bluie West 1. To be sure, the location was ideal, almost exactly the same distance of 775 miles from air bases in Goose Bay, Labrador, and Reykjavik, Iceland, respectively. This meant that there were enough stops on the transatlantic route that even fighter planes with their shorter ranges would be able to fly to the British Isles.[39] However, the American vice consul George West visited the troops and got first-hand knowledge of the challenges the construction teams faced, including a topography that did not exactly invite the construction of large airfields. "Although there was a little gravel on the top, you got down a bit and you had these [...] boulders," he recalled later.[40] "They had an awful time getting equipment ashore [...] All kinds of ships were sent up with heavy equipment. They were stuck there sometimes for over a month just because of the tempestuous weather."[41] It was perhaps some consolation that the Americans were not the first to try to make the area habitable, since Bluie West 1 was close to Erik the Red's old farm, as Brun, the southern governor explained during a visit. "I once told a Catholic clergy, which was with the army up there, that just across the fjord were the ruins of the oldest Catholic church in the Western Hemisphere," he said. "This made a deep impression on him."[42]

***

Penfield, the American consul, had soon grown tired of Greenland. The entire island was a backward place that was not helped by having been deliberately isolated for generations, he wrote in a dispatch to the State Department in May 1941. "There are a lot of false reports and rumors always current in a country like Greenland which is so cut off from world events. These rumors and reports are often repeated, even though obviously inspired to a considerable extent by active imaginations, by reliable Greenlanders and even the more sophisticated Danes," he said.[43] As for the Greenlanders, he commented disparagingly in another report, "in their childlike way, they invariably approve of anyone who gives them things."[44]

Greenland politics was no better than you might expect against this background, Penfield said, describing a meeting of elected representatives with utter disdain. "The session as a whole gave more the impression of a class in school than of a deliberative assembly in operation," he wrote. "It is only natural, however, that a people which has lived under the extremely paternal Danish colonial system for over two hundred years should be characterized by an immature provisionalism, and the tone of the Council meetings is certainly no reflection on the native intelligence or character of the people."[45] There was little interest among the local population in the work of the assemblies, evidenced in the lack of spectators at the meetings, even though they were open to the public, he complained.[46]

Some of the unhappiness that permeated Penfield's reports back to Washington DC was also noticed on the other side of the enforced cultural encounter that evolved as more and more Americans traveled to Greenland in the course of 1941, most visibly when Coast Guard cutters were making brief stops at its major harbors. "The visits of the American inspection vessels did not happen without friction everywhere," said Christian Sørensen, a Danish sailor. "Overall, the Greenlanders felt somewhat uncomfortable with the Americans."[47] Some of the Greenlanders complained about what they saw as racial prejudice. "When we trade with them, they treat us as if we have no brains," a Greenlander said angrily.[48]

Still, the arrival of the Americans in ever greater numbers in the course of 1941 also meant pleasant surprises. They brought hitherto unknown prosperity to the Greenlanders. The new ties with the United States meant a drastic increase in the consumer items available. "The Greenlanders were fond of several American products, clothes and so on, which were completely different from what they were used to from Denmark," an eyewitness said.[49] Catalogues from American department stores were distributed among the population, who were able to order a variety of consumer items, although they often had to wait months for delivery. As US trading companies were unable to meet the demand for the ubiquitous fish-oil lamps, kerosene lamps were permitted. Home by home, the Greenlanders were bathed in a bright modern light during the dark winter months. It was "the single biggest technical advance in Greenland history," according to Brun, the governor.[50]

War was a welcome change to some. The workers at the cryolite mine in Ivigtut had a strange feeling of liberation. "We didn't feel very bothered by our isolation," said Erik Juhl, an engineer. "Especially it helped that the rest of Greenland was opened up, so that workers and managers could go traveling, and in addition we were allowed to visit the United States and Canada."[51] Aksel Svane found out that the Aluminum Company of Canada was often better placed at sourcing supplies than anyone else. "The company is a 'great power' and could often provide supplies which [...] our contacts in New York could not," he told a reporter.[52]

American censors reading the mail of the Greenlanders reported that they were happy, "adapting themselves easily to the changing conditions, and are, on the whole, contented. This is no doubt due to the fact that they are materially well provided for. Their connections with American and Canadian ships have added interest and excitement to their lives."[53] Godthaab was experiencing a craze for everything American, a local Dane reported. "Everyone wants to learn English, also many Greenlanders, and a female lecturer from the teachers' training college is busy teaching classes."[54]

Kirkwood, the Canadian consul, was also giving private lessons, stating that the English fad was triggered by frequent visits by Coast Guard vessels, but not only that. "[It] is also a reflection of the subconscious feeling here (sometimes expressed but often not admitted) of a possible future drift of Greenland into a North American orbit, and misgivings as to Greenland's future political affiliation," he noted.[55] Many Greenlanders, especially the young, became enthusiastic about the United States. "The United States, this huge and immeasurably prosperous country, had many fans among the Greenlanders, and some people even thought that it would be better and more beneficial if Greenland was ruled by the United States after the war," a resident of Greenland recalled six decades later.[56]

There was another, and more immediate cause of concern which the Greenland governors explained in a meeting with Penfield in May 1941. If US servicemen in Greenland spent too much money, it could create dangerous divisions in local society, they argued. Those with access to the Americans could become richer than the rest too fast and "abandon their normal ways of life for others less suitable to their unsophisticated nature."[57] Secretary of State Cordell Hull voiced similar concerns to Henry Morgenthau, the treasury secretary, in a letter sent one month earlier: "You will be interested to know that the German propaganda has already made much of the assertion that the contact of Greenlanders with Americans will result in the enslavement, miscegenation and ultimate extinction of the native population."[58]

***

Sentiments such as those described by Hull might have more of an audience in Greenland than he knew. In a surprising development, an embryonic Nazi movement emerged among indigenous youth in at least some settlements along Greenland's west coast. "There were local fans of the Nazis during the early years of the war, when Germany was still victorious. In a certain settlement there were rumors that a local Nazi association was to be formed. A teacher at the teachers' training college was from southern Denmark and was rooting for the Germans. It rubbed off on some of his students," an eyewitness testified much later.[59]

Once he observed a surprising episode: "During a dance in the college gym, the Nazi students stepped onto the stage, wearing homemade armbands. They showed a portrait of the Führer and talked about his excellent qualities. The demonstration ended when the young people held the arm straight in front of them, yelling 'Heil Hitler!'"[60] The extant sources of this peculiar phenomenon are scarce,[61] providing little basis for speculating about its origins. However, as it appears that most followers were young, it may have been part of a youthful rebellion against traditional society, while lingering resentment over Danish colonial rule may also have fed admiration of Hitler's Germany, the occupier of Denmark, based on the idea that "my enemy's enemy is my friend."

An eyewitness said many years later that there had been rivaling pro-American and anti-American groups among the students at the college. The principal of the college was also rumored to have been a Nazi sympathizer and possibly to have facilitated the emergence of pro-Nazi sentiments.[62] A Greenlander who was young then explained the varieties of opinion. "As was the case with rationing, the war divided the Greenland population into three different categories: Those loyal to Denmark, the pro-Americans, and the Nazi sympathizers," he said. "The Nazis also had fans among the Greenland youth during the war, especially during the first period when Germany was victorious. Young students at the teacher training college even demonstrated in favor of Adolf Hitler."[63]

The issue was not limited to Godthaab. In the settlement of Holsteinsborg further up the west coast, a group of young people attempted to set up a Nazi chapter, introducing Nazi armbands and the Nazi greeting. It became influential and ambitious enough that its members wanted to take over the leadership of a local community association which was in charge of organizing cultural events and similar activities. "It seemed the young people were so aggressive that the older community members couldn't stop them," a junior official reported in a letter from the town. "It all seemed very cunning with an 'underground' force seeking to fan the flames without surfacing itself." However, Leif Regnar Hagensen, the local representative of the colonial administration, managed to quell the movement.[64]

Possibly related to this, Holsteinborg appears to have been the scene of considerable tension throughout the war years. An account from the early war years includes the following passage: "Colonial chief Schultz had experienced major trouble with the local population. At one point it had gone so far that the Greenlanders had threatened to kill the colonial chief, and it was rumored that the Coast Guard ship *Northland* was to be dispatched. However, the assistant had allegedly managed to settle the dispute before the arrival of the ship."[65] Brun in a letter also described that some "combative fellows" had threatened to shoot a representative of the colonial power in Holsteinsborg.[66] The fact that a Nazi movement, most likely embryonic, emerged in a town with a history of tension between the locals and the Danish administrators, strengthens the suspicion that Nazi sympathies were primarily a means of expressing antipathy against Danish colonial rule. As the war progressed, and knowledge about the crimes of Hitler's regime spread, these sentiments, born out of ignorance about actual conditions in Europe, faded away.

CHAPTER 11

Of Dogs and Men

Summer and Fall 1941

On August 25, an American seaplane landed at the police station on Ella Island on the east coast of Greenland. It picked up one of the station's two occupants, Aage de Lemos, the man who had observed the German aircraft in November the previous year seeking news about the lost *Furenak* expedition. De Lemos, 45 years of age, was tiring of his work in the isolated outpost, and as the seaplane was taking him north for talks with representatives of the US Coast Guard, he was preparing what he planned to say. The station was poorly equipped. The clothing that he could obtain from the Americans was inadequate and better suited for the tropics. There was no tobacco and no fresh fruit. And worst of all, the job was meaningless. The station was 60 miles from the ocean, squeezed in between high mountains, which he thought rendered the meteorological observations that he had had to contribute of questionable value.[1]

After flying for about 100 miles, the seaplane carrying de Lemos touched down at the scientific station at Eskimoness. Edward "Iceberg" Smith, commander of the Northeast Greenland Patrol, the renamed Task Force 11, was awaiting him there on board the Coast Guard cutter USS *Northland*. Immediately upon seeing Smith, de Lemos launched himself into a lengthy tirade about why the police station on Ella Island ought to be closed down and he himself sent to the more populated west coast where he could act as a translator between English and Danish and would be of greater value for the money that he was paid. Smith listened patiently and then replied that the station was to stay. It was needed more than ever, he explained, as it was designated to become one of the bases for a new sledge patrol which was to be formed from scratch with the chief responsibility of keeping a watch on the entire northeast coast of Greenland.[2]

Smith handed de Lemos a freshly typewritten document which got right down to business. "Sledge patrols of Northeast Greenland during the cold months of the year (October–June) have been found desirable," the opening paragraph stated. "They should be regarded as confidential." It then went on to outline the responsibilities of the new unit. "The patrol should be essentially one of reconnaissance and

Sledge patrol's stations in northeast Greenland.

search, first of the closed hunting stations and numerous huts and then of the more remote places and secluded fjords which would naturally be suspected of providing concealment," read the document, which was addressed to de Lemos personally. "The patrol should be devoted to the detection, and notification to the proper officials, of the presence of any radio, military, naval, or air activity by persons of a belligerent power."[3]

De Lemos accepted, as did the handful of other Danish police officers and trappers along the northeast coast contacted at the same time. Norwegian nationals were given the opportunity to join the patrol in order to signal that it was not a Danish attempt to reinforce sovereignty over the area. Initially, just one Norwegian applied and was accepted.[4] A few Greenlanders were also employed as helpers, but it was decided from the outset that they would not be required to take part in any combat operations.[5] The patrol was to man three stations along the east coast: Scoresby Sound in the south, Ella Island in the center, and Eskimoness furthest up north.[6] The equipment was basic, and the members were issued Springfield rifles used in World War I.[7] "The original plans for the sledge patrol were rather extensive and required a great number of small patrols in order to cover the very great area assigned to the service," Brun later wrote. "The patrols were therefore relatively small, mostly consisting of one patrolman accompanied by one or two native sledge drivers."[8]

The background of the sledge patrol was a gap in understanding of conditions on the northeast coast of Greenland, felt as far away as in Washington DC. Amid the slew of intelligence reports in spring of actual or impending German attempts to set up weather stations in Greenland, the secretaries of war and the navy, Henry Stimson and Frank Knox, had written a memorandum to Roosevelt in April, listing the likely German moves in the months ahead. "When the ice conditions permit, in July, Germany may attempt to establish new weather stations and to send supplies to any which may now be in operation," they warned. "Since the region involved is slightly less than 1,000 miles from German bases in Norway, attempt may also be made to establish aviation facilities."[9] In his reply, Roosevelt concurred: "I think Germany will probably seek to get a definite foothold even if this foothold can only defend its own location. Therefore, our own expedition should be fitted out with sufficient guns to hold the Scoresby Sound area until early September, leaving just before the ice closes in," the president wrote.[10]

Four reconnaissance flights carried out in late May and early June by American PBY Catalina planes, led to the conclusion that whatever the Germans might be planning, they were not present in Greenland yet. "There was absolutely no sign of any kind of habitation [...] This entire section is by far the most barren, desolate and unhabitable area that can be imagined," one of the pilots reported afterwards.[11] Roosevelt was undeterred and so was Brun, the governor of Greenland. "It appeared obvious that the Germans were interested in establishing stations in that part of the coast," Brun wrote later.[12]

The question was how to keep an eye on a part of the world that was this remote and inaccessible, trying to detect what would likely be a small band of men within the vast wilderness. New airbases were soon to be built, but it would be difficult to institute routine reconnaissance flights of an area this huge, and naval patrols were limited to only parts of the year because of the ice.[13] In this situation, the idea of a sledge patrol was promoted by the Coast Guard and was accepted by the War Department after some hesitation.[14]

The official decision to set up a sledge patrol service appears to have been made in the middle of the summer, possibly on July 19, 1941, during a meeting in Julianehaab attended by Smith, Penfield and Brun.[15] According to Max Dunbar, the later Canadian consul in Godthaab, the impetus to set up the patrol came from Brun, who saw a need for the unit following the German attempts to establish a weather reporting system on the Greenland east coast. "These operations inspired Eske Brun to the establishment of a small 'Greenland army' composed of Danes, Norwegians and Greenlanders based on the northeast coast," he wrote in short memoirs from his time in Greenland.[16]

It is disputed if Brun indeed took the first initiate to the sledge patrol as claimed by Dunbar. Predictably, Coast Guard historians credit Smith. "As founder and champion of the concept within the U.S. military and senior officer with control of the needed resources and logistic support, Iceberg Smith was indeed the 'founding father' of the North-East Greenland Sledge Patrol," says one.[17] Smith was "largely responsible for the creation of the Greenland Sledge Patrol," writes another.[18] It appears likely that the original initiative to set up the sledge patrol did indeed come from the Americans. "The American side proposed the establishment of an expanded police force along the coastline, with the responsibility of reporting all alien activity to the American military authorities," wrote Niels Ove Jensen, one of the officers placed in charge of the new unit.[19]

Whether or not he was the originator of the idea, Brun was eager. He had been frustrated that American papers reported extensively about Norway's resistance against Germany while saying very little about Danish efforts.[20] "The administration felt that it would be possible to play an active role in the area against the German war effort," Brun recalled later.[21] The sledge patrol that would monitor the inhospitable northeast was just the right opportunity to show off Danish activism. Penfield, on the other hand, was skeptical about the usefulness of the new unit.[22] It would soon be put to the test, although the challenge would not come from Germany, but from Norway.

***

The Norwegian foray into Greenland had ended in failure in the fall of 1940 with the capture of *Veslekari*, but the dream of a future on the island had not died. This was true for Norwegians on both sides of the Axis-Allies divide. In June 1941, the Norwegian government-in-exile in London contacted the US government with a proposal to have the remaining Norwegian trappers on the east coast of Greenland supplied by a Norwegian warship. On the surface, it was a humanitarian gesture, but it could easily be seen as a repetition of earlier tactics of increasing Norway's footprint in Greenland in preparation of later territorial claims, and Washington turned the proposal down.[23] The United States had got what it wanted in terms of access to Greenland from Denmark, and while America was not yet a belligerent nation, it identified increasingly with the Allied cause, and in this light, it did not wish to facilitate friction inside the Allied camp between two nations that were arguably its members, Denmark and Norway.[24]

It was in consequence of the same policy that Secretary of State Cordell Hull had sent his stern letter the previous fall to Morgenstierne, the Norwegian envoy in Washington DC, criticizing the overactive Norwegian moves in Greenland waters, but in early 1941, it had resulted in a reply from the Norwegian diplomat which was remarkably unapologetic in tone. "What has been done by the Norwegian Navy at Greenland has been only to prevent the sending of weather reports and other radio messages which might benefit exclusively countries with which Norway is at war," Morgenstierne wrote. Norway was not planning to change Greenland's status, he claimed, but could not guarantee that it would stay out of the island: "As long as the war lasts [...] the Norwegian Government cannot admit that Germany should be given the opportunity, directly or indirectly, to utilize Greenland for German purposes."[25] Even later, Morgenstierne continued to push for Norwegian interests on the island.[26]

Parts of the Norwegian establishment exiled to Britain saw the war, in which Norway had fought hard to resist German invasion whereas Denmark had been overrun in one morning, as an opportunity to use its new-won prestige to push Denmark out of the North Atlantic.[27] Trygve Lie, the foreign minister of the Norwegian government-in-exile in London, was harboring hopes of a post-war cooperative arrangement that would give Norway a major role in the area. "To preserve peace, it is important for Great Britain, the United States and Norway to be jointly responsible for the defense at sea, on land and in the air of Greenland, Iceland and the Faroe Islands by having bases there," Lie told Sir Cecil Dormer, the British envoy to Oslo prior to the German invasion.[28] In this respect, he was picking up from thoughts about abandoning Nordic cooperation in favor of a "Norse" area of collaboration involving territories around the North Atlantic, that had been circulating among some Norwegian intellectuals in the interwar years.[29]

Lie made the Norwegian interest in Greenland known on several occasions. In a letter to a Norwegian exile in Stockholm dated May 3, 1941, he wrote that "Norway's future security primarily depends on cooperation with Great Britain, the United States, Canada and Iceland. The Faroe Islands and Greenland will also be of significance."[30] In a speech at Oxford in October of the same year, he elaborated on this idea, seeing Greenland as part of an ambitious vision for Atlantic defense cooperation in the post-war world: "What I would like to see would be an agreement on Eastern Atlantic defense between Britain, the U.S.A. and Canada, covering Greenland and Iceland. Norway would then wish to come in for the sake of her own defense."[31] Summarizing his position, Lie told Alexander Cadogan, the permanent undersecretary of the Foreign Office, that Norway "had special interests to tend to in all matters relating to Greenland."[32]

The British Foreign Office was somewhat lukewarm to Lie's ideas, believing that it was premature this early in the conflict with Germany to speculate about US policies in a post-war world. The Foreign Office asked the Admiralty for its view on the matter. The Admiralty, too, considered any thinking about US long-term policies on the North Atlantic to be speculative, but emphasized Greenland's strategic importance along with the Faroe Islands and Iceland, suggesting that the security of these areas should in future be managed by people who not only were friendly towards Britain but were also willing to be cooperative with it on their own defense.[33]

Meanwhile, similar sentiments were playing out in occupied Oslo. Kauffmann's deal with the Americans caused the Norwegian Arctic Seas Committee, a nationalist pressure group associated with the Greenland cause,[34] to voice concerns about the long-term prospects for the island. It had echoes of Hamsun's words the year before about the mercenary attitude of the Danes. "It seems evident that Denmark is not exerting itself to keep Greenland in European hands," the committee wrote to Quisling, Norway's Nazi party leader, in July. "They have handed over to the United States a great and valuable piece of Arctic land which thanks to Norway has so far been linked to the Nordic region and to Europe."[35] Quisling, whose passion for Greenland predated his Nazi sympathies, was completely on the same page. "I do not doubt that the final defeat of Britain and America will bring the old Norwegian possessions back to the Nordics: Svalbard, Greenland, Iceland, the Faroe Islands, as well as the Shetland and Orkney Islands," Quisling said in a radio message. "This will guarantee our natural living space and also the basis for our exertions in the world and on the oceans."[36] In private conversations, Quisling said later that the Norwegian claim to Greenland was for the entire island, not just parts of it.[37]

In May 1941, Quisling met with two leading members of the Arctic Seas Committee, Gustav Smedal, the activist who had been involved in Hamsun's attempt to reach the Berlin leadership the year before, and Adolf Hoel, a geologist and prominent polar researcher. They discussed plans to send an expedition to northeast Greenland to support and supply the seven Norwegian trappers who remained there, with the hardly disguised ulterior motive of showing the flag in the disputed territory. Quisling was eager and proposed a major undertaking, sending 100 Norwegian trappers to northeast Greenland as reinforcement on board the same ships. While

Quisling had no official position at the time, the two activists believed he could pull the strings. "Without a doubt, he was the right man to break down the resistance that the expedition was likely to meet from the Germans," Hoel remarked.[38]

After additional work, Hoel handed over a detailed plan for the expedition to Quisling in late June. Clearly, memories of *Veslekari*'s fate the previous year were still vivid. "The dispatch of such an expedition under the present conditions entails a certain risk that the expedition may be captured," Hoel wrote.[39] Therefore, the ambitions were scaled down somewhat, and the suggestion was now to send four ships with altogether 50 trappers, who were to be spread along the northeast coast of Greenland to make it, to all intents and purposes, Norwegian land. Detection should be avoided. "The expedition should be dispatched in such a way so as to ensure that the ship will arrive off northeast Greenland at a time when navigation in those waters has usually stopped," Hoel advised.[40]

In early July, Hoel met with Ragnar Skancke, a member of a Nazi-installed council with a rank similar to a Cabinet member, only to receive disappointing news. The Germans were not keen on the whole enterprise, as they feared that a Norwegian expedition to northeast Greenland could be seen as "a German offensive."[41] Once again, Hitler's reluctance to upset the Americans showed. Over the next few days, the planned expedition was further reduced to 30 people on board one ship,[42] and it now received the required permission from the German-dominated Norwegian authorities, which also agreed to provide the necessary financing.[43]

A ship was chartered—the steam-driven sealer *Buskø*, owned by the shipping magnate Elling Aarseth who also owned *Veslekari*, now confiscated and in Allied service—and to head the expedition, the organizers opted for Hallvard Devold, the polar explorer who had led the private occupation of a piece of northeast Greenland in 1931.[44] Some discussion arose about whether the expedition should carry a radio station as on the one hand, it was considered vital for surviving in arctic conditions, while on the other, the crew could risk being accused of espionage if caught by the British or the Americans. The upshot was that no land radio station was to be transported to Greenland.[45] It was now August, and *Buskø* was ready to depart from the Norwegian port of Ålesund, where *Veslekari* had also been sent off a year earlier. There was one last snag. The Germans did not want to give out an exit permit. Only after Hoel met with General Admiral Hermann Boehm, the commanding admiral of the German Navy in Norway, was the permission granted. On August 19, 1941, *Buskø* with 29 men and one woman on board, finally steamed out of Ålesund.[46]

***

Germany only got a stake in the *Buskø* venture almost as an afterthought and at the initiative of the military intelligence service, which unlike the navy wanted to be involved.[47] During part of the preparations ahead of *Buskø*'s departure,

Obersturmführer Werner Krause of the Abwehr, German military intelligence, had been breathing down the organizers' necks, inquiring incessantly about the mission and especially the backgrounds of the participants.[48] Again, on August 20, the day after *Buskø* had sailed out of Ålesund, Krause ordered a meeting with Hoel and now demanded that the expedition should also carry along a radio station and a radio operator in order to send weather reports to the Luftwaffe from Greenland. Hoel protested, but to no avail, and on August 25, he was informed by Krause that the radio operator had already been found and would be placed on board *Buskø*, which was still in Norwegian waters, picking up expedition members from various ports.[49]

His name was Iacob Bradley, 26 years old and with a past in the Norwegian Nazi party. In the middle of August, he had been contacted by a member of the German security police with an offer to be employed as a radio operator and meteorologist for an expedition to Greenland. After having suggested he was interested, he had been taken to a private home in Oslo, where he had been subjected to a five-day crash course in basic radio handling and weather forecasting and instructed to send weather reports four times a day. He had also been issued a pistol with 50 bullets. Upon completing the course, he was put on a plane and flown to Tromsø in northern Norway before being taken the last part of the way to *Buskø* on a small fishing vessel, accompanied by Krause.[50]

The arrival of Bradley and Krause, with the radio equipment packed in several suitcases, was not welcomed by the expedition members, who protested loudly but were quickly silenced by Krause. "We have a long arm and can reach anyone who doesn't want to do it our way," the *Obersturmführer* said menacingly, before sailing back to the mainland.[51] The suitcases were carried on board, but placed on deck, so they could be thrown overboard immediately if *Buskø* was to be stopped by Allied ships. Finally, on August 29, the ship left Norwegian waters for Greenland. Boehm, the naval commander, made sure to emphasize in his war diary that the mission went ahead "without German assistance," thus seeking to relieve the navy of any blame if things were to go wrong.[52] Bradley was treated coldly by the rest of the crew. He was not assigned a bunk, and the other participants avoided him. Devold told him there was no way the radio station would be set up once they reached Greenland as it would jeopardize the entire mission. "He was very dispirited and also angry at the Germans for having put him in this idiotic situation," Devold reported later.[53]

The voyage across the Atlantic proceeded smoothly, and on September 2, *Buskø* anchored in Peter's Bay on the east coast of Greenland, dropping off Bradley and two trappers near a hunting station. Once again, Bradley was ordered not to attempt to use his radio, while the two other Norwegians made sure he understood that he would not get a share in any of the profit they might make from their catch in the coming months. *Buskø* immediately continued south in the direction of Mosquito Bay, intending to let off personnel along the way according to the plan. The few Norwegians already in place were elated to see compatriots for the first time in

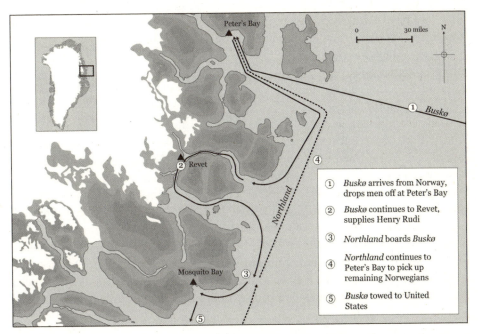

The hunt for *Buskø*.

months. Henry Rudi, a Norwegian trapper, eyed the *Buskø* on the horizon on September 8. "There's a ship! There's a ship!" the lonely man thought to himself. He ran around in his cottage, making everything ready for receiving guests, as he saw the vessel approach. "So they are still sending ships from Norway. They haven't forgotten us after all!"[54]

This was, however, when everything started falling apart. A motorboat from the newly formed sledge patrol spotted *Buskø* and informed the US Coast Guard cutter *North Star*.[55] In turn, it informed "Iceberg" Smith on board *Northland*, which went searching for the mysterious ship. On September 12, it caught sight of *Buskø*. Smith sent a boarding party, which directed the ship into Mosquito Bay, where a thorough search was undertaken. The Americans counted 27 people on board, including the woman, who said she was a nurse.[56]

"Have you dropped off any men?" a Coast Guard officer asked.

"No," was the universal answer from anyone on board.[57]

After some further questioning, members of the crew owned up to the fact that Bradley and the two trappers had disembarked at Peter's Bay, and while *North Star* towed the Norwegian ship to Scoresby Sound, *Northland* sailed north to arrest the remaining three expedition members.[58] Lieutenant Carlton Skinner, who was on board, described what happened next: When in the vicinity of the station, *Northland* was stopped and at about 2am a motorboat put over the side with a force equipped with rifles and tommy guns. "The motorboat proceeded to the hunting station landing at about 3am, surrounding the hut and immediately took possession. There was no resistance. The hut contained three men all of whom were asleep," Skinner said.[59]

From Scoresby Sound, *Buskø* was towed by *Bear* all the way to Boston. It was the first US capture of the war, in fact happening even before the United States was officially a belligerent, and the arrival of *Buskø* was a sensation. *The New York Times* reported the unprecedented arrest of "authenticated Nazi operatives," including "a man described as a member of the German Gestapo."[60] Interrogations of those on board by Norwegian officials led to the conclusion that all except four, including Bradley and Devold, had decided to participate out of unpolitical motives. "As for the others, based on the impression I have, I see no problem in releasing them," a Norwegian official reported.[61] One problem remained. It was unclear under what justification anyone on the *Buskø* could be held, since the United States was not at war, and so they were not prisoners of war. "The unembarrassed Justice Department, which knows a lot about the law, smoothly ruled that the *Busko*'s crew could be held 'because they are not in possession of the proper traveling documents'," according to a report in *Time* magazine.[62]

***

When the war came to Greenland, the human presence along the island's harsh northeastern coastline was extremely limited. There had been two Danish police stations at Eskimoness and Ella Island, a Norwegian weather station at Mosquito Bay, a Danish research station in Dove Bay, and, scattered along the entire vast emptiness, 13 Norwegian and 12 Danish trappers.[63] During the ensuing months, that number had fallen further, as the Norwegians were removed from Mosquito Bay,[64] and the majority of trappers were also evacuated.[65] In the summer of 1941, Governor Brun issued the final order to vacate the northeastern coastline completely of people. Presumably he wanted to get a better grasp of all activities in the area. Once the evacuation was complete, any person still observed there could automatically be assumed to be an enemy. The task was assigned to US Coast Guard vessels patrolling the area, and they were equipped with powers to use force if anyone refused to be moved.[66]

Initially, the order only applied to Danes, which caused a great deal of discontent. Six Norwegians had been evacuated to Iceland by *Fridtjof Nansen*, but by 1941, seven remained in northeast Greenland, and for the time being they were allowed to stay despite Brun's decision, in order not to upset the Norwegian government-in-exile. By October 1941, four Norwegians remained in northeast Greenland, but now they also had to go.[67] One of them was Henry Rudi, the trapper who had been pleasantly surprised by the arrival of *Buskø*. He was now visited by two vessels from

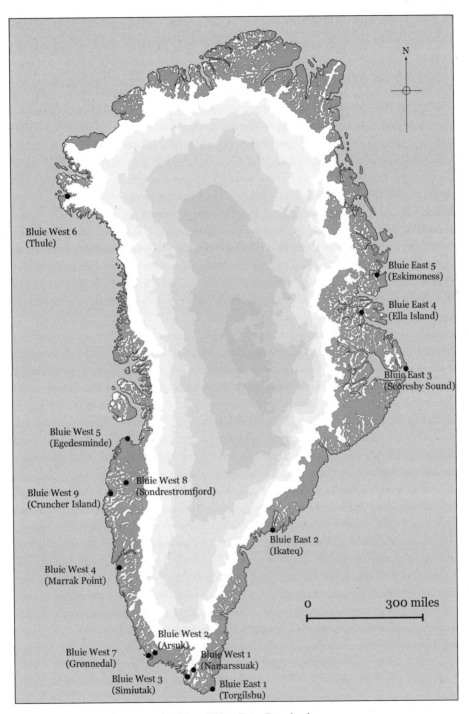

US bases ("Bluies") in Greenland.

the US Coast Guard. The American commander on board addressed Rudi with great politeness and confronted him with an ultimatum. He could either join the sledge patrol, or he could be sent to the west coast.

"There is no third alternative," the American said with a smile. Rudi opted for the sledge patrol.[68]

Once the last Norwegian had been evacuated in the fall of 1941, the entire area was nearly deserted apart from the odd appearance of military personnel. As a theater of war, it was more desolate than even the most remote and inaccessible areas of the world. The most distant ocean, the most impenetrable jungle, the most isolated desert had more people than this. It was to give the war in Greenland, as it would play out over the next almost four years, a very special character.

The US Coast Guard, by contrast, was boosting its presence. Alongside Northeast Greenland Patrol, consisting of *Northland*, *North Star* and *Bear*, the South Greenland Patrol had been established in the summer, made up of Coast Guard cutters *Modoc*, *Comanche* and *Raritan* as well as the geodetic ship *Bowdoin*, and charged among other things, with protecting the mine at Ivigtut.[69] In October, the two patrols were consolidated into Greenland Patrol, named Task Force 24.8 under the command of "Iceberg" Smith.[70]

In the meantime, the practical work of building the airbases that were foreseen in the April agreement signed by Kauffmann and Hull kicked into gear. The construction of Bluie West 1, designed to be a main refueling stop on the ferry route bringing aircraft to Britain, was already well underway, and now the Army Air Force wanted a second base on the west coast, further up north at Sondrestromfjord later to be named Bluie West 8. It was to provide an alternative in cases when the capricious arctic weather closed down the more southerly route.[71] The commander of the Army Air Force, Henry H. Arnold, knew exactly where to look for the right person to handle the task.

"Where's Bernt Balchen?" Arnold asked.

"Sir, I haven't the faintest idea where Bernt Balchen is," one of his senior aides replied.

"Well, find him! Get him in; I want to commission him in the Air Force. I want to send him to Greenland."[72]

Balchen was an officer in the Norwegian air force, flying for the Allies, and was also a well-known polar aviator. He was in the Pacific at the time when Arnold summoned him and once he appeared in the United States, he was informed about his new mission in Greenland.

"But the United States isn't in the war," Balchen pointed out.

The Army Air Force officer who briefed him shrugged: "It will be."[73]

Before he left in September 1941, Balchen received a letter from Arnold hailing his mission as unprecedented, given how high north it was. "The thin paths beaten in the snow by courageous explorers have been obliterated by time. It is up to us to establish detachments to serve as stepping stones to the far-flung areas we must reach," Arnold wrote.[74]

The route through Bluie West 8 actually turned out to be used more frequently than the southern route via Bluie West 1, as unexpectedly the weather further north turned out generally to be better suited for flying.[75] Balchen and his men could not know this in late 1941, and for them it was mostly dreary work in complete isolation. "Came our first Christmas, and I saw what I had expected: faces around me expressing a quiet gloom. There was no mail from home—the last had come in with the last ship; none would arrive until spring," Balchen recalled.[76]

The loneliness felt by the Americans was self-imposed to an extent. Squadron Leader R. A. Logan from the Royal Canadian Air Force had participated in an Arctic expedition in 1922 to assess the feasibility of aviation in the area and recommended in the report he completed upon his return to cooperate with the local population. "It will be found advisable to employ Eskimos for work around the air station—in various ways, but especially in connection with hunting for food and clothing," he wrote. In actual fact, the opposite was true when the Americans settled down in Greenland two decades later.[77] Reflecting the concerns expressed in Hull's letter to Morgenthau, the Americans embarked on the Greenland venture with a basic principle of minimizing contact with the Greenlanders.

The Germans had excellent information about Balchen's activities. One afternoon he was listening to a broadcast by Lord Haw-Haw, the American-born propagandist William Joyce working for the Germans: "I say, there, Bernt Balchen," Lord Haw-Haw chided in his distinctly recognizable intonation, "how are you doing way up there at Sondrestromfjord in Greenland? We know all about the new 6,000-foot airfield you have built, and we will be taking care of it in due time, old chap. Cheerio."[78]

The harsher tones from Germany reflected one fact: The United States was now at war with Germany. There had been dense snow over Godthaab on December 7, and a strong wind had been blowing in from the southwest, as if to emphasize that this was arguably the most isolated capital in the world. And yet, it was more connected to the outside world than ever on that fateful Sunday. The radio reports were all about the Japanese attack on Pearl Harbor. Christian Vibe, the young polar explorer who had now become a journalist based in Godthaab, met Eske Brun, the governor. "Now we're at war," Brun said. He did not seem concerned.[79]

In his post-war memoirs, the governor confirmed that the war had actually come as a relief. Any doubts that the Americans were not on the island for serious reasons had disappeared. "The mood at the American bases changed completely. People turned resolute and serious. The storm that caused America's vast potential in productive capacity and human skill to be mobilized entirely for the struggle was also felt on our shores. The dice had been cast, and everybody and everything was in the fight," Brun recalled.[80] Penfield, the American consul, put it succinctly when describing his reaction to the war: "It's awful but, still, I feel a great deal better."[81]

CHAPTER 12

Amerika-Bomber

Winter to Summer 1942

At 10am on Tuesday, May 12, 1942, senior members of the German Luftwaffe convened at Rechlin, a testing ground for new aircraft models 60 miles northwest of Berlin. Among the topics that were discussed: Greenland. Field Marshal Erhard Milch, the top officer responsible for aircraft production in Germany, presided over the meeting. Now that the United States was an active belligerent and had joined the enemies of the Reich, the gloves had come off, and the Luftwaffe was looking into ways to bring the war to the American homeland. The search was on for an "Amerika-Bomber" that could cross the Atlantic, deliver its deadly load on the big cities on the US east coast, and return safely.[1]

"As for long-distance aircraft, what airplanes do you have, when will they be ready, and in what numbers?" Milch asked.

"We have Messerschmitt Me 264, Junkers Ju 390, Junkers Ju 290, and a Focke-Wulf project which has not yet been assigned a number yet," replied Walter Friebel, a leading aviation engineer.

"The question is: What are the tasks at hand, and which aircraft can solve them, and which cannot?" Milch continued.

"One task that has emerged with renewed urgency recently is the need for an Amerika-Bomber. With this in mind, all ongoing projects involving long-distance aircraft have been reviewed. The most interesting project is the Me 264, because it has advanced the furthest," Friebel said.

"But can it really deal with the America challenge?" Milch asked.

"With the current means at our disposal, it is not possible to reach America by air. There are partial solutions that can only be handled with relatively complicated procedures, for example mid-air refueling," Friebel replied.

The back and forth between Milch and Friebel resulted in the conclusion that mid-air refueling at the time was not a feasible option.

"If the general staff changes its mind about mid-air refueling, I would like to be informed. Until then, I would ask that the idea be put aside," Milch said. Then he raised a completely different solution.

"There is also the idea of landing in Greenland and have a submarine bring fuel. I'm not sure what people are thinking. It would be better to fly over, drop the bombs, crash the plane, and then ask, 'What POW camp have you planned for me'?"

The stenographic record that was produced for the meeting is the only source that has surfaced from the Luftwaffe archives after the war, suggesting that officers in the German air force did indeed consider using Greenland as a refueling base for bombing raids on the United States. Milch's brief reference to the idea of a refueling stop in Greenland lacks any detail, but it is possible that these thoughts might be connected to the tests on the Finse glacier in Norway in 1940.

Technology had not yet reached a level where intercontinental flight for large bomber aircraft was feasible, and therefore other solutions had to be found. Since mid-air refueling apparently was also not realistic in mid-1942, it would seem that a refueling stop in Greenland was the most promising option, for lack of better alternatives. However, Milch's remark suggests that he also did not favor this approach, although the rationale for his thinking is unclear. Perhaps it was a simple question of timing. While an end to the 11-month invasion of the Soviet Union was nowhere in sight, an offensive against the United States was entirely out of the question, and even tentative planning for a strategic bombing campaign against North American cities was a waste of resources.

Later during the same meeting at Rechlin, Colonel Dietrich Schwenke, another aeronautical engineer, was invited to introduce various long-term projects connected to the Western Hemisphere. He mentioned the Panama Canal as an obvious target, as well as the aircraft being flown from America to Britain, but again, the problem of mid-air refueling posed an obstacle. And then Greenland suddenly was back on the agenda:

"The cryolite deposits at Evigtok [Ivigtut, ed.] in southern Greenland would be of special importance as the United States, Canada and England use them for the production of aluminum. We are talking about the only major cryolite reserves in the whole world. The United States can't produce aluminum synthetically the way we do," Schwenke said.

Remarkably, given the amount of time spent by American, British, and Canadian planners agonizing over the risk of attack against the crucial mine at Ivigtut, this is the only example in the sources of senior Luftwaffe officers actually discussing this option. And it was put aside immediately as not feasible, likely because of the refueling problem. Schwenke briefly raised another possibility:

"Practically speaking, it would hardly be possible to interrupt the operation of the mine, but it should be possible to disrupt the shipping going to the mine and back," he said. That, too, was dismissed as not realistic. A secondary reason why the Luftwaffe officers dismissed the topic may have been that the German submarine fleet was already carrying out a campaign to deprive the Allies of their access to vital resources, including cryolite. It was a campaign that was underway, and was costing lives, even as the Luftwaffe officers were meeting.

***

Public concerns in the United States and Britain persisted about the vulnerability of Greenland and its cryolite. "If Germany should capture the Greenland cryolite deposit, the only one in the world, it might seem that our Achilles heel had been cut," Harry N. Holmes, the president of the American Chemical Society, told members in 1942, going on to state, however, that "fortunately we know how to make synthetic cryolite from our own fluorspar, soda and sulfuric acid."[2] Still, the aluminum makers of North America remained uninterested in this option. This made men like Niels Oluf Petersen, the experienced captain of the steamship *Hans Egede*, which carried cryolite from Ivigtut, essential to the war effort. But in early 1942, Petersen had an uncanny premonition. "I don't think I'll return from my next voyage," he told an acquaintance.[3]

He was right. *Hans Egede* left Ivigtut on February 27 with a cargo of 560 tons of cryolite, bound for Philadelphia. It never made it to its destination but disappeared without a trace. Only three months later, on June 1, did the newspaper *Grønlandsposten* report its loss, with Petersen and 22 other men on board, 17 Danes, four Greenlanders, and one Norwegian.[4] Memorial services were held both in Greenland and in occupied Denmark.[5] What had caused the tragedy was open to speculation, but the Greenland newspaper wrote what most were probably thinking: "Unfortunately, there is no doubt that the ship, like so many others, has fallen victim to a Nazi submarine."[6]

Only after the war was it confirmed that *Hans Egede* had indeed been sunk by a U-boat, the *U-587* commanded by 32-year-old Corvette Captain Ulrich Borcherdt, south of Newfoundland on March 6. Borcherdt reported that the sunk ship was a camouflaged Greenland patrol vessel, misreading its name as "*Hawse Gude*."[7] *U-587* was only on its second patrol and was itself sunk at the end of the same month by a group of four Royal Navy destroyers. There were no survivors.

Sailing in Greenland waters was hazardous even in the absence of German submarines, when the elements were the main foe. Magnus Magnusson, the captain on board *Nanok*, a converted fishing vessel that joined the Greenland Patrol, described the daily hardship on board. "Cold weather, ice, fogs, snowstorms, and plenty of hard work were far worse than any of the expectations of my crew of 'green', potential sailors," said Magnusson, called "Maggie" by his men. "But there they were, cooped up in that little tub month after month, in bad weather, wet to their skins, regardless of whether they were on the lookout watch or in their sacks."[8]

"I saw those kids stand in water up to their armpits," he continued, "in water that had a temperature of 34 degrees, working from six in the morning to almost midnight, floating and rolling oil barrels ashore. I saw them work all day and well into the night, unloading tons of shark meat whose odor could be smelled for miles; their hands torn and bleeding from the sharp needles on the shark skin. I saw them hang on with one hand and break ice with the other, 20 out of 24 hours, in a 65-mile-per-hour gale, with the ship on her beam ends, and the temperature at five degrees below zero. Cold, hungry, tired, and sleepy, but they worked with a grin on their faces, not for one day but for three days."[9]

Thaddeus D. Novak, a young seaman who joined the *Nanok*'s crew in 1942, recorded the endless dreariness endured for months on end, depicting the lonely bow watch that had to be undertaken at all times of the day. "My back aches and tires under continuous pounding of heavy, solid waves that manage to fall upon me." To cope with the pressure, he began daydreaming about solid ground under his feet and clothes that were not wet, about picnics and walks in the sun. "How can I dream these things with ice water dripping off my face and drenching the inside of the collar of my parka?" he wrote in his diary. "I think of civilization as something unreal, something I'd only read about."[10]

***

To many Americans, Greenland did not feel like part of the Western Hemisphere. Indeed, it might as well have been as far away as China. Getting there was an achievement in itself. C. Gray Bream, an official at the American consulate, described the epic voyage he had to undertake in order to return to his post after an appendectomy in the United States: "I hitchhiked my way back to Greenland, but I spent three months getting to my post. I think I set a record en route to post. I got from Washington to the South Base in Greenland, but from there it was another story. This was in the wintertime. I got as far as Ivigtut which was where the cryolite mine was and I was there for six weeks and finally an ice breaker came through and took me up to a little emergency landing field which had been established 50 miles south of Godthaab, and from there I was picked up by a local motorboat which took me to Godthaab."[11]

Still, even a few months into the war, the Americans were beginning to build small enclaves throughout Greenland's vast arctic wilderness. Bluie West 1 and Bluie West 8, which Balchen had been busy building since late 1941, was joined by a number of other bases—or "Bluies"—up the west and east coast of Greenland. Extensive surveys of the east coast had been carried out by Captain Elliott Roosevelt, the president's son, without any luck in locating a suitable spot for an airfield, but one was finally found in 1942 at Ikateq near the settlement of Angmagssalik.[12] The base, known as Bluie East 2, doubled as a weather station, and while its military purpose was paramount, the planners also made sure that a few modern amenities were available. "It was a very odd place. There were 800 people and a movie theater was operating around the clock," wrote a visitor.[13]

The original plan had been to expand the ferry program to an extent where 1,000 planes could be shipped from North America to Britain every month. However, the material requirements were so massive that they threatened to undermine other priorities such as the buildup of American forces on the British Isles in preparation for the attack across the Channel, and the project was scaled back significantly.[14] Even though the ambitions were reduced, the local commanders in Greenland still faced major logistical problems, as most of what was needed had to be shipped in. "Nothing is available locally, except drinking water, and sand and rocks for construction," the base commander at Bluie West 1 complained in July 1942.[15] One of the problems was that despite gradually improving harbor facilities, cargo was being unloaded at an unsatisfactory rate. In a desperate move to reduce the backlog, the military authorities decided to hire 32 experienced longshoremen from Baltimore and Philadelphia. Their presence during the last three months of 1942 brought about a visible reduction in the unprocessed cargo, but even though the workers were paid excellent wages none of them wanted to stay on in Greenland beyond their original contract.[16]

There was a reason why the civilian workers were out again the moment they could. Endless monotony, a lack of normal social contacts and a resulting intense sense of isolation meant that neuropsychiatric cases made up 18 percent of all cases of servicemen being repatriated stateside, second only to those sent back home due to accidents of various kinds.[17] "From early autumn, when the northern ice forced the last ship to retreat to civilization, until the thaws of late spring permitted the first vessel to return, the men saw no living thing except their dogs and perhaps a few Eskimos," the official Army Air Force history reports.[18] After more than a year in Greenland, a majority of the men developed a vacant, emotionless expression that was commonly referred to as "The Arctic Stare."[19]

George C. Marshall, the army chief of staff, sent a memorandum to Roosevelt in September 1942 pointing out the issue of morale in the outposts: "We have isolated garrisons scattered throughout the Pacific from Alaska to Australia. We have them in Labrador, Greenland, Iceland and many other places. Many of the men on this duty have been in position for more than a year and will probably continue in their present positions until the end of the war. We hope there will be no fighting in most of these garrisons but we must be ready for action. Morale is therefore an important factor and the difficulty of maintaining morale increases with the length of stay without active operations."[20]

In a letter to a senator, Marshall pointed out the responsibility borne by the higher-ups: "The soldier overseas in many of the theaters is utterly dependent on the activity of the War Department in providing for him recreation, and reading and off-duty educational opportunities. This is particularly true in the many isolated stations such as in Greenland and the Aleutians, small islands in the Pacific and Atlantic, Equatorial Africa and in the Himalayan Mountains in Burma and China."[21]

The suffocating isolation motivated some to take matters into their own hands. Radio operators seized any opportunity to get in touch with the outside world.

During a single night in July 1942, a total of 11 "urgent" messages were sent from Bluie West 1 to the airbase in Goose Bay, Labrador. "Nothing short of the melting of the Greenland Ice Cap" could have justified that number, an observer noted tersely.[22] Others sought alternative ways to combat boredom. "I was able to read *War and Peace* among other things," said C. Gray Bream, the American diplomat who had taken three months to get to Godthaab.[23] A few snapped. The US-installed chief of police at the cryolite mine in Ivigtut lost his mind and had to be sent home. "I had been sensing it for several days, when he came to me with all kinds of trifles and looked weird. Religious stuff," engineer Oscar Corp wrote to his wife. "It came out into the open yesterday, and we had to put him under guard around the clock. He was violent, but we took away his revolver immediately. He expresses a wish to be crucified and die for the sake of us all. He will now be returning to the United States."[24]

***

Erik Frederiksen, a teenager when the war broke out, was impressed with the American efficiency he encountered at Narsarssuak, or Bluie West 1: "Immediately after they arrived, the Americans started constructing the airfield and building houses. They had cleared the entire plain in a matter of days … We were a little concerned when they arrived but also happy, since we feared the Germans."[25] Little by little, as more Americans trickled in, the exchanges became more numerous and more profitable, despite the official policy frowning upon fraternization. "There was a lively barter, allowing us access to candy, cigarettes and other small items," said Jehu Davidsen, a young man in Narsarssuak.[26]

By 1942, a small building boom was taking place in Godthaab, especially in order to house the American and Canadian consular personnel in suitable buildings, featuring toilets, hot water and modern kitchens.[27] The arrival of the foreigners meant new opportunity. Young Greenlanders got jobs on ships plying routes in North America and were exposed to the outside world to an unprecedented extent.[28] "The straightforward manner of the Americans appealed to the Greenlanders, and cigarettes, jewelry and silk stockings inevitably made an impression on the women," a wartime observer wrote.[29]

At least among some, it all fed into even stronger pro-American sentiments than had been observed the year before. When American planes appeared in the sky over Godthaab, the Greenlanders would emerge out of their houses, waving and shouting "America, America!"[30] Local Danes were not pleased to see the welcoming attitude. "How many Greenlanders really see themselves as Danes?" Christian Vibe, the young polar explorer who had now found a job as a journalist in Godthaab, wrote to an acquaintance. "It does hurt to see young Greenlanders flashing American flag lapel buttons or using the flags to decorate their homes, because to the Greenlanders it is something special, and the Americans have little tact and hand them out by the hundreds."[31] Kirkwood, the Canadian consul, reported to Ottawa about the mixed feelings among the Danes: "They regard [...] the Allied cause as their own hope. This feeling is not strong enough, however, to make them welcome any Allied action or intervention in Greenland, which they would strongly deprecate unless it were to counteract an actual enemy attack. On this point they are most sensitive."[32]

Vibe was rather suspicious of US designs on Greenland, and his feelings often seemed to veer into actual anti-Americanism. "Every now and then we see some Coast Guards or airplanes that we are not allowed to write about, but that's ok, we are not interested at all, more like the opposite. We rush out and hoist the Danish flag whenever such a devil shows up, not to greet but to show that we live here, and we are not Americans," he wrote in a letter to a friend.[33] Likewise, Vibe was critical of the US consul, Penfield, as reflected in a letter to an acquaintance sent in October 1942: "We have all had more than enough of American ways. Penfield is definitely not very popular. He sticks his nose into all kinds of matters that aren't his business, and he exhibits a curious interest in the Greenlanders. Maybe he just wants to see if he can pick up some gossip about us Danes. Maybe he is paving the road for the United States. I have given him a cold shoulder more than once."[34]

The Americans, too, developed a fascination with the Greenlanders, fueled by their radically different culture. Thaddeus Novak, the enlisted man on board *Nanok*, the converted fishing vessel, described the elaborate hairdos of the Inuit women. "It shines as if varnished," he wrote. "The varnish is really whale, seal, or musk oxen oil. It has an unpleasant odor but the artistic results justify the odor."[35] Mutual attraction was increased by tolerant attitudes among the Greenlanders towards sex. "In the past, it was very common that the designations for the sexual organs were used as personal names," according to a Danish account. The report also noted that it was widely accepted among Greenlanders to discuss intimate sexual issues without anyone feeling offended. "However," the report added, "they are reluctant to discuss such matters in the presence of more prominent Greenlanders or of Danes."[36]

The US military, reckoning that sexual relations involving the American servicemen and local women were inevitable, attempted initially to introduce an organized approach that could facilitate control and policing. Soon after the American arrival, US officers suggested to Brun that the establishment of brothels staffed with Greenlander women would be beneficial for the morale of the troops. Brun rejected the idea.[37] The result was that the matter was left to personal initiative. At Narsarssuak, two young servicemen had girlfriends in a nearby settlement, sailing across the fjord to meet them in the summertime, and walking on the ice in winter.[38] A US Army weather observation sergeant was said to have "gone native." "He wears an Eskimo jumper and boots and has several Eskimo women pregnant," a Coast Guard sailor wrote in his diary.[39]

This behavior could be costly, he added, citing a rumor among the men: "If any serviceman impregnates a native woman he must pay the Danish government the sum of five hundred dollars to provide medical attention at the child's birth and thereafter."[40] There were other costs as well. "During the war, the Americans arrived in Angmagssalik [near Bluie East 2], and so did gonorrhea," according to an account. The local nurse, Signe Vest, received much appreciated assistance from the American infirmary, but the disease proved impossible to eradicate.[41]

No precise figure exists for the number of children fathered by American servicemen, but statistics suggest they were in the hundreds. A total of 1,401 children were born out of wedlock in Greenland during the 1940s, up from 600 during the previous decade. As a proportion of total number of births, the figure also went up. Whereas during the decades prior to the war, the percentage of children born out of wedlock never exceeded 8.7 percent, during the 1940s, it rose to 16.6 percent.[42] It is also likely that some pregnancies, perhaps a large number, were terminated even though abortions were illegal at the time. One report describes a Greenland woman who had become pregnant out of wedlock and provoked an abortion by carrying a heavy bucket of water out of her home and emptying it, before walking around barefoot in the snow, while there were also several instances of newborn babies being killed.[43] The sanctions against unmarried women who decided to go ahead with a pregnancy could be severe. Some were denied entry to the local church and had to listen in on the service through an open window. One unmarried mother reported having her national costume burned and her hair cut off.[44]

The Danish authorities were keen to put up as many obstacles as possible to this exchange, and courts in Greenland handed down sentences for actions that in Denmark proper were not considered illegal. A woman in Godthaab was punished for allowing sailors and women to have intercourse at her home against pay, while a person in Jakobshavn was sentenced for allowing a couple to spend the night at his house in exchange for cigarettes and chewing gum.[45] But as an observer noted: "While having little else in common, Americans and Greenlanders at least share an aversion to the rigorous enforcement of bans."[46]

Jehu Davidsen, the young resident of Narsarssuak involved in barter, was soon employed in the municipal government and was put in charge of controlling access to the American base. "Only people on official business were allowed to enter. Yet, it happened pretty often that I had to go to the base to pick up girls who stayed there illegally," he recalled later. "I was impressed that my modest insignia as a municipal official had this much of an impact on these huge, uniformed foreigners. They always obeyed me when I arrived to pick up their girls."[47]

CHAPTER 13

The Reluctant Commander

Fall and Winter 1942

Hermann Ritter was excited about the prospect of traveling to his beloved north. It was a chance to escape the war he hated. Born in 1891 in the Bohemian city of Karlsbad, then part of the Austro-Hungarian Empire, he was from a generation that was too old to be thoroughly carried away by Hitler, and with an Austrian father and a Finnish mother, his background was perhaps a little too cosmopolitan for Nazi tastes. Now as an officer in the Kriegsmarine, he had been ordered to head the first German attempt to set up a weather station on the east coast of Greenland. All previous meteorological missions to the island had been funded or otherwise supported by Germany, but they had been staffed by Norwegians and Danes. This time it would be a purely German undertaking.

The rationale for not sending German expeditions to Greenland had disappeared with Pearl Harbor and the state of war that now existed between the United States and the Axis powers.[1] Soon after the United States officially joined the ranks of the Allies, Germany's naval leadership began making concrete plans for a permanent or semi-permanent weather service located in Greenland. In April 1942, a proposal was discussed to send the polar ship *Zenith* on a weather reporting mission in waters off Greenland. In the summer months, it would operate in the open sea, moving to a stationary position, possibly near the east coast of Greenland, during the winter.[2]

After some debate, the naval planners decided instead to equip the weathership *Coburg* for the expedition, but soon changed their minds and eventually settled on the weathership *Sachsen* as more suitable for the mission. Meanwhile, they gave the operation a name: "Holzauge."[3] In an odd and unnecessary decision that could only risk compromising attempts to keep details secret to the enemy, this was in reference to the officer who was originally picked to lead the expedition: Rupert Holzapfel, the same officer who had attempted and failed two years earlier to get the Danish government's approval for a mission to Greenland. Since his services were fully needed by the Luftwaffe, he could not be spared for the mission, and the next choice was Ritter, incidentally captain on board *Zenith*.[4]

On paper, at least, Ritter seemed to have all the right qualifications. Given the unusual nature of the mission—to survive in Greenland's harsh climate for at least one winter while avoiding enemy contact—polar experience was considered paramount, and Ritter had that in droves. Fresh out of high school, he had taken part in an Arctic expedition organized by Prince Albert of Monaco, only to volunteer for the Austro-Hungarian Army and serve as an officer specializing in mountain artillery on the Italian front during World War I. After the war, when Austria-Hungary fell apart, he had become a citizen of the newly emerging republic of Czechoslovakia. He became a sailor, traveling extensively in the Arctic region, often spending prolonged periods as a trapper.[5]

In 1933, when Hitler came to power, Ritter was employed as a teacher at the Nautical College in Altona near Hamburg. The Nazis were extremely distasteful to him, and to keep his Czech citizenship, he went home to Bohemia.[6] Shortly afterwards, he was back in the polar regions, appearing in the Norwegian city of Tromsø, where he befriended Henry Rudi, the Norwegian trapper who would later move to Greenland.[7] Ritter ended up spending most of the 1930s in the region. "Hermann Ritter had arrived as a typical order-loving Austrian, but you cannot be like that and live long in the Arctic," wrote the American polar explorer Willie Knutsen, who knew about Ritter through a friend. "He quickly adapted and was soon a true arctic man, enthusiastically tolerant of the most primitive—and life-threatening—conditions."[8] In 1934 and 1935, Ritter had passed the winter in the Norwegian island of Spitsbergen with his wife Christiane Ritter, who subsequently wrote a bestselling book about their exploits, *Eine Frau erlebt die Polarnacht*, or *A Woman in the Polar Night*, which was also translated into Swedish.[9]

When the war broke out, Ritter was the master on the whaling ship *Wikinger*, which was now converted into a tanker to serve the German military. He continued in this capacity until the fall of 1941, when he was suspected by the Gestapo of spreading anti-Nazi propaganda and of carrying out espionage for Russia. This caused him to be dismissed by his employer, the whaling company Hamburger Walfang-Kontor, but he was ultimately cleared of any overt anti-Nazi activity, and in February 1942, he was called into active service and commissioned *Leutnant zur See*, the equivalent of ensign in the United States.[10] It was a rare, twisted road that had led him to command in the German war-time navy, and it would turn out to entail far more complications than anyone had expected.

***

Not long after Hermann Ritter had been named to lead the "Holzauge" expedition to Greenland, the ship was to carry him and his men across the Atlantic, *Sachsen*, was renamed *Hermann* in his honor, in another inexplicable breach of security.[11] Slowly, his team came together. Eventually, it consisted of 18 men, counting himself.

A US Coast Guard tug has pulled up alongside a freighter off Greenland. The guard in the foreground keeps a wary eye. (National Archives)

US Coast Guard sea planes, of the type Grumman J2F Duck, patrol the coast of Greenland. (National Archives)

Extreme weather conditions greeted the Americans in Greenland. A Coast Guard cutter completely covered in ice. (National Archives)

US Coast Guard combat cutter blasts its way through thick ice off the coast of Greenland. (National Archives)

Coast Guard cutter navigates through the ice-covered ocean at night. (National Archives)

A Coast Guard officer is greeted by members of Greenland's Inuit. The American authorities did their best to prevent fraternization, partly at the urging of the Danes, but also, ironically, out of fear that the Germans, of all people, could use it to accuse the United States of pressuring an original people. (National Archives)

Coast Guard men assist Inuit women in carrying coal up a hillside. Among the Inuit, the females often had the worst conditions, forced to do the most backbreaking work. (National Archives)

American servicemen with a dog team. Driving a dog sledge is indispensable in Greenland's harsh nature but is a complicated skill that takes a long time to learn to perfection. Both US and German troops discovered this to their chagrin. (National Archives)

Boeing B-17s in Greenland. The island was originally meant to be a refueling stop for airplanes sent to Britain from the still neutral United States, but with the American entry into the war, it also became a transit base for building up US armed might in the European theater. (National Archives)

American troops carry out live fire drill at the base known as Bluie East 2 on the Greenland east coast. (National Archives)

American troops during a trek through glacier country in Greenland. (National Archives)

Nazi armbands featuring polar bears. A small Nazi movement emerged during the war among Greenland's Inuit community, likely as a form of protest against Danish colonial rule. (Nunatta Katersugaasivia Allagaateqarfialu ©NKA, Grønlands Nationalmuseum og Arkiv)

Hermann Ritter, left, the commander of the "Holzauge" expedition on board *Hermann*, the ship named after him, probably late 1942. The man to his right is Rudolf Kasper, a deck officer, who was shot and injured during a hunting accident during the expedition's early days. (Bundeswehr Military History Museum, Dresden)

Members of the "Holzauge" expedition in Hansa Bay, East Greenland, release a meteorological balloon from the deck of the weather ship *Hermann*. (Bundeswehr Military History Museum, Dresden)

Members of the "Holzauge" expedition set up an emergency camp following a US air raid on their base on land, carried out in May 1943. (Bundeswehr Military History Museum, Dresden)

An unarmed Dornier Do 26 flying boat extracts members of the "Holzauge" expedition in June 1943. Sledge dogs captured from the Danish sledge patrol are also taken on board for breeding in Germany in preparation of future expeditions. (Bundeswehr Military History Museum, Dresden)

Coast Guard men head for Sabine Island, East Greenland, to search for remnants of the German "Holzauge" expedition. (National Archives)

Coast Guard men move in skirmish formation towards Sabine Island's Hansa Bay, where Germans had maintained a weather station for months. (National Archives)

Rudolf Sensse, physician on the German "Holzauge" expedition in East Greenland in 1942 and 1943. The photo is taken after his capture by American Coast Guard men. (National Archives)

Coast Guard man wipes snow off PBY Catalina plane on a base in Greenland. Combating the furious elements made service in Greenland unique and unlike any other place visited by Americans during World War II. (National Archives)

Coast Guard men examine an abandoned German parachute cannister dropped to supply weather teams on the ground. (National Archives)

B-17 Flying Fortress after emergency landing in Greenland. Numerous planes ended up on the icecap on their way to Europe or back. Most are still encased in ice eight decades later. (National Archives)

Coast Guard gun crews at their stations as their ship heads out for patrols in the shipping lanes off Greenland. (National Archives)

Victims of the *Dorchester* disaster are buried. In one of the war's worst maritime catastrophes, the troop transport was torpedoed by a German U-boat on the way to Greenland. Out of 900 men on board, altogether 675 lost their lives. (National Archives)

Machine gun crew in live-fire drill at night, near an American base in Greenland. The photo was originally marked as "Restricted." (National Archives)

US soldiers at a medal award ceremony on a windswept base in Greenland. (National Archives)

Johann Rodebrügger, captain of the ship *Coburg*, which was used to transport the "Bassgeiger" expedition to Greenland. He is with one of the polar bear cubs that the members of the expedition adopted but had to shoot before departure. (Bundeswehr Military History Museum, Dresden)

The members of "Bassgeiger" expedition allowed their beards to grow to considerable lengths, partly as protection against the Arctic cold. (Bundeswehr Military History Museum, Dresden)

Members of "Bassgeiger" expedition on their way back to Europe on board a four-engine Junkers Ju 290 transport plane. (Bundeswehr Military History Museum, Dresden)

The "Bassgeiger" expedition is at an end, and its members pose after their return to Norway, being greeted as heroes on the German airfield at Trondheim. (Bundeswehr Military History Museum, Dresden)

Members of the US Coast Guard disembark on the east coast of Greenland. (National Archives)

German Lieutenant Gerhard Zacher's grave on Shannon Island, close to where he was shot by a member of the sledge patrol. (National Archives)

Crew from the scuttled German ship *Kehdingen*, used to transport the "Edelweiss I" expedition across the Atlantic, surrender to the US Coast Guard off the east coast of Greenland. (National Archives)

Coast Guard walk across ice towards the abandoned German "Bassgeiger" base on Shannon Island. (National Archives)

German trawler *Externsteine*, the ship used for the "Edelweiss II" expedition. It was the only surface vessel to be captured by the US Navy in World War II. (National Archives)

German troops from the "Edelweiss II" expedition after their surrender to US troops on the island of Little Koldewey, October 4, 1944. (National Archives)

"Movie night" on board US Coast Guard cutter *Eastwind*. The five men seated in the top row are German prisoners captured from Operation "Edelweiss II." "We were being directly spoiled," one of the prisoners said after the war. (National Archives)

German-born film star Marlene Dietrich with US Army Major R. C. Calef in Greenland in September 1944. Dietrich was on her way to entertain US troops in Europe. (National Archives)

The meteorologist Gottfried Weiss was named scientific leader of the expedition, essentially also becoming Ritter's second-in-command. The naval command had left the exact position of the weather station to Ritter's discretion, and while the ship was being prepared in the north German port city of Kiel, on July 10, Weiss was taken in a Focke-Wulf Fw 200 Condor long-range airplane to survey the future operation area.[12]

The 15-hour flight, conducted out of the Norwegian city of Trondheim, led Weiss across the Atlantic and up the east coast of Greenland past Eskimoness. "A thin mist spread below us, but through it I saw a flagpole with the Danish flag flying from it," he wrote later. "So there were people here." He did not know at the time that it was in fact one of the stations of the Northeast Greenland Sledge Patrol, but later learned that the inhabitants had been alerted by the low-flying airplane, reacting by throwing their sleeping bags out of the windows, and would have jumped out themselves if it had turned out to be an air raid, following a basic Arctic rule of survival: "Sleeping bag first, man second."[13] Back in Trondheim, Weiss analyzed his observations and came to the conclusion that the best area to set up the weather station was between 74th and 75th northern latitudes.[14] The fact that this was close to Eskimoness, which was obviously manned, did not seem a major issue to him, possibly because travel across anything but the shortest distances would be almost impossible to undertake during the winter.

Hermann departed from Kiel in early August, heading for the port of Tromsø in Norway, where the last preparations were carried out. Among other things, the crew removed the antiaircraft gun, as *Hermann* was to make the voyage to Greenland disguised as a Norwegian fishing vessel. While the gun was left on the dock, a dummy was placed in its stead. "A couple of boards and a broomstick," wrote Helmut Scherer, the radio operator, in his diary.[15] This was merely for show. While the ship was still sailing in waters close to Norway's coastline, there was a risk that it would be spotted by local resistance members, who would pass their observations on to the Allies, and the absence of the gun would be seen as a hint that the vessel was to be put to special uses.[16]

The ship sailed out of Tromsø at 11am on August 22, accompanied by the minesweeper *M-251*, heading for the east coast of Greenland.[17] A few hours later, in the afternoon, two polar dogs, Agar and Bello, were carried over from the minesweeper. Waiting until now was also a security measure, as the appearance of the dogs on *Hermann* while in the harbor would have been an indication about the purpose of the mission. "The two dogs can't stand each other and whine at each other the entire evening," Scherer wrote. At 7:30pm, *Hermann* reached the open sea, and the dummy gun was now torn down, while the Norwegian flag was painted on the hull. This was part of the cover while the ship crossed the Atlantic.[18] "It is particularly important that the crew does not act in a way that attracts attention if overflown by enemy aircraft or meeting enemy submarines. It can contribute to

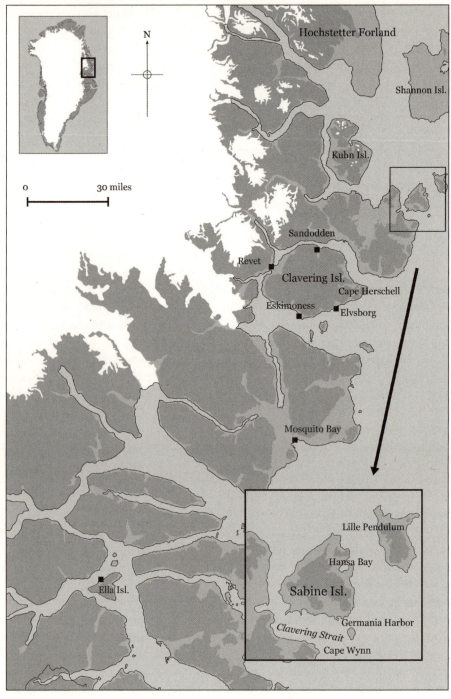

"Holzauge" operation area, 1942 and 1943.

the deception if they wave or show Norwegian flags," the Naval Group Command North, a naval station based in the north German port of Wilhelmshaven, said in a confidential written order.[19]

The crew on *Hermann* reached the pack ice off the East Greenland coastline on August 25.[20] Two days later, the ship arrived at Sabine Island, which was separated from the mainland by Clavering Strait and part of the area previously reconnoitered by Weiss by plane. At the north side of the island, the ship entered Hansa Bay, which Ritter decided would be ideal for spending the winter. The anchorage in the bay had a depth of 130 feet, and its entrance was concealed by another, smaller island called Little Pendulum. Ritter also decided to split the team in two. One was to stay on board the ship, and the other to build a hut on land near water's edge. [21] Landfall was made the day after, on August 28. Five crew members sailed to the coastline in a boat. "All of them are heavily armed with submachine guns, pistols and hand grenades," Scherer wrote in his diary. "They step onto Greenland soil as the first ever German soldiers."[22]

***

One thing was abundantly obvious as the Germans started settling in at Hansa Bay. Ritter was not a popular commander. Belonging to a different generation than his men, he was considered old and out of touch. Weiss, the scientific leader, recognized Ritter's arctic expertise, but considered him a fiasco as a leader. "Because of age, background and inner convictions, he was not on the same page as his men. He failed to bond with them, and he did not enjoy their confidence," Weiss wrote after the war.[23] It would have been a problem under any circumstances, but in the crushing isolation of the Arctic, where a handful of men had to endure each other's company for months within a tightly confined environment, it became magnified to a point where the entire mission was endangered.

Some of the distrust was out of professional shortcomings. Whether it was because of his lack of experience as a military leader, or just sheer bad luck, Ritter made a series of wrong choices, and his men had to pay for it. His decision after anchoring in Greenland to wait until the bay froze to unload the stores, proved costly. The ice turned out to be so uneven that transporting the heavy supplies onto land proved more trouble than if a boat had been used right at the outset.[24] Scherer and Ritter also disagreed on where to place the antenna, but Ritter overruled Scherer, requiring it to be attached to the railing, where it soon threatened to fall into the water. "He has regretted making that decision," Scherer wrote in his diary.[25]

Ritter did not seem to cope well with unexpected challenges. The expedition members on land soon settled in after they had built a hut, but a mishap broke the routine. In September, Rudolf Kasper, deck officer and part of the crew that was housed on land, was shot twice in the thigh during a hunting accident, when the man next to him accidentally fired his double-barreled rifle.[26] After this incident, the men were told to hand back their weapons, and skiing was prohibited. The measures were seen as too stern, and thinly veiled criticism of the commander emerged. "Ritter is afraid of accidents," Scherer wrote. "My view is if something is bound to happen, it will happen no matter what, maybe just in a different way."[27]

Ritter was the opposite of the ideal officer as promoted by the Wehrmacht during the war years. While there should be no question of the officer's authority, he was supposed to be his men's best comrade and lead by his example. Instead, Ritter often isolated himself. When *Hermann* was being refurbished to make it ready for spending the winter in Hansa Bay, arrangements were being made for the entire staff to spend their time in one big space in the hull, except for Ritter himself, who stayed aloof in his cabin. Although he tried to connect with his men, for example by leveraging his teaching experience by giving algebra classes, it was the kind of paternalistic behavior that did not necessarily appeal to all his crew.[28] The only expedition member that seemed to really get along with him was Wenzel Novotny, a fellow Bohemian.[29] The rest of the crew soon gathered around another leader, helmsman Fritz Koch, "owing to his resoluteness, his experience as a sailor and his skill in all work required on board," Weiss wrote.[30] "Even though there was no feeling of confidence with the commander, the men had enough sense to maintain discipline by themselves."[31]

Most devastatingly, Ritter had incessant arguments with his closest deputies. There were frequent disagreements with Kasper, the injured deck officer, after he was transported from the camp on land to *Hermann* for treatment.[32] Rudolf Sensse, the expedition's physician, also found himself at odds with Ritter. "Since I often contradicted him, he became more withdrawn. He did his duty, but at the same time expressed his sadness that the war was now also being waged in the Arctic. He was an 'Arctic fool'," Sensse said.[33] Finally, Weiss had to struggle to conceal the bad blood between the commander and himself. "Ritter and I disagreed on most professional matters. But both of us made sure not to create a scene or ever to exchange any angry words," he noted.[34]

Although it was a subject that the participants in "Holzauge" were reluctant to address directly in the postwar era, it appears that Ritter's anti-Nazi views were a source of considerable acrimony. "He did not agree with a number of aspects of the system then," Sensse remarked after the war, carefully choosing his words.[35] Weiss' somewhat nebulous reference to Ritter's "inner convictions" seems to point in the same direction. The Americans put it more bluntly. Ritter, in the words of a US Army report completed later during the war, "hates Prussian militarism and glories in the fact that he is Austrian not German."[36]

The problems with Ritter as a leader were eventually noted by the naval command in Germany. He was the "amiable kind of Austrian officer with all his recognized flaws and weaknesses," according to a critical evaluation report written about him later.[37] The report did not go into detail, but it probably referred to an attitude regarded as laid-back and complacent by the standards of the military of World War II. In the dense prose of a German officer who later filed a report on conditions in Hansa Bay, Ritter had numerous flaws: "The very reserved attitude of the expedition leader towards almost all expedition participants right from the outset, combined with the decisions he made regarding the location for the anchorage of the ship and the construction of the huts on land, as well as the mostly unclear directions he gave when carrying out special missions soon dealt heavy blows to the confidence in Lieutenant Ritter's leadership skills."[38]

***

It was more than a month before "Holzauge" was ready to perform its task and act as a meteorological observation post. Scherer, the radio operator, had been working overtime for weeks to get the wireless connection established with Europe, with no luck. "I'm almost going crazy: It still doesn't work," he wrote in his diary nearly five weeks after they had arrived.[39] He was beginning to feel the anger among the other members of the expedition, some questioning his qualifications. It was not until early October that it finally worked out. The first weather report from Hansa Bay was sent to Tromsø on October 6, and reached Seekriegsleitung H, the hydrographic unit of the German naval command, the following day.[40]

Hermann was gradually pulled apart to make it less conspicuous from the air. The mast was taken down and the chimney cut in half, the other half thrown into the bay. "In the last couple of days, the ship has almost turned into a wreck," Scherer wrote in his diary. "They are going to wonder when we return to Germany in this condition."[41] Soon the bay started freezing, and before long, *Hermann* was completely surrounded by pack ice. Then the snow started, and the ship was "so completely buried in snow that the thought of being on board a floating, mobile vessel was completely alien," Weiss wrote.[42] Meanwhile, on land a second hut was built next to the existing one, allowing accommodation for the people on *Hermann* if they had to be evacuated for whatever reason.[43]

The sun disappeared below the horizon on November 7 and did not show itself again until February 3 the following year.[44] Helmut Scherer described the sinister mood that spread amid the perpetual darkness. "The bad weather continues, and every once in a while, one wishes with all one's heart to be somewhere else," he wrote in his diary on November 13. "The comrades also often dream of Hamburg or of being lifted out by airplane. But that's just dreams. Still, I hope—and do so persistently—that I will be able to go home next year. Now, when the nights are completely dark, life here becomes even more monotonous."[45] The following day, he noted: "With mixed feelings we hear about heavy fighting in Africa and other events in the Mediterranean. Then we are cheered up by the successes of German

U-Boats in all oceans around the world. For a sailor it is nice to hear that comrades have done well against the enemy. That way, our (boring) task becomes less of a drag, since we know that we are working for them."[46]

Ritter led a four-man expedition attempting to reach the mainland across the ice from Sabine Island with a sledge pulled by the two dogs, but it was back after a week, without having achieved the crossing. "They returned rather exhausted and disappointed," Scherer wrote. "They had thrown away half their equipment along the way."[47] Another foray closer to Hansa Bay was more successful. It was just six miles from the camp, on the southern tip of the island. At a place called Germania Harbor, named after a German expedition in the 1860s,[48] they found a hut built by Danish trappers. A note left inside showed that the last time it had been visited was in April 1940, when a sledge driver from Eskimoness 50 miles to the south had passed by. "It was confirmation that we had company at some distance from us!" Weiss remarked.[49] It was also confirmation that visits from the outside were infrequent, and that there was a good chance no one would notice the Germans. Over the next months, the Germania Harbor hut became a coveted retreat for the Germans. Especially Hans Röttger, second deck officer, who became an avid visitor, using the hut as a base for fox hunting.

With limited abilities to escape from the narrow area around *Hermann* and the hut on land, cabin fever became worse. "In the afternoon," Scherer wrote in a typical entry in his diary, "once again a state of war reigned on board. Kasper was furious at the old man, simply because he wanted to use his cabin, and later he had an argument with Dr. Sensse. Hardly a day passes without someone throwing a tantrum."[50] Another entry: "We play cards this evening, but a small dispute between Kasper and Hoffman ends the fun"[51] In particular, Heribert Wenglorz, leading engineer, was a source of considerable tension.[52] One evening, when too much alcohol was consumed, things got out of hand, Scherer recorded. "It all ended on a bad note, and [Wenglorz], totally wasted, was to blame."[53] Weiss, who tried to keep morale high with frequent lectures on topics such as polar exploration, described how maintaining one's sanity became a priority. "Experience shows that passing the winter during the polar night results in a certain nervous tension and restrained irritability. The reasons are the darkness and especially the lack of incident and constricted space," he wrote. "The only way to overcome it is to stay active and demand absolute self-discipline from everyone [...] It was important that sufficient numbers of good books, a scientific library, games, musical instruments and radios were available during the expedition."[54]

Christmas marked a brief interruption in the monotony of the three-month-long polar night. In the afternoon of December 24, the inhabitants in the hut on land walked out to *Hermann*, carrying a Christmas tree made from pieces of wood. The men listened to radio from home. An officer had made a small present to each of them. Scherer received a wooden "Sabine Cross, 1st Class."[55] A member of the expedition had written a song for the occasion, with humorous descriptions of each of his comrades, and a refrain they could all agree on:

> Greenland, Greenland, land of snow,
> We will remember, that I know![56]

Just 50 miles south of Hansa Bay, at Eskimoness station, members of the Danish sledge patrol were also marking Christmas, eating a meal of porridge, steak and ice cream. A few had too much to drink. There were greetings from home, sent to Greenland by radio from occupied Denmark. Among those present was Henry Rudi, Ritter's old friend from his adventures in the Arctic, years before.[57] Ritter, of course, did not know. Meanwhile, the Danes had no idea that within a distance that could be covered in a couple of days by dog sledge, the German enemy was also celebrating Christmas. It was testimony to the cold and the darkness, closing everything down. That would change in spring, once the darkness lifted, and long-distance travel was again possible.

CHAPTER 14

The Hunt

Winter and Early Spring 1943

On March 11, 1943, Marius Jensen of the Northeast Greenland Sledge Patrol and his two Inuit companions, William Arke and Mikael Kunak, were on the third day of their spring patrol up the east coast, each driving their own sledge.[1] It was a clear day, and at minus 16 degrees Fahrenheit it was not unusually cold for the year. Moving towards Sabine Island across the frozen Clavering Strait at mid-afternoon, they were surprised to see footprints in the snow, and when they eyed the lonely trapper's hut at Germania Harbor on the southern tip of the island, they noticed a thin trickle of smoke emerging from the chimney.[2] "As we approached, we saw two men and a dog run off into the distance," Jensen wrote in his diary.[3] Searching the house, they found a green tunic with the German eagle and swastika as well as two down sleeping bags.[4] "We found no provisions, no radio and no equipment of any kind. Only the fur and meat from a polar bear was to be found," Jensen noted.[5]

The two men that Jensen and his companions had seen hastily run north, Hans Röttger and Friedrich Littmann, had been in the hut resting in a break during a fox-hunt expedition.[6] They covered the roughly six miles to the German main camp in Hansa Bay on foot, bringing the bad news that after more than six months of operation, "Holzauge" had been revealed to the Allies. Röttger was reprimanded sternly for not seeking to engage the sledge patrol,[7] and Ritter ordered three reconnaissance patrols to return south to Germania Harbor by different routes in order to ascertain if there was a larger enemy presence. A patrol headed by Gottfried Weiss, the scientific leader of "Holzauge," took the shortest route straight south and reached Germania Harbor before the other two, finding the hut abandoned but with sledge tracks leading south across the ice on Clavering Strait.[8]

Weiss proposed that he and the members of his patrol continue following the tracks. Ritter, who was also on the scene at Germania Habor, agreed to the proposal before himself returning north to Hansa Bay. Once back in the camp, the Germans undertook comprehensive work to strengthen their defenses, while Ritter sent a radio message via the German radio station in Tromsø to Group North, the naval command station based in the north German port of Wilhelmshaven: "Three men with dog team discovered us this evening. They fled, likely in the direction of Eskimoness. They will arrive there in two days at the earliest. We try to catch up with them."[9]

To Ritter, it was inconceivable that the men who had discovered the German presence on Sabine Island would not immediately set out for Eskimoness. In fact, Marius Jensen, described by another patrol member as "an old East Coast rat,"[10] had been in severe doubt how to proceed once he had come across the first clear evidence of Germans in Greenland. Remarkably, it appears that the sledge patrol had issued no detailed orders about what to do in this eventuality. "We had no idea what to do," he told interviewers many years later. "I had been given no instructions. If you meet the Germans, then what are you to do? Are you to try and contact them, or to get away unnoticed? We didn't have the slightest inkling. But I found it to be the wisest choice to withdraw."[11]

Still, he and his two companions had moved no further than five miles to a hut at Cape Wynn, just across Clavering Strait, where they decided to make a halt because of the gathering darkness. "We are going to spend the night here," Jensen told the Greenlanders. "We'll drive to Eskimoness tomorrow. We have driven too much already to be able to drive all the way back today."[12] They had only settled in—just long enough for Jensen to write the day's entry in his diary while a fire was started in the stove[13]—when towards 10pm, Weiss' patrol, seeing the light in the window from a distance, approached across the ice. The dogs outside the hut sensed the presence of the strangers and began stirring and becoming unruly, alerting the three inside. They saw the dark shadows in the distance and immediately understood that there was no time to get the dog sledges ready. Instead, they made a swift decision to flee the hut on foot. They only had time to quickly grab the clothes they needed to survive in the severe cold. Jensen put on an Icelandic sweater and a pair of Inuit boots.[14]

There was no hesitation in Jensen's mind now. "Get back to Eskimoness as soon as possible and report about what has happened," Jensen told the two Greenlanders. "I'll follow you later." He found a spot near the hut and lay down in the snow, planning to observe the Germans and get an idea what they would do next, but he soon gave up because of the cold and started his own desolate trek by foot through ice and snow towards Eskimoness, 50 miles to the southwest. He found that the boots were no good for the long walk, and when after long, bitter hours struggling through the snow he reached an empty hut at Cape Herschell, he was able to trade them for a pair of ski boots. He finally caught up with the two Greenlanders at Elvsborg, a Norwegian hunting station on Clavering Island.[15]

Meanwhile, the German patrol under the command of Weiss had burst into the hut at Cape Wynn, deciding not to pursue the fleeing occupants as they feared running into an ambush.[16] Instead they searched the building, finding the nearly complete equipment of the three men as well as, crucially, Marius Jensen's diary, which he had left behind in the rush to get out. Waiting out the night in the hut, the Germans returned north to Hansa Bay at dawn on March 12, bringing the three dog sledges that had been abandoned. They had little experience handling dogs, except for the two canines they had brought from Norway. "The dogs would pull with great eagerness, but run in whichever direction they wanted, and then would suddenly stop, looking at their new masters with an expression as if to say: 'Aren't you happy with us? Aren't we doing a great job?'" Weiss reminisced.[17] The short journey took most of the day.[18]

The captured diary was an intelligence triumph for Ritter, giving him an almost complete picture of the people he was up against and who had passed the dark winter months within just a few hundred miles of Hansa Bay. Many were identified by name, and at least one—that of his old friend Henry Rudi from a decade earlier—must have surprised him. After spending several hours perusing the diary, Ritter reported the coup in a telegram to Group North in Wilhelmshaven in the early hours of March 13: "From a base at Eskimoness, Greenland is patrolled up till 72° 00' N. Last [enemy] patrol order: A trip to Sabine Island and Pendulum." A threat such as this could not be tolerated, he continued: "Eskimoness appears to be occupied by five police officers and several Greenlanders. Elimination seems called for, as we can be observed from there and reported by radio. Awaiting instructions."[19]

***

Exhausted and cold, Marius Jensen and the other two men reached Eskimoness in the middle of the day on March 13 after having walked for 36 hours with only a few breaks in between. The station was thinly staffed as several members were on patrols with the sledges in the surrounding area, but Ib Poulsen, the leader of the unit, was there, and surprise at seeing the men in this condition soon gave way to anger at how Marius Jensen had handled the situation. "When I asked Marius why he did not go straight on to Eskimoness he answered that the dogs were tired and that he did not consider it dangerous to stay the night at Cape Wynn, even though it is only eight kilometers [five miles] from Sabine island. This decision was of course absolutely wrong," Poulsen commented later.[20] After listening to the three men's account, Poulsen wrote a lengthy telegram to Eske Brun in Godthaab, describing the dire situation that had now emerged. "Unfortunately, diaries and instructions have been left behind," he said. "Unless I receive orders to the contrary, I intend to depart myself in order to investigate further."[21]

In his reply, Brun ordered Poulsen to stay put at Eskimoness for the time being until the various patrols had returned and the station was fully staffed. At the same time, he left no doubt that he wanted him to act aggressively and proactively. "Your task for the time being is to gather as much reliable information as possible, and also to eliminate the enemy force by capturing or killing its members, as long as it does not compromise the ability to obtain information," Brun wrote. "You have the authority to use any means to achieve this objective. While taking prisoners, you must use your weapons rather than run the slightest risk, and the same applies if there is the slightest indication that prisoners will resist or attempt escape … An energetic response is crucial for our future position in east Greenland. Remember that the enemy is probably highly resolute. Therefore, take no chances, but shoot first."[22]

The situation immediately set off a crisis atmosphere at Eskimoness. In the daytime, the Inuit members patrolled the area around the station, scouring the horizon for any human activity. At night, the Danes kept a watch, while one team of dogs was placed at a distance to provide early warning if someone approached. Meanwhile, the personnel worked around the clock to strengthen the defenses, placing sacks of flour near the doors and windows of the main building. Kurt Olsen, a member of the sledge patrol, was on a two-day expedition at the time, and when he returned without knowledge of what had happened, he was surprised by the scenery that met him. "As I approached, I noticed eight metal pipes sticking out of the snow around the building. When I got even closer, I realized they were the muzzles of guns. They were retracted when the chaps recognized me," he wrote in his diary.[23]

The situation did not look good. Poulsen had requested support from the Americans the moment the German presence was known, but none had arrived. Besides, there was widespread recognition that the Germans were now directly privy to information about the sledge patrol after having captured Marius Jensen's diary. "The Germans could not have wished for any better intelligence about our tasks here," Olsen remarked drily.[24] Nevertheless, for the young men, confirmation that the Germans were now standing on Greenland soil boosted morale and the will to fight immensely. Some thought of the day three years earlier when Germany had occupied Denmark and little actual resistance had taken place. Now was the chance for revenge many had been waiting for. "We are now actually at war. The Germans are 60 miles from here, and we have no other choice but to throw them out. Well, we will get them," Olsen wrote in his diary.[25]

The members of the sledge patrol had little idea about the German capabilities. They did not know if the opposing force also was able to call in air support, and one of their main concerns was that they would be targeted by an air attack. Therefore, they built a bomb shelter with room for the entire personnel, from old coal sacks filled with sand, while also preparing a reserve depot near the station, containing sledges, tents, skis, and food, so that they would be able to travel even if the main huts were destroyed. The station's accounts, instructions and reports as well as all telegrams sent and received since 1939, were put in a cache amongst the rocks that only three men knew about, while the codes were placed in a different location, also known only to a few.

Eskimoness was not fully manned. One member of the sledge patrol, Peter Nielsen, was on patrol almost 100 miles to the north in an area known as Hochstetter Forland, and Poulsen sent Marius Jensen and Eli Knudsen, another patrol member, to retrieve him. Besides, from the outset nearly two years earlier, it had been understood that the sledge patrol was only to employ native Inuit as helpers, not as combatants, and this was not going to change now. Two Inuit at Eskimoness, who had been hired as factotums, were a cause of concern. "[They] began to show considerable anxiety, and it was clear that it was useless to count on them in action," Ib Poulsen said.[26] Henry Rudi made the same observation. "Their faith prohibited them from using arms against another person under any circumstances," he said. "Now they were nervous and were mostly in the way."[27] The upshot was that there were only three men at Eskimoness in a position to fight: Poulsen, Olsen and Rudi.

Still, the mood lightened somewhat as the days passed with no Germans in sight. "We felt quite at ease, since the Germans did not come during the first days after Marius' arrival, as we had expected them to do," Poulsen wrote later.[28] There was an explanation for this, and had he known about it, Poulsen would not have been reassured. At Hansa Bay, Ritter had received orders back from Group North little more than an hour after his original telegram reporting about the existence of a sledge patrol at Eskimoness. The reply was brief and to the point, and in its unforgiving attitude, it was remarkably similar to the message Brun had sent to the Danish sledge patrol: "Eliminate Eskimoness, even if it means that you will temporarily be unable to send weather reports. The implementation is up to you."[29]

Having been given a free hand to organize the attack on Eskimoness as best he could, Ritter spent more than a week making the necessary preparations. Having discovered the efficiency of dog sledges in Greenland conditions, the men under his command took their time getting to know the ropes and becoming accustomed to the three dog teams they had captured at Cape Wynn. Only on March 21, despite suffering from a slight fever, did Ritter take off, accompanied by Novotny, his favorite, as well as the doctor Sensse, and two sailors, Karl Kaiser and Littmann. It was a small team, but it was heavily armed with one light machine gun, six automatic rifles, six pistols and a dozen hand grenades.[30]

***

Ritter's team reached the area near Eskimoness in the afternoon of March 23, making a temporary camp at the Breivik Hut, a small shelter built by Norwegian trappers a few miles to the east. After sunset, they left their dogs behind and began the short trek towards Eskimoness, armed and on foot.[31] The evening had started out somewhat overcast, with weak moonlight, and by the time they reached the station about an hour before midnight, the sky was completely covered by clouds, and the darkness was nearly impenetrable.[32] Noticing that the hut was inhabited, Ritter moved forward, positioning his men with weapons ready to fire.[33]

Inside, Poulsen was wrapping up an inspection tour of the station and its vicinity. Olsen was busy completing weather observations, which were to be transmitted at

11:20pm, and Rudi was standing outside on night watch duty. At 11:12pm, the dogs started barking and Rudi could hear footsteps on the ice. He saw that it was an entire group of people, trying to walk in step over the uneven ground.[34] Rudi slammed open the door, alerting the others. Poulsen rushed through the hut, past Olsen, who had not yet realized that the enemy was just outside.

"Do you want me to finish the weather report first?" he asked.

"No!" Poulsen yelled at him before leaping out of the hut.

Olsen now also ran out to his action station at one corner of the building but remained unaware of the seriousness of the situation, omitting to burn the code books on his desk, although this was his primary responsibility in case of enemy attack.[35] The two Inuit hastily disappeared behind the back of the building, leaving Eskimoness as had been decided beforehand. No one had fired a single shot yet.

"*Wer da*?" Poulsen shouted in German into the darkness, seeking cover behind a box filled with ice while grasping his rifle firmly with the safety off: "Who is there?"

"The German Wehrmacht," a voice said, also in German.

Poulsen replied that one man could approach, unarmed. The reply from the dark was now in perfect Norwegian:

"Is Poulsen present?"

"No, he is away on a sledge expedition," Poulsen replied. "Why don't you come back tomorrow?"

"Is Henry Rudi or Olsen there?"

"No!"

Poulsen wondered where the German had got the names, and in the heat of the moment he did not make the obvious connection with the captured diary. Instead, he suspected with growing unease that the enemy might have listened in on the sledge patrol's radio communication and broken the codes. Rudi, meanwhile, was shocked by the voice from the dark, but for completely different reasons. "It was Ritter. Ritter whom I knew as a friend. Now he was confronting me, armed. It's either me or you. That was the motto now. I hated it," he recalled later in his memoirs.[36]

Poulsen now heard movement in the dark, and he yelled:

"You must pull back immediately."

"We need to talk to Mr. Poulsen, Mr. Rudi or Mr. Olsen," the voice in the darkness replied.

"One man, unarmed, may come forward," was Poulsen's reply.

"Are you prepared to offer armed resistance," the voice now asked.

"You bet," was Poulsen's answer.[37]

At this point, the Germans suddenly opened fire. Both Rudi and Olsen got the impression that they were aiming their weapons chest-high, intending to kill.[38] Poulsen raised his rifle and fired towards a spot where he had noticed movement a few moments earlier, but it was so dark that he was unable to use the sights of his weapon. The flash from his own muzzle, on the other hand, immediately gave away his position, and a hail of projectiles slammed into the ice-filled box in front of him. The German tracers flew in confused patterns across the night sky, and it was now impossible to determine where the shooting was coming from.

When the firing eased up for a brief moment, Poulsen ran back to the hut. He found Rudi in his firing nest at one corner of the building, standing bolt upright as if paralyzed, perhaps not yet fully recovered from realizing that it was Ritter he had just heard. Poulsen gave the older man a nudge and then ran to the other side of the building where Olsen's position was located. Olsen was under heavy fire and did not respond when Poulsen called out to him. The Germans were now shooting in a nearly uninterrupted fashion, with one or two automatic weapons in use at a time, causing splinters from the woodwork to fly through the air. Especially the machine gun made a difference. "The fire was so intense now that I could hear nothing else," Rudi recalled. "If one of my comrades was hit, I wouldn't be able to hear it."[39]

After the shooting had lasted for several minutes, Poulsen decided to abandon the building and run into the mountains behind it. He believed that Rudi had joined him in the retreat but was also under the impression that Olsen had been hit and remained in the building. At a depot placed about a mile behind the station, he was relieved to see that a rifle and other objects had recently been removed, showing that someone, probably Rudi, had already got away. However, he was concerned about Olsen and walked back towards the station, hiding on high ground at a distance of about half a mile from the main building. He kept observing Eskimoness for several hours but registered no activity except for one person moving about outside the main building for a while, and as the cold was severe, he pulled out at 3:30am.[40]

When they broke into the hut and searched it, Ritter and his men found governor Brun's belligerent note, calling on the patrol members to "shoot first." Even more seriously, they discovered so-called "dumdum" bullets, with their tips hollowed out and therefore designed to expand on impact, creating a larger wound on the target. While the sledge patrol most likely intended to use this ammunition while hunting for large game such as polar bears, it had been banned from use in war since the late 19th century. Furious at what he had uncovered, Ritter ordered the entire station to be burned down. Even though the Germans left a small shed next to the main building, where they stored the personal effects of the Danes as well as a large number of furs, it was a clear breach of the code of conduct among travelers in the Arctic, where even the tiniest shelter can mean the difference between life and death in severe weather.[41]

Ritter knew this better than most, and left a handwritten note in English on the wall of the small shed, justifying his actions:

March 23:
    The U.S.A. protects its defence interests in Greenland. We do the same also. We are not at War with Denmark. Now the administration on Greenland gave orders to capture or shoot us, and you are giving weather reports to the enemy. You are making Greenland into a place

of War. We have stayed quietly at our post without attacking you. Now you want war, so you shall have war. But remember that if you shoot with illegal weapons (dum-dum bullets) which you have at hand here in the loft of the radio station, then you must take full responsibility for the consequences, because you are placing yourselves outside the rules of war. Note we have put all personal effects of the hunters and all furs in this hut, while we have destroyed the radio apparatus operating for the U.S.A.

Sign. H. Ritter

Commander of the Wehrmacht Unit, Eskimoness.[42]

While the Germans were collecting supplies from the destroyed Danish station in preparation for their return to Hansa Bay, Poulsen was making his way on foot to Revet, a hunting station 20 miles due north. So were the two others. For Olsen had not been hit after all. He had escaped at about the same time as Poulsen and run into Rudi a small distance from the hut. The following day, the two arrived at Revet independently of Poulsen, and Olsen sent a lengthy message to Brun in Godthaab. Eskimoness had fallen, he explained, and went on: The enemy had better weapons. The dogs had been captured by the Germans. And yet more news, now really bad: In the confusion of the battle, Olsen had left behind his diary, and he had failed to destroy the codes, causing new secrets to fall into the hands of the Germans.[43]

***

From Olsen's diary and other documents left behind at Eskimoness, Ritter learned that the station had not been fully manned, and that Marius Jensen and Eli Knudsen were on an expedition to the north to find Peter Nielsen. The German commander was also given their route back south: From Hochstetter Forland via Kuhn Island to the station Sandodden. Sandodden was on the route the Germans planned to follow as they traveled back to Hansa Bay, and Ritter decided to organize an ambush. Having covered the roughly 25 miles from the charred buildings at Eskimoness to Sandodden, they camped there waiting for the Danish patrol to pass by, wanting to take its members prisoner. Sensse was manning the machine gun from inside the hut, while Novotny had found a well-camouflaged position in the terrain in front.[44]

The first to arrive at Sandodden on March 26, unaware of the German presence, was Eli Knudsen on his dog sledge. At the last moment, he appeared to sense that something was not right and tried to steer the dogs away from the hut. The Germans opened fire, aiming for the dogs and hitting several of them. Novotny, who had hidden near Knudsen's path, stood up pointing a submachine gun at him. This prompted Knudsen to reach forward into his sledge for his rifle. Sensse was handling the machine gun, felling Knudsen with a single shot before his weapon jammed. "He had to be stopped from firing at Novotny," he said.[45] Knudsen fell on a snowdrift while the dog team continued, dragging the dead and injured dogs along, while the Germans rushed up to his lifeless body. "He was lying face down in the snow groaning softly. He was unconscious," Ritter said later.[46]

Knudsen was carried inside, and Sensse, who had fired the projectile, was also the one now trying to save him. It was to no avail, and he died within 30 minutes. The German knew it was impossible to bury him because the soil was frozen solid, and instead they carried his body to a small sod-house next to the main building where food had previously been stored. They put his body in his sleeping bag and wrapped it in the Danish flag, and in front of the building, they placed a wooden cross along with his name and date of death, as well as the message: "He died for his country."[47]

The Germans expected the two other Danes, Marius Jensen and Peter Nielsen, to turn up shortly afterwards, but they waited for hours, and nothing happened. It turned out that Jensen and Nielsen had got separated from Knudsen and had decided to raise a tent roughly 10 miles from Sandodden, continuing only on the following day, March 27.[48] Marius Jensen was the first to arrive. What was left of Eli Knudsen's dog team was placed outside the building to leave the impression that he was inside waiting for the other two. It was a ruse, and it worked. Jensen drove right into the trap. When he had almost reached the building, several Germans who had been hiding on the ground stood up, pointing their weapons at him. Shortly afterwards, Nielsen was captured in the same way.[49]

Ritter assembled the two Danish captives in the hut. He wanted no uncertainty about who was in charge, and his anti-Nazi leanings were far from obvious to his captives. "You are prisoners now," he said in Norwegian. He then explained that they would be going back to Germania Harbor, divided into two teams. Each of the teams would be driven by a captured Dane, as the Germans had still not developed the necessary skill. "If one of you makes trouble, the other one will have to pay," he said menacingly, making a movement with his hands as if he was twisting a small animal's head around.[50]

Soon afterwards, the two teams took off. It was a clear German victory. One enemy had been killed, and two had been taken prisoner. The sledge patrol's main station in the area had been burned to the ground, and its members were on the run. Six sledges and six teams of dogs had been captured. And all with no losses to the Germans, not even a single injury. It seemed that Ritter had finally proven himself as an efficient leader of men in times of crisis. He had been vindicated after six difficult months holed up with a group of argumentative men in the claustrophobic darkness of the Arctic night. And yet, everything was not right. The unit under Ritter's command was much more fragile than it seemed. At the moment when it appeared stronger than ever, it was in fact reaching breaking point. This would have fatal consequences only a few days later.

CHAPTER 15

The Escape

Late Spring 1943

In early April, Ritter's achievement received recognition from the very highest level of the German military hierarchy. Grand Admiral Karl Dönitz, who had been commander-in-chief of the navy since late January, sent a telegram to Hansa Bay via the radio station in Tromsø: "Your work has been extremely valuable for our war effort at sea and in the air. The raid on Eskimoness was a sound success."[1] On the face of it, this ought to be final confirmation of Ritter's ability, removing the last bit of doubt about his suitability for the role as commander of the isolated outpost. Quite to the contrary, it came at a time when his authority as leader, already challenged in the escalating tension of the long, dreary winter months, was falling apart, and his relationship with his men, always tenuous, was rapidly deteriorating to a point where there was no turning back.

Despite the triumphant mood in Dönitz's telegram, Ritter knew he was in a difficult position, not just vis-à-vis his own men, but also the enemy. The Danes and by extension the Americans now knew that the Germans had a presence on Sabine Island, and it was just a question of time before *Hermann*, squeezed in place by huge masses of ice and unable to move, was spotted from the air along with the two huts. They could move the camp on land to a new position, but the tracks left in the snow would be all too easy to detect. And even if he managed to find a place to set up a new weather station, would he be able to survive a second winter with a group of much younger men who were grumbling behind his back, rejecting him as an old man hopelessly out of touch?

After arriving back at Germania Harbor from Sandodden, Ritter dropped off the two Danish prisoners, Marius Jensen and Peter Nielsen, along with a few armed guards, while he himself continued on to Hansa Bay. He did not give any explanation as to why the prisoners were not to come along for the last six miles of the journey to the German camp. Perhaps he wanted to keep his options open. At any rate, there were incipient signs that he was a changed person. The other members of "Holzauge" sensed it, and they linked it to the killing of Eli Knudsen. "Ritter was shaken by the death of the Dane. It was an outcome he had not wanted at all," wrote Gottfried Weiss, while noting that it meant a blow to him to find out that his old friend Henry Rudi was fighting on the other side.[2] Rudolf Sensse, the doctor, also observed a drastic change in Ritter's behavior. "He was very depressed that Eskimoness had been destroyed. And after Eli Knudsen's death, he shut himself off. He didn't say much," he recalled.[3]

The sources do not give any details about what happened in the short period while Ritter was in Hansa Bay, and the captured Danes remained at Germania Harbor. Perhaps his depressed mood deteriorated further after he found that his leadership problems remained. Perhaps he found that his men were not as impressed by the successful raid on Eskimoness as he had hoped, and that an unbridgeable gulf still existed between them. Perhaps his fellow officers had used his absence to plot against him. His colleagues at Hansa Bay later voiced the suspicion that Ritter "had lost his nerve after realizing his weak position among the other expedition members and wanted to distance himself physically from the station."[4] To some of the younger more military-minded men it also added to their frustration over Ritter that he had failed to discipline Hans Röttger, who had been in command of the two-man hunting expedition that had been interrupted by Marius Jensen and fled the scene rather than seeking to oppose and capture the approaching team.[5] He even feared that members of his expedition might report him to the Gestapo for not being a loyal German.[6]

Marius Jensen and Peter Nielsen were not aware of the internal tensions among the Germans. Initially during their stay at Germania Harbor, they and their captors killed time with card-play inside the cabin. It turned out that one of the Germans even spoke reasonable Danish, having grown up in a part of Germany close to the border with Denmark. "I wouldn't say we were friends, but they treated us correctly," Marius Jensen recalled later.[7] The relationship developed as the days went by, and Jensen commanded grudging admiration from the Germans because of his experience in arctic conditions. They were also looking to him for advice about what to do with the dogs captured from the sledge patrol, now numbering about 100. One day, one of the Germans, the Danish speaker, stepped inside the cabin with an excited look on his face.

"I've just seen seven polar bears pass by just outside," he said.

"Why don't we go hunting together? Shoot a polar bear?" Jensen asked. Bear meat was sorely needed, not least for the dogs.

"Will you promise that you won't shoot me while we are hunting?" the German replied.

"Why the hell would I shoot you? My dogs and all my gear is here," Jensen replied. This convinced the German, and soon Jensen was carrying a rifle, hunting side by side with his German captors.[8]

Ritter returned to Germania Harbor from Hansa Bay after a few days. He, too, was developing a rapport with Marius Jensen. As was perhaps to be expected, he enjoyed the company of the young Dane, feeling that since they both had a history in the Arctic, he had more in common with him than with his own compatriots. Marius Jensen sensed the subtle change in attitudes towards him, reasoning that with his deep knowledge of life in Greenland's harsh nature, he was of value to the less experienced Germans. He decided to turn it to his advantage.

"Can we make a deal?" Ritter asked him.

"It depends on what it's about," Jensen replied.

"Will you drive me around in this area to find a new camp site?" Ritter asked.

"We can talk about that, if you hand back Peter Nielsen's equipment and his dogs," Jensen replied, suggesting that the other Dane should be allowed to return to Sandodden to give Eli Knudsen a proper burial before his body was eaten by wild animals.[9]

Ritter wanted to think it over. Agreeing to the proposal could ease his nagging sense of guilt over the killing of Knudsen. On the other hand, there was an obvious risk that Nielsen would simply make a run for it. In the end, Ritter decided to return the sledge to the Dane, fully equipped with weapons, ammunition, medical supplies and provisions—in short, everything needed for survival in arctic conditions—against his word of honor that he would not try to escape.[10] Marius Jensen was the last person to talk to Peter Nielsen before he left, speaking out of earshot of the Germans:

"Just go south. Find the others. Don't stay at Sandodden," he told him before he disappeared into the distance.[11]

Ritter's decision was received with disbelief by his men, and any goodwill the commander might have earned from the successful raid against Eskimoness evaporated, instead deepening the gulf that had existed since the previous fall. Few of Ritter's men saw any need to release Nielsen, pointing out that it would be impossible to dig a grave in the frozen soil.[12] Instead, Nielsen could easily have been brought to Hansa Bay and placed under guard there, and even if it had been impossible to keep him as a prisoner, he should not have been let go, they thought. "If a prisoner cannot be transported and becomes a burden on the other members of the expedition, the commander must have the courage to shoot him," said Novotny, otherwise one of Ritter's few allies. "You cannot just release him."[13]

***

A few days after Peter Nielsen's departure, it was Marius Jensen's turn to fulfill his part of the deal, acting as Ritter's sledge driver during a reconnaissance mission in the area around Hansa Bay, looking for a new place to establish the German camp. On April 5, the two left Germania Harbor on two sledges, accompanied by Karl Kaiser, the sailor who had also taken part in the raid on Eskimoness. Initially, they headed north in the direction of Hochstetter Forland. On the same day, a separate sledge mission, Stosstrupp Ella Insel or Combat Patrol Ella Island, consisting of

Weiss, Sensse, Littmann and Novotny, moved south. Its aim was to search the station at Ella Island for members of the Danish sledge patrol and, if needed eliminate it.[14] Ritter's group soon ended up in a local snowstorm, and the sledge driven by the inexperienced Kaiser was so far behind that he lost visual contact with the other two.[15] It was becoming clear that Kaiser was a drag on the expedition, and Ritter ordered him to return to Hansa Bay.[16]

Ritter and Jensen continued on their own sledge and got along well. Ritter suggested only half in jest that they should try to reach the west coast of Greenland by moving anti-clockwise following the coastline to the north. Jensen thought it could be done.[17] Ritter let it shine through in the conversations that he found himself in a desperate situation. "I don't think he expected to survive with the other Germans," Jensen recalled later.[18] Suddenly, only three days into the journey, Ritter made an astonishing proposal: He would swap roles with Jensen. Captor would become captive, and vice versa, weapons would change hands, and they would head south, aiming for the southernmost sledge patrol station at Scoresby Sound, well inside territory controlled by US forces. Jensen agreed.[19]

It was a momentous decision and one with potentially enormous personal consequences for Ritter. An officer handing himself over to the enemy without offering any resistance was at such odds with the expectations in the German military, or any military for that matter, that it is hard to imagine that it would result in anything but a court martial and a probable death sentence. Equally important, it entailed abandoning his men to their own devices at a time when it was likely that their position had been compromised, or soon would be, and the result could very well be an Allied air raid, against which the German station had almost no defenses.[20] They were young men with families back home in Germany—Novotny was informed by radio in April that his wife had given birth to a daughter[21]—and the fact that their commander would leave them to an uncertain fate, possibly death, reveals the extent of the acrimony between them.

On the way south, Ritter and Jensen aimed to make a stop at the Mosquito Bay station, incidentally the spot occupied by 12 Royal Marines nearly three years earlier during the hunt for *Veslekari*. They were surprised to find it occupied by the members of Stosstrupp Ella Insel, who had not got any further because of their lack of familiarity with sledge travel. "It didn't seem to suit him that he ran into us at Mosquito Bay during our journey to Ella Island. He seemed affected," Sensse recalled later.[22] Most likely his awkwardness reflected embarrassment at being found so far south when he was supposed to be much further up north reconnoitering for a new camp site. Weiss and the other Germans also noticed that Ritter had approached the station unarmed. Their reading of the situation was that he had been worried that he might come across people that he had known before the war but were now on the other side. They did not realize that he had already handed over control of the mission, and his weapons, to his captive. Both he and Jensen wisely kept quiet about this fact, as it could potentially cost them their lives.[23]

Ritter had a heated argument with the members of Stosstrupp Ella Insel. He did his utmost to dissuade them from following through with the mission against Ella Island. Jensen, he said disingenuously, had divulged to him the fact that the station had a garrison of 16 men, so that an attack would be suicide. Weiss insisted on carrying out the mission, and Ritter now proceeded to show him a route to Ella Island twice as long as the direct way, which, he said, contained dangerous crevices.[24] Hardly had the German combat patrol disappeared along the longer route before Jensen jumped on his own sledge, leaving Ritter behind at Mosquito Bay while going the straight way to Ella Island in the hope of warning any Danes who might be staying there. A furious race was on.[25]

Jensen, the more skilled sledge driver taking the shorter route, got to Ella Island first, finding it empty. Persuaded that there was no danger to any Danes, he returned directly to Mosquito Bay in order to pick up Ritter. He circled the station in a radius of one and half miles in order to ensure that there were no fresh sledge tracks before being assured that Ritter was alone. He picked him up and resumed the journey to the south in the direction of Scoresby Sound.[26] Meanwhile, Weiss and the other Germans turned up at Ella Island, finding it deserted but noticing the prints of a sledge, as well as one lonely sledge dog running around bewildered near the empty huts. Since they recognized the dog from Ritter's and Jensen's dog team—each of the canines had distinct appearances and personalities—they put two and two together, realizing that the others had been there before them.[27]

Beyond that, they were left guessing what had transpired. One of the possibilities, they reluctantly agreed, was that Ritter had voluntarily surrendered to Jensen, but they immediately dismissed the idea, stating that "a German officer doesn't do that."[28] In fact, of course, this was exactly what had happened. Ritter and Jensen were now on their way south, the Dane headed for freedom, the German for captivity. For the next three weeks, the two covered 300 miles. It was "quite a job," remarked Poulsen, the head of the sledge patrol.[29] Just before the two reached Scoresby Sound, at the small settlement at Cape Hope, Ritter made a halt, tearing the military insignia from his uniform in a dramatic gesture.

"Now the war is over for me," he said.[30]

***

Ritter spent more than two months at Scoresby Sound.[31] He was not interrogated, and he was allowed to roam freely in the settlement, although he was constantly watched by a guard, mostly his own former prisoner Peter Nielsen.[32] In the German camp at Hansa Bay, Ritter's former subordinates were still questioning what might have become of him. His return was expected in mid-May, possibly because that was what he had told the members of Stosstrupp Ella Insel when he met them at Mosquito Bay.[33] When he had still not turned up by the middle of the month, the naval command in Germany ordered "Holzauge" to launch a sledge expedition to look for him.

On May 17, just a few days after returning as part of the Stosstrupp, Sensse took off with a team of five sledge dogs. "As we were not many people, I left on my own," he said later.[34] Another reason why it was a one-man expedition was the likelihood that it would lead only to death. There was a high probability of running into enemy forces, and the incipient thaw meant sledge travel was becoming riskier. In other words, according to his own testimony, Sensse was prepared to sacrifice himself but would not let other members of the expedition follow him on what could very well be a doomed mission. Exactly what Sensse was supposed to achieve is unclear from the contemporary sources. Perhaps the Germans thought Ritter had been in an accident. In that case, however, it was unlikely he was still alive. Novotny's testimony a quarter century later was more straightforward in this respect: "Sensse was in pursuit of Ritter [...] in order to arrest or kill him, as this had been clearly ordered by Group North."[35]

From the outset, Sensse's lonely expedition was marred by bad luck, and possibly also by his lack of experience with dog sledges. He was only on the second day of his journey and had just passed Sandodden, where he had killed a man only recently, moving in the direction of a Norwegian trapper station known as Herschellhus, when near the coastline, he suddenly passed over a stretch of thin ice, and the sledge broke through. The dogs struggled but all five were pulled into the deep by the heavy sledge, as Sensse himself fought for his life. "I pulled myself onto firmer ice and reached a shed that I knew between Sandodden and Herschellhus. I dried my gear there and walked back to Sandodden," he explained later. "From the depot there I built a light sledge from skis and a frame, loaded it with necessities and pulled it after me in a harness. I found a pair of good skis for myself and moved faster than I had expected."[36]

A few days into his lengthy trek, Sensse observed three American bombers on their way north.[37] Most likely, they were aircraft under the command of Norwegian aviator Bernt Balchen, who was carrying out a brief campaign against the Germans in northeast Greenland during that month. The campaign was ultimately the result of Ultra, the top-secret Allied ability to read encoded German messages after the Enigma cypher had been cracked. British intelligence read communication from Group North revealing that it wanted the "Holzauge" weather station to continue its meteorological reports even though it had been discovered by the sledge patrol, and that it prepared a relief expedition.[38] This information was passed on to Washington DC, prompting General George C. Marshall to issue an order to "annihilate" the German stations in East Greenland.[39]

On May 14, Balchen led a group of two Boeing B-17 Flying Fortresses taking off from their base at Keflavik in Iceland in a raid of Eskimoness, as it was assumed the Germans might still be using the station as a base. Apparently, there had been no attempt to reconnoiter by air in advance, and when Balchen arrived with his Fortresses over Eskimoness, he got his first inkling that it had in fact been deserted. From his cockpit, he could see how thorough the destruction at the hands of Ritter's men had been: "Doors swung open, windows were broken and vacant [in] half-burned and wrecked buildings." Still, Balchen decided to go ahead with his mission, completing the work that the Germans had begun. "We carried out our orders, dropped our bombs, strafed the buildings, and left them burning as we headed back to Iceland," he wrote later.[40]

The raid had taken the B-17s to the limit of their range, and they had even had to allocate space in their bomb bays for reserve fuel tanks. Balchen realized that for the next raid, against Hansa Bay at an even greater distance from his base in Iceland, he would need B-24 Liberators with longer-range tanks. While he was waiting for two Liberators to arrive from stateside, he prepared what he later termed "the northernmost bombing ever attempted by the Army Air Forces." The B-24s had only six defensive positions compared to the B-17s' nine, and therefore the Fortresses would still be needed for the raid on Hansa Bay as added protection against possible enemy fighters, he decided, fearing that the Luftwaffe might be able to interfere from bases in Norway.[41]

On May 25, at 4am, the two B-17s, one of them carrying Balchen, took off from Keflavik base, followed 30 minutes later by the two B-24s, with full bombloads. One of them also carried the base mascot, a six-month-old Icelandic sheepdog by the name of "Tailspin". The four aircraft rendezvoused at Bontekoe Island, south of Mosquito Bay, at 9am. While Balchen went ahead in his B-17 to carry out reconnaissance of Hansa Bay, presumably in order not to repeat the disappointment earlier that month of bombing a deserted target, the three others assembled 50 miles to the southeast, awaiting his orders. As he flew over the area at 5,000 feet, Balchen noticed two large wooden huts, as well as the German ship, the *Hermann*. He also noticed small figures like ants running around frantically. So, it was still occupied, unlike Eskimoness.[42]

Balchen returned to the other aircraft and led the way back to Hansa Bay, arriving shortly before noon. To make it easier for the B-24 crews to recognize the target, Balchen dived towards the two buildings. "We gave it everything we had with our forward machine guns; the tail-gunner took over as we passed," he wrote. "Looking back, we could see smoke from our incendiary bullets pouring out of both buildings."[43] Now the scene was set for the B-24s. The first of the two, the one carrying "Tailspin," made a perfect run over the German camp but did not drop its bombs. It turned out the Icelandic puppy had fallen asleep in the bomb-bay and would have been released onto the Germans along with the bombs if the crew had not hesitated. Instead, the B-24 circled back and emptied its load in the second try.[44]

On the ground, the Germans counted 16 bombs from the two B-24s and noted that none of them hit any target. But long minutes of terror ensued after the bombs were dropped, and all four aircraft made repeated runs at low altitude firing their machine guns. "I pressed myself motionless against the ground, and every time the planes approached, I felt as if the projectiles were going to hit me straight in the back," Gottfried Weiss recalled. The larger of the two buildings was ablaze when the four aircraft disappeared over the horizon. "Since we were all lying on the ground, they probably thought we were dead," Weiss wrote. They now counted the damage. The building was burnt to the ground, but the other building was largely undamaged, and the same was true for *Hermann*.[45] "No injured, no dead," Scherer wrote in his diary. "Troubled days are behind us, and there are surely difficult days ahead as well."[46]

Sensse, hundreds of miles to the south, was oblivious to these events. At the time of the raid on Hansa Bay, he was still on his way to Mosquito Bay on his skis and with his home-made sledge. Some days later, he finally reached Mosquito Bay, hoping that perhaps this would be the end of his search, but he was quickly disappointed. "Ritter wasn't there," he recalled. "The sledge tracks didn't tell me much, as the thaw had already begun."[47] He now decided that he could go no further, and he returned north. After yet more days struggling through the barren landscape, he reached Eskimoness, the target of the first American air raid. It was the first indication he had got of the bombings that had taken place. "Balchen had shot the Danish flag from the pole," he remarked matter-of-factly many years later.[48]

***

On June 7 at 4:25am, an unarmed German Dornier Do 26 flying boat landed at Hansa Bay under an overcast sky. On board were *Fregattenkapitän* Reinhold Bürklen of the navy and *Oberregierungsrat* Richard Becker from the military weather service, in addition to a radio operator and the aircraft's four-member crew.[49] The mission, which was also aimed at evacuating three members of "Holzauge" who had fallen ill, had been in preparation since May, even before the American raid. Headquarters back home in Germany had read between the lines in the stream of telegrams that had arrived from Greenland, and it was clear that a dangerous rift had developed between Ritter and the other officers. Ritter's behavior was also considered increasingly odd. Releasing a prisoner who would almost certainly escape back to his own lines and divulge the location of the German station was one thing but following this up by then going on a reconnaissance patrol alone with another prisoner showed severe lack of judgment. It was impossible to get to the bottom of the case through the exchange of telegrams, and therefore, the naval command had decided that inspection on the spot was needed.[50]

The flying boat's journey across the North Atlantic from its base in Norway had lasted for eight hours as the bulky hull had made its way slowly through the dim light of the polar summer night, with headwinds forcing speeds down to 100 miles per hour. Flying as low as 15 feet over the ocean, the crew had enjoyed limited visibility, and twice icebergs had been mistaken for enemy warships. When the rugged coastline of Greenland finally emerged in the distance, navigation had been made difficult by the accumulation of pack ice, blurring well-known contours. Only after the peculiar shape of Shannon Island appeared in front of the plane was the pilot able to find his bearings, and shortly afterwards, he landed the plane in ice-free water off Hansa Bay. A group of "Holzauge" expedition members were lined up, along with a dog sledge containing the equipment of the men who were to be evacuated home.[51] "It was exciting and a great feeling to suddenly see new people," Weiss, among those welcoming the plane, wrote in his memoirs.[52]

There was little time to waste, and Bürklen and Becker immediately sat down with Weiss and Kasper to discuss the problems encountered by the Germans in Greenland. From the testimony of the two officers, it was clear that Ritter had "failed almost consistently in making the right choices at decisive moments," Becker wrote in a report afterwards. The mistrust between Ritter and his men had reached a level where some of them even thought he had been behind the American air raid. It was understandable that such suspicions would arise, Becker remarked, but added dutifully: "There is no evidence for this."[53] Further Allied attacks, most likely from the air, were almost sure to happen, and since the men had little means to defend themselves, the conclusion was straightforward: "Taking everything into account, *Fregattenkapitän* Bürklen and I were convinced beyond any doubt that the station could no longer continue under the present circumstances," Becker wrote.[54]

As a result, it was decided that the flying boat would return to Norway with a total of six "Holzauge" members rather than the three originally slated for evacuation. The 10 Germans left behind would be flown out at the earliest date possible. If the thaw meant that *Hermann* could be extricated from the ice, the skeleton crew was to attempt sailing it back to Europe. Hans Röttger was put in temporary charge of the expedition, with Weiss as his deputy and scientific leader. If Ritter by some miracle returned to Hansa Bay, he was to be arrested. It was now mid-morning, and a wind started blowing in from the sea, necessitating a swift departure of the Dornier Do 26. By the time the flying boat took off after five hours and 15 minutes of talks, carrying a large number of Germans home from Greenland, "Holzauge" was history.[55]

The same Dornier Do 26 was back 10 days later to pick up the last expedition members. It was shortly after midnight, and in the eternal day of the arctic summer, the sun was shining from a clear blue sky as the plane landed. One of the last actions of the expedition members before they boarded the aircraft for the long journey back across the Atlantic was to blow up the remaining building and sink the *Hermann*, only leaving emergency supplies for the possibility that Ritter or Sensse were to return. "Relief at going home in one piece mixed with sadness at leaving the island we had come to know so well," Weiss wrote.[56]

Sensse was still far south while all this was taking place, only returning to the German camp more than a month later. Towards the end of his journey, the melting snow made large parts of the coastal area lakes of mud, and trekking across open land was now an impossible endeavor, forcing him to cover the last distance in a small flat-bottomed boat he had found. He arrived near Hansa Bay in late July, finding the camp deserted. Furious at what seemed to be the defeat of the German mission to Greenland, all he found was a record player and a potato-masher hand grenade. Dejected, he sat down, waiting to strike one last blow for the fatherland.

Incidentally, the US Coast Guard cutter *North Star* under the command of Captain Carl Christian von Paulsen arrived off Hansa Bay just a short while afterwards. A landing party led by von Paulsen himself was put ashore and quickly encountered problems. "They had a real tough time of it, the mud being so thick the men sank to their knees with almost every step," Coast Guard photographer Hyman Rothman recalled.[57] They walked in this manner for six or seven miles until they discovered the deserted German station, finding abandoned clothing, food, wrecked machine guns, and plenty of ammunition.[58] The search parties found no people, and at night they returned to the cutter, while only von Paulsen and two others stayed behind.

Late the next day, the three heard the strange sound of a German love song across the empty, barren wilderness. Following the sound, they came upon Sensse who was sitting next to the record player, clutching the hand grenade.[59] Sensse stood up and made the Nazi greeting, but surrendered to the Americans without following through with his plan to fight to the last.[60] Sensse was under suspicions of being a Gestapo agent, but no evidence to this effect ever emerged. "I was taken onboard and placed in the sickbay, where I was treated well," Sensse later recalled.[61]

Meanwhile, Ritter was picked up from Scoresby Sound and flown on board a US Navy Catalina seaplane on July 20 to Iceland, where he was handed over to US Army authorities in the capital of Reykjavik. While in Iceland, he was visited by Balchen, who told him how he personally had bombed the camp at Hansa Bay in late May, destroying all buildings and sinking the ship. The Norwegian aviator was unable to inform Ritter what had happened to his men. Surprisingly, they became friends, and Balchen saw to it that the prisoner was able to read books about polar science. In early August, Ritter was taken back across the Atlantic to the United States, arriving at Camp Crossville, Tennessee, on August 15.[62]

CHAPTER 16

Crossroads

Summer 1943

On May 22, 1943, the Canadian consul Maxwell Dunbar returned to Godthaab after having spent several months in Ottawa. It had been a lengthy journey. A Royal Canadian Air Force plane had transported him to a US Army Air Force base at Goose Bay, Labrador, and he had continued by aircraft to Bluie West 1 at Narsarssuak in western Greenland. The last part of the journey had been on board US Coast Guard cutter *Escanaba*, a 1,021-ton vessel with a crew of 103, which had formed part of the Greenland Patrol since the beginning of the war.[1] "Shortly after she put me ashore and was on her way back to sea again, she was blown to bits by a German torpedo that hit the ship's magazine; only two of her crew survived," Dunbar later recalled.[2]

After departing from Godthaab, *Escanaba* on June 10, had joined convoy GS-24 from Narsarssuak to St. Johns, Newfoundland. On June 12, with the west coast of Greenland barely out of sight, two of the convoy's Cost Guard vessels conducted a search for a U-boat reported to be in the area but found nothing.[3] It seemed it was going to be uneventful convoy, but it was not to be. The following day, at 5:10am, less than 100 nautical miles off the cryolite mine at Ivigtut, a powerful blast ripped through the entire body of *Escanaba*. On board, Melvin A. Baldwin, a 21-year-old boatswain's mate second class, was at the wheel and was "blown upward and hit the overhead of the wheelhouse," he explained later. "I staggered out the door and was washed overboard." Meanwhile, Seaman First Class Raymond F. O'Malley was below deck. "I reached the main deck and started for No. 1 gun and the ship went down from under me."[4]

Observers on other ships from the convoy reported a column of dense black and yellow smoke rising from *Escanaba*, and it was no more than three minutes before the cutter had sunk below the waves. It had not even had time to send out a signal. Baldwin and O'Malley struggled through water filled with pieces of wreckage, eventually clinging desperately to a strongback, a 38 foot log that had been used to keep the lifeboats from banging against the side of the ship. The last they remembered was being joined at the log by three other members of the crew, including the ship's skipper, Lieutenant Commander Carl U. Peterson, and then they passed out. When Baldwin and O'Malley came to, they were on board the Coast Guard cutter *Raritan*. The three others had been washed away before help arrived, and there was no trace of them. The two were the sole survivors out of a crew of more than 100.[5]

It was a mystery then what had hit *Escanaba* and remains so to this day. Perhaps it was a torpedo as claimed by Dunbar, or more likely it hit a mine. Either way, it was a matter of bitter irony that it should be sunk just at the time when the Battle of the Atlantic was finally on the verge of being won by the Allies. *Escanaba* had taken part in this battle since its earliest beginnings, and as late as in February of that year, the ship's crew had witnessed one of the campaign's greatest tragedies, the sinking of *Dorchester*, a 5,252-ton coastal passenger ship converted into a US Army troop transport, while on its way from Newfoundland with more than 900 men on board, mostly soldiers who were to reinforce the Greenland garrison.[6]

In the intense darkness of the early hours of February 3, *Dorchester*'s small convoy, which also consisted of two Norwegian freighters, was in a position roughly 150 miles west of Greenland, protected by an escort consisting of *Escanaba* and two other Coast Guard cutters. The convoy had been warned of the presence of German U-boats in the area but was nevertheless caught by surprise when *U-223*, commanded by 26-year-old Karl-Jürgen Wächter, crept up from behind and sent five of its torpedoes against *Dorchester*, of which two found their target. The ships were placed so far apart that none of the others noticed the blasts and sailed on, inadvertently leaving the doomed ship to its own devices.

Many who died on *Dorchester* could have survived. "Abandon ship" was ordered almost immediately, but a large number did not hear the command and never made it out in time. The ones who did hear the message joined a panicked chaos on deck. The lifeboats were lowered into the water in an inefficient and disorganized manner, and only two out of 14 were filled to capacity. Amid the frantic scramble to escape the sinking ship, no one released any distress signals, and the other ships in the convoy simply continued on their course towards Greenland, ignorant of the disaster playing out behind them.

"My God, I forgot my life preserver," a soldier on *Dorchester* burst out in despair when he stepped onto the deck. "Here, take mine," said George L. Fox, a Methodist minister and one of four chaplains on board.[7] The other three chaplains—a rabbi, a Catholic priest and a Reformed Church minister—did the same thing, offering their life jackets to others and condemning themselves to certain death. "The last I saw of the chaplains they were standing on deck praying," Anthony J. Povlak, one of the survivors, remembered later. "By that time the ship had capsized and was at a forty-five degree angle."[8] James A. Ward, who also survived, recalled the chaplains' last moments before the ocean devoured *Dorchester*: "They were singing songs, hymns. I knew they couldn't get off. The next time I looked, it was like slipping away under water."[9]

Sixteen Danes were on board *Dorchester* on the way to the Ivigtut mine, and only three survived. One of the survivors, Knud Knudsen, described his plight in the water along with two other Danes after their lifeboat had capsized, struggling to stay afloat. "First Andreassen gave up, and five minutes later Doctor Hansen. After that, I saw a rubber boat with three soldiers who helped me up," he said later.[10] Only much too late was the rest of the convoy alerted to *Dorchester's* plight. While the two Norwegian transports continued on to Greenland guarded by one Coast Guard cutter, the two remaining vessels of the escort, including *Escanaba*, were ordered back to hunt for the German U-boat and pick up survivors. When they arrived, the U-boat was long gone, and with the ocean temperature just above freezing point, many of the men who had escaped *Dorchester* but had been unable to haul themselves onto one of the half-empty lifeboats had already died. Altogether 675 men lost their lives that night.

More was to come. As the saying goes, the darkest hour is just before the dawn, and the spring of 1943, with the turning point imminent, saw the bloody culmination of the Battle of the Atlantic. The effort to haul cargo across the ocean to the British Isles reached new highs and was countered by an unforgiving and determined German U-boat force still at the height of its powers, while Allied intelligence was momentarily incapacitated by a change in the secret German code. The ocean around Greenland was part of this war-deciding drama, due to the existence of the "Greenland air gap", a zone of no Allied air cover south of the island.[11]

In a shocking example of what this entailed, the eastbound convoy SC-121 was attacked off the southern tip of Greenland by a pack of 27 German U-boats in early March. Strong winds shattered the convoy's formation, leaving the individual ships to fend for themselves, as the escort's detection systems were rendered useless by the weather. The result was a loss of 13 ships, and not a single German U-boat sunk in return.[12] It was part of a larger story. In a note on air operations in the antisubmarine effort issued in the spring of 1943, George C. Marshall pointed out the severity of the situation: "During the first three weeks of March 1943 German submarines sank over three-quarters of a million tons of shipping in the North Atlantic southeast of Greenland 'in an area not yet covered by air search'."[13]

Greenland was at the edge of the Battle of the Atlantic, but the special natural conditions added extra hardship on top of what was endured by sailors and soldiers elsewhere on the vast ocean. More serious than anything were the arctic temperatures, meaning no one could survive exposed to the elements for long, as the death toll from *Dorchester* showed. This was an ongoing hazard even during routine operations, reflected in the official record of Coast Guard cutter *North Star* for an otherwise unremarkable day during the war: "On the 5th [of February 1943] a man fell overboard and was unconscious when recovered, dying at 1535."[14]

The Coast Guard did develop methods to speedily recover men from the ocean before the cold claimed them. Lieutenant Robert H. Prause, the executive officer on board the *Escanaba*, designed and tested what he termed the "*Escanaba* retriever method of rescue," describing it in a letter home: "A man in a rubber suit with a parachute harness about him and a line attached is sent over the side. The retriever swims out, ties on another line about the victim or raft and it's hauled into the ship's side."[15] The retriever system was put to the test in the *Dorchester* disaster, helping in hauling many of those who had not yet died from exposure to safety.[16]

Prause went down with *Escanaba* in June and did not live to see his system widely implemented. It was in use again towards the end of the year, when sailors of US Coast Guard cutter *Comanche* dressed in rubber suits, braved raging waves near Greenland to rescue survivors from transport ship *Nevada*, which had capsized in a violent storm. The official history describes what happened as Fireman First Class Robert C. Vile jumped into the ocean, showing only too clearly that even when Hitler's U-boats had been beaten back, the elements remained a formidable foe that still claimed lives: "After reaching his man and towing him to the side of the *Comanche*, [...] Vile was so battered and beaten that he lapsed into a state of helplessness and his man slipped away from him. When last seen the man was floating, supported by a life preserver, with his face down on the water, apparently dead."[17]

***

The war had thrown several surprises at Norwegian trapper Johan Johansen. He had arrived at Mosquito Bay in northeast Greenland on August 1, 1939, and exactly one month later, the German invasion of Poland had made it clear that his stay at the isolated station would take much longer than expected. The occupation of Norway in April the following year had made a return home an even more distant prospect. As the months passed, he had concentrated on his work of hunting animals and preparing furs, as well as simple survival. Then in August 1941, Coast Guard cutter *North Star* had anchored off his lonely abode at Mosquito Bay with orders to evacuate him. He had protested, but to no avail.[18]

By 1943, Johansen was employed as a sledge driver at Base Ice Cape Detachment, south of Angmagssalik. He was accompanied by his team of eight dogs, which he had brought from Mosquito Bay. "We had been through many rough patches together, and I knew I could trust them if it really mattered," he wrote later.[19] Still, he was a rough and sometimes brutal master of his dogs. The dominant male in his dog team had a large scar where he had temporarily wired his mouth shut as punishment for attacking him.[20] Johansen's main responsibility now was to help search for air crews that had been forced to land on the icecap. It was testimony to how much Greenland had changed since he had arrived four years earlier, as in the meantime the island had become a vital station on the air routes between North America and Britain. "Planes would disappear," he wrote. "Sometimes they were able to send off signals, so we knew where to look for them. On other occasions they didn't and there was no other choice but to start looking for them, a bit like a needle in a haystack."[21]

Greenland aviation was one of the great unsung heroic endeavors during the war, similar in many respects to the epic struggle to supply China by air via "the Hump," the treacherous route across the Himalayas. Also similar to "the Hump," the adversary was not enemy aircraft, but the forces of nature. "Our fliers hated Greenland's snow, rain, sleet, fog, wind, and ice," remarked William S. Carlson, a special Arctic consultant for the US Army Air Forces.[22] Flying across the icecap, pilots often found themselves in a situation known as "whiteout," described as reminiscent of flying through milk, where the featureless landscape below caused any depth perception to disappear.[23] "The Northeast ferrying route is the world's second worst ferrying route," according to Lieutenant Colonel Milton W. Arnold, weather officer at Air Transport Command in Washington DC.[24] Only "the Hump" was worse.

From the beginning of the war until its very last days, aircraft ended up on the icecap due to mishaps of various kinds.[25] In July 1942, in the largest forced landing to date, two B-17 Flying Fortresses and six escorting Lockheed P-38 Lightnings crash landed wheels up on the icecap after being caught in a bad storm and being unable to find an emergency airfield. According to reports that have never been entirely validated, the pilots were being deliberately led in the wrong direction by a German radio operator posing as Greenland ground personnel.[26] After three days on the icecap, the crews were rescued without injury, but the planes were abandoned. "There's a bonding that occurs between a young pilot and his own plane, and when you left you were saying goodbye to it in a sense, and that was a very sentimental moment," said one of the pilots, Bradley McManus.[27]

In what was to become the longest rescue effort in any theater during the entire conflict, a B-17 crashed in southeastern Greenland in November 1942, ironically as it had been diverted to assist in the search for another crashed aircraft, a Douglas C-53 transport, which was never found. The nine men of the B-17—the six-member crew plus two volunteer observers and one passenger—were left stranded on the icecap for five months, while the US military worked tirelessly to save the men. The wreckage of the Fortress was in an area characterized by seemingly bottomless crevasses covered by thin layers of ice and snow, meaning it was associated with grave risk to attempt rescue overland. The stranded men were airlifted out in phases, but the entire rescue operation was only definitively brought to an end in early April 1943, when the last men were transported out, "in silence, still unable to believe their ordeal [was] ending," according to the Norwegian aviator Bernt Balchen, who led the effort.[28]

While most aircraft in the air over Greenland were involved in ferrying planes to the European Theater of Operations, the Coast Guard carried out local responsibilities ranging from antisubmarine patrols to observation of ice conditions with a designated air squadron, VP-6. Established in the summer of 1943, it was equipped with PBY-5A Catalina flying boats and based at Bluie West 1. John Redfield, one of the squadron pilots, said. "Most of the time, our return to BW-1 during bad weather conditions was an exercise in nail-chewing," said John Redfield, one of the squadron pilots. "We had very few instrument landing aids. Sometimes when we were inbound with one-quarter to one-half mile visibility we would receive a report that another plane had just departed BW-1 on a priority mission!"[29]

The hazards were not limited to time spent in the air. Occasionally, Bluie West 1 and other bases would be hammered by epic gales worse than those that even farm boys used to midwestern tornadoes had ever seen. "I saw buildings lifted from their foundations and carried yards away," an eyewitness reported.[30] An air inspector's report from Narsarssuak described what happened to aircraft left in the open when exposed to the violent arctic storms: "Paint was sand-blasted from propellers, leading edges of wings, etc. Propellers were nicked by flying sand and rocks. All engine covers were torn to shreds by the high wind."[31]

***

November 1943 was a special time in the settlement of Egedesminde, a small community of just over 2,000 people close to Bluie West 5, a radio and weather station built by the Americans. US Army Air Force Sergeant Arthur Burgess of Sonora, California, was engaged to Alice Hansen, the ethnic Danish daughter of a local shipmaster.[32] The subsequent wedding was one of the biggest events of the year. "It's tough to be married far away from one's loved ones, in a foreign country," one of the invitees, the teacher Inge Agerschou, wrote in a letter to an acquaintance. "The entire community contributed to the wedding, and it ended up a grand celebration."[33] The wedding was even more special than any of those in attendance realized. It was the only Danish-American marriage to result from more than three years of US military presence in Greenland during the war. In addition, one marriage between an American citizen and a member of the island's Inuit community was also recorded.[34]

The explanation seemed straightforward. American and Danish authorities had agreed on discouraging fraternization from the outset. However, that was not the whole story. Although the United States and Denmark were allies in the war against the Axis, the relationship between the Americans and the locals in Greenland had both ups and downs, and sometimes the downs attracted more attention. On the one hand, the United States was a symbol of technological advance in a society such as Greenland that was still stuck in the 19th century in many ways. When the first American truck arrived in Godthaab in June 1943, the whole city turned out to follow it through the streets.[35] At the same time, among many of the Inuit, there seemed to be a genuine feeling of friendship towards the American government. At the beginning of the year, the residents of Scoresby Sound donated a haunch of musk ox, described as "more delectable than beef," to President Roosevelt to express gratitude that the US Coast Guard had arrived at the isolated community with much-needed supplies early in the conflict.[36]

Uncomplicated positive encounters and exchanges such as these were, however, not the norm. In the same letter that described the wedding of Sergeant Burgess and Miss Hansen, Agerschou vented considerable frustration at the way relations with the Americans had developed. She cited strong indications that the enlisted men in the bases had become convinced that the Danes in Greenland were pro-Nazi. "Their logic goes like this: 'Why did we Americans have to go to Greenland? Because Greenland was in danger of being occupied by the Germans. There were already Germans on the east coast, and who got them there? The Danes, of course, who else, so the conclusion must be that the Danes are Nazis'," she wrote.[37] She put it down to lack of communication between the Americans and the Danes, pointing out that the average GI had never met a member of the Danish community, leaving him with the impression that Danes were only semicivilized and did not live in proper buildings. "I think this ban against leaving the bases has both positive and negative effects, but it could probably have been handled in a better way," she wrote. "In any case, it can also be construed as demonstrating that we don't want anything to do with the Americans because we are Nazis."[38]

The Danes in Greenland maintained ambiguous feelings towards the Americans partly out of a quiet concern that they might outstay their welcome. "Danes in Greenland will consider any American attempt to continue the occupation after the war in the Atlantic to be a violation and breach of earlier promises," Brun wrote to Kauffmann in June 1943, revealing with his choice of words—"occupation"—his true feelings about the American presence.[39] Brun's suspicious attitude was partly triggered by what he observed in situations where Americans did come into contact with Greenlanders, despite the policy of preventing interaction. US Coast Guard vessels often anchored off Julianehaab, a settlement close to the base Bluie West 1, with unwanted consequences, Brun noted: "These Americans were all extremely wealthy by our standards, and they were not used to getting anything for free. Once the opportunities dawned on the girls, matters exploded. For the first time in Greenland's history, we had full-scale prostitution on our hands. Significantly it encompassed an alarmingly large proportion of the population in the area."[40] As a result, in October 1943, Brun moved the American authorities to impose a blanket ban on all US personnel's visit to inhabited areas in Greenland.[41]

***

Gustav Smedal, the campaigner for Norway's right to Greenland, had continued his unceasing campaign for his country's territorial claims throughout most of 1943, but by September it was time to rest. After undergoing surgery, he traveled to unoccupied Sweden to recuperate at a spa, but his stay left him with little reason to relax. Anti-German sentiments ran high among the officially neutral Swedes, reflecting the shifting fortunes at the battlefronts, with the Wehrmacht on the defense in Russia and facing Allied invasion forces in Italy. When Smedal passed through the capital Stockholm at the end of his visit, he was in for yet another disappointment. He paid a call on Sven Hedin, Sweden's most famous explorer and notorious Hitler admirer, hoping to persuade him to speak to his German connections on behalf of Norway and its position in the world. Hedin politely declined, stating now was not the time, as Germany in its current difficult situation would be loath to make any concessions that could be construed as a sign of weakness.[42]

Smedal took one final, remarkable step on the eve of his return to Norway. "Before I left, I sent a letter by airmail to Ambassador Wilhelm Morgenstierne in Washington DC. I provided a brief description of what had been done in Oslo to support Norway's claim in Greenland, and he was asked to do what he could to look after Norwegian interests in this cause," Smedal wrote in his memoirs. It was a highly unusual move, and he knew it could potentially land him in serious trouble: "The letter was anonymous. It was dangerous to put one's own name under it. If it had been intercepted by the Germans, they would not look mildly on the fact that I had used a stay in Sweden to get in touch with King Haakon's representative in the United States."[43]

No record has surfaced about whether Morgenstierne received the letter, and if so, what he thought about it. However, it marked an extraordinary instance of attempted policy coordination between individuals who were otherwise at war with each other and had been so for over three years. It was testimony to the depth of commitment to the Greenland cause among certain members of the Norwegian elite that even though they had ended up on different sides in the global conflict, representing groups that were prepared to kill each other, and did kill each other when they met in open combat, they were united by one, fundamental issue: the shared conviction that Greenland had been taken from Norway in an unjust fashion, and the belief that the war had created new conditions that could set things right.

For Smedal, the attempt to reach out to the opposite side in Washington DC may very well have been a sign of growing desperation. After years of efforts, the community of nationalistic Norwegians that he represented had very little to show for them. To be sure, some Germans had voiced early support for the Norwegian claim. In February of 1942, Smedal had been given the chance at a dinner party hosted by friends to explain the Norwegian point of view to Hermann Boehm, the senior commander of the German Navy in Norway and the man who had allowed the *Buskø* to leave. "Outrageous," was the German officer's reaction when told how in Kiel in 1814, Norway had been robbed of the chance of taking Greenland with it into the union with Sweden.[44]

Still, it did not translate into solid German support at the official level. Other Germans—arguably Germans who mattered more in terms of setting policy in the field—were growing decidedly unenthusiastic about the Norwegian bid for Greenland, if they had ever had any genuine interest in what they probably considered petty arguments at the periphery of their empire. Frustratingly for Smedal, these Germans seemed to favor the status quo over any experiments that might complicate politics in Scandinavia, and with their actions they had demonstrated that they did not want to rock the boat. Indeed, in December 1941, the Danish envoy to Berlin had complained to the German authorities about Norway's interest in Iceland and Greenland, resulting in a temporary German ban on any mention of the two islands in the Norwegian press.[45]

SS-*Obersturmführer* Georg Wolff, a ranking officer in Division III at the security police in Oslo and responsible for feeding regular, detailed reports on the Norwegian situation to his masters in Berlin, sent a damning dispatch in early 1942, describing the Greenland dream as an aspect of Norwegian megalomania. The Norwegian claim to Greenland was based on "extremely vague historical arguments," as were parallel claims to parts of northern Russia, islands in the Polar Sea and even the Faroe Islands, he argued. "Such demands can only be explained by an almost unlimited overestimation of one's own capabilities and possibilities," Wolff wrote. "Without a doubt, an extraordinarily painful lesson is in store for the Norwegian people in this particular field."[46]

Ignorant of this harsh assessment, Smedal had been involved in May 1942 in the preparation of a secret memorandum on the establishment of Norwegian weather stations in Greenland, seeking to draw lessons from the *Buskø* debacle the year before. The document argued that the weather missions should be small-sized—consisting of one meteorologist and two telegraphers—and should be transported to Greenland by seaplane. The stations should be placed "as far removed as possible from enemy stations to lower the risk of attack," the memorandum said.[47]

Shortly afterwards, Smedal and other leading members of the Arctic Seas Committee wrote a letter to Quisling, who had become the leader of a puppet government, calling for his assistance in effecting German acquiescence to a new deal on Greenland that would divide the island between the Norwegians and the Danes. They pointed out that Cecil von Renthe-Fink, the head of the German mission in Copenhagen, had allegedly suggested giving eastern Greenland to the Norwegians, while letting the Danes keep the western half. Ideally a new arrangement for Greenland would have to be pushed through now and could not wait until a post-war settlement, when the great powers would be occupied with other issues of more imminent importance to their national interest, the committee members argued.[48]

In November 1942, Smedal met Quisling in person, following up on the earlier letter and discussing the idea of sharing Greenland "fifty-fifty" with Denmark. Not surprisingly, the talk ended up revolving around Danish intransigence, despite what both men considered to be the evidently reasonable Norwegian demands.

"Why are the Danes so stubborn in this matter?" Quisling asked at the meeting. "Is it because they don't understand the issue at hand and actually think they are right?"

"The [Danish] public in general just don't understand it," Smedal said, "but the people in government do, and they realize that Greenland is actually Norwegian territory."[49]

While the Arctic Seas Committee had high hopes for what Quisling could achieve, its members did not want to stake all on just one person, however powerful, and they decided on a multi-pronged approach. In a parallel effort to impress the Norwegian point of view on the Germans, the committee also attempted appealing to public opinion in Germany. In late 1942, Smedal published a collection of articles translated into German, titled *Greenland and the Nordic Region*. Knut Hamsun wrote the preface, and copies were sent to Hitler and Ribbentrop as well as a number of German scholars.[50]

This step ended up backfiring badly. On May 20, 1943, five months after the book had been sent to the Nazi leaders, Smedal attended a dinner party hosted by Albert Viljam Hagelin, the minister of domestic affairs in Quisling's government. Eighteen people were invited to the dinner, including Rudolf Schiedermair, a legal advisor to Terboven, the German governor of Norway. After the dinner, Schiedermair pulled Smedal aside to bring bad news: Ribbentrop had not liked the book. He considered it to betray insufficient will to compromise. Hamsun's preface was also "not good." Smedal said nothing but was certain that once again the Danish envoy in Berlin had complained and got his way with the Germans.[51] Schiedermair had more bad news. It was impossible at the moment to consider a division of Greenland between Norway and Denmark. If Norway obtained any Greenland territory under the present circumstances, with Norway under German occupation, the outside world would consider Germany to be the real beneficiary.[52]

The bottom-line was this: even if the Germans had been winning the war, they would have been lukewarm towards facilitating the transfer of part of Greenland to Norway. Now, by 1943, the war was no longer going their way, and they had even less inclination to allocate time and sparse resources to an issue they had always considered peripheral. The achievements that Smedal and the other Greenland campaigners could boast of, never anything but modest and few in number, now faded into insignificance.

In the months that followed Smedal's visit to Sweden and his desperate letter to Washington DC, the Norwegian attempts at strengthening claims to Greenland became increasingly unreal. The Arctic Seas Committee now zeroed in on postage tables. Its members noted that the Faroe Islands and Greenland—destinations that Norwegians could no longer mail letters to anyway due to the war—were placed in parentheses behind Denmark: "Denmark (with the Faroe Islands and Greenland)", suggesting that they were part of Denmark. The committee pushed through a change, causing the table to be reissued with a new wording: "Denmark, Faroe Islands and Greenland." The committee members saw it as a major victory.[53]

CHAPTER 17

"Bassgeiger"

Fall 1943 to Spring 1944

Born in 1901 in the city of Innsbruck as a citizen of the Austro-Hungarian Empire, Heinrich Schatz was just months away from being drafted into World War I when it ended. Having narrowly avoided being sent to the frontline in that global conflict, he spent the 1920s advancing rapidly in the world of academe, excelling as a mathematician and physicist with a special interest in glaciology. By the time war broke out again in 1939, Austria had already been incorporated into the Reich and he was now a German citizen, liable for military service. Initially, the Wehrmacht wasted his skills by using him as a truck driver, but in 1942, after a brief return to life civilian life, he was drafted back into the army, and this time around, the powers-that-be decided to assign him to responsibilities more in line with his qualifications: as a meteorologist specializing in arctic conditions.[1]

In the spring of 1943, Schatz was sent to a newly established school on Goldhöhe, a mountain just south of the former border with Czechoslovakia in an area that had now become part of Germany. There the German Navy was training future batches of weathermen before sending them to polar regions. "This included instruction on the meteorological work to be undertaken, and in the duties of a radio operator; further, there was training in practical matters relating to the actual expeditions, such as how to build snow-huts and handle dog teams and sleighs, the transport of wounded or sick men, medical training and so on," said Wilhelm Dege, a meteorologist with polar experience, who was part of a team planning the education.[2] The attendants were also given lectures about the history and topography of the region as well as an introduction to plant and animal life. Those who were going to Greenland had additional classes in the culture of the Inuit.[3]

In a reflection of the intense inter-service rivalry existing in the German military, the Luftwaffe had established a separate training facility at Finse, the location in the Norwegian mountains where, back in 1940, it had experimented with building airfields on glaciers. The overall direction of the education was in the hands of Rupert Holzapfel, the meteorologist who had attempted had attempted the same year to get Danish permission for an expedition and had originally been tapped to head "Holzauge".[4] At both Finse and Goldhöhe, the priorities were the same, and the focus was on scientific observation, not combat. The teams were valuable for as long as they kept sending meteorological reports, and this was only possible as long as they remained unseen. Detection would mean death, imprisonment or hasty evacuation. "The orders were clear and to the point: you are to make weather observations; you are to desist from attacking enemy weather groups," said Dege.[5]

The new weathermen would soon be put to use, as "Holzauge" was considered a success even though it had been revealed in the end. Less than a fortnight after the last men from that mission had been flown out from Hansa Bay, the naval high command met in early July 1943, agreeing to establish a network of weather stations in the Arctic, including one on the east coast of Greenland.[6] The Greenland operation was codenamed "Bassgeiger" or "Double Bass Player," and Schatz was put in charge. He was allowed to handpick the members of his team from among the other men who had taken the course at Goldhöhe. Their motivation for joining up were surprisingly similar. "They were looking for a life of adventure, liberated from the strict rules of the military, and first and foremost they were happy to be able to escape the monotony and compulsion associated with military service," wrote the expedition's meteorologist, Günter Triloff, in post-war memoirs.[7]

The expedition members, eight altogether, left Goldhöhe in early August. Still, no one knew their ultimate destination and had only been informed it would be somewhere in the Arctic. They passed through Berlin, where they met a senior naval officer who almost revealed where they were going as he wished them "a good hunt for muskoxen." Since muskoxen just appeared naturally in two places, Greenland and Canada, it was a giveaway, but only one member of the team was sufficiently knowledgeable about zoology to realize it, and anyway he thought it was a deliberate smokescreen to confuse them about their objective.[8] They moved on to Rostock, a harbor on the Baltic, boarding the 420-ton weathership *Coburg* whose crew of 18 was to take them to Greenland, help establish the weather station, and then return to Europe. Just prior to departure, yet another expedition member boarded. It was Lieutenant Gerhard Zacher of the Germany Navy, who was to provide military expertise in case of contact with the enemy, a likely eventuality, given the "Holzauge" experience. On Saturday, August 14, 1943, *Coburg* steamed out of Rostock with 27 men on board, heading north.[9]

***

In fact, *Coburg* had been ready to sail one day earlier, on Friday the 13th, but Johann Rodebrügger, the captain, had been worried this might upset superstitious crew members, and he found excuses to postpone the departure by one day. Still, the ship was beset with bad luck from the outset. The final stop before heading to Greenland was the port of Narvik in northern Norway, and *Coburg* only arrived after having been in a powerful storm which damaged part of the supplies that had been stored on deck. Once in Narvik, *Coburg* had to wait several days as the navy had omitted equipping the expedition with items essential for survival in the arctic, including sleeping bags, outdoor cookers, and petroleum lamps. These had to be flown in from Germany, and only on August 28, at 4am, was the ship able to depart Narvik for Greenland. "In three weeks, we'll be back in Narvik," Rodebrügger told his men.[10]

Coburg's delayed departure had two unfortunate consequences. It meant that it was unable to rendezvous in the North Atlantic with the U-boat *U-355*, which was to have escorted it across, as the submarine's captain had already given up and had returned back to his base in Norway. More importantly, the late journey meant that a belt of drift ice, floating slowly in a southerly direction and forming a massive barrier off the Greenland coast, threatened to freeze solid before *Coburg* had made it through. An additional consequence was that the ship might be unable to return to Europe with its crew that same year. The root of this problem was inherent in the entire design for the mission. The expedition was to be disembarked at Germanialand, about 200 miles north of Hansa Bay to avoid detection by the Americans and their Danish helpers. The usual way to reach that far north in peacetime would be to sail up along the eastern coastline, inside the ice belt. In times of war this was, of course, impossible, and therefore *Coburg* had to pass through the drift ice the hard way, at a 90 degree angle to the belt.[11]

Reconnaissance flights by the Luftwaffe prior to *Coburg*'s departure from Narvik had led to the conclusion that the ice belt was still passable, but by the time the ship reached the eastern edge of the belt on August 31, the low temperatures had already had an effect, and the crew could only navigate among the ice floes with some difficulty. The day after, on September 1, *Coburg* was already stuck in three feet of ice, and a seemingly impenetrable expanse of white was stretching from one end of the horizon to the other in front of the men. Now explosives, which had also had to be flown in while *Coburg* was waiting in Narvik, proved irreplaceable. The crew simply had to blow up the ice in front of the ship, while the 590 horsepower of its engine squeezed its way through. "It was a unique feeling when the ice was pushed apart by the body of the ship, and the ice sheets reached as high as the railing," recalled Johann Zima, a 21-year-old radio operator. "Sometimes [...] *Coburg* passed through ice that was pressed upwards all the way to the level of the bridge."[12] Progress was now extremely cumbersome. On some days, *Coburg* advanced by as little as 200 yards, and on no day did it move more than three nautical miles.[13]

By September 9, *Coburg* was at a distance of roughly 20 nautical miles from Ile de France, an island off the east coast of Greenland. As the ship was still moving at a snail's pace, the meteorologists on board decided on doing their work, setting up a makeshift weather station on the ice nearby. The crew had now consumed so many explosives that new supplies had to be flown in. A first attempted airdrop failed on September 16, but two days later, a Focke-Wulf Fw 200 Condor transport plane managed to deliver eight drop cannisters parachuted down onto the ice. A further delivery of explosives on September 28 was also necessary. "With great effort, we pull the cannisters to the ship," Schatz wrote in his diary. "Then we open the cannister, each of us hoping secretly [but in vain] to also find letters from home inside."[14]

On October 2, the ice suddenly began breaking up, and *Coburg* slowly drifted south carried along by the current. The weather station on the ice next to its hull was hastily dismantled, and the equipment pulled on board before it was too late. If *Coburg* simply continued on this course, a quick look at the map showed that it would end up at Shannon Island, much further south than originally planned, and dangerously close to the northernmost American and Danish settlements. Schatz radioed the naval command on October 12 requesting permission to set up the weather station on Shannon instead of further north, receiving the green light the following day, while also being warned that under these circumstances, contact with the enemy would be a likely outcome sooner or later. After a few days of further drift, *Coburg* came to halt amid thickening ice about seven nautical miles east of Shannon. As the ship was locked inside solid ice and was unlikely to move any further, Schatz decided to make this his weather station. The expedition started preparing for the winter. There was no going back this year, also not for the 18-member crew who had been told it would only be a mission of three weeks.[15]

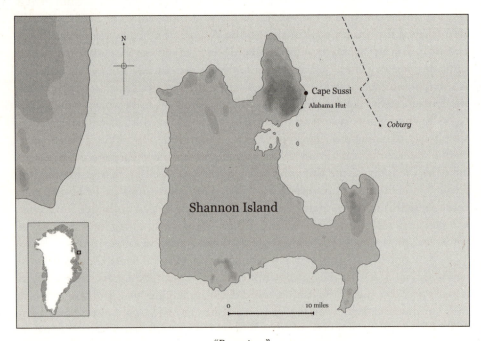

"Bassgeiger."

***

In Germany, the naval command was in touch with the Luftwaffe to arrange continued supply to "Bassgeiger", and to this end, the air force agreed to deploy one of its largest aircraft, the six-engine flying boat Blohm & Voss BV 222 Wiking. After several false starts, a BV 222 took off from Tromsø on November 17, piloted by Captain Adolf Mlodoch. More cargo was squeezed into the aircraft's hull than was allowed, and when it departed shortly after 6am, the total weight was 52 tons, four tons more than the maximum. After five hours over the Atlantic, the BV 222 was approaching the area where *Coburg* was known to be located, but even though the radio operator got in touch with members of "Bassgeiger" on the ground, the ship was hidden by a thick fog cover. "To carry out a somewhat safe drop of the supply cannisters in the middle of this endless ice desert, it was absolutely necessary to have visual contact with the ship," Mlodoch wrote later. "The whole operation had been planned for good weather, so a drop was not feasible."[16]

The bad weather that Mlodoch encountered was only the beginning. On the day after, November 18, a powerful storm swept through the area, reaching force 10 on the Beaufort scale. The wind also set the ice floes in motion, and large sheets of ice pressed against the hull of *Coburg*, causing it to list 30 degrees. Fearing that it would be forced under water, the crew began hurriedly to salvage the most important equipment. Battered by the violent, freezing winds and shrouded in darkness, the men were helped to orient themselves by the ship's searchlight, but without warning it was extinguished, and the night devoured them all. The men huddled in groups, trying to keep warm, and hoping for the storm to weaken. It was "a night of terror," one of them recalled later.[17]

The following day, the men continued their attempts to salvage supplies from the ship, and although it now seemed that it had come to a rest in its new inclined position, Schatz decided to move the expedition onto land on Shannon. The following weeks were taken up with a slow, back-breaking effort to haul most of the supplies from *Coburg* across the ice to the new station area. Meanwhile, a skeleton crew remained on board the ship, headed by captain Rodebrügger, who still dreamed of being able to somehow extricate his ship and bring it safely back to Germany.[18]

The new camp found for "Bassgeiger" was at a place called Cape Sussi, at the base of a peninsula on the north end of Shannon Island. Reconnaissance established the presence of a large snowdrift, measuring 100 feet by 130 feet, and with snow in a depth of up to 15 feet. It was decided to set up the camp here by digging tunnels and caves into the solid snow. This had the added advantage of offering natural camouflage. It would be almost impossible to spot from the air, and scouts on the ground would have to literally stumble over the camp to discover it.[19] The transfer of supplies from *Coburg* was not completed until late February, and then for the first time in five months, a resemblance of routine finally set in. "During the polar night almost our whole life was spent inside the glacier; we only left it if the weather permitted movement over the ice, or if a weather observation had to be made," wrote Triloff, the meteorologist.[20]

Gerhard Zacher, the lieutenant who had been seconded to *Coburg* at the last moment, turned out to be a liability for the team. He was the belligerent sort and seemed frustrated at the lack of action. Instead, he vented steam over the relaxed atmosphere among the expedition members and tried repeatedly to instill more military decorum especially into the younger ones. "It was a clear mistake by the naval command to bother us with a man like that," commented Zima, the radio operator. "I'm sure they could have found better ways to use him."[21] Or perhaps there would be a use for Zacher. Contrary to the initial plans calling for the "Bassgeiger" weather station to be set up so far north that it was unlikely to be detected, it was now located only 50 miles north of Hansa Bay, where "Holzauge" had established its camp a year earlier. It was so close to the operation area of the Northeast Greenland Sledge Patrol that contact could be hard to avoid. "All the enemy, who was not too far away, had to do was to send a patrol our way to establish our exact location," wrote Zima. "If we came under attack, and if we were not alert, we had no chance of escaping."[22] The following months were to show that he had good reason to be concerned.

***

A little to the south of "Bassgeiger"—at a distance that could be covered by dog sledge within just a few days—the sledge patrol was going about its day-to-day business, with a certain feeling of vindication. The deployment against "Holzauge" and in particular, the success in capturing the enemy commander, had given the unit a sudden prestige and silenced some of the doubters. When news of the sledge patrol's success reached the governor of Greenland, Eske Brun, it was a source of unexpected relief. "It was a real pleasure to be able to demonstrate what could be done when the odds were in favor of those who knew the area intimately and possessed courage, sang-froid, stamina and experience in using whatever means were at their disposal," he wrote in his memoirs. "We felt a certain pride, and the Americans, too, learned a little."[23]

The patrol was initially organized along civilian lines, but Brun saw to it that this was changed once enemy activity was confirmed in the winter of 1942 and 1943. "As soon as I received reports on this, I ordered that battle should be joined, and at the same time I reorganized the entire service as a military unit as I did not want to run the risk that the members were to be treated as partisans if they fell into enemy hands," Brun wrote after the war.[24] Each of the members received a military rank and an armband showing his place in the hierarchy. In this way, one of the smallest and most irregular armies in the world had been created.

The sledge patrol was already alerted to the German presence at the end of 1943. Peter Nielsen, the patrol member who had been captured by "Holzauge" and then released by Ritter to the consternation of his men, was part of a team manning a new station at Dead Man's Bay. It was located eight miles east of Eskimoness, which had been burned down by the Germans and then bombed by the Americans. In late fall 1943, Nielsen and another patrol member, Carl Henrik Schultz, were on a journey that on November 22 took them past Shannon Island. They planned to spend the night at a trapper's cabin known as the Alabama Hut just a couple of miles south of Cape Sussi. While Schultz made the cabin ready, Nielsen reconnoitered the area. He noticed traces in the snow that could be from a fox, but also could be human. He moved a bit further north and again saw traces. "I walked over and found three fresh traces in the snow, left by three men, who had been here two or three hours ago," Nielsen said.[25] He rushed back to pick up his colleague, and the two immediately drove west with their dogs to report the discovery. "He was under strict orders not to be taken prisoner before reporting his observations," Kurt Olsen, another patrol member, wrote in his memoirs. "If he had been taken out before the news had been passed on, the consequences could have been unimaginable."[26]

A four-member team from the sledge patrol returned to Shannon Island in early February 1944 to gain further intelligence about the Germans. The four men made camp on the island about four miles south of Alabama Hut. Creeping into a tent, one of them pulled out a card deck, and they took turns drawing cards. The one with the highest card "won": He was the one who was to cover the last part of the way to reconnoiter Alabama Hut and Cape Sussi. Carlos Ziebell, a veteran patrol member, was chosen. Wearing a white anorak to avoid discovery, he carefully moved north. "Suddenly I was standing in the middle of a veritable avenue of footsteps leading from the ice onto land. I immediately threw myself behind some pack ice while my heart started pumping like crazy. It was five or six years since I had seen human footsteps which did not belong to either myself or my comrades," he recalled later. He moved closer and discovered the entrance into one of the Germans caves, so well camouflaged that he almost walked on top of it. "I probably had been lying there for a quarter of an hour, when a man walked towards me. I grabbed my handgun and turned the safety off. He was just below me, roughly 80 feet away." He saw a flash of light as the man opened the entrance to the cave and closed it quickly again. Then Ziebell moved back to the other three, as fast as he could without attracting attention. He had seen enough, and they knew enough. There was a significant German presence.[27]

The expedition members of "Bassgeiger" were blissfully unaware that the enemy now had complete information about their whereabouts, and that an attack could be expected at any time. Instead, they continued their routines, sending daily weather reports and otherwise trying to mitigate the boredom of isolated Arctic life. Lieutenant Zacher went on frequent hunting trips. A couple of polar bear cubs had been adopted by the men. Two of the expedition members were convinced they had found a copper deposit and started considering how best to extract it and transport it to Europe, planning to return after the war and make a fortune.[28] In the morning of April 20, the soldiers of the camp assembled in front of the glacier to mark Hitler's birthday. "No one knew that this was the last time we would be together in this way," Triloff wrote.[29]

***

In the early hours of April 22, six men were moving stealthily across the northern tip of Shannon Island in the direction of Cape Sussi. They were members of the Northeast Greenland Sledge Patrol, under command of Niels Ove Jensen, the head of the station at Dead Man's Bay. They had left their sledges and dogs on the ice west of Shannon Island, guarded by two of their comrades. If they were not back within 36 hours, the two were to take the sledges and return to Dead Man's Bay. The team headed by Jensen was heavily armed: rifles, submarine guns, a machine gun with 1,000 rounds, and hand grenades. Prior to the operation, the Americans had also been supposed to airdrop additional equipment, including walkie-talkies, but for some reason the plane never turned up. Jensen hoped this would not matter, and that he would be able to fulfill his mission: to wipe out the German weather station.[30]

It was still early in the day when Cape Sussi appeared in the distance. They also discovered a sentry, forcing them to make their further approach very slowly in order not to be seen. After a couple of hours, they were approximately 300 yards from the German camp. Taking advantage of a moment when a new sentry took over guard duty, Jensen and one of his men crawled closer and were now only 50 yards away. Jensen realized that from this position, he and his group would be able to control the entire area and have a direct line of fire towards all exits from the German caves. They could pick them off one after the other as they exited. Jensen sent his man back to alert the rest of the group and summon them to the position. "I quietly cursed the Americans for having let us down and not giving us the supplies we needed," Jensen said later. "A couple of walkie-talkies could really have come in handy now."[31]

While Jensen was waiting for his men to catch up, he suddenly was face-to-face with a German carrying a hunting rifle. Jensen pointed his submachine gun at him and told him to put his hands in the air. The German threw his rifle to the side, exclaiming: "This makes no sense! We are brothers and shouldn't fight. Germany is not at war with Denmark." Having uttered these words, he pulled out a pistol from his pocket and fired several shots at the Dane. He missed, which made this his last move. Jensen fired a burst from his submachine gun, felling the German. He was dead on the spot.[32]

The German that Jensen had killed was Lieutenant Zacher. The sentry was radio operator Henrich Schmidt. Zacher had passed him on his way out of the camp, saying he was going hunting for ptarmigans. Schmidt had seen the entire situation from the distance and immediately called in reinforcements with his field telephone, then firing his weapon towards the stranger. Having used up his ammunition, he ran through the camp, alarming the men inside the caves:

"The Americans are here. The lieutenant is dead. I have no more ammunition. Give me some!"[33]

The camp only came to life slowly. Triloff, the meteorologist, was still asleep in his cave when he was awakened by his deputy, Kurt Pritsch, who shouted: "*Achtung, Achtung*, the lieutenant has been shot." The first thought that went through Triloff's still-sleepy mind was that Lieutenant Zacher had been talking about arranging a drill to test the defenses and he figured this was probably it, although he thought it was an unusual way to kick off the exercise. Without rushing, Triloff got dressed and stepped outside his cave, looking at his comrades, who were standing, still sleepy, outside their caves. The enemy was nowhere to be seen. Triloff crawled on top of the snowdrift to get a better view. At the same moment, a series of projectiles hit the snow in front of him. So, it was for real after all![34]

The Germans now rushed into their prepared positions, firing in the general direction of the enemy. The Danes in the position 300 yards away shot back, and especially the machine gun was able to deliver suppressing fire, which allowed Jensen to hastily move back and join his men. As he soon realized that he was facing a superior force and was not able to deliver effective fire from this distance, he ordered his men to withdraw west. In the rush to escape, they left behind the machine gun. As mist covered the island, and the Germans were reluctant to pursue, expecting an ambush, it was possible for the Danes to reach their two comrades guarding the dog sledges, and the entire group disappeared across the ice towards the mainland.[35]

On board *Coburg*, seven nautical miles out to sea, no one had any inkling of the drama unfolding at Cape Sussi. In the mess, Captain Rodebrügger and several of the officers were involved in a heated argument about how to salvage the ship. Another was sitting nearby reading the book *Farthest North* by Norwegian polar explorer Fridtjof Nansen, pretending not to notice. Yet another was silently smoking his pipe, also assuming an indifferent air. Suddenly, the radio operator entered, not saying a word. He walked straight over to Rodebrügger and handed him a piece of paper. The captain read it, jolting with a startled look on his face. It was a telegram from Cape Sussi. He read it aloud: "The camp has been attacked by the enemy. The attack has been repelled. The enemy has withdrawn for the time being. Lieutenant Zacher has fallen. Schatz."[36]

***

During the first days after the attack on April 22, the Germans at Cape Sussi expected a renewed assault at any time. The sentries were reinforced, and more patrols were sent out in the surrounding area. Some of the men perhaps started seeing ghosts. On April 25, enemy troops were observed in mountains close to the camp. On April 30, patrols from both sides met at Alabama Hut but there was no shooting as the weapons on both sides malfunctioned.[37] A member of the Danish sledge patrol later categorically denied this could have been possible, saying there were no patrols in the area at the time, and that the closest Dane was separated from the German camp by 125 miles.[38]

The small crew remaining on board *Coburg* were ordered by the naval command to abandon the ship and move inland to strengthen the defenses at Cape Sussi. This was a tough command for Captain Rodebrügger, whose priorities in terms of loyalties seemed to be: ship first, country second. Contrary to the order he had received, he initially seconded only two of his men to the camp on Shannon Island, waiting on *Coburg* in the hope that a sudden thaw might allow him to recover his ship. "We will get out of the ice soon," he told his petty officer, Kurt Koos. "I can feel it in the weather!"[39] Eventually, however, he received yet another direct order to destroy the ship and then leave it behind, and he could not ignore it without making himself guilty of insubordination. Close to tears, he obeyed.[40]

Meanwhile, the Germans on land, being constantly reminded of the dangers involved by the sight of the wooden cross placed over Zacher's grave, started fearing that they might never return home. "We had absolutely no illusions that any prisoners could be taken. Prisoners who had to be dragged around for several days while on the move, or who, in our case, would have to be kept at our station, would be a great risk for both sides," Zima wrote.[41] They did what little they could to improve the chances of survival at the hands of their enemies. Schatz noticed that one of the hunting rifles was loaded with "dumdum" bullets, which were better able to stop a polar bear. If the rifle were found by the Allies, it could easily be misunderstood, and Schatz ordered his men to change for regular ammunition instead. They readily complied.[42]

The initial order from Germany was to stay put. The camp had of course been compromised and further attacks were likely, but the weather reports were essential for the war effort and had to continue, the naval command explained. Then on May 10, a new telegram from Germany stated that an evacuation would be attempted with a huge BV 222 flying boat, along with a request to find a hole in the ice big enough for it to land. "We were totally confused. A few days earlier we had received a radio message saying we could not be evacuated because our weather reports were very important. Now they wanted to evacuate us after all," Zima remarked.[43]

It turned out that a hole in the ice big enough for a BV 222 could not be found. Instead, the Luftwaffe arranged for the dispatch of a four-engine Junkers Ju 290, a maritime patrol aircraft and the largest land plane it had. The men at "Bassgeiger" found a suitable landing area on the ice near the camp. After thorough reconnaissance and confirmation that the ice was thick enough, about three feet, the evacuation of all 26 surviving men of the mission took place on June 3.[44] It was a bittersweet departure. The Germans destroyed everything that they had built up with much energy and ingenuity over the preceding months. All the caves dug into the snow were blown up. Even the machine gun captured from the Danes was destroyed with a hand grenade. The two polar bear cubs, who were considered too wild for a long plane ride, were shot.[45]

The plane took off late in the afternoon, just managing to clear a wall of ice at the end of the makeshift runway, before flying in the direction of Trondheim, Norway. Rodebrügger, still mourning the loss of *Coburg*, was looking out of the window, staring at the unbroken expanse of white passing by under the plane. After 20 minutes of flight, the ice underneath started breaking up into large sheets, and a little further on, they were over open water. "Look, Koos," said Rodebrügger, patting the petty officer on the shoulder. "We wouldn't have had to wait long, and then we would have been able to get out with the ship!"[46]

CHAPTER 18

"Meteorology's Finest Hour"

Summer to Winter 1944

June 6, 1944, was "meteorology's finest hour," according to Sverre Petterssen, a Norwegian weather forecaster in British service who played a pivotal role in picking the right day for the Allied invasion of Europe.[1] Timing was crucial and marked the difference between success and failure. After the window of opportunity in early June, long-term predictions indicated that the next opportunity was a fortnight later. If that window had been picked instead, the invasion would have run into a "gale, the like of which had not been known in June for forty years," to quote Churchill.[2] General Dwight D. Eisenhower had no doubts about the importance of the weather. "Thank the gods of war that we went when we did," he commented when receiving a report about the storm that hit later that June.[3]

Information from Greenland was a big piece in the elaborate puzzle that the Allied weathermen put together in order to be able to provide Eisenhower with useful forecasts. For example, a high-pressure system that had developed over Greenland was key in predicting a brief spell of quiet weather on the morning of June 6. "What we most needed for our longer range predictions were weather observations made at regular intervals on the ocean south of Greenland," reminisced James Martin Stagg, a Royal Air Force meteorologist who was instrumental in moving the Allied supreme commander to make his final decision on when to give the go-ahead.[4] Still, there was a great deal of uncertainty, as the senior officers were keenly aware. "Well, you guys will be making history if we get there, and if we don't we'll all be busted to privates," General Carl Spaatz, commander of US Strategic Air Forces in Europe, told his meteorologists.[5]

The Germans had little understanding of the Allied weather service but could only observe an almost magical ability to pick the right time to launch the invasion, during a short gap between two storms. "We [...] assumed that they had much more and better data over the Atlantic than we had," commented Hermann Flohn, a weather forecaster for the Luftwaffe. "We apparently overestimated the meteorological technique used in the Allied Forces."[6] Against this backdrop, and in order not to lag too far behind the enemy's capabilities in the field, the German commanders continued to prioritize weather forecasting in the summer of 1944, even as they were pressured on all fronts and had to make tough decisions about allocation of scarce resources.

Early in the war, before the US entry, the German intelligence service, the Abwehr, had been involved in the dispatch of weather teams to Greenland. This was natural since there was not yet a formal state of war between the United States and Germany, and therefore, using Greenland, a territory covered by the Monroe Doctrine, as a base for German meteorological observations had necessarily had the character of a clandestine operation. With American participation in the war, the Germans could abandon these pretenses and conduct weather operations in Greenland as an overt military activity primarily involving the navy but with frequent assistance from the air force.

By 1944, the intelligence services again got involved. The Reich Security Main Office, a large bureaucracy inside the SS which also had a hand in intelligence matters, sent a proposal to the Luftwaffe in July to cooperate in the field of meteorology. Under the codename "Laubfrosch," or "tree frog," three small units were to be put together and transported to different areas in the Arctic region. One of these, "Laubfrosch I," was to be made up of Norwegians hired by the Abwehr and be sent to Greenland by long-distance plane. The details were agreed on at a meeting between the Reich Security Main Office and the air force on August 19. On August 24, the entire operation was given up again due to lack of aviation fuel. The foray of the SS into Greenland meteorology began late, and it lasted just five days.[7]

***

On August 27, three days after the SS decided to abandon its project, the trawler *Kehdingen* departed from Tromsø, also headed for Greenland. On board was a 12-member expedition in addition to the ship's own crew of 14. The operation, codenamed "Edelweiss," aimed to resume the meteorological work that had been abruptly cut short earlier that summer when the men of the "Bassgeiger" mission had to be evacuated out. The twelve men participating in "Edelweiss" were expected to spend nine to 10 months on the Greenland coast and had been carefully selected among the personnel that had passed the demanding course at Goldhöhe on the former Czech border. To an even larger extent than earlier graduates from the facility, they had received extensive training in marksmanship and mountain warfare, since the experience of past expeditions to Greenland had demonstrated that clashes with the enemy were more than likely.[8]

Gottfried Weiss, who had been the scientific leader of "Holzauge" in 1942 and 1943, was in overall command of "Edelweiss." Lieutenant Hans-Jürgen Alleweldt had been assigned as the officer in charge of military matters in case of enemy contact. Weiss was not the only "Holzauge" veteran on board *Kehdingen*: the

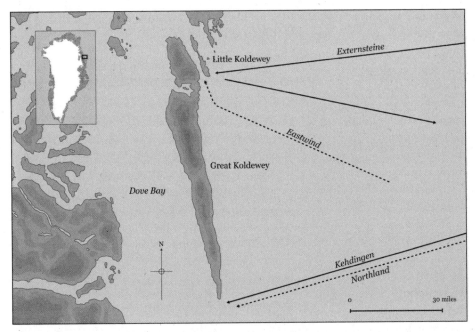

The "Edelweiss" expeditions.

Germans also brought sledge dogs, partly bred from the ones brought home from Greenland at the end of the mission in Hansa Bay in 1943.[9] The expedition was expected to make landfall at Dove Bay and then move inland to set up a station that could not be easily detected from a passing ship. Given the fast-changing weather and ice conditions in the area during the fall, the naval command had not made a prior decision about the exact location but left it to Weiss' discretion once he had arrived with his men.[10]

Shortly after putting out to sea, *Kehdingen* rendezvoused with the U-boat *U-703* under the command of First Lieutenant Joachim Brünner, which was to escort the trawler at some distance and defend it if it was attacked. In the afternoon of August 30, an unwelcome report ticked in based on Luftwaffe reconnaissance: a ship, estimated at 400 tons, had been spotted off Greenland. "Perhaps it will get in our way," Brünner wrote in his war diary.[11] Thirty-six hours later, in the morning of September 1, the ice belt shielding off Greenland from the Atlantic was sighted on the horizon in the dim light of the Arctic summer night. On the ice border, *U-703* sailed up alongside *Kehdingen* to take on board much needed fuel for the return journey. When the work was just completed, at 5:20am, a mast was sighted over the horizon. It was an enemy ship.[12]

U-703 immediately submerged but kept close to the surface maintaining visual contact with the approaching ship through periscope. After 20 minutes, the full profile of the approaching ship was visible.[13] "We immediately guessed that it had to be the ship that was reported during the aerial reconnaissance, but there must have been a mistake when it came to tonnage. The ship that was steering in our direction measured about 2,000 tonnes," wrote Alleweldt.[14] It was US Coast Guard cutter *Northland*, commanded by Lieutenant Commander R. W. Butcher. *Kehdingen* attempted to escape into the pack ice, and the American vessel commenced the pursuit. The German ship was faster, but not built to navigate in ice-filled waters and had to dodge the larger ice floes, while *Northland* could steer straight through the water, compensating for its slower speed. Butcher signaled the German trawler to halt, and as it ignored the message, he ordered the forward gun to fire at it continuously while the distance was gradually reduced.[15]

It was Weiss' decision, made against Alleweldt's advice, to steer through the ice in order to reach the Greenland coast as soon as possible. The predetermined plan for contingencies such as this was to drag the pursuing enemy ship into a vulnerable position where the submerged *U-703* would be able to fire its torpedoes at it. "I suggested steering towards the open sea, as it was to be assumed that the U-boat would not be able to get in a shot because of the pack ice," Alleweldt wrote.[16] He turned out to be right. *U-703* fired two torpedoes at *Northland*, both hitting ice floes that knocked them off course and saved the Coast Guard cutter from what could otherwise have been a devastating hit. After waiting for 30 minutes to be out of immediate artillery range, *U-703* surfaced, but *Kehdingen* was now out of sight.[17] "We [on board the trawler] were on our own and had to find our own way to handle *Northland*," Alleweldt wrote. "The situation I had feared had arisen. We had no escape door any longer."[18]

With *Northland* still in pursuit and closing in, Weiss and Alleweldt quickly conferred about what to do next. They were approaching the large island Great Koldewey, and they decided to attempt sailing around its southern tip in hopes of reaching the ice-free waters of Dove Bay between the island and the Greenland east coast, where *Kehdingen* could again take advantage of its higher speed. Meanwhile, a signal was sent to Tromsø: "Pursued by enemy ship. Preparations made to destroy secret documents and code keys." It was now noon. Two crew members with binoculars posted on the highest point of the German trawler reported the entrance into Dove Bay blocked by pack ice. "We were trapped. The situation was hopeless, and we had to abandon ship," Alleweldt said.[19]

Three explosive charges were prepared—two in the engine room and one in the magazine—and the three lifeboats were lowered into the water. The fuses for the explosives had been set for nine minutes, but only after 11 minutes did the first of the charges go off, followed by the second and the third. At 12:47pm, *Kehdingen* disappeared under the sea. The crew on *Northland* had ceased fire once it was clear the German trawler had been evacuated and now approached the Germans in their lifeboats. The engines in two of the lifeboats had broken down, and therefore it was hopeless to try to reach Great Koldewey and make a stand there. The German surrendered immediately.[20]

With a certain sense of drama, Weiss handed his dagger to Butcher, who saw to it that it was framed and hung as a trophy in *Northland's* wardroom.[21] Space aboard was tight, since it also carried more than 100 infantrymen specially trained for arctic warfare, and the German officers and non-commissioned officers had to be placed in the sickbay.[22] The treatment was decent, but there was some dissatisfaction among the prisoners with the situation. Wilhelm Gockel, the expedition's chief meteorologist, blamed Weiss and the U-boat commander Brünner for the capture: "Transfer of fuel at the ice border of all places!" he wrote in an account after the war, suggesting that *Kehdingen* had been unnecessarily vulnerable there.[23] After some time, Weiss was transferred to the Coast Guard cutter *Storis*. While the vessel stayed within a narrow space along the east coast of Greenland for the next few weeks, he saw no fewer than eight American observation ships, all equipped with aircraft. "It became clear to me that this summer it would hardly have been possible to land any mission, at most a small station from a U-boat," he wrote in post-war memoirs.[24]

***

When the German naval command received confirmation that "Edelweiss" had ended in failure, it made a hasty decision to redirect another expedition that was being made ready in Norway. Codenamed "Goldschmied," or "Goldsmith," it had 12 members including its commander, Lieutenant Karl Schmid, who was a geographer in civilian life. It had originally been meant to be deployed on Franz Josef Land, an archipelago north of Russia. It was now renamed "Edelweiss II," a decision that seemed popular with the men. "To be honest, we were only too happy to swap 'Goldsmith' for 'Edelweiss' and Franz Josef Land for Greenland. I'd been wanting to go to Greenland for ten years. Now it had suddenly become our destiny," a member of the expedition recalled.[25] The ship that was to take "Edelweiss II" to Greenland was *Externsteine*, with a crew of 20.[26]

Externsteine left Norway late in the afternoon of September 26 in thick fog, and was joined off the Norwegian coast by U-boat *U-965* early the following day.[27] In the night between September 29 and 30, the expedition reached the ice belt east of Greenland, and the U-boat returned home.[28] Initially, *Externsteine* only made slow progress through the ice, but suddenly it chanced upon a clear path of ocean leading all the way to the Koldewey archipelago off the Greenland coast.[29] Despite the constant risk of detection, the men almost started enjoying the voyage. "If it wasn't for the mountains and the ice, this could almost be a beautiful autumn day on a ferry on [Lake Constance] between Konstanz and Meersburg," said Hans Wagner, a private first class.[30] Anchoring off the island of Little Koldewey early on October 1, Schmid decided to immediately begin unloading the expedition's supplies in order for *Externsteine* to return to Norway before the operation was spotted by a bypassing reconnaissance plane. In the course of 35 hours of uninterrupted work, all supplies were put on shore, and the ship made ready to depart in the afternoon of October 2. "Now came the fateful moment when we started having as much bad luck as we had so far had good luck," Schmid said.[31]

When the engine started, the ship released a column of thick black smoke into the air. It was the result of allowing the crude engine oil to cool down while the supplies were being unloaded.[32] Standing on Little Koldewey, Schmid momentarily worried about the risk of being spotted by an American plane, but then calmed down, telling himself the chances were tiny. He knelt down to get a snapshot of the picturesque motif: the white icebergs, the black plume—and then he heard the distant noise of an aircraft. They had been detected after all. He had previously been planning to give his men 48 hours of rest after the grueling work of unloading ship, but now they were back at it again, struggling to spread the supplies over a large area so they would not form an easy target in an air raid. The following day, on October 3, Schmid and his men were again overflown by a reconnaissance aircraft. It was just a question of time before they were attacked.[33]

Meanwhile, US Coast Guard cutter *Eastwind* was on its way towards Little Koldewey from the south. "This was the *Eastwind*'s first real test in heavy, polar-packed floes," recalled its commander, Charles W. Thomas. "The speed with which she chewed her way through fascinated me."[34] The ship moved up the west coast of the island, disembarking two platoons of infantry in the early hours of October 4. The American soldiers moved across the island, spotting the German camp. The Germans had heard strange sounds in the darkness, and they were on the alert. Schmid could have made a stand, and he knew the higher-ups in the navy would have approved of it if he had done so. Still, suddenly seeing him and his men surrounded by what appeared to him to be "250 Americans," he decided against it. He ordered his men to put down their weapons and surrender without firing a shot. "I knew the war was lost," he argued later. "I wanted to give our boys a good, healthy start in the post-war world."[35]

Externsteine was still unaccounted for. After more than a week of unsuccessful searches, it was spotted at 4:20pm on October 15 by *Eastwind*'s seaplane, located off Cape Borgen at the northern tip of Shannon Island. Both *Eastwind* and *Southwind*, another Coast Guard cutter, headed to the area, and *Eastwind* got there first. The cutter made radar contact with *Externsteine* at 8pm, and two hours later, at a distance of 4,000 yards, fired three broadside salvos at the German ship, deliberately aiming for the shells to fall 50 yards short. After the end of the third salvo, the German ship signaled "We give up." *Eastwind* moved in on the Germans, signaling that if they made any move to scuttle the ship, it would trigger fire from the American heavy machine gun battery. Shortly after midnight, when the two ships were separated by just 300 yards, a boarding party rounded up the prisoners and transferred them to the Coast Guard cutter, while a prize crew took over the Nazi vessel.[36] It was the only American capture of an enemy surface vessel in World War II.[37]

A chapter in the history of warfare in the arctic regions was about to be closed. The Germans would not again attempt to land men on Greenland soil for the purpose of carrying out weather observations. For the members of "Edelweiss II" it was the end of the war, and the beginning of a prolonged period of relative comfort. The officers were occasionally invited to dine with the commander of *Eastwind*. The enlisted men were put up in spacious quarters and given fiction books and games. One fourth of them, in turns, were allowed to attend movie showings alongside the regular American crew.[38] "I must say that we were being treated correctly by the Americans," Karl Schmid remarked later. "After a few days we were being directly spoiled."[39]

***

Schmid, Weiss and their men were not the only Germans in Greenland in 1944. In what was perhaps the clearest sign that the war had connected Greenland with the outside world, silver screen star Marlene Dietrich, born in Berlin but now an American citizen, visited the island twice during the year. In April, the 42-year-old celebrity, who was not allowed to fly in peacetime to avoid any risk to her expensively insured legs, landed for a refueling stop before moving on to the Azores and then further to her final destination in the Mediterranean, where she entertained the American troops.[40] Then once again in September, she stopped over in Greenland en route to Europe and newly liberated Paris, and this time she stayed a little longer.[41] She gave four concerts at Bluie West 1 in Narsarssuak, performing a number of songs, but none more popular than "Lili Marleen."[42] This was the same everywhere she went. "I sang if for three long years," she said. "All through Africa, Sicily, Italy; through Alaska, Greenland, Iceland; through England, through France, through Belgium and Holland, through Germany and into Czechoslovakia."[43]

The GIs in Greenland needed cheering up. Corporal Albert Henry Soar, a former football player with the New York Giants now serving on Greenland, wrote a letter to his former teammates in late 1944, describing his joy at a recent win: "I am the happiest guy in Greenland—if you ever can get happy up here in this God-forsaken country of ice, snow, icecaps and rocky mountains. They ought to give this place back to Denmark and get us all the hell out of here."[44] He was not alone. After more than three years in Greenland, many Americans thought it was time to go home. Some Danes thought the same about the visitors, allies or not.

Eske Brun, the governor who had exerted all his influence the previous years to try and root out prostitution, was frustrated to see that American soldiers were still walking freely in the vicinity of their bases. "Without prior consultation, base command has completely undermined the preconditions for our effort to prevent the occupation from having harmful effects on the population," he wrote in a telegram to the Danish mission in Washington DC in August 1944. "Lest four years of hard work on this matter be wasted, the US government must be made to understand that this has to stop."[45] Not everyone agreed on the gravity of the problem. When an official from the Danish consulate in New York visited Greenland in 1944, he did not see excessive fraternization. "American influence, through the various regulations of the armed forces limiting contacts with the native settlements [...] has been small," he wrote.[46]

Sometimes the pernicious American influence was so subtle that many were unable to see it, perhaps because it was not there in the first place. On Friday, September 22, at 8pm, the doctor was called to Godthaab's Teacher Training College. A student, Moses Wille, had been shot in the abdomen by one of his classmates. Despite all the doctor's efforts, he died within one hour. An op-ed writer in a local newspaper linked the tragic incident to the growing exposure to Hollywood movies imported into Greenland as part of a general increase in US clout. "[We can] never tolerate that the children use each other for target practice or play cowboys using American movie methods," the unnamed writer stated.[47]

In a different way, Bluie East 2 on the east coast of Greenland, came to exemplify some of the negative consequences of the cultural clash between Americans and Inuit. The base was established close to a traditional hunting ground for the locals, and as the strange pale-faced newcomers grew more numerous, eventually reaching a number of 800, they inevitably attracted interest. The Americans at the base only worsened the problem when out of an understandable and very human wish to share their wealth with the less fortunate they handed out cigarettes and candy to the Inuit. A shantytown developed on the outskirts of the base, where entire families settled down inside large wooden crates that had been used for transporting vehicles.

The situation that developed was probably not unlike what Secretary of State Hull had in mind when back in 1941 he warned against practices that could fuel Nazi propaganda of "enslavement" of original peoples. Many of the hunters turned into scavengers, sifting through the base dump for edible items. When the activity was explicitly banned for health reasons, they turned to doing it after dark. Often at night, the lights carried by visitors could be seen over the dump. The Danish authorities had foreseen this problem, and when the base had initially been negotiated, one precondition had been that the contents of the dump would be burned at regular intervals. The people in charge at the base omitted doing this, and the results were sadly predictable: food poisoning among the Inuit was widespread. In one particular notorious episode, seven Inuit died and 22 were severely sickened after eating meat from the dump that had gone bad.[48]

CHAPTER 19

The End

1945

In late April 1945, Hitler's favorite architect Albert Speer was holed up with what remained of the Nazi government in the North German city of Flensburg. As Speer, also armaments minister, was awaiting the arrival of the victorious British Army, he was alerted to a remarkable plan: he and a few other members of the political elite were to fly to Greenland, find a quiet fjord, and evade the first tumultuous months of Allied occupation of the Reich. The suggestion came from Werner Baumbach, the commander of Kampfgeschwader 200, a Luftwaffe unit veiled in secrecy that focused on special operations and clandestine missions. "Boxes full of books were packed, medical supplies, a lot of stationery (since I planned to begin my memoirs already there), hunting gear, my collapsible boat, skis, tents, hand grenades for catching fish and provisions," Speer wrote later.[1]

One of Kampfgeschwader 200's most experienced pilots, Peter Wilhelm Stahl, was let in on the plan. It was to involve the unit's 3rd Squadron, which controlled a considerable transportation capacity on the island of Rügen in the Baltic, including the huge, six-engine BV 222 flying boats. "They had been made ready to bring a large group of people—they had the political leadership of the Reich in mind—to a hidden place on the coast of Greenland," Stahl wrote in his memoirs. "There, in the safety of geographic isolation—or so they thought—it would be possible to survive for a long period of time and then at a later date to discreetly slip back into society." It never materialized, and he never heard any further details about the project. "It was an adventurous plan, which reflected boy scout romantics rather than any sense of reality," he remarked.[2]

Another adventurous plan landed on the desk of Professor Johannes Georgi, one of Germany's best-known polar explorers, in March 1945. It was a proposal written by Franz Nusser, a naval meteorologist, for continued weather observations from Greenland. The expeditions to the island, from "Holzauge" to the failed "Edelweiss" missions, had shown two things: first, to get weather observations from Greenland that were useful in continental Europe, where the war was now being fought, it was necessary to move further south than had been possible so far. Second, moving too far south was bound to trigger detection by the ever more numerous Americans.

Nusser had an unconventional solution to this dilemma. Instead of establishing a station near the coastline, where an American patrol would stumble on it sooner or later, it should be set up on the icecap.

Similar to the way that German and Austrian troops had lived inside glaciers during the war in the Alps from 1915 to 1918, the station should be built inside the ice. It would require fewer building materials to be ferried in from Europe, and it would be naturally camouflaged. The experience of "Bassgeiger" on Shannon Island would also be useful in this respect. The only feasible method would be to fly in the expedition members, Nusser argued, possibly having in mind the earlier experiments with landing on glaciers carried out almost five years earlier in Norway. Therefore, the expeditions had to be small, consisting of one commander doubling as a meteorologist, one technical assistant and two radio operators. Georgi pointed out certain practical difficulties, as the extent of American patrolling was unknown, but fundamentally signed off on the project as sound. The plan, to be implemented during the winter of 1945 and 1946, never got beyond the drawing board.[3]

Meanwhile, Alfred Saalwächter, a general admiral in the German Navy, put the finishing touches to a bizarre document in early 1945. It was a memorandum on how Germany should project its naval power across the world's oceans in order to regain the upper hand against the Allies. "Despite the tense military situation in which we seem to have lost all gains won in the early years of the conflict," he wrote in the introduction to the document, "I believe in final victory."[4] It is hard to imagine that this senior officer, with all his privileged access to information on the situation at the strategic level, truly was convinced that the war could still be won. Perhaps he was making plans for a future in which Germany would be allowed to unleash its destructive potential on the world for a third time. Perhaps he was simply meditating fancifully on what Germany should have done in a parallel universe where the strongest powers were not closing in on its borders from all sides.[5]

It is impossible to tell. What can be said for a certain is that if the German commanders had known in 1940 what they knew in 1945 and had at their disposal technologies that at the beginning of the war had been in an embryonic state but had come to full fruition five years later, Greenland would play a bigger role in their strategy. "Iceland, Greenland and the Azores must be removed from the American sphere of interest, just like Africa, as they, too, are unsinkable aircraft carriers or bases for long-distance weapons, which may threaten Europe once they have developed further," he wrote.[6] He pointed out that Greenland was of paramount importance in the future as a bulwark against American invasion plans against Europe. At the same time, it could be used offensively as a "launch base for rocket-type weapons fired at the United States," Saalwächter wrote, in all likelihood thinking of future versions of the V-2 rocket that the Germans had used against Allied targets in Britain and Western Europe since the fall of 1944.[7]

***

By April 1945, the people of Greenland and especially the Danes were waiting for the news they knew could come at any time, about the capitulation of Germany and the liberation of Denmark. Instead, news of an entirely different and unexpected kind arrived on April 12, about the death of US President Franklin D. Roosevelt. His frail health had been kept a carefully guarded secret, and therefore his demise came as an even bigger shock, in Greenland as elsewhere. The Greenland governor, Brun, sent his condolences and received a reply from Secretary of State Edward Stettinius, stating that the late president had appreciated the friendship of the Greenland people. "Never before a foreign death had struck so deeply as was the case on April 12, 1945," wrote Mikael Gam, a Danish educator in Greenland. "The resolute way that Roosevelt had acted in 1940 after the German occupation of Denmark [...] had made a lasting impression on the Greenlanders."[8]

Three weeks later, in the evening of May 4, it was finally reported in Greenland that German officers had met with British Field Marshal Bernard Law Montgomery, agreeing to the surrender of all forces in the Netherlands, northwest Germany and Denmark. The spread of the news could be directly observed in Godthaab, as people hoisted their flags the moment they were informed. Officers from the transport ship *Julius Thomsen*, which was anchored in the port, produced signal rockets and fired them into the air. "The only shooting we have experienced during the entire war," a newspaper reporter commented.[9] In the small community of Fiskeness, Apollus Noassen, the local politician who had quit smoking on the day that Germany occupied Denmark five years earlier, produced a cigar and lit it, to the applause of those around him.[10]

Governor Brun spoke about the sacrifices that had been necessary. "Let us commemorate [...] the brave Greenlander and Danish sailors, who disappeared with their ships while doing their duty," he said. Referring to Eli Knudsen, the member of the sledge patrol who had been killed in March 1943, he talked about "the lonely grave at Sandodden, where a brave soldier rests after having given his country everything."[11] A common theme in all the speeches that were held in May of 1945 was the alleged harmony between Greenlanders and Danes. Any divisions that existed during the war years were only hinted at: "All through these difficult years, which have also been difficult for the Greenlanders, they have sympathized with the Danes, even if they have not always found the right way to express this," said Jørgen Chemnitz, a member of the Greenland national council.[12]

Relations between Greenlanders and Danes had been characterized by a certain tension throughout the war years. For justification of this claim, one just had to look at King Christian X, a figure popular with both Greenlanders and Danes and therefore, on the face of it, not a bone of contention. In May 1940, for example, the provincial councils sent a greeting to the king in recently occupied Copenhagen:

"In this dark time, we feel a need to ask your Majesty to accept our promise of unending loyalty to our country and to our rightful king. We look forward to the day when nothing will again separate us from our king."[13] An eyewitness remembered how three years later, in the fall of 1943, the residents of Greenland had a rare opportunity to listen to the Danish Broadcasting Corporation transmitting a speech by the king. "An old woman next to me was sobbing uncontrollably. She probably did not understand a word of what the king was saying. Still, it was a major and touching moment being able to hear his sorrowful voice," he said.[14]

It was widely understood that the king and the royal family were powerful symbols that could help maintain inter-ethnic harmony in Greenland, and the media were employed to magnify this effect. Some Danes thought it went too far in its attempt to placate the Greenlanders. When Godthaab radio sent a special broadcast to mark the king's birthday, some listeners noted that there was no special greeting to the Danes in Greenland. "You shouldn't be so afraid of rubbing the Greenlanders the wrong way so as to forget that we Danes are a community unto ourselves and are tied closer together than Greenlanders and Danes," a listener in the Jakobshavn settlement complained in a letter to the radio station.[15] The ethnic division remained, in spite of all official efforts to tone it down. It was a message about the future awaiting Greenland and its inhabitants, a future very different from its pre-war past.

***

Maxwell Dunbar, who had been Canadian consul until 1943, returned to Greenland in 1945 for yet another stint and found society much changed. The standard of living had risen as a result of peace, and morale was high. But it also seemed as if the island had turned a corner. "So many of the people I had learnt to know so well had gone home to Denmark; a community structure had been broken," he said.[16] Especially the Danes that had been stranded in Greenland in 1940 and had been forced to wait out the war were no longer there. Still, they had left behind a legacy. While they had been in Greenland, they had participated in the governance of the small society and contributed to a feeling of having matured to a level where Copenhagen was no longer needed as much as in the past. "They had been governing themselves for five years. They had the ability themselves," complained an official with the Greenland Board in the Danish capital. "The idea of leading the Greenlanders gradually and cautiously towards greater development and independence belonged to the past. Copenhagen and the Greenland Board had become more and more distant. They talked about the Board with growing contempt. 'The Board'—they were laughing a little every time someone mentioned it," said a former senior official.[17]

A big part of the explanation for the growing confidence among the Greenlanders was to be found further to the west. The United States emerged as one of the two superpowers in 1945—arguably the stronger one—and Greenland was an immediate neighbor. A Dane who had not been to Greenland since before the German occupation and returned in early 1945, noticed that the Greenlanders seemed much better off and in the middle of a US-fueled consumer boom. "They were better dressed than before primarily in American clothes, especially colorful cotton garments which one had never seen before in Greenland," he wrote. "I also saw Greenlanders wearing second-hand American uniform items, but as far as I remember not a single American soldier."[18] The American presence was subtle. Draconian measures to keep the GIs at a distance from the local population had had an impact, even if they had not worked perfectly. Still geography was an inescapable fact, and geography had made Greenland an indispensable piece in the strategic game the United States was now involved in at the dawn of the Cold War.

Geography only meant something because of technology—aeronautical technology, to be more precise. When he left Greenland in 1943, Penfield, the US consul, was asked about his predictions for the island after the war. He expected it would be important in aviation. "If transarctic air routes should be adopted, it will naturally be very significant. Also, it may be used for air freight, with the idea that the shorter the jump, the bigger the pay load. It is hard to say now just what the situation will be," he said.[19] Others had made similar forecasts even before. "Quite possibly Greenland may in the future be useful as a stepping stone from the American Middle West to Scandinavia and Russia, and, as the land mass nearest the North Pole, it may acquire value through the development of trans-polar airlines," wrote Philip Mosely, an international relations scholar, in 1940.[20]

Mosely was optimistic, evidentially having civilian aircraft in mind when thinking about reaching Russia. As it turned out, he was almost right insofar as his vision turned out to be true for military aircraft. Greenland did become important as part of a vast, globe-spanning infrastructure that formed the Western response to the Soviet challenge. It had all begun in 1941 when the Americans arrived and kickstarted Greenland's journey into the modern world, for better or for worse. "The war had seemed likely to lower Greenland even deeper into its dark past when the ties with Denmark were cut short by the brutal German attack on our motherland, the absence of the ships, and the silence of the radio. But it was to turn out quite differently," wrote Christian Vibe, the young journalist.[21]

Postscript

Greenland impressed itself on most people who passed through or stayed for a longer period during the war years. One of them was Canadian diplomat Hugh Keenleyside. "My own most lasting memento of the Greenland episode is a charming small polar bear carved by an Eskimo out of pure white cryolite! Due to the passage of time and the perils of family life it has lost one of its rear paws, but it is still cherished for both its beauty and the memories it evokes," he wrote in his memoirs.[1] It is an amusing coincidence that this piece of original Greenland art should be made out of cryolite, "the ice that will not melt," which had such an important role to play in pushing the island to center stage from early on in World War II.

The cryolite mine at Ivigtut was one of the weak spots of the Western Allies in the initial stages of the conflict. It was the one place in Greenland where the Germans, by landing just a single successful blow, could have caused serious trouble for their enemies, not least in the crucial field of aircraft production. To be sure, the Allies knew how to make synthetic cryolite, but if, for example, the mine had been flooded by an explosion, it would have taken them months and absorbed precious resources from elsewhere to reset their production accordingly.

The question is: why did the Germans not do it? The short answer is: first they would not and then they could not. In 1940, when a U-boat could have disembarked a sabotage team with relative ease, because the mine essentially had no one to protect it, any plans, if they did exist, would be stopped by Hitler's reluctance to upset the Americans. Attacking Greenland would have meant war with the United States. He wanted that war eventually, but not at a time when Britain and more importantly, the Soviet Union, had not been beaten yet. Later, after the United States had entered the war, the Luftwaffe, which had the most to gain by putting obstacles in the way of Allied airplane manufacturing, deemed it technically impossible to send a bomber to Ivigtut. But why not launch a commando raid? The sources only allow us to speculate, but perhaps it was an instance of inter-service rivalry, since the assistance of the German Navy would have had to be called upon to help take the small team of specially trained soldiers to Greenland.

Cryolite represented one of three ways in which Greenland had strategic significance in World War II, and the only area where, in theory at least, there was some parity between Germany and the Allies, as Germany had it in its power to cause serious damage to its opponents. In the second of the three respects, Greenland as a station on the ferry route for airplanes from North America to Britain, Germany's ability to do anything but minor harassment was severely curtailed. As consultation among Luftwaffe planners showed, the threat of German attack on the Allied aircraft while in the air, could force them to boost their armament, thus spending more fuel, but that was it.

Finally, in the third of the three aspects, Greenland as a base for weather forecasts, Germany was at a severe disadvantage throughout the war. There was no question of Greenland's value for meteorological observations, as the preparations for the Normandy landings demonstrated, but the Allied ability to secure a continued stream of data was also never in doubt. The Germans could do nothing about it, and never even considered disrupting their enemies' activities in the field. The real question was whether they themselves were also in a position to obtain weather data from Greenland.

They definitely tried, again and again. Six attempts, wholly or partly supported by the Germans, were made to strengthen weather reporting from Greenland: *Furenak*, *Buskø*, "Holzauge," "Bassgeiger," "Edelweiss I" and "Edelweiss II." In addition, *Veslekari* partly had meteorological aims, carrying a telegrapher to Mosquito Bay. "Laubfrosch I," set for August 1944, was canceled at the last moment. Of these, only "Holzauge" and "Bassgeiger" managed to become operational, but they did lead to the result that Germany received regular weather reports from Greenland during the period from August 1942 until June 1944, with a six-month hiatus between June and December 1943.[2] Given the uneven odds at the outset, this must count as a qualified German success.

There was one fourth respect in which Greenland could potentially have been important, but was not: as a staging ground for a German invasion of North America. It has been claimed that the US government never really feared a German attack via Greenland, and that this was only mentioned in statements to sway American public opinion in favor of a growing presence on the island. The evidence, however, suggests real worries in the leadership among Roosevelt. Assistant Secretary of State Berle voiced the concern that Germany could attempt to establish a presence in Greenland. "We should have to contemplate the possibility that the Germans might try to interrupt the place," he wrote on August 27, 1940.[3]

To the extent that Hitler's views can be gauged from the rather modest sources to his thinking on cross-Atlantic invasion, he saw the Azores as the main stepping stone and did not accord Greenland major significance in plans for taking America. Still, in the compartmentalized decision-making of the Third Reich, it was entirely possible that for example the Luftwaffe, building an experimental airfield on a Norwegian glacier, might be making plans of its own, possibly with a view to eventually persuading the Führer. Anyway, a German offensive against the American homeland was far off in the future, after the Soviet Union had been beaten, and much could change, including the priority given to Greenland.

General Admiral Saalwächter was looking into an even more distant future, when amid the catastrophe of 1945 he described Greenland's importance in a coming era, then still only dimly foreseen, where intercontinental bombers and even missiles would have the power to decide wars. The general admiral may have been dreaming about what a Fourth Reich might be able to achieve, and in this sense his vision was doomed to fail, as the Allies would never allow the Germans to bring war to the rest of the world a third time in a row. However, he did envision with some accuracy a future where the Soviet Union had taken over the role as America's main adversary, and new aviation and missile technologies gave Greenland unprecedented importance.

Inuit Equivalents of Geographical Names Appearing in This Book

Traditional names	Inuit equivalents
Egedesminde	Aasiaat
Fiskeness	Qeqertarsuatsiaat
Godhavn	Qeqertarsuaq
Godthaab	Nuuk
Greenland	Kalaallit Nunaat
Holsteinsborg	Sisimiut
Julianehaab	Qaqortoq
Kutdligssat	Qullissat
Scoresby Sound	Ittoqqortoormiit
Sondrestromfjord	Kangerlussuaq
Sukkertoppen	Maniitsoq

Notes

Chapter 1: "Greenland's Ice-girt Shore"

1 Paul Burkert, *Weisser Kampf* [*White Struggle*] (Berlin: Gustav Weise Verlag, 1938), 12–13.

2 Hans Christian Gulløv (ed.), *Grønlands forhistorie* [*The Prehistory of Greenland*] (Copenhagen: Gyldendal, 2004), 14–15.

3 Ibid., 16.

4 Ibid., 64.

5 Maanasa Raghavan et al., "The genetic prehistory of the New World Arctic," *Science*, vol. 345, no. 6200 (August 29, 2014): 1020.

6 *Eirik the Red's Saga: A Translation*, translated by John Sephton (Liverpool: D. Marples & Co., 1880), 8.

7 Henrik M. Jansen, *A Critical Examination of the Written and Archaeological Sources' Evidence Concerning the Norse Settlements in Greenland* (Copenhagen: C. A. Reitzel, 1972), 35.

8 Robert W. Park, "Stories of arctic colonization," *Science*, vol. 345, no. 6200 (August 29, 2014): 1005.

9 *Eirik the Red's Saga: A Translation*, translated by John Sephton (Liverpool: D. Marples & Co., 1880), 28.

10 Ibid., 30.

11 Niels Lynnerup, "Life and Death in Norse Greenland," in *Vikings: The North Atlantic Saga*, eds. William W. Fitzhugh and Elisabeth I. Ward (Washington DC and London: Smithsonian Institution Press, 2000), 290–292.

12 L. K. Barlow, J. P. Sadler, A. E. J. Ogilvie, P. C. Buckland, T. Amorosi, J. H. Ingimundarson, P. Skidmore, A. J. Dugmore and T. H. McGovern, "Interdisciplinary investigations of the end of the Norse Western Settlement in Greenland," *The Holocene*, vol. 7, no. 4 (December 1997): 491.

13 Inge Kleivan, "Grønlandske sagn om nordboerne" ["Greenlandic Legends About the Norsemen"], *Tidsskriftet Grønland*, vol. 30, no. 8–9 (September 1982): 316–317; C. Pingel, "Antiquariske Efterretninger fra Grønland" ["Antiquarian Information from Greenland"], *Annaler for Nordisk Oldkyndighed* (1838–1839): 237–241.

14 Gunnar Karlsson, *The History of Iceland* (Minneapolis MN: University of Minnesota Press, 2000), 103.

15 Eilert Sundt (ed.), *Egedes Dagbog i Uddrag* [*Excerpts of Egede's Diary*] (Christiania (Oslo): P. T. Mallings Bogtrykkeri, 1860), 15–17.

16 Sundt (ed.), *Egedes Dagbog*, 17.

17 Ibid., 18.

18 Hans Egede, *Det gamle Grønlands nye Perlustration eller Naturel-Historie* [*A New Survey or Natural History of Old Greenland*] (Copenhagen: Johan Christoph Groth, 1741), 66 and 68.

19 Gulløv (ed.), *Grønlands forhistorie*, 223; Sven Svensson, *Kristian den Andres planer på en arktisk ekspedition och deras förutsättningar* [*Christian II's Plans for an Arctic Expedition and Their Preconditions*] (Lund: C. W. K. Gleerup, 1960).

20 Louis Bobé (ed.), *Diplomatarium Groenlandicum 1492–1814* (Copenhagen: C. A. Reitzels Forlag, 1936), 153–154.

21 Sundt (ed.), *Egedes Dagbog*, 110.

22 Ibid., 130.

23 Ibid., 135.

24 Ibid., 137.

25 Bobé (ed.), *Diplomatarium*, 266.

26 Ibid.

27 Louis Bobé (ed.), *Peder Olsen Walløes Dagbøger fra hans Rejser i Grønland* [*Peder Olsen Walløe's Diaries From His Travels in Greenland*] (Copenhagen: G. E. C. Gad, 1927), 14.

28 Bobé (ed.), *Diplomatarium*, 327–328.

29 H. Ostermann, "Et engelsk overfald paa et dansk etablissement i Grønland under krigen 1807–14" ["An English Attack on a Danish Establishment in Greenland During the War of 1807–14"], *Det Grønlandske Selskabs Aarsskrift* (1931–32): 39–51; Finn Gad, "Tasiussaq-affæren af 1811" ["The Tasiussaq Affair of 1811"], *Tidsskriftet Grønland*, vol. 28, no. 6 (August 1980): 175–184.

30 Gad, "Tasiussaq-affæren," 183.

31 Ibid., 184.

32 Ostermann, "Et engelsk overfald," 44.

33 Finn Gad, "'La Grönlande, les Isles de Ferröe et l'Islande non comprises': A new look at the origins of the addition to Article IV of the Treaty of Kiel of 1814," *Scandinavian Journal of History*, vol. 4 (1979): 187–205; Thorkild Kjærgaard, "Freden i Kiel, Grønland og Nordatlanten 1814–2014" ["The Peace of Kiel, Greenland and the North Atlantic 1814–2014"] *Fund og Forskning*, vol. 54 (2015): 382–383.

34 Robert W. Rix, *The Vanished Settlers of Greenland: In Search of a Legend and Its Legacy* (Cambridge: Cambridge University Press, 2023), 161–162.

35 Rix, *Vanished Settlers*, 145, 163–164.

36 Ibid., 152.

37 Ibid., 163.

38 George Sculthorpe Morris, *Convicts and Colonies: Thoughts on Transportation & Colonization, with Reference to the Islands and Mainland of Northern Australia* (London: Hope and Company, 1853), 5.

39 George Sculthorpe Morris, *Convicts and Colonies: Thoughts on Transportation & Colonization, with Reference to the Islands and Mainland of Northern Australia* (London: Hope and Company, 1853), 6.

40 William Earl Weeks, *The New Cambridge History of American Foreign Relations, vol. 1: Dimensions of the Early American Empire, 1754–1865* (Cambridge: Cambridge University Press, 2013), 114–120.

41 Ingo Heidbrink, "'No One Thinks of Greenland': US-Greenland Relations and Perceptions of Greenland in the US from the Early Modern Period to the 20th Century," *American Studies in Scandinavia*, vol. 54, no. 2 (December 2022): 12–13.

42 "Greenland," *The United Brethren's Missionary Intelligencer, and Religious Miscellany, Containing the Most Recent Accounts Relating to the United Brethren's Mission among the Heathen, with Other Interesting Communications from the Records of that Church*, vol. 3, no. 9 (1830): 452.

43   "Greenland," *The United Brethren's Missionary Intelligencer,* 451.

44   Benjamin Mills Peirce, *A Report on the Resources of Iceland and Greenland* (Washington DC: Government Printing Office, 1868), 3.

45   Ibid., 3–4.

46   Ibid., 48–49.

47   Vilhjalmur Stefansson, *Greenland* (Garden City NY: Doubleday, Doran & Co., 1942), 294–295.

48   Edward W. Chester, *The United States and Six Atlantic Outposts: The Military and Economic Considerations* (Port Washington NY: Kennikat Press, 1980), 185.

49   Walter Stahr, *Seward: Lincoln's Indispensable Man* (New York NY: Simon & Schuster, 2012), 516.

Chapter 2: *Terra Incognita* No Longer

1   Vilhjalmur Stefansson, *Greenland* (Garden City NY: Doubleday, Doran & Co., 1944), 1.

2   Robert E. Peary, "Greenland as an American Naval Base," *The New York Times*, September 11, 1916: 8.

3   Ibid.

4   J. D. Hazen to Lord Curzon's Sub-Committee on Territorial Desiderata in the Terms of Peace, Report, 20 April 1917, CAB 24, 11, The British National Archives, 1–2; quoted from Dawn Alexandrea Berry, "The North Atlantic Triangle and the Genesis and Legacy of the American Occupation of Greenland During the Second World War," (PhD diss., University of Oxford, 2013), 54.

5   See, for example, Robert E. Peary, *Northward over the 'Great Ice'* (New York NY: Frederick A. Stokes Co., 1898), xxix–xxx.

6   Quoted from *Congressional Record: Proceedings and Debates of the 76th Congress, Third Session, vol. 86, part 7* (May 26, 1940 to June 12, 1940) (Washington DC: United States Government Printing Office, 1940), 7687–7688.

7   *Papers relating to the foreign relations of the United States with the address of the president to Congress December 4, 1917* (Washington DC: Government Printing Office, 1926), 561.

8   Ibid., 566.

9   Caroline Patrice Peck, "Maurice Francis Egan: Writer, Teacher, Diplomat" (Master's diss., College of William & Mary, 1969), 53–54; *Papers relating to the foreign relations of the United States with the address of the president to Congress December 4, 1917* (Washington DC: Government Printing Office, 1926), 561–566.

10   See for example *Papers relating to the foreign relations of the United States with the address of the president to Congress December 4, 1917* (Washington DC: Government Printing Office, 1926), 645–646.

11   *Papers relating to the foreign relations of the United States, 1922, Volume II* (Washington DC: Government Printing Office, 1938), 1.

12   Ibid., 1–3.

13   Løkkegaard, Finn, *Det danske gesandtskab i Washington 1940–1942* [*The Danish Mission in Washington 1940–1942*] (Copenhagen: Gyldendal, 1968), 54; Lothar Burchardt, *Amerikas langer Arm: Kontroversen um die Nutzung von Grönland in Zweiten Weltkrieg* [*America's Long Arm: Controversies over the Exploitation of Greenland in World War Two*] (Frankfurt am Main: Peter Lang, 2017), 43.

14   Løkkegaard, *Danske gesandtskab*, 54; *Papers relating to the foreign relations of the United States, 1922, Volume II* (Washington DC: Government Printing Office, 1938), 1–3.

15   *Papers relating to the foreign relations of the United States, 1929, Volume I* (Washington DC: Government Printing Office, 1943), 698–719.

16 E. J. Overbye, "Flyvning på Grønland" ["Aviation in Greenland"], in *Grønlandsbogen* [*The Greenland Book*], vol. 2, ed. Kaj Birket-Smith, Ernst Mentze and M. Friis Møller (Copenhagen: J. H. Schultz Forlag, 1950), 147–153.

17 Vilhjalmur Stefansson, "The American Far North," *Foreign Affairs*, vol. 17, no. 3 (April 1939): 523.

18 Løkkegaard, *Danske gesandtskab*, 56–57.

19 Paul E. Ancker, "Narsarsuaq Air Base (B. W.-1), 1941–1958," *Tidsskriftet Grønland*, vol. 41, no. 4–5 (August 1993): 9.

20 Philip E. Mosely, "Iceland and Greenland: An American Problem," *Forign Affairs*, vol. 18, no. 4 (July 1940): 745–746.

21 *The Public Papers and Addresses of Franklin D. Roosevelt*, 1938 volume, ed. Samuel I. Rosenman (New York NY: The Macmillan Company, 1941), 258. The reference to the "Great Circle Route" in the context of German planning in the late war years may be somewhat anachronistic, as the concept only entered into public parlance during the 1930s. I am indebted to Charles Dusch, command historian emeritus, US Air Force Academy, for making this point.

22 *Hearings Before the Committee on Naval Affairs of the House of Representatives on Sundry Legislation Affecting the Naval Establishment 1923–1924* (Washington DC: Government Printing Office, 1924), 469.

23 In the words of Jürgen Bleibler, historian at the Zeppelin Museum Friedrichshafen, the "concrete route described by Roosevelt across Iceland and Greenland in 1919 would have been suicidal for a craft such as the L-72, whether from the point of view of meteorology or navigation." I am grateful to Bleibler for his detailed research into claims of planned German Zeppelin attacks on the Western Hemisphere towards the end of World War I.

24 Douglas H. Robinson, *Giants in the Sky. A History of the Rigid Airship* (Henley-on-Thames: Foulis & Co., 1973), 139, n25.

25 Ernst A. Lehmann and Howard Mingos, *The Zeppelins: The Development of the Airship, with the Story of the Zeppelin Air Raids in the World War* (New York, NY: J. H. Sears & Company, 1927), 306–310.

26 Burchardt, *Amerikas langer Arm*, 22–23.

27 William Barr, "Gyrfalcons to Germany: Herdemerten's expedition to west Greenland, 1938," *Polar Record*, vol. 48, no. 2 (April 2012): 113–122. See also Burchardt, *Amerikas langer Arm*, 22–23.

28 Account by Knud Oldendow, December 1961, Finn Løkkegaard papers, Håndskriftssamlingen, Danish National Archives.

29 William S. Carlson, *Lifelines Through the Arctic* (New York NY: Duell, Sloan and Pearce, 1962), 42.

30 Peter Freuchen, *The Vagrant Viking: My Life and Adventures* (New York NY: Julian Messner Inc., 1953), 168.

31 Wolfgang von Gronau, *Im Grönland-Wal: Dreimal über den Atlantik und einmal um die Welt* [*In the Grönland-Wal: Three Times Across the Atlantic and Once Around the World*] (Berlin: Verlag Reimar Hobbing, 1933), 28.

32 Richard Becker, "Das Flugklima Grönlands" ["Greenland's Flying Weather"] *Aus dem Archiv der deutschen Seewarte*, vol. 52, no. 4 (1933): 7.

33 Wolfgang von Gronau, *Im Grönland-Wal: Dreimal über den Atlantik und einmal um die Welt* [*In the Grönland-Wal: Three Times Across the Atlantic and Once Around the World*] (Berlin: Verlag Reimar Hobbing, 1933), 28.

34 Becker, "Das Flugklima Grönlands," 3–32; and Gerhard Heinz Baumann, "Grönland-Flug von Gronau 1931" ["Gronau's Greenland Flight in 1931"] *Aus dem Archiv der deutschen Seewarte*, vol. 52, no. 4 (1933): 33–48.

35 Account by Knud Oldendow, December 1961, Finn Løkkegaard papers, Håndskriftssamlingen, Danish National Archives.

36   Daniel Nagelstutz, "'I dette sataniske Evangelium'" ["'In This Satanic Gospel'"], *European Journal of Scandinavian Studies*, vol 51, no. 2 (2021): 311–312, Burkert, *Weisser Kampf*, 72.

37   Burkert, *Weisser Kampf*, 74.

38   Account by Agnar Jonsson, November 1965, Finn Løkkegaard papers, Håndskriftssamlingen, Danish National Archives. See also Solrun B. Jensdottir Hardarson, "The 'Republic of Iceland' 1940–44: Anglo-American Attitudes and Influences" *Journal of Contemporary History*, vol. 9, no. 4 (October 1974): 30; Philip E. Mosely, "Iceland and Greenland: An American Problem," *Foreign Affairs*, vol. 18, no. 4 (July 1940): 745; and *Congressional Record: Proceedings and Debates of the 76th Congress, Third Session, vol. 86, part 7* (May 26, 1940 to June 12, 1940) (Washington DC: United States Government Printing Office, 1940), 7690.

39   Account by Agnar Jonsson, November 1965, Finn Løkkegaard papers, Håndskriftssamlingen, Danish National Archives.

40   Ibid.

41   Hans-Liudger Dienel and Martin Schiefelbusch, "German Commercial Air Transport until 1945," *Revue belge de Philologie et d'Histoire*, vol. 78, no. 3–4 (2000): 965.

42   Account by Agnar Jonsson, November 1965, Finn Løkkegaard papers, Håndskriftssamlingen, Danish National Archives.

43   Einar Arne Drivenes, "Ishavsimperialisme" ["Arctic Ocean Imperialism"], in *Norsk Polarhistorie* [*Norwegian Polar History*], vol. 2, eds. Einar Arne Drivenes and Harald Dag Jølle (Oslo: Gyldendal Norsk Forlag, 2004), 215.

44   Drivenes, "Ishavsimperialisme," 234–235.

45   Ida Blom, *Kampen om Erik Raudes Land* [*The Struggle for Erik the Red's Land*] (Oslo: Gyldendal Norsk Forlag, 1973), 54–56.

46   Blom, *Kampen*, 18.

47   Ibid., 59.

48   Quoted from M. Rudolph, "Geopolitische Überseeprobleme des dänischen Staates II" ["Geopolitical Problems for the Danish State Overseas II"], *Zeitschrift für Geopolitik*, vol. 7, no. 5 (1930): 391–392.

49   Blom, *Kampen*, 59.

50   Ibid., 60–61.

51   Drivenes, "Ishavsimperialisme," 243.

Chapter 3: War

1   Christian Vibe, *Ene ligger Grønland* [*Greenland Alone*] (Copenhagen: Gyldendal, 1946), 16.

2   Mikael Gam, *Een gang Grønland—altid Grønland* [*Greenland Stays With You*] (Copenhagen: Fremad, 1972), 132.

3   Troels Brandt, *Dagbog fra Grønland 1938–1945* [*Diary from Greenland 1938–1945*] (Nuuk: Forlaget Atuagkat, 1999), 68.

4   Brandt, *Dagbog*, 68.

5   Vibe, *Ene ligger Grønland*, 16.

6   Ibid., 22–23.

7   Finn Gad, *Grønland under Krigen* [*Greenland During the War*] (Copenhagen. G. E. C. Gads Forlag, 1945), 7–8.

8   Ejnar Mikkelsen, *Svundne Tider i Østgrønland: Fra Stenalder til Atomtid* [*Times Long Gone in Eastern Greenland: From the Stone Age to the Nuclear Age*] (Copenhagen: Gyldendal, 1960), 173.

9   Herbert Feith, *The Decline of Constitutional Democracy in Indonesia* (Ithaca NY: Cornell University Press, 1962), 5.

10 Troels Riis Larsen, "Grønland på vej—adskilt fra Danmark 1940–1945" ["Greenland on its Way: Separated from Denmark 1940–1945"] in *Tro og samfund i Grønland i 300-året for Hans Egedes ankomst* [*Faith and Society in Greenland at the 300th Anniversary of Hans Egede's Arrival*], eds. Aage Rydstrøm-Poulsen, Gitte Adler Reimer and Annemette Nyborg Lauritsen (Aarhus: Aarhus Universitetsforlag, 2021), 302.

11 Gam, *Een gang Grønland*, 61.

12 Løkkegaard interview of Oldendow, December 13, 1961, 3. Finn Løkkegaard papers, Danish National Archives.

13 Ole Vinding, *Grønland 1945* [*Greenland 1945*], (Copenhagen: Gyldendal, 1946), 8–9.

14 James K. Penfield to the Secretary of State, October 1940, quoted from Hanna i Horni, "British and U.S. post-neutrality policy in the North Atlantic area 09.04.1940–1945: The role of Danish representatives" (PhD diss., Swansea University, 2010), 271–272.

15 Brandt, *Dagbog*, 70.

16 Report on the American-Greenland Commission from April 1940 until August 1941, quoted from Hanna i Horni, "British and U.S. post-neutrality policy in the North Atlantic area 09.04.1940–1945: The role of Danish representatives" (PhD diss., Swansea University, 2010), 269.

17 Max Dunbar, *Essays from a Life: Scotland, Canada, Greenland, Denmark* (Montreal: McGill University Libraries, 1995), 67.

18 William L. Langer and S. Everett Gleason, *The Challenge to Isolation: The World Crisis of 1937–1940 and American Foreign Policy* (New York NY: Harper &Row, 1952), 201.

19 *The Public Papers and Addresses of Franklin D. Roosevelt*, 1939 volume, ed. Samuel I. Rosenman (New York NY: The Macmillan Company, 1941), 463.

20 Langer and Gleason, *Challenge to Isolation*, 206–207.

21 *Foreign relations of the United States. Diplomatic Papers, 1939*, vol. 5, *The American Republics* (Washington DC: The United States Government Printing Office, 1957), 36–37.

22 Remark made at press conference on April 25, 1941. "Press Conference #738." Press Conferences of President Franklin D. Roosevelt, 1933–1945. Franklin D. Roosevelt Presidential Library & Museum, 5.

23 Langer and Gleason, *Challenge to Isolation*, 211.

24 Burchardt, *Amerikas langer Arm*, 69.

25 Aluminium Limited, *Aluminium Panorama*, 1953, 32.

26 Ibid., 13.

27 Cited in Matthew Evenden, "Aluminum, Commodity Chains, and the Environmental History of the Second World War," *Environmental History*, vol. 16, no. 1 (January 2011): 69–70.

28 Albert J. Baime, *The Arsenal of Democracy: FDR, Detroit, and an Epic Quest to Arm an America at War* (Boston MA and New York NY: Houghton Mifflin Harcourt, 2014), 96.

29 James K. Penfield, "Northward Ho!" *American Foreign Service Journal*, vol. 18 no. 2 (February 1941): 66.

30 Eigil Knuth, "Grønland under Krigen," in *De Fem Lange Aar. Danmark under Besættelsen 1940–1945* [*The Five Long Years: Denmark During the Occupation 1940–1945*], eds. Johannes Brøndsted and Knud Gedde (Copenhagen: Gyldendalske Boghandel, 1945), 1414.

31 James K. Penfield, "Northward Ho!" *American Foreign Service Journal*, vol. 18 no. 2 (February 1941): 66.

32 Wendy Dathan, *The Reindeer Botanist: Alf Erling Porsild, 1901–1977* (Calgary: University of Calgary Press, 2012), 396–397.

33 Burchardt, *Amerikas langer Arm*, 69–70.

34 *Kriegstagebuch der Seekriegsleitung 1939–1945* [*War Diary of the Naval Command 1939–1945*], *Part A, vol. 1* (Herford and Bonn: Verlag E. S. Mittler & Sohn, 1988), 20 and 24.

35   S. W. Roskill, *The War at Sea*, vol. 1, *The Defensive* (London: Her Majesty's Stationery Office, 1954), 112.

36   Roskill, *War at Sea*, vol. 1, 112.

37   Klaus H. Schmider, *Hitler's Fatal Miscalculation Why Germany Declared War on the United States* (Cambridge: Cambridge University Press, 2021), 84.

38   *Kriegstagebuch der Seekriegsleitung 1939–1945* [*War Diary of the Naval Command 1939–1945*], Part A, vol. 6 (Herford and Bonn: Verlag E. S. Mittler & Sohn, 1988), 226.

39   Asbjørn Lindboe, *Fra de urolige trediveårene* [*From the Turbulent Thirties*] (Oslo: Johan Grundt Tanum Forlag, 1965), 180.

40   Oddvar K. Hoidal, *Quisling: A Study in Treason* (Oslo: Norwegian University Press, 1989), 144.

41   Ibid., 302.

42   Alfred Rosenberg's Diary, United States Holocaust Memorial Museum Accession Number: 2001.62.14 | RG Number: RG-71, 351–353. The document shown to Hitler by Quisling has since been lost, see for example Jürgen Matthäus and Frank Bajohr, *The Political Diary of Alfred Rosenberg and the Onset of the Holocaust* (Lanham MD: Rowman & Littlefield Publishers 2015), 179.

43   Hans Fredrik Dahl, *Vidkun Quisling: En fører for fall* [*Vidkun Quisling: A Leader Destined to Fall*] (Oslo: Aschehoug, 1992), 44.

44   Alfred Rosenberg's Diary, United States Holocaust Memorial Museum Accession Number: 2001.62.14 | RG Number: RG-71, 351–353. The document shown to Hitler by Quisling has since been lost, see for example Jürgen Matthäus and Frank Bajohr, *The Political Diary of Alfred Rosenberg and the Onset of the Holocaust* (Lanham MD: Rowman & Littlefield Publishers 2015), 179.

45   Translation of report by Maurice Reddy, American Red Cross, August 1940. Director K. H. Oldendow's papers. Greenland 1940–1945. Danish National Archives.

46   Knuth, "Grønland under Krigen," 1414.

47   Penfield, "Northward Ho!" 68 and 96.

48   Translation of report by Maurice Reddy, American Red Cross, August 1940. Director K. H. Oldendow's papers. Greenland 1940–1945. Danish National Archives.

49   Eske Brun, *Mit Grønlandsliv* [*My Life in Greenland*] (Copenhagen: Gyldendal, 1985), 24.

50   Penfield, "Northward Ho!" 96.

51   Mikkelsen, *Svundne Tider*, 88.

52   Sylv. M. Saxtorph, "Sundhedsforhold" ["Health Conditions"], in *Grønlandsbogen, vol. 2*, eds. Kaj Birket-Smith, Ernst Mentze and M. Friis Møller (Copenhagen: J. H. Schultz Forlag, 1950), 164.

53   Ibid., 164.

54   "Een Kvinde alene gjorde det hele" ["One Woman Did It All Single-Handedly," *Berlingske Tidende*, July 22, 1951: 9.

55   Saxtorph, "Sundhedsforhold," 168.

56   Gam, *Een gang*, 106.

57   Brun, *Mit Grønlandsliv*, 32.

58   James F. Abel and Norman J. Bond, *Literacy in the Several Countries of the World* (Washington DC: United States Government Printing Office, 1929), 50. Eske Brun also claims that literacy was effectively universal, Brun, *Mit Grønlandsliv*, 31.

59   Sarah Helms, "Signe Vest," in *Tasiilaq. Angmagssalik*, ed. Jørgen Fisker (Umanak: Nordiske Landes Bogforlag, 1984), 238.

60   Brun, *Mit Grønlandsliv*, 31.

61   Ibid.

62   Women's suffrage was not introduced until 1948, Gam, *Een gang*, 108.

63 Guldborg Chemnitz, "Kvinden i Grønland" ["The Woman in Greenland"], in *Kvinderne og valgretten* [*The Women and Suffrage*], ed. Ellen Strange Petersen (Copenhagen: Schultz, 1965), 266.

Chapter 4: Orphan Island

1 Brandt, *Dagbog*, 100.

2 Gad, *Grønland under Krigen*, 8.

3 Brandt, *Dagbog*, 100.

4 Brun, *Mit Grønlandsliv*, 56; "Grønland under sidste krig," *Atuagagdliutit*, January 1, 1961: 8.

5 Gad, *Grønland under Krigen*, 8.

6 Eske Brun, "Grønland i Adskillelsens Aar," *Grønlandsposten*, December 1, 1945: 258.

7 Claus Bundgård Christensen, Joachim Lund, Niels Wium Olesen and Jakob Sørensen, *Danmark besat: Krig og hverdag* [*Denmark During the Occupation: War and Everyday Life*] (Copenhagen: Informations Forlag, 2015), 93–112.

8 Gad, *Grønland under Krigen*, 8.

9 "Danmark befriet: De tyske Tropper kapitulerer betingelsesløst," *Grønlandsposten*, May 16, 1945: 110. Another source attributes this act to Egede Motzfeldt, also a local politician from Fiskenæsset, see Bjarne Rasmussen (ed.), *Tilbageblik—2. bog: Tidligere telegrafister fortæller erindringer fra Grønland* [*Looking Back, vol. 2: Former Telegraphers Describe Memories from Greenland*] (e-book, 2019), 206–207. https://slaegtsbibliotek.dk/911191.pdf. Since the article in *Grønlandsposten* is much closer in time to the events, I have opted to use this source.

10 Jørgen Fleischer, *Forvandlingens år: Grønland fra koloni til landsdel* [*Years of Change: Greenland from Colony to Part of the Country*] (Nuuk: Atuakkiorfik, 1996), 80.

11 Michael Gam, *Een gang Grønland*, 133.

12 Gam, *Een gang Grønland*, 142.

13 Vibe, *Ene ligger Grønland*, 24.

14 Gad, *Grønland under Krigen*, 8.

15 Gam, *Een gang Grønland*, 133.

16 "Summary of conversation with Ms. Balle, returned from Greenland on January 11, 1941." Director K. H. Oldendow's papers. Greenland 1940–1945. Danish National Archives.

17 Gad, *Grønland under Krigen*, 10.

18 "Summary of conversation with Ms. Balle."

19 Gad, *Grønland under Krigen*, 7.

20 "Summary of conversation with Ms. Balle."

21 Vibe, *Ene ligger Grønland*, 32.

22 "Meetings of the United Greenland Councils 1940," Director K. H. Oldendow's papers. Greenland 1940–1945. Danish National Archives, 4.

23 Gad, *Grønland under Krigen*, 10.

24 "Meetings of the United Greenland Councils 1940," 4–5.

25 "Meetings of the United Greenland Councils 1940," 2.

26 Summary of conversation with van Hauen, January 7, 1941. Director K. H. Oldendow's papers. Greenland 1940–1945. Danish National Archives.

27 "Summary of conversation with Ms. Balle."

28 "Meetings of the United Greenland Councils 1940," 5.

29 Løkkegaard, *Gesandtskab*, 17–18; "Da ambassadøren selv maatte handle spontant" ["When the Ambassador Himself Had to Act Spontaneously"], *Politiken*, November 27, 1958: 4.

30 Account by Agnar Klemens Jonsson, September 23, 1965. Finn Løkkegaard papers, Håndskriftssamlingen, Danish National Archives.

31 Account by Anna Andersen, February 5, 1963. Finn Løkkegaard papers, Håndskriftssamlingen, Danish National Archives.

32 Beatrice Bishop Berle and Travis Beal Jacobs (eds.), *Navigating the Rapids 1918–1971: From the Papers of Adolf A. Berle* (New York NY: Harcourt Brace Jovanovich, 1973), 303.

33 Berne disclosed this to the Danish governor Aksel Svane during a conversation in 1941. Aksel Svane, "En 'uafhængig' gesandt," ["An 'Independent' Envoy"], *Historisk tidsskrift*, 12, vol. 4, no. 3 (1970): 529.

34 Moffat diary, April 9, 1940. Quoted from Løkkegaard, *Gesandtskab*, 510–511 n26.

35 "Danes' Envoy Here Defies Nazi Rule," *The New York Times*, April 10, 1940: 12.

36 Quoted from Løkkegaard, *Gesandtskab*, 510–511 n29.

37 Conversation with foreign ministry official Adam Tscherning, May 4, 1962. Finn Løkkegaard's papers. Håndskriftsamlingen. IV, T 38.9. Danish National Archives.

38 Ibid.

39 Cordell Hull, *The Memoirs of Cordell Hull*, vol. 1 (New York NY: The Macmillan Company, 1948), 753.

40 "Miss MacDougall Marries Diplomat," *The New York Times*, November 19, 1926: 28.

41 Svane, "Uafhængig," 527.

42 "Press Conference #634." Press Conferences of President Franklin D. Roosevelt, 1933–1945. Franklin D. Roosevelt Presidential Library & Museum, 4.

43 Cordell Hull, *The Memoirs of Cordell Hull*, vol. 1 (New York NY: The Macmillan Company, 1948), 753.

44 "Greenland Raises Hemisphere Issue," *The New York Times*, April 11, 1940: 1.

45 William L. Langer and S. Everett Gleason, *The Challenge to Isolation: The World Crisis of 1937–1940 and American Foreign Policy* (New York NY: Harper &Row, 1952), 430.

46 "Press Conference #635." Press Conferences of President Franklin D. Roosevelt, 1933–1945. Franklin D. Roosevelt Presidential Library and Museum, 4.

47 "Press Conference #636A." Press Conferences of President Franklin D. Roosevelt, 1933–1945. Franklin D. Roosevelt Presidential Library and Museum, 17.

48 "Press Conference #635." Press Conferences of President Franklin D. Roosevelt, 1933–1945. Franklin D. Roosevelt Presidential Library and Museum, 5.

49 "Press Conference #636A." Press Conferences of President Franklin D. Roosevelt, 1933–1945. Franklin D. Roosevelt Presidential Library and Museum, 17–18.

50 Ibid., 28–29.

51 *Congressional Record: Proceedings and Debates of the 76th Congress, Third Session, vol. 86, part 5 (April 18, 1940 to May 8, 1940)*. (Washington DC: United States Government Printing Office, 1940), 4641.

52 Ibid., 5054.

53 Quoted from Løkkegaard, *Gesandtskab*, 86.

54 *Foreign relations of the United States. Diplomatic Papers, 1940, vol. 2: General and Europe* (Washington DC: Government Printing Office, 1957), 361.

55 Transcript of telephone conversation between Morgenthau and Berle on April 20, 1940. Jr. Diaries of Henry Morgenthau, Jr., book 256 (April 20–23, 1940), 54–55. Franklin D. Roosevelt Presidential Library and Museum.

56 Løkkegaard, *Danske gesandtskab*, 88.

Chapter 5: Force X

1   The account here of the complex events leading up to the standoff at Ivigtut in June of 1940 leans on a number of sources, including Gordon Smith, "'This was not the time for this type of 1890 imperialism': Cryolite, Control, and Canada-US Relations over Greenland, 1940," *The Northern Mariner/Le marin du nord*, vol. 31, no. 3 (Autumn 2021): 249.

2   David R. Murray (ed.), *Documents on Canadian External Affairs,* vol. 7 (Ottawa: Department of External Affairs, 1974), 947–948. The extent of Alcan's involvement in the Ivigtut incident in 1940 has been the subject of speculation. Even while events were still unfolding, several of the involved individuals sensed the company pulling the strings. "The rather unfortunate Nascopie Expedition to Greenland of June 1940 was proposed and practically organized by Canadian Aluminum," the US Consul Penfield reported shortly afterwards, quoting his Canadian counterpart in Greenland, see Burchardt, *Amerikas langer Arm*, 110. Since then, Alcan's role has also been discussed by historians. The German historian Lothar Burchardt, who specializes in business history among other things, gives great emphasis to the role played by the Canadian company, see *Amerikas langer Arm* throughout. Gordon Smith, on the other hand, alleges that "contrary to a widely-held supposition among non-Canadians at the time, it was not true that the Company was the actual organizer and director of the expedition behind the scenes," Smith, "'This was not the time'," 275 n136. The interpretation adopted here is that Alcan was one of several important actors.

3   Burchardt, *Amerikas langer Arm*, 90–91.

4   Murray (ed.), *Documents*, 948.

5   Ibid., 951.

6   Diaries of William Lyon Mackenzie King, 1893 to 1950. Library and Archives Canada. April 11, 1940.

7   Murray (ed.), *Documents*, 949–950.

8   Ibid., 954. In the original document, "Eskimos" is spelled "Esquimaux" but has been adjusted here for ease of reading.

9   Gordon Smith, "'This was not the time for this type of 1890 imperialism': Cryolite, Control, and Canada-US Relations over Greenland, 1940," *The Northern Mariner/Le marin du nord*, vol. 31, no. 3 (Autumn 2021): 249.

10   Maurice A. Pope, *Soldiers and Politicians* (Toronto: University of Toronto Press, 1962), 144.

11   Burchardt, *Amerikas langer Arm*, 91.

12   Jay Pierrepont Moffat's diary, April 12, 1940. Quoted from Løkkegaard, *Gesandtskab*, 63 and 518 n37.

13   *Congressional Record. Proceedings and Debates of the 76th Congress, Third Session, vol. 86, part 5*, 4641.

14   "U.S. to Establish Ties with Iceland," *The New York Times*, April 17, 1940: 13.

15   Berle and Jacobs (eds.), *Navigating the Rapids*, 305–306.

16   *Papers relating to the foreign relations of the United States, Japan: 1931–1941, vol. 2* (Washington DC: United States Government Printing Office, 1943), 281.

17   Ibid., 283–284. The US fear that Japan would see equivalence between an occupation of Greenland and its own actions in East Asia, was not unfounded. On July 26, 1941, Mackenzie King met with the Japanese ambassador to Ottawa, Yoshizawa Seijiro, who made remarks to this effect: "The Minister said that if the Prime Minister would allow him to say it, just between ourselves, he would say that there was no difference in what Japan was doing [in Indochina] than in what the United States had done in sending troops to Iceland and taking Greenland

and Iceland under her protection." Diaries of William Lyon Mackenzie King, 1893 to 1950. Library and Archives Canada. July 26, 1941, 2. Significantly, Yoshizawa reported back to Tokyo from the same meeting, quoting himself as having made the following remark: "The United States stretched forth her hand and seized Greenland and Iceland, proclaiming that this was necessary in the interests of hemisphere defense. Well, now our ideal is an East-Asian sphere of co-prosperity and by the same logic as was used by the United States, say in Iceland, we occupied French Indo-China." *The Magic Background of Pearl Harbor*, vol. 2, Appendix (Washington DC: United States Government Printing Office, 1978), A-256.

18 Letter from Danish mission in Tokyo to Kauffmann, May 14, 1940. Washington DC Diplomatic Representation. 1930–1946. 8 V 5—V5/1. Danish National Archives.

19 Hugh L. Keenleyside, *Memoirs of Hugh L. Keenleyside, Vol. 2: On the Bridge of Time* (Toronto: McClelland and Stewart, 1982), 190.

20 Tony McCulloch, "Mackenzie King and the North Atlantic Triangle in the Era of Munich, 1938–1939," *London Journal of Canadian Studies*, vol. 36, no. 1 (2021): 3.

21 Diaries of William Lyon Mackenzie King, 1893 to 1950. Library and Archives Canada. April 29, 1940, 1.

22 Diaries of William Lyon Mackenzie King, 1893 to 1950. Library and Archives Canada. April 24, 1940, 3.

23 Murray (ed.), *Documents*, 968–969.

24 Diaries of William Lyon Mackenzie King, 1893 to 1950. Library and Archives Canada. April 29, 1940, 1–2.

25 Ibid., 3.

26 The American fears that US or Allied moves on Greenland could be used as a pretext by Japan was seen as genuine by at least some Canadian officials, Keenleyside, *Memoirs*, 190–191.

27 Keenleyside, *Memoirs*, 191.

28 Cordell Hull, *The Memoirs of Cordell Hull*, vol. 1, 757.

29 Quoted from Smith, "'This was not the time'," 256.

30 Diaries of William Lyon Mackenzie King, 1893 to 1950. Library and Archives Canada. April 29, 1940, 1–2.

31 Berle and Jacobs (eds.), *Navigating the Rapids*, 308.

32 Løkkegaard, *Danske gesandtskab*, 74–80.

33 Ibid., 523 n90.

34 Quoted from Smith, "'This was not the time'," 255 n62.

35 Ibid., 255 n62.

36 Burchardt, *Amerikas langer Arm*, 114.

37 Diaries of William Lyon Mackenzie King, 1893 to 1950. Library and Archives Canada. May 2, 1940.

38 Ibid.

39 Quoted from Smith, "'This was not the time'," 259.

40 Shelagh D. Grant, "Why the *St. Roch*? Why the Northwest Passage? Why 1940? New Answers to Old Questions," *Arctic*, vol. 46, no. 1 (March 1993): 85.

41 Pope, *Soldiers and Politicians*, 144–145.

42 Smith, "'This was not the time'," 259–260.

43 High Commissioner for Canada in London to Secretary for External Affairs, No. 527 (May 2, 1940), Public Archives of Canada, W. L. M. King Papers, MG 26 J4, Vol. 394, 277347–277349, quoted in Michael F. Scheuer, "On the Possibility That There May Be More To It Than That," *The American Review of Canadian Studies*, Vol. 12, No. 3 (Fall 1982): 74–75.

Chapter 6: Standoff at Ivigtut

1   Murray (ed.), *Documents*, 987.
2   Smith, "'This was not the time'," 260.
3   Ibid.
4   Hudson's Bay Company History Foundation, "R. M. S. Nascopie," accessed June 19, 2024. https://www.hbcheritage.ca/things/technology/rms-nascopie.
5   Berry, "North Atlantic Triangle," 259–260 n764.
6   Quoted from Scheuer, "On the Possibility," 75.
7   Quoted from Smith, "'This was not the time'," 260.
8   Smith, "'This was not the time'," 269–270. According to Berry, "North Atlantic Triangle," 264, there were eight members of the Royal Canadian Mounted Police on board the *Nascopie*.
9   "Consul to Greenland Is Leaving on Cutter," *The New York Times*, May 10, 1940: 6.
10 George L. West, oral history, interviewed by Charles Stuart Kennedy, Foreign Affairs Oral History Collection, Association for Diplomatic Studies and Training, Arlington, VA, adst.org, 8.
11 *The American Foreign Service Journal*, vol. 17, no. 6 (June 1940): 321.
12 Penfield, "Northward Ho!" 65.
13 Ibid., 66.
14 Patrick Abbazia, *Mr. Roosevelt's Navy: The Private War of the U.S. Atlantic Fleet, 1939–1942* (Annapolis MD: Naval Institute Press, 1975), 87.
15 *Foreign relations of the United States. Diplomatic Papers, 1940, vol. 2: General and Europe* (Washington DC: Government Printing Office, 1957), 364.
16 Løkkegaard, *Danske gesandtskab*, 167.
17 "Summary of conversation with Ms. Balle, returned from Greenland on January 11, 1941," Director K. H. Oldendow's papers. Greenland 1940–1945. Danish National Archives.
18 Penfield, "Northward Ho!" 67.
19 "Dansk Sømand Hjem fra Grønland" ["Danish Sailor Has Returned Home from Greenland"], *Nationaltidende*, June 25, 1941: 7.
20 *Foreign relations 1940, vol. 2*, 365.
21 Ibid., 365–366.
22 *The Public Papers and Addresses of Franklin D. Roosevelt*, 1940 volume. ed. Samuel I. Rosenman (New York NY: The Macmillan Company, 1941), 199.
23 Cable from Svane to Brun, May 30, 1940. Aksel Svane, 1940–1945, Telegrams, 1940 5 29–9 2. Danish National Archives.
24 Berle and Jacobs (eds.), *Navigating the Rapids*, 319–320.
25 Ibid., 313.
26 "Da 'Jutho' bragte til Grønland under sidste verdenskrig" ["When 'Jutho' Carried Supplies to Greenland During the Recent World War"], *Atuagagdliutit*, December 23, 1965: 14.
27 Smith, "'This was not the time'," 270.
28 Berry, "North Atlantic Triangle," 264; Burchardt, *Amerikas langer Arm*, 112–113.
29 Quoted from Smith, "'This was not the time'," 276 n143.
30 Quoted from Burchardt, *Amerikas langer Arm*, 113.
31 Cable from Svane to Brun, May 30, 1940. Aksel Svane, 1940–1945, Telegrams, 1940 5 29–9 2. Danish National Archives.
32 Burchardt, *Amerikas langer Arm*, 115, Løkkegaard, *Gesandtskab*, 165.
33 Løkkegaard, *Danske gesandtskab*, 165.
34 *Foreign relations, 1940, vol. 2*, 368; cable from Svane to Ivigtut, June 6, 1940. Aksel Svane, 1940–1945, Telegrams, 1940 5 29–9 2. Danish National Archives.
35 *Foreign relations, 1940, vol. 2*, 370.

36   Burchardt, *Amerikas langer Arm*, 117.
37   Cable from Svane to Ivigtut, June 3, 1940. Aksel Svane, 1940–1945, Telegrams, 1940 5 29–92. Danish National Archives.
38   Cable from Svane to Ivigtut, June 4, 1940. Aksel Svane, 1940–1945, Telegrams, 1940 5 29–92. Danish National Archives.
39   *Foreign relations, 1940*, vol. 2, 369.
40   Berle and Jacobs (eds.), *Navigating the Rapids*, 321.
41   Ibid.
42   Burchardt, *Amerikas langer Arm*, 118
43   Berry, "North Atlantic Triangle," 270.
44   Cable from Svane and Brun to Kauffmann, June 3, 1940. Washington DC Diplomatic Representation. 1930–1946. 8 V 5–V5/1. Danish National Archives.
45   Løkkegaard, *Danske gesandtskab*, 168. For Penfield accompanying Svane, see also *Foreign relations, 1940*, vol. 2, 368.
46   Cable from Svane to Brun, June 14, 1940. Aksel Svane, 1940–1945, Telegrams, 1940 5 29–9 2. Danish National Archives.
47   Quoted from Berry, "North Atlantic Triangle," 271.
48   Burchardt, *Amerikas langer Arm*, 118.
49   Quoted from Berry, "North Atlantic Triangle," 272.
50   *Foreign relations, 1940*, vol. 2, 369–370.
51   Ibid., 371.
52   Langer and Gleason, *Challenge to Isolation*, 685.

Chapter 7: The First German Mission

1   Dag Indebø and Anders Nøkling, "Den hemmelege flyplassen på isbreen" ["The Secret Airfield on the Glacier"], NRK, March 17, 2019.
2   Ibid.
3   "Menschlich abgestimmt", *Der Spiegel*, March 1, 1950. The report in the periodical is the only source that has emerged so far linking the airfield on the Norwegian glacier to German designs for Greenland. The article points out that Madelung was the head of the Graf Zeppelin Research Institute, which undertook various scientific projects in the war years within the field of aeronautics. However, there is no mention of Greenland-related projects in the most comprehensive treatment yet of the activities of the research institute and its predecessor organizations, Christian Elsässer, *Die Forschungsanstalt Graf Zeppelin 1937–1945: Ein Überblick* [*The Graf Zeppelin Research Institute 1937–1945: An Overview*] (Berlin: Logos Verlag, 2022). As described in Elsässer's book, a large number of records associated with the research institute were destroyed at the end of the war. It is thus possible but speculative, that the research institute "had some form of connection to Greenland, as it would offer the right kind of very adverse test conditions in a non-combat environment." Elsässer, personal communication May 12, 2023.
4   On Madelung's biography, see Elsässer, *Die Forschungsanstalt*, 84–89.
5   "Menschlich abgestimmt", *Der Spiegel*, March 1, 1950.
6   Indebø and Nøkling, "Hemmelege."
7   Rupert Holzapfel, "Deutsche Polarforschung 1940/45" ["German Polar Exploration 1940–1945"], *Polarforschung*, vol 21, no. 2 (1951): 89.
8   Holzapfel's wish that a ship be placed at his disposal is not mentioned directly in the sources but can be deduced from Oldendow's remark at the meeting in the Foreign Ministry that such an arrangement was out of the question.

9 *Parlamentariske Kommissions Beretning* [*Report of the Parliament Commission*], XIII, addenda, vol. 6 (Copenhagen: J. H. Schultz, 1954), 1045.

10 Account by Knud Oldendow, December 13, 1961. Finn Løkkegaard papers, Håndskriftssamlingen, Danish National Archives.

11 Ibid.

12 Ibid.

13 *Parlamentariske*, XIII, addenda, vol. 6, 1045.

14 Ibid.; Rupert Holzapfel, "Deutsche Polarforschung 1940/45" ["German Polar Exploration 1940–1945"], *Polarforschung*, vol 21, no. 2 (1951): 89; "Wetterdienst im Nordmeer," September 16, 1940. *Kriegstagebuch der Seekriegsleitung 1939–1945* [*War Diary of the Naval Command 1939–1945*], *Part A, vol. 13* (Herford and Bonn: Verlag E. S. Mittler & Sohn, 1989), 215–216.

15 Ebbe Munck, *Døren til den frie verden* [*The Door to the Free World*] (Copenhagen: Det Schønbergske Forlag, 1967), 28. A detailed account of the Furenak expedition, which has been an important help in preparing parts of this chapter, is John T. Lauridsen, "' …et uhyre vindende væsen …' Nazisten som gik sine egne veje—Curt Carlis Hansen" ["'… An Extremely Likable Character …' The Nazi Who Chose His Own Path—Curt Carlis Hansen"] in *Over stregen—under bevægelsen* [*Crossing the Line During the Occupation*], ed. John T. Lauridsen (Copenhagen: Gyldendal, 2007), 198–204.

16 "Danner spillet en rolle ved Kuhlmanns Kidnapning" ["Danner Played a Role in the Kidnapping of Kuhlmann"], *Politiken*, June 12, 1934: 2. See also Lauridsen, "Uhyre," 189–193.

17 Mabel Carlis Hansen, "En beretning om Curt Carlis Hansens liv og mærkelige skæbne" ["An account of the Life and Strange Fate of Curt Carlis Hansen"], unpublished manuscript, Carlis Hansen papers, Danish National Library.

18 *Parlamentariske*, XIII, addenda, vol. 6, 1052.

19 Edward Thomas, "Norway's role in British wartime intelligence," Newcastle University, accessed February 1, 2024, https://www.staff.ncl.ac.uk/j.p.boulton/xread/thomas.htm

20 Lauridsen, "… uhyre," 198.

21 Summary of interrogation of three members of *Furenak*'s crew, Danish Mission in Reykjavik, September 13, 1940. Carlis Hansen papers. Danish Royal Library.

22 Ibid.

23 Jørgen Tvermose to Franz Selinger, May 29, 1982. Franz Selinger archive, Bundeswehr Military History Museum, Dresden.

24 Summary of interrogation of three members of *Furenak*'s crew, Danish Mission in Reykjavik, September 13, 1940.

25 Jørgen Tvermose to Franz Selinger, May 29, 1982. Selinger archive.

26 Report from Sicherheitsdienst in Oslo, August 12, 1940, published in Stein Ugelvik Larsen, Beatrice Sandberg and Volker Dahm, *Meldungen aus Norwegen 1940–1945: Die geheimen Lageberichte des Befehlshabers der Sicherheitspolizei und des SD in Norwegen* [*Intelligence from Norway 1940–1945: The Secret Reports from the Commander of the Security Police and Security Service in Norway*], vol. 1, (Munich: Oldenbourg Wissenschaftsverlag, 2008), 52.

27 Munck, *Døren*, 32.

28 Summary of interrogation of three members of *Furenak*'s crew, Danish Mission in Reykjavik, September 13, 1940.

29 Munck, *Døren*, 32.

30 F. H. Hinsley, *British Intelligence in the Second World War: Its Influence on Strategy and Operations*, vol. 1 (London: Her Majesty's Stationery Office, 1979), 286.

Chapter 8: The Norwegian Connection

1   Susan Barr, *Norway—A Consistent Polar Nation? Analysis of an image seen through the history of the Norwegian Polar Institute* (Oslo: Kolofon, 2003), 205–206; John Giæver, *Fra 'Little Norway' til Karasjok* [*From 'Little Norway' to Karasjok*] (Oslo: Tiden Norsk Forlag, 1975), 7–16.

2   Giæver, *'Little Norway,'* 11.

3   Ibid., 9–10.

4   Løkkegaard, *Gesandtskab*, 306.

5   Ib Poulsen to Franz Selinger, May 24, 1982. Selinger archive.

6   Magnus Sefland, "Runne-familien frå Brandal: Nokre hendingar i krig og fred" ["The Runne Family from Brandal: Some Events in War and Peace"], *Isflaket: Polarmagasin frå Ishavsmuseet*, vol. 23, no. 4 (2021): 6. The standard multi-volume work on Norway's history in World War II goes further than warranted by the sources when stating that the Veslekari mission was organized by Abwehr. Magne Skodvin (ed.), *Norge i krig: Fremmedåk og frihetskamp 1940–1945* [*Norway at War: Foreign Yoke and Freedom Fight*], vol. 3, Tim Greve, *Verdenkrig* [*World War*] (Oslo: Aschehoug, 1985), 48.

7   28 Giæver, *'Little Norway,'* 9; E. A. Steen, *Norges Sjøkrig 1940–1945* [*Norway's War at Sea 1940–1945*], vol. 7, *Marinens operasjoner i arktiske farvann og i Island, på Grønland, Jan Mayen og Svalbard* [*Naval Operations in Arctic Waters and at Iceland, Greenland, Jan Mayen and Svalbard*] (Oslo: Forsvarets krigshistoriske avdeling and Gyldendal Norsk Forlag, 1960), 28.

8   Kåre Rodahl, "Med 'Polarbjørn' til Grønland og med fallskjerm til Norge" ["With *Polarbjørnen* to Greenland and by Parachute into Norway"], in *Polar-Årboken* [*The Polar Yearbook*], ed. Odd Arnesen (Oslo: Gyldendal Norsk Forlag, 1945), 61.

9   Sophie Jackson, *British Interrogation Techniques in the Second World War* (Cheltenham: The History Press, 2012); Kjell-G. Kjær and Magnus Sefland, "The Arctic ship *Veslekari*," *Polar Record*, vol. 41, no. 1 (2005): 62; Nigel West, *Hitler's Nest of Vipers: The Rise of the Abwehr* (Barnsley: Pen and Sword Books, 2022), 65–66.

10   Giæver, *'Little Norway,'* 10.

11   Ibid., 11.

12   Norges Svaldbard-og Ishavs-Undersøkelser, *Report on the Activities of Norges Svalbard-og Ishavs-Undersøkelser 1936–1944* (Oslo: Jacob Dybwad, 1945), 33 and 35.

13   Ib Poulsen to Franz Selinger, May 24, 1982. Selinger archive.

14   Giæver, *'Little Norway,'* 8–9, 11.

15   Steen, *Norges Sjøkrig*, 24–25.

16   Rodahl, "Med 'Polarbjørn'," 63. Giæver has a different version, saying that the telegrapher was watching puzzled and "with his hands in his pockets" when the Marines landed, Giæver, *'Little Norway,'* 15.

17   Steen, *Norges Sjøkrig*, 26.

18   Giæver, *'Little Norway,'* 13; Steen, *Norges Sjøkrig*, 28.

19   N. O. Jensen, "Aarsberetning Eskimonæs 1940–41," Grønlands Styrelse Hovedkontoret. 1942–1945. Landsfogeden Sydgrønland, Jnr. 122: Begivenheder Østkysten: 4.

20   Jon Ulvensøen, *Brennpunkt Nord: Værtjenestekrigen 1940–45* [*Flashpoint North: The Weather War 1940–45*] (Oslo: Forsvarsmuseet, 1991), 12.

21   Adolf Hoel, "Norges Svalbard-og Ishavsundersøkelsers ekspedisjoner til Svalbard og Grønland under de to verdenskriger" ["The Expeditions of the Norwegian Svalbard and Arctic Ocean Survey to Svalbard and Greenland During the Two World Wars"], in *Polarboken 1956* [*The Polar Book 1956*], eds. Helge Ingstad and Søren Richter (Oslo: Norsk Polarklubb, 1956), 188.

22 N. O. Jensen, "Aarsberetning Eskimonæs 1940–41", Grønlands Styrelse Hovedkontoret. 1942–1945. Landsfogeden Sydgrønland, Jnr. 122: Begivenheder Østkysten: 4; N. O. Jensen, "Patruljetjenestens oprettelse" ["The Establishment of the Patrol Service"], *Grønlandsposten*, December 31, 1945: 286.

23 *The Coast Guard at War: Greenland Patrol* (US Coast Guard Headquarters, 1945), 8.

24 Giæver, *'Little Norway,'* 14.

25 Løkkegaard, *Gesandtskab*, 308–309.

26 State Department archive F. W. 859B. 01/283, memo on conversation on August 14, 1940, quoted from Løkkegaard, *Gesandtskab*, 564 n23.

27 State Department archive F. W. 859B. 01/283, quoted from Løkkegaard, *Gesandtskab*, 564 n24.

28 Willie Knutsen and Will C. Knutsen, *Arctic Sun on My Path: The True Story of America's Last Great Polar Explorer* (Guilford CT: The Lyons Press, 2005), 182.

29 Steen, *Norges Sjøkrig*, 30.

30 Norges Svaldbard- og Ishavs-Undersøkelser, *Report*, 34–35.

31 Summary of interrogation of three members of *Furenak*'s crew, Danish Mission in Reykjavik, September 13, 1940.

32 Jørgen Tvermose to Franz Selinger, May 29, 1982. Selinger archive.

33 Summary of interrogation of three members of *Furenak*'s crew, Danish Mission in Reykjavik, September 13, 1940; Steen, *Norges Sjøkrig*, 31.

34 Ibid.

35 Lauridsen, "…uhyre," 202.

36 Ibid.

37 Summary of interrogation of three members of *Furenak*'s crew, Danish Mission in Reykjavik, September 13, 1940.

38 Jørgen Tvermose to Franz Selinger, May 29, 1982. Selinger archive.

39 Steen, *Norges Sjøkrig*, 31.

40 Ibid., 31–32.

41 Jørgen Tvermose to Franz Selinger, May 29, 1982. Selinger archive.

42 Jørgen Tvermose to Reventlow, Danish mission in London, October 1940. Carlis Hansen papers. Danish Royal Library.

43 Jørgen Tvermose to Reventlow, Danish mission in London, October 1940.

44 Ib Poulsen, Begivenhederne i Nordøstgrønland under den anden verdenskrig [Events in Northeastern Greenland during World War Two], 1946, Selinger archive.

45 Carlis Hansen, "En beretning," 18.

46 Ibid.

47 Summary of interrogation of three members of *Furenak*'s crew, Danish Mission in Reykjavik, September 13, 1940.

48 Brun to Kauffmann, September 18, 1940. 2–0516 Washington DC, Diplomatic Mission, 8 U27—U30/1, Danish National Archives.

49 Radiogram sent from de Lemos to Aksel Svane, November 12, 1940. 2–0516 Washington DC, Diplomatic Mission, 8 U27–U30/1, Danish National Archives. See also Løkkegaard, *Gesandtskab*, 317; Steen, *Norges Sjøkrig*, 32.

50 Lauridsen, "…uhyre," 203–204.

51 Hull to Morgenstierne, September 23, 1940. Record Group 59, Entry A1 205-E General Records of the Department of State. Central Decimal File, 1940–1941, 859B.01/293B.

52 Ibid.

53 Ibid.

54 Letter from Fr. de Fontenay to Henrik Kauffmann, November 20, 1940. 2–0516 Washington DC, Diplomatic Representation. 1930–1946. 8 U27–U30/1. Danish National Archives.

55   Olav Riste, 'London-regjeringa': Norge i krigsalliansen 1940–1945 ['The London Government': Norway in the War Alliance 1940–1945], vol. 1, 1940–1942: Prøvetid [Period of Trial] (Oslo: Det Norske Samlaget, 1973), 33.

56   Bo Lidegaard, I Kongens Navn [In the Name of the King] (Copenhagen: Samleren, 1996), 181–182.

57   Jørgen Haugan, Solgudens fall: Knut Hamsun—en litterær biografi [Fall of the Sun God: Knut Hamsun, a Literary Biography] (Oslo: Aschehoug, 2004), 309–310; Tore Rem, Knut Hamsun: Rejsen til Hitler [Knut Hamsun: Journey to Hitler] (Vordingborg: Vild Maskine, 2015), 115.

58   Haugan, Solgudens fall, 308.

59   Harald S. Næss (ed.), Knut Hamsuns Brev [Knut Hamsun's Letters], vol. 6, 1934–1950 (Oslo: Gyldendal, 2000), 255–256.

60   Gustav Smedal, Patriotisme og Landssvik [Patriotism and Treason] (Oslo: Self-published,1949), 18. It is possible that the diary was written retrospectively. However, it is likely to reflect Smedal's thoughts at the time relatively precisely, see Næss ed., Knut Hamsuns Brev, vol. 6, 254.

61   Næss (ed.), Knut Hamsuns Brev, vol. 6, 256; see also Haugan, Solgudens fall, 309.

62   Hamsun wrote the original letter in the Norwegian language on June 15, but the German version was sent off to Ribbentrop on June 21, Næss ed., Knut Hamsuns Brev, vol. 6, 257–258 and 260–262.

63   Næss (ed.), Knut Hamsuns Brev, vol. 6, 257–258; see also Haugan, Solgudens fall, 310.

64   Næss (ed.), Knut Hamsuns Brev, vol. 6, 259–260; see also Rem, Knut Hamsun, 115.

65   Næss (ed.), Knut Hamsuns Brev, vol. 6, 265. Ribbentrop's reply has not been found, but the gist of his message can be understood from Hamsun's letter to Smedal dated August 12, 1940.

66   Næss (ed.), Knut Hamsuns Brev, vol. 6, 271–272.

67   Ibid., 273.

68   Ibid., 274.

69   Hamsun had noted repeatedly before his departure that Ribbentrop's attention was probably directed towards Romania at the time. Næss (ed.), Knut Hamsuns Brev, vol. 6, 269 and 271.

70   Smedal, Patriotisme, 22–23.

71   Ibid.

72   Haugan, Solgudens fall, 310.

73   Lidegaard, I Kongens Navn, 181–182.

Chapter 9: Preempting the Nazis

1   Kauffmann to Munch, "De Forenede Staters Holdning specielt forsaavidt angaar Grønland" ["The US Position Especially with Regards to Greenland"], September 4, 1940, 14. Director K. H. Oldendow's papers. Greenland 1940–1945. Danish National Archives.

2   Løkkegaard, Danske gesandtskab, 311. Berle note quoted from ibid., 565 n34.

3   Note from Einar Blechingberg, December 7, 1940. Washington DC, diplomatic representation, 1930–1946. 8 U27 U30/1. Danish National Archives.

4   Phoebe Kornfeld, Passionate Publishers: The Founders of the Black Star Photo Agency (Bloomington IN: Archway Publishing, 2021), 23.

5   Gerhard Wagner (ed.), Lagevorträge des Oberbefehlshabers der Kriegsmarine vor Hitler 1939–1945 [Briefings of Hitler by the Supreme Commander of the Navy, 1939–1945] (Munich: J. F. Lehmanns Verlag, 1972), 154.

6   Kriegstagebuch der Seekriegsleitung 1939–1945 [War Diary of the Naval Command 1939–1945], Part A, vol. 12 (Herford and Bonn: Verlag E. S. Mittler & Sohn, 1989), 99.

7   Tilo Krause, "Tyskernes Grønlandsplaner under 2. Verdenskrig" ["German Plans for Greenland during World War Two"], Tidsskriftet Grønland, vol. 55, no. 5–6 (December 2007): 206–207.

8   Knutsen and Knutsen, *Arctic Sun*, 181.

9   Malcolm Willoughby, *The U.S. Coast Guard in World War II* (Annapolis MD: United States Naval Institute, 1957), 96.

10 *The Coast Guard at War: Greenland Patrol* (US Coast Guard Headquarters, 1945), 8; Langer and Gleason, *Challenge to Isolation*, 685–686.

11 Aksel Svane, "Beretning angaaende den politiske Udvikling i Grønland i Aarene 1940–41" ["Account of the Political Development in Greenland during the Years 1940–41"], quoted from Paul E. Ancker, "Narsarsuaq Air Base (B.W.-1), 1941–1958." *Tidsskriftet Grønland*, vol. 41 no. 4–5 (August 1993): 134.

12 *The Papers of George Catlett Marshall, vol. 2, "We Cannot Delay," July 1, 1939–December 6, 1941* (Baltimore and London: The Johns Hopkins University Press, 1986), 303–304.

13 *Foreign Relations of the United States. Diplomatic Papers, 1940*, vol. 2, *General and Europe* (Washington DC: United States Government Printing Office, 1957), 372.

14 Summary of conversation with Einar Nørager Olsen, January 15, 1941. Director K. H. Oldendow's papers. Greenland 1940–1945. Danish National Archives.

15 When a Coast Guard cutter visited Ivigtut in October, the gun had still not been assembled, see Langer and Gleason, *Challenge to Isolation*, 685.

16 Summary of conversation with sailor Christian Sørensen, 1941. Director K. H. Oldendow's papers. Greenland 1940–1945. Danish National Archives.

17 Berle and Jacobs (eds.), *Navigating the Rapids*, 331.

18 Stetson Conn, Rose C. Engelman and Byron Fairchild, *Guarding the United States and Its Outposts* [*United States Army in World War II: The Western Hemisphere*] (Washington DC: Center of Military History, 1964), 443.

19 Berle and Jacobs (eds.), *Navigating the Rapids*, 332.

20 The account of the meeting is based on *Foreign Relations of the United States. Diplomatic Papers, 1940*, vol. 2, *General and Europe* (Washington DC: United States Government Printing Office, 1957), 372–376.

21 Svane, "Uafhængig," 542.

22 "Summary of conversation with Ms. Balle, returned from Greenland on January 11, 1941," Director K. H. Oldendow's papers. Greenland 1940–1945. Danish National Archives.

23 George L. West, oral history, interviewed by Charles Stuart Kennedy, Foreign Affairs Oral History Collection, Association for Diplomatic Studies and Training, Arlington, VA, adst.org, 8.

24 Quoted from Jens Heinrich, "Eske Brun og det modern Grønlands tilblivelse 1932–64" ["Eske Brun and the Emergence of Modern Greenland 1932–64"], PhD diss., University of Greenland, 2010, 80.

25 "Greenland Governor Calls U.S. Aid Prompt," *The New York Times*, August 13, 1940: 23.

26 Quoted from Hanna i Horni, "British and U.S. post-neutrality policy in the North Atlantic area 09.04.1940–1945: The role of Danish representatives" (PhD diss., Swansea University, 2010), 271.

27 "Summary of conversation with Ms. Balle, returned from Greenland on January 11, 1941," Director K. H. Oldendow's papers. Greenland 1940–1945. Danish National Archives.

28 Quoted from Løkkegaard, *Danske gesandtskab*, 544 n114.

29 Quoted from ibid., 544 n119.

30 Troels Fink, "Det danske gesandtskab i Washington 1940–42" ["The Danish Mission in Washington 1940–42"], *Historie*, vol. 8, no. 3 (1970): 323.

31 George L. West, oral history, interviewed by Charles Stuart Kennedy, Foreign Affairs Oral History Collection, Association for Diplomatic Studies and Training, Arlington, VA, adst.org, 9.

32 "Summary of conversation with Ms. Balle, returned from Greenland on January 11, 1941," Director K. H. Oldendow's papers. Greenland 1940–1945. Danish National Archives.

Chapter 10: The Yanks Are Coming

1   *The Public Papers and Addresses of Franklin D. Roosevelt*, 1940 volume. ed. Samuel I. Rosenman (New York NY: The Macmillan Company, 1941), 689.

2   William L. Langer and S. Everett Gleason, *The Undeclared War 1940–1941* (New York NY: Harper & Brothers, 1953), 189.

3   Quoted from Løkkegard, *Danske gesandtskab*, 567 n59.

4   *Foreign Relations of the United States. Diplomatic Papers, 1941*, vol. 2, *Europe* (Washington DC: United States Government Printing Office, 1959), 35.

5   Svane to Penfield, February 1, 1941, Aksel Svane's private archive, quoted in Heinrich, "Eske Brun," 93.

6   Berle and Jacobs (eds.), *Navigating the Rapids*, 356.

7   Quoted from Løkkegard, *Gesandtskab*, 569 n74.

8   Løkkegard, *Gesandtskab*, 327–328.

9   Berle and Jacobs (eds.), *Navigating the Rapids*, 356–357; *Foreign Relations of the United States. Diplomatic Papers, 1941*, vol. 2, *Europe*, 36–37.

10 Conn, Engelman and Fairchild, *Guarding the United States and Its Outposts*, 444.

11 *The Coast Guard at War: Greenland Patrol*, 10.

12 Fink, "Danske gesandtskab," 326. There is no consensus among historians on this interpretation, but I consider it plausible.

13 Løkkegard, *Danske gesandtskab*, 350–351.

14 Note from Prime Minister's office, Denmark, March 20, 1941. Director K. H. Oldendow's papers. Greenland 1940–1945. Danish National Archives.

15 *Foreign Relations of the United States. Diplomatic Papers, 1941*, vol. 2, *Europe*, 44–45.

16 Quoted from Løkkegard, *Danske gesandtskab*, 573 n110.

17 Svane, "Uafhængig gesandt," 533.

18 Quoted from Løkkegard, *Danske gesandtskab*, 580 n153.

19 Werner Schwerdtfeger and Franz Selinger, *Wetterflieger in der Arktis 1940–1944* [*Weather Pilot in the Arctic Region 1940–1944*] (Stuttgart: Motorbuch Verlag, 1982), 54–55.

20 Ibid., 48–49.

21 Ibid., 206.

22 *Foreign Relations of the United States. Diplomatic Papers, 1941*, vol. 2, *Europe*, 43.

23 This particular sentence was amended prior to publication of the war memoirs, since the Ultra Secret, the ability of British intelligence to read encoded German messages, had not yet been divulged to the public. David Reynolds, "The Ultra Secret and Churchill's War Memoirs," *Intelligence and National Security*, vol. 20, no. 2 (June 2005): 215–216.

24 Samuel Eliot Morison, *History of United States Naval Operations in World War II*, vol. 1, *The Battle of the Atlantic September 1939–May 1943* (Boston MA: Little, Brown and Company, 1947), 60.

25 Dathan, *Reindeer Botanist*, 425. Berle to Knox, April 25, 1941.

26 Winston S. Churchill, *The Second World War*, vol. 3, *The Grand Alliance* (New York NY: Houghton Mifflin, 1950), 121.

27 Conn, Engelman and Fairchild, *Guarding the United States and Its Outposts*, 451.

28 "Amerikanske Formodninger om tyske Tropper paa Grønland" ["American Assumptions about German Troops in Greenland"], *Nationaltidende*, April 27, 1941: 1.

29 *Den Parlamentariske Kommissions Beretninger*, vol. 5, (Copenhagen: J. H. Schultz, 1948), 252.

30 *Trial of the Major War Criminals Before the International Military Tribunal. Nuremberg 14 November 1945–1 October 1946, vol. 10: Proceedings 25 March 1946–6 April 1946* (Nuremberg: International Military Tribunal, 1947), 296.

31 Transcript of meeting on April 11, 1941, hosted by Henry Morgenthau, Jr. Diaries of Henry Morgenthau, Jr., book 388, 62. Franklin D. Roosevelt Presidential Library and Museum.

32 Quoted in Joseph P. Lash, *Roosevelt and Churchill 1939–1941: The Partnership That Saved the West* (New York NY: W. W. Norton & Co, 1976), 325.

33 Morison, *History of United States Naval Operations,* vol. 1, 61.

34 *The Public Papers and Addresses of Franklin D. Roosevelt*, 1941 volume. ed. Samuel I. Rosenman (New York NY: The Macmillan Company, 1950), 189.

35 Morison, *History of United States Naval Operations*, vol. 1, 61.

36 Conn, Engelman and Fairchild, *Guarding the United States and Its Outposts*, 452.

37 Telegram from United Kingdom High Commissioner in Canada to Dominion Office, May 31, 1941. National Archives.

38 *Papers of George Catlett Marshall*, vol. 2, 488–489.

39 John D. Carter, "The Early Development of Air Transport and Ferrying," in *The Army Air Forces in World War II*, vol. 1, *Plans and Early Operations: January 1939 to August 1942*, eds. Wesley Frank Craven and James Lea Cate (Chicago IL: University of Chicago Press, 1948), 343.

40 George L. West, oral history, interviewed by Charles Stuart Kennedy, Foreign Affairs Oral History Collection, Association for Diplomatic Studies and Training, Arlington, VA, adst.org, 10.

41 Ibid.

42 Vibe, *Ene ligger Grønland*, 110.

43 Report from American consulate, Godthaab, sent to Secretary of State, May 4, 1941, quoted from Horni, "British and U.S. post-neutrality policy," 268.

44 Report from American consulate, Godthaab, sent to Secretary of State, October 7, 1940, quoted from Horni, "British and U.S. post-neutrality policy," 268.

45 Report from American consulate, Godthaab, sent to Secretary of State, July 15, 1941, quoted from Horni, "British and U.S. post-neutrality policy," 268.

46 Ibid.

47 Summary of conversation with sailor Christian Sørensen, 1941. Director K. H. Oldendow's papers. Greenland 1940–1945. Danish National Archives.

48 Gam, *Een gang Grønland*, 141.

49 Summary of conversation with sailor Christian Sørensen, 1941. Director K. H. Oldendow's papers. Greenland 1940–1945. Danish National Archives.

50 Brun, *Mit Grønlandsliv,* 24.

51 "Ivigtut kryolitbrud," *Grønlandsposten*, March 1, 1947: 45–46.

52 "Foran Afskeden med Grønland" ["Before the Departure from Greenland"], *Grønlandsposten*, March 1, 1946: 46.

53 PRO, FO 371/24790, Postal Censorship Reports, New Series no. 98, 19.12.40, quoted from Horni, "British and U.S. post-neutrality policy," 270.

54 "Summary of conversation with Ms. Balle, returned from Greenland on January 11, 1941." Director K. H. Oldendow's papers. Greenland 1940–1945. Danish National Archives.

55 Dathan, *Reindeer Botanist*, 422.

56 Jørgen Fleischer, "Grønland under krigen," *Sermitsiak*, no. 19 (2005): 22.

57 Telegram from US consul, Godthaab, May 13,1941. Diaries of Henry Morgenthau, Jr., book 400, 182–183. Franklin D. Roosevelt Presidential Library and Museum.

58 Letter from Cordell Hull to Henry Morgenthau, Jr., April 28, 1941. Diaries of Henry Morgenthau, Jr., book 393 (April 30, 1941), 302–303. Franklin D. Roosevelt Presidential Library and Museum.

59 Fleischer, "Grønland under krigen," 22.

60 Ibid.

61 In 2005, when the National Museum of Greenland organized an exhibition on the war years, the organizers were surprised to come across several Nazi armbands, some showing a swastika and a polar bear. When approaching the public in hopes of obtaining testimony from people who might still have memories of what had happened, no one came forward.

62 Heinrich, *Eske Brun*, 172.

63 Fleischer, *Forvandlingens år*, 111.

64 J. M. Sehested to Vibe, April 5, 1945. Grønlands Styrelse. 1942–1945. Grønlands radio og Grønlandsposten, redaktionelle papirer, Danish National Archives.

65 Summary of conversation with sailor Christian Sørensen, 1941. Director K. H. Oldendow's papers. Greenland 1940–1945. Danish National Archives.

66 Heinrich, "Eske Brun," 112.

Chapter 11: Of Dogs and Men

1 Letter from Aage de Lemos to Eske Brun, August 31, 1941. 0030 Grønlands Styrelse. Hovedkontoret. 1942–1945. Landsfogeden Sydgrønland, Jnr. 122: Begivenheder Østkysten. 1942 mm. Danish National Archives.

2 Ibid.

3 Letter from Smith to Niels Ove Jensen, Aage de Lemos and Henryk Hoegh, August 25, 1941. 0030 Grønlands Styrelse. Hovedkontoret. 1942–1945. Landsfogeden Sydgrønland, Jnr. 122: Begivenheder Østkysten. 1942 mm. Danish National Archives.

4 Eske Brun, "Nordøstgrønlands danske Slædepatruljetjeneste 1941–45" ["The Danish Sledge Patrol in Northeast Greenland 1941–45"], *Grønlandsposten*, June 16, 1945: 133; Vibe, *Ene ligger Grønland*, 106.

5 Brun to Ocheltree, February 14, 1944. 0030 Grønlands Styrelse. Hovedkontoret. 1941–1945. Landsfogden Sydgrønland, Jnr. 124: Meteorologi. 1943–1944.

6 N. O. Jensen, "Patruljetjenestens oprettelse" ["Establishment of the Patrol"], *Grønlandsposten*, December 31, 1945: 286.

7 Kurt Olsen, *Et hundeliv* [*A Dog's Life*] (Copenhagen: Gyldendal, 1965), 18.

8 Brun to Ocheltree, February 14, 1944. 0030 Grønlands Styrelse. Hovedkontoret. 1941–1945. Landsfogden Sydgrønland, Jnr. 124: Meteorologi. 1943–1944.

9 Stimson and Knox to Roosevelt, April 22, 1941. US Navy, Naval History Division, Operational Archives, Office of the Chief of Naval Operations, Records of the Strategic Plans Division (formerly War Plans Division), Box 81. File: Signed Letters April 1941. Selinger Archive.

10 Roosevelt to Stimson and Knox, April 30, 1941. Selinger Archive.

11 Abbazia, *Mr. Roosevelt's Navy*, 179.

12 Brun to Ocheltree, February 14, 1944. 0030 Grønlands Styrelse. Hovedkontoret. 1941–1945. Landsfogden Sydgrønland, Jnr. 124: Meteorologi. 1943–1944.

13 Conn, Engelman and Fairchild, *Guarding the United States and Its Outposts*, 457–458.

14 Ibid.

15 Smith to Penfield, October 22, 1941. 0030 Grønlands Styrelse. Hovedkontoret. 1942–1945. Landsfogeden Sydgrønland, Jnr. 122: Begivenheder Østkysten. 1942 mm. Danish National Archives.

16 Max Dunbar, "Grønlandsårene" ["The Years in Greenland"], *Tidsskriftet Grønland*, vol 40, no. 9–10 (December 1992): 274.

17 Bob Desh, "The North-East Greenland Sledge Patrol," Foundation for Coast Guard History.

18 John A. Tilley, "The Coast Guard and the Greenland Patrol," 6.

19   N. O. Jensen, "Patruljetjenestens oprettelse" ["The Establishment of the Patrol Service"], *Grønlandsposten*, December 31, 1945: 286.

20   Heinrich, "Eske Brun," 140.

21   Dathan, *Reindeer Botanist*, 425.

22   Burchardt, *Amerikas langer Arm*, 283 n11.

23   Ibid., 281.

24   Ibid.

25   Morgenstierne to Hull, February 12, 1941. NA RG.59, 859B.01/339 National Archives.

26   For example, in January 1942, Morgenstierne signaled Norwegian interest to the US government when it was rumored that Greenland's postwar status was up for discussion Burchardt, *Amerikas*, 281.

27   Thorkild Kjærgaard, "Freden i Kiel, Grønland og Nordatlanten 1814–2014" ["The Peace of Kiel, Greenland and the North Atlantic 1814–2014"] *Fund og Forskning*, vol. 54 (2015): 394.

28   Olav Riste, 'London-regjeringa,' vol. 1, 72–73.

29   Blom, *Kampen*, 152–153.

30   Trygve Lie, *Med England i ildlinjen 1940–42* [*With England in the Firing Line 1940–42*] (Oslo: Tiden, 1956), 297–298.

31   Quoted from Olav Riste, "Solidarity at Home and Abroad: The Norwegian Experience of World War II," in *The Second World War as a National Experience*, ed. Sidney Aster (Ottawa: The Canadian Committee for the History of the Second World War, 1981), 96.

32   Lie, *Med England*, 176.

33   Riste, 'London-regjeringa,' vol. 1, 73. See also Frank Esmann Jensen, *Da fornuften sejrede. Det britiske udenrigsministeriums politik overfor Danmark under 2. Verdenskrig* [*When Common Sense Prevailed: The Policy of the British Foreign Office Toward Denmark During World War Two*] (Copenhagen: Fremad, 1972), 38–41.

34   Barr, *Norway*, 221.

35   Letter from the Norwegian Arctic Seas Committee to Quisling, June 7, 1941. Trial for treason 4208. Box 1. Norwegian National Archives. Quoted from Ketil Edgar Stordalmo, "Grønlandssakens utvikling under den andre verdenskrig" ["The Evolution of the Greenland Issue During World War II"] (Masters thesis, University of Tromsø, 2006), 48.

36   Smedal, *Patriotisme*, 38.

37   Ibid., 44.

38   Stordalmo, "Grønlandssakens utvikling," 48.

39   Letter from Hoel to Quisling, Smedal's archive. Quoted from Ivar Lohne, "Grønlandssaken 1919–1945: Fra borgerlig nasjonalt samlingsmerke til nasjonalsosialistisk symbolsak" ["The Greenland Issue 1919–1945: From Conservative National Rallying Point to Symbolic Cause of National Socialism"] (Masters thesis, University of Tromsø, 2000), 106.

40   Stordalmo, "Grønlandssakens utvikling," 48.

41   Ibid., 48–49.

42   Various sources give the number of people on board as 27 when *Buskø* was seized by *Northland*, see for example Willoughby, *U.S. Coast Guard*, 98. In addition, one must add three men dropped off on the east coast of Greenland before that.

43   Stordalmo, "Grønlandssakens utvikling," 49.

44   Frode Skarstein, "*Buskø*-affæren" ["The *Buskø* Incident"], *Historie*, no. 1 (2007): 12.

45   Stordalmo, "Grønlandssakens utvikling," 51.

46   Ibid., 52.

47   The standard Norwegian history of the war years exaggerates the German role in the *Buskø* expedition, stating it was directly organized by Abwehr. Skodvin (ed.), *Norge*, vol. 3, 50. A similar error is made in that work with regards to the *Veslekari* expedition.

48 Skarstein, "*Buskø*-affæren," 12.

49 Stordalmo, "Grønlandssakens utvikling," 52.

50 Skarstein, "*Buskø*-affæren," 13–14.

51 Selinger, *Von 'Nanok,'* 64.

52 Ibid., 65.

53 Skarstein, "*Buskø*-affæren," 14; Stordalmo, "Grønlandssakens utvikling," 53.

54 Henry Rudi with Lars Normann Sørensen, *Isbjørnkongen* [*The Polar Bear King*] (Oslo: Gyldendal Norsk Forlag, 1961), 206.

55 Poulsen, "Begivenhederne," 8.

56 Willoughby, *U.S. Coast Guard*, 98.

57 Ibid.

58 *The Coast Guard at War: Transports and Escorts*, vol. 5, part 1, *Escorts* (Washington, DC: US Coast Guard Headquarters, 1949), 84–85.

59 Carlton Skinner, oral history, National Archives.

60 "Brings Seized Ship from Greenland," *The New York Times*, October 15, 1941: 6.

61 Skarstein, "Buskø-affæren," 17.

62 "Prisoners of Defense," *Time*, October 27, 1941.

63 N. O. Jensen, "Patruljetjenestens oprettelse" ["The Establishment of the Patrol Service"], *Grønlandsposten*, December 31, 1945: 286.

64 Brun, *Grønlandsliv*, 96.

65 Jensen, "Patruljetjenestens oprettelse, 286.

66 Ibid.

67 Smith to Penfield, October 22, 1941. 0030 Grønlands Styrelse. Hovedkontoret. 1942–1945. Landsfogeden Sydgrønland, Jnr. 122: Begivenheder Østkysten. 1942 mm. Danish National Archives.

68 Rudi with Sørensen, *Isbjørnkongen*, 214.

69 Willoughby, *U.S. Coast Guard*, 98.

70 Ibid.

71 Carter, "Early Development," 343.

72 Transcript of oral history conducted October 22–23, 1975. Air Force Historical Research Agency, Maxwell AFB, file K239.0512–875. Quoted from Carroll V. Clines, *Bernt Balchen: Polar Aviator* (Washington DC and London: Smithsonian Institution Press, 1999), 130.

73 Bernt Balchen, *Come North With Me* (London: Hodder and Stoughton, 1958), 214.

74 Quoted from Clines, *Balchen*, 131.

75 Clines, *Balchen*, 136.

76 Undated notes from talk by Balchen, Balchen Collection, Maxwell AFB, file 168.7053–89. Quoted from Clines, *Balchen*, 142.

77 Edward P. Wood, *Per Ardua at Arcticum: The Royal Canadian Air Force in the Arctic and Sub-Arctic* (Antigonish: Mulroney Institute, 2007), 117.

78 Balchen, *Come North*, 228.

79 Vibe, *Ene ligger Grønland*, 104.

80 Brun, *Grønlandsliv*, 89.

81 Ibid.

Chapter 12: Amerika-Bomber

1 This section is based on "Stenographische Berichte über die GL-Besprechungen," May 12, 1942. RL3/14. Bundesarchiv. Militärachiv, Freiburg.

2 Harry N. Holmes, "National Survival through Science," *Science*, vol. 96, no. 2498 (November 13, 1942): 437.

3 Philip Lauritzen, "De fleste var bange for at udtale sig" ["Most Were Afraid to Speak Their Minds"], *Grønlandsposten*, May 6, 1992: 2.

4 "S/S '*Hans Egede*' forlist" ["*Hans Egede* Sunk"] *Grønlandsposten*, June 1, 1942: 61.

5 "Mindehøjtidelighed for '*Hans Egede*'" ["Memorial Service for *Hans Egede*"], *Grønlandsposten*, June 16, 1942: 76; "Mindehøjtidelighed for '*Hans Egede*'," *Grønlandsposten*, September 16, 1942: 153.

6 "Vi mindes" ["We Commemorate"], *Grønlandsposten*, June 1, 1942: 62.

7 Jürgen Rohwer, *Die U-Boot-Erfolge der Achsenmächte: 1939–1945* [*U-Boat Successes of the Axis Powers, 1939–1945*] (Munich: J. F. Lehmanns Verlag, 1968), 83.

8 *The Coast Guard at War: Greenland Patrol*, 44.

9 Ibid.

10 Thaddeus D. Novak, *Life and Death on the Greenland Patrol* (Gainesville FL: University Press of Florida, 2005), 129.

11 C. Gray Bream, oral history, interviewed by Charles Stuart Kennedy, Foreign Affairs Oral History Collection, Association for Diplomatic Studies and Training, Arlington, VA, adst.org, 8.

12 Carter, "Early Development," 344.

13 Poul Hennings, "Ikateq-basen under 2. verdenskrig" ["The Ikateq Base During World War Two"], in *Tasiilaq. Angmagssalik*, ed. Jørgen Fisker (Umanak: Nordiske Landes Bogforlag, 1984), 257.

14 Richard M. Leighton and Robert W. Coakley, *Global Logistics and Strategy* (*United States Army in World War II: The War Department*) (Washington DC: US Government Printing Office, 1955), 372.

15 Leighton and Coakley, *Global Logistics and Strategy*, 335.

16 Joseph Bykofsky and Harold Larsen, *The Transportation Corps: Operations Overseas* (*United States Army in World War II: The Technical Services*) (Washington DC: US Government Printing Office, 1957), 16.

17 Charles M. Wiltse, *The Medical Department: Medical Service in the Mediterranean and Minor Theaters* (*United States Army in World War II: The Technical Services*) (Washington DC: US Government Printing Office, 1965), 21–22.

18 Jonas A. Jonassen, "Weather and Communications," in *The Army Air Forces in World War II*, vol. 7, *Services Around the World*, eds. Wesley Frank Craven and James Lea Cate (Chicago IL: University of Chicago Press, 1958), 348.

19 Wiltse, *The Medical Department*, 21–22.

20 *The Papers of George Catlett Marshall, vol. 3, "The Right Man for the Job," December 7, 1941–May 31, 1943* (Baltimore and London: The Johns Hopkins University Press, 1991), 369.

21 *The Papers of George Catlett Marshall, vol. 4, "Aggressive and Determined Leadership," June 1, 1943–December 31, 1944* (Baltimore and London: The Johns Hopkins University Press, 1996), 185–186.

22 Jonassen, "Weather and Communications," 348.

23 C. Gray Bream, oral history, interviewed by Charles Stuart Kennedy, Foreign Affairs Oral History Collection, Association for Diplomatic Studies and Training, Arlington, VA, adst.org, 9.

24 Letter from Oscar Corp to Mrs. Corp, June 17, 1941. Danish National Archives. Grønlands Styrelse. Papers of Director K. H. Oldendow. Greenland during the War.

25 Ole Guldager, "Træk af Narsarsuaqs historie" ["Features of Narsarsuaq History"], *Tidsskriftet Grønland*, vol. 47, no. 4–5 (August 1999): 166.

26 Guldager, "Træk," 167.

27 Summary of article in *Christian Science Monitor* by Naomi Jackson, April 17, 1942. Director K. H. Oldendow's papers. Greenland 1940–1945. Danish National Archives.

28 Vibe, *Ene ligger Grønland*, 188.
29 Ibid., 187.
30 Summary of article in *Christian Science Monitor* by Naomi Jackson, April 17, 1942. Director K. H. Oldendow's papers. Greenland 1940–1945. Danish National Archives.
31 Christian Vibe to Gam, June 25, 1942. 0030 Grønlands Styrelse Hovedkontoret. 1942–1945. Grønlands radio og Grønlandsposten, redaktionelle papirer.
32 Dathan, *Reindeer Botanist*, 423.
33 Christian Vibe to Eli Henriksen, October 9, 1942. 0030 Grønlands Styrelse Hovedkontoret. 1942–1945. Grønlands radio og Grønlandsposten, redaktionelle papirer.
34 Ibid.
35 Novak, *Life and Death*, 123.
36 "Den juridiske ekspedition til Grønland" ["The Legal Expedition to Greenland"], vol. 5, (1948–1949), 48.
37 Heinrich, "Eske Brun," 126–127.
38 Guldager, "Træk," 167.
39 Novak, *Life and Death*, 105–106.
40 Ibid.
41 Sara Helms, "Signe Vest," in *Tasiilaq. Angmagssalik*, ed. Jørgen Fisker (Umanak: Nordiske Landes Bogforlag, 1984), 240.
42 Børne- og socialministeriet, "Notat om antallet af juridisk faderløse" ["Notice about the Number of Legally Fatherless"], December 5, 2016.
43 "Den juridiske ekspedition til Grønland" ["The Legal Expedition to Greenland"], vol. 5, (1948–1949), 50.
44 Jens Heinrich, "Historisk udredning om retsstillingen for børn født uden for ægteskab i Grønland 1914–1974 Afgivet til Statsministeriet d. 1. juni 2011," 54.
45 "Den juridiske ekspedition til Grønland" ["The Legal Expedition to Greenland"], vol. 5, (1948–1949), 46.
46 Vibe, *Ene ligger Grønland*, 112.
47 Guldager, "Træk," 167.

Chapter 13: The Reluctant Commander

1 J. D. M. Blyth, "German Meteorological Activities in the Arctic, 1940–45," *Polar Record*, vol. 6, no. 42 (July 1951): 198.
2 *Kriegstagebuch der Seekriegsleitung 1939–1945* [*War Diary of the Naval Command 1939–1945*], Part A, vol. 32 (Herford and Bonn: Verlag E. S. Mittler & Sohn, 1992), 280.
3 *Kriegstagebuch der Seekriegsleitung 1939–1945* [*War Diary of the Naval Command 1939–1945*], Part A, vol. 33 (Herford and Bonn: Verlag E. S. Mittler & Sohn, 1992), 126.
4 Franz Selinger, *Von 'Nanok' bis 'Eismitte': Meteorologische Unternehmungen in der Arktis 1940–1945* [*From 'Nanok' to 'Eismitte': Meteorological Undertakings in the Arctic*] (Hamburg: Convent, 2001), 119–120.
5 Extract of report of interrogation no. 208, August 28, 1943, 1.
6 Ibid., 2.
7 Knud Ernsted, "Hermann Ritter sagaen" ["The Hermann Ritter Saga"], in *Polarboken 2011–2012* [*The Polar Book 2011–2012*], eds. Susan Barr, Ian Gjertz and Fridtjof Mehlum (Oslo: Norsk Polarklubb, 2012), 124.
8 Knutsen and Knutsen, *Arctic Sun*, 66–67.

9   After the war, it was also published in English with the title *A Woman in the Polar Night*. Extract of report of interrogation no. 208, August 28, 1943, 2.

10 Extract of report of interrogation no. 208, August 28, 1943, 3.

11 Selinger, *Von 'Nanok,'* 119.

12 Gottfried Weiss, *Das arktische Jahr: Eine Überwinterung in Nordostgrönland* [*The Arctic Year: Spending the Winter in Northeast Greenland*] (Braunschweig: Georg Westermann Verlag, 1949), 9–19.

13 Weiss, *Das arktische Jahr*, 18.

14 Selinger, *Von 'Nanok,'* 120; Gottfried Weiss, "Bericht über die Ostgrönland-Expeditionen des Marine-Wetterdienstes 1942/43 und 1944" ["An Account of the East Greenland Expeditions of the Naval Weather Service in 1942–43 and 1944,"]2.

15 Scherer, Diary, August 22, 1942. Selinger archive.

16 Selinger, *Von 'Nanok,'* 120.

17 Ibid. Scherer, Diary, August 22, 1942. Selinger archive.

18 Scherer, Diary, August 22, 1942. Selinger archive.

19 "Operationsbefehl das Wetterbeobachtungsschiff 'Hermann'," August 7, 1942, 5.

20 Selinger, *Von 'Nanok,'* 120.

21 Blyth, "German Meteorological Activities," 199; Scherer, Diary, October 24 and 26, 1942. Selinger archive.

22 Scherer, Diary, August 28, 1942. Selinger archive.

23 Gottfried Weiss, "Bericht über die Ostgrönland-Expeditionen des Marine-Wetterdienstes 1942/43 und 1944 ["Account of the East Greenland Expeditions of the Naval Meteorological Service in 1942–1943 and 1944"], January 1947, 29.

24 Blyth, "German Meteorological Activities," 199.

25 Scherer, Diary, September 16, 1942. Selinger archive.

26 Ibid., September 1.

27 Ibid., September 14.

28 Ibid., October 19 and 20.

29 Selinger, *Von 'Nanok,'* 125.

30 Weiss, "Bericht," 5.

31 Ibid., 30.

32 Scherer, Diary, December 15, 1942. Selinger archive.

33 Account by Rudolf Sensse, October 10, 1986. Selinger archive.

34 Weiss, "Bericht", 30.

35 Account by Rudolf Sensse, October 10, 1986. Selinger archive.

36 Extract of report of interrogation no. 208, August 28, 1943, 2.

37 Confidential report on Ritter. August 20, 1943, 3.

38 "Bericht über den Sondereinsatz für 'Holzauge'," June 18, 1943. "Holzauge. Ostgrönland 1942–1943." Selinger archive.

39 Scherer, Diary, October 1, 1942. Selinger archive

40 *Kriegstagebuch der Seekriegsleitung 1939–1945* [*War Diary of the Naval Command 1939–1945*], *Part A, vol. 38* (Herford and Bonn: Verlag E. S. Mittler & Sohn, 19932), 133.

41 Scherer, Diary, September 16, 1942. Selinger archive.

42 Weiss, *Das arktische Jahr*, 80.

43 Jens Fog Jensen and Tilo Krause, *Slagmarksarkæologi i Nordøstgrønland: En arkæologisk-historisk undersøgelse af allierede og tyske vejrstationer fra Anden Verdenskrig* [*Battlefield Archeology in Northeast Greenland: An Archeological and Historical Investigation of Allied and German Weather Stations from World War Two*] (Copenhagen: The Arctic Centre at the Ethnographic Collections, The National Museum of Denmark, 2009), 88.

44 Weiss, "Bericht," 5.
45 Scherer, Diary, November 13, 1942. Selinger archive.
46 Ibid., November 14.
47 Ibid., October 26 and November 2.
48 Peter Schmidt Mikkelsen, *Nordøstgrønland 1908–60: Fangstmandsperioden* [*Northeast Greenland 1908–60: The Trapper Era*] (Copenhagen: Aschehoug, 2001), 348–349.
49 Weiss, *Das arktische Jahr*, 61–62.
50 Scherer, Diary, December 10, 1942. Selinger archive.
51 Ibid., November 16.
52 In his diary, Scherer describes him almost exclusively as "der Leitende" or "the leading (engineer)," but in his entry for October 31, explicitly states that he is referring to Wenglorz.
53 Scherer, Diary, November 22, 1942. Selinger archive.
54 Weiss, "Bericht," 30.
55 Scherer, Diary, December 24, 1942. Selinger archive.
56 Weiss, *Das arktische Jahr*, 92.
57 Kurt Olsen's diary, December 24, 1942. Selinger archive.

Chapter 14: The Hunt

1 The account of the showdown between the sledge patrol and the German participants in "Holzauge" described in this chapter and the next, is based mainly on primary sources in the form of contemporary documents, diaries and memoirs. The sources for these events are unusually rich, but not always internally consistent, and in some cases, they directly contradict each other. Therefore, any attempt to write a history of these dramatic events must necessarily be based on the author's personal interpretations and choices must be made when the sources do not agree. This is also the case here. Other recent attempts to describe the events from March to June 1943 include Anders Odsbjerg, *Nordøstgrønlands slædepatrulje 1941–45* [*The Northeast Greenland Sledge Patrol 1941–45*] (Copenhagen: Forlaget Komma, 1990); Jens Erik Schultz, *Krigen i Nordøstgrønland* [*The War in Northeast Greenland*] (Rønde: XSirius Book, 2020); and Selinger, *Von 'Nanok,'* 118–127, 145–149 and 160–170. Of particular note is Jens Fog Jensen and Tilo Krause, *Slagmarksarkæologi i Nordøstgrønland: En arkæologisk-historisk undersøgelse af allierede og tyske vejrstationer fra Anden Verdenskrig* [*Battlefield Archeology in Northeast Greenland: An Archeological and Historical Investigation of Allied and German Weather Stations from World War II*] (Copenhagen: The Arctic Centre at the Ethnographic Collections, The National Museum of Denmark, 2009), which in addition to a detailed chronological reconstruction of the events contains a careful assessment of the sources available.
2 Interview with Marius Jensen, March 1, 2001, by Leif Vanggaard, Mogens Guldbrandsen and Jens Erik Schultz. https://www.arktiskebilleder.dk/pages/search.php?search=%21collection26796#
3 Marius Jensen's diary, March 11, 1943. German translation; Selinger, 145, 160.
4 Ib Poulsen telegram to Brun, March 13, 1943. Grønlands Styrelse Hovedkontoret, 1941–1945. Landsfogden Sydgrønland, jnr. 124: Meteorologi. 1943–1944. Marius Jensen's diary, which is only available in a German translation, describes the discovery of a "German military sweater," not a tunic.
5 Marius Jensen's diary, March 11, 1943. German translation; Selinger, *Von 'Nanok,'* 145, 160.
6 Selinger, *Von 'Nanok,'* 160. At least one source claims that the person at the hut with Röttger was not Littmann but Heribert Wenglorz, Letter from Novotny to Kurt Olsen, August 16, 1967.
7 Letter from Novotny to Kurt Olsen, August 16, 1967.
8 Selinger, *Von 'Nanok,'* 160.

9   Transcript of message in Selinger archive.

10   Olsen, *Hundeliv*, 19.

11   Interview with Marius Jensen, March 1, 2001.

12   Ibid.

13   The last entry in Marius Jensen's diary is for March 11.

14   Interview with Marius Jensen, March 1, 2001.

15   Ibid.; Selinger, *Von 'Nanok,'* 145.

16   Selinger, *Von 'Nanok,'* 160.

17   Weiss, *Das arktische Jahr*, 100.

18   Selinger, *Von 'Nanok,'* 160, 162.

19   Transcript of message in Selinger archive.

20   Ib Poulsen, "Report of Events in Northeast Greenland in the Spring of 1943," Grønlands Styrelse Hovedkontoret, 1941–1945. Landsfogden Sydgrønland, jnr. 124: Meteorologi. 1943–1944. Danish National Archives.

21   Ib Poulsen telegram to Brun, March 13, 1943. Grønlands Styrelse Hovedkontoret, 1941–1945. Landsfogden Sydgrønland, jnr. 124: Meteorologi. 1943–1944. Danish National Archives.

22   Brun telegram to Poulsen, March 15, 1943. Grønlands Styrelse Hovedkontoret, 1941–1945. Landsfogden Sydgrønland, jnr. 125: Forsvarsforanstaltning. 1942–1945. Danish National Archives.

23   Kurt Olsen's diary, March 17, 1943.

24   Ibid.

25   Ibid.

26   Ib Poulsen, "Report of Events in Northeast Greenland in the Spring of 1943," Danish National Archives, Grønlands Styrelse Hovedkontoret 1941–1945 Landsfogden i Sydgrønland. Jnr. 124: Meteorologi 1943–1944: 2.

27   Henry Rudi, 223.

28   Ib Poulsen, "Report of Events in Northeast Greenland in the Spring of 1943," Danish National Archives, Grønlands Styrelse Hovedkontoret 1941–1945 Landsfogden i Sydgrønland. Jnr. 124: Meteorologi 1943–1944: 2.

29   Transcript of message in Selinger archive, 41.

30   Extract of report of interrogation no. 204, Karl Ritter, August 28, 1943.

31   Jensen and Krause, "Slagsmarksarkæologi," 20. On Breivikhytten, see Mikkelsen, *Nordøstgrønland*, 335.

32   Ib Poulsen, "Report of Events in Northeast Greenland in the Spring of 1943," Danish National Archives, Grønlands Styrelse Hovedkontoret 1941–1945 Landsfogden i Sydgrønland. Jnr. 124: Meteorologi 1943–1944: 3.

33   Selinger, *Von 'Nanok,'* 162.

34   Poulsen, "Report of Events," 3; Rudi, *Isbjørnkongen*, 225.

35   Poulsen, "Report of Events," 3.

36   Rudi, *Isbjørnkongen*, 225

37   The conversation is a combination of information contained in Rudi, *Isbjørnkongen*, 224 and Poulsen, "Report of Events," 3.

38   Poulsen, "Report of Events," 3.

39   Rudi, *Isbjørnkongen*, 225

40   Poulsen, "Report of Events," 4.

41   Selinger, *Von 'Nanok,'* 162.

42   The note is reproduced in almost identical versions in Bernt Balchen, *War Below Zero: The Battle for Greenland* (London: George Allen & Unwin, London, 1945), 26 and Selinger, *Von 'Nanok,'* 147.

43 Olsen to Brun, March 25, 1943. Grønlands Styrelse Hovedkontoret, 1941–1945. Landsfogden Sydgrønland, jnr. 124: Meteorologi. 1943–1944. Danish National Archives.

44 Ritter interrogation; Sensse to Erling Selnes, May 4, 1987.

45 Rudolf Sensse described the incident in a letter to Selinger in 1987: "I was the shooter, and Novotny was standing below with his submachine gun. I had only shot the dogs, but as Knudsen reached for his rifle, he had to be stopped from firing at Novotny." Sensse to Selinger, September 7, 1987.

46 Ib Poulsen, "Report of Events in Northeast Greenland in the Spring of 1943," Danish National Archives, Grønlands Styrelse Hovedkontoret 1941–1945 Landsfogden i Sydgrønland. Jnr. 124: Meteorologi 1943–1944: 6.

47 Poulsen, "Report of Events," 6; Ritter interrogation; Gottfried Weiss, "Bericht über die Ostgrönland-Expeditionen des Marine-Wetterdienstes 1942/43 und 1944 ["Account of the East Greenland Expeditions of the Naval Meteorological Service in 1942–1943 and 1944"], January 1947, 8.

48 "Oversigt over begivenhederne marts—august 1943."

49 Interview with Marius Jensen, March 1, 2001.

50 Ibid.

Chapter 15: The Escape

1 Telegram from Dönitz to "Holzauge," April 5, 1943. "Holzauge. Ostgrönland 1942–1943." Selinger archive.

2 Weiss, "Bericht," 7.

3 Account of "Holzauge" operation, written by Sensse on October 10, 1986. "Holzauge. Ostgrönland 1942–1943." Selinger archive.

4 "Bericht über den Sondereinsatz für 'Holzauge'," June 18, 1943. "Holzauge. Ostgrönland 1942–1943." Selinger archive.

5 Preliminary investigation of Ritter by German Navy, August 20, 1943, 5. "Holzauge. Ostgrönland 1942–1943." Selinger archive.

6 Extract of report of interrogation no. 204, Karl Ritter, August 28, 1943.

7 Interview with Jensen, March 1, 2001.

8 Ibid.

9 Ibid.

10 Preliminary investigation of Ritter by German Navy, August 20, 1943, 5–6.

11 Interview with Jensen, March 1, 2001.

12 Letter from Novotny to Kurt Olsen, July 6, 1967.

13 Preliminary investigation of Ritter by German Navy, August 20, 1943, 6.

14 Weiss, "Bericht," 8. According to a contemporary source, the departure took place on April 4.

15 Interview with Jensen, March 1, 2001.

16 Extract of report of interrogation no. 204, Karl Ritter, August 28, 1943.

17 Interview with Jensen, March 1, 2001.

18 Ibid.

19 Extract of report of interrogation no. 204, Karl Ritter, August 28, 1943.

20 "Bericht über den Sondereinsatz für 'Holzauge'," June 18, 1943. "Holzauge. Ostgrönland 1942–1943." Selinger archive.

21 Transcript of message in Selinger archive, 42.

22 Account of "Holzauge" operation, written by Sensse on October 10, 1986. "Holzauge. Ostgrönland 1942–1943." Selinger archive.

23 Preliminary investigation of Ritter by German Navy, August 20, 1943, 8.

24 "Bericht über den Sondereinsatz."

25 Interview with Jensen, March 1, 2001.

26 Poulsen, "Report of Events," 8.

27 "Bericht über den Sondereinsatz."

28 Preliminary investigation of Ritter by German Navy, August 20, 1943, 9.

29 Poulsen, "Report of Events," 8.

30 Interview with Jensen, March 1, 2001.

31 Extract of report of interrogation no. 204, Karl Ritter, August 28, 1943, 10.

32 Interview with Jensen, March 1, 2001.

33 Transcript of telegram from *Marinewetterdienst* (Naval Weather Service) to Group North, May 12, 1943, in Selinger archive.

34 Letter from Sensse to Selinger, August 1, 1985, Selinger archive

35 Letter from Novotny to Kurt Olsen, August 16, 1967.

36 Letter from Sensse to Selinger, August 1, 1985, Selinger archive.

37 Ibid.

38 F. H. Hinsley, *British Intelligence in the Second World War: Its Influence on Operations*, vol. 3, part 1 (London: Her Majesty's Stationery Office, 1984), 527.

39 Balchen, *Come North*, 247.

40 Balchen, *War Below Zero*, 28; Glines, *Balchen*, 163.

41 Balchen, *War Below Zero*, 28.

42 Ibid., 30.

43 Ibid., 31.

44 Ibid.

45 Weiss, *Das arktische Jahr*, 152, 157.

46 Scherer diary, May 25, 1943.

47 Letter from Sensse to Selinger, August 1, 1985, Selinger archive.

48 Ibid.

49 "Bericht über den Sondereinsatz"; Weiss, *Das arktische Jahr*, 159–160.

50 Ibid.

51 Ibid.

52 Weiss, *Das arktische Jahr*, 160.

53 "Bericht über den Sondereinsatz."

54 Ibid.

55 Ibid.

56 Weiss, *Das arktische Jahr*, 161.

57 *The Coast Guard at War: The Greenland Patrol* (US Coast Guard Headquarters, 1945), 178.

58 Ibid.

59 Ibid., 172.

60 Ib Poulsen to Selinger, May 17, 1985. Selinger archive.

61 Letter from Sensse to Selinger, August 15, 1985, Selinger archive.

62 Extract of report of interrogation no. 204, Karl Ritter, August 28, 1943, 10.

Chapter 16: Crossroads

1 Dathan, *Reindeer Botanist*, 477–478.

2 Dunbar, *Essays from a Life*, 72.

3   *The Coast Guard at War: Transports and Escorts*, vol. 5, part 1, *Escorts* (Washington, DC: US Coast Guard Headquarters, 1949), 67.

4   "2 Tell of Cutter Sinking," *The New York Times*, June 20, 1943: 27.

5   "U.S. Cutter Sinking Revealed by Navy," *The New York Times*, June 19, 1943: 5; "2 Tell."

6   The account of the sinking of *Dorchester* is based on Clay Blair, *Hitler's U-boat War: The Hunted, 1942–1945* (New York NY: Random House, 1996), 179–180, and Samuel Eliot Morison, *History of United States Naval Operations in World War II, vol. 1, The Battle of the Atlantic September 1939—May 1943* (Boston MA: Little, Brown and Company, 1947), 331–334.

7   Affidavit sent to the US Army by Nace F. Darnell, reproduced in Dan Kurzman, *No Greater Glory: The Four Immortal Chaplains and the Sinking of the* Dorchester *in World War II* (New York NY: Random House, 2004), 223.

8   Affidavit sent to the US Army by Anthony J. Povlak, reproduced in Kurzman, *No Greater Glory*, 222.

9   Affidavit sent to the US Army by James A. Ward, reproduced in Kurzman, *No Greater Glory*, 223.

10   Paul E. Ancker, "Narsarsuaq Air Base (B.W.-1), 1941–1958," *Tidsskriftet Grønland*, vol. 41 no. 4–5 (August 1993): 175–176.

11   S. W. Roskill, *The War at Sea, vol. 2: The Period of Balance* (London: Her Majesty's Stationery Office, 1956), 207.

12   Marc Milner, *North Atlantic Run: The Royal Canadian Navy and the Battle for the Convoys* (Toronto: University of Toronto Press 1985), 235; Marc Milner, "The Atlantic War," in *The Cambridge History of the Second World War*, vol. 1, *Fighting the War*, ed. John Ferris and Evan Mawdsley (Cambridge: Cambridge University Press, 2015), 480.

13   *The Papers of George Catlett Marshall*, vol. 3, 649–650.

14   *The Coast Guard at War: Transports and Escorts*, vol. V, part 1, *Escorts* (Washington, DC: US Coast Guard Headquarters, 1949), 87.

15   Quoted from William H. Thiesen, "The Long Blue Line: 80 years ago— *Escanaba* saves hundreds of lives and then perishes," United States Coast Guard, accessed March 8, 2024, https://www.mycg.uscg.mil/News/Article/3436978/the-long-blue-line-80-years-ago-escanaba-saves-hundreds-of-lives-and-then-peris/

16   Thiesen, "The Long Blue Line."

17   *The Coast Guard at War: Greenland Patrol* (US Coast Guard Headquarters, 1945), 86.

18   Dagbok for Myggbukta fangststasjon N.Ø. Grønland: begynt den 1 august 1939 ført av Johan Johansen [Diary for Mosquito Bay Trapper Station, Northeast Greenland, Commenced on August 1939 by Johan Johansen], Norwegian Polar Institute.

19   Johan Johansen, "Med amerikanske soldater på Grønlands innlandsis" ["With American Soldiers on Greenland's Ice Cap"], in *Polarboken 1949: Liv og virke ved polene* [*The Polar Book 1949: Life and Work at the Poles*], ed. Søren Richter (Oslo: Norsk Polarklubb, 1949), 53–54.

20   Wallace Hansen, *Greenland's Icy Fury* (College Station, TX: Texas A&M University Press, 1994), 130.

21   Johansen, "Med amerikanske soldater," 53.

22   Carlson, *Lifelines*, 69.

23   Ibid., *Lifelines*, 91.

24   Ibid., 72.

25   Ibid., 101.

26   Glines, *Bernt Balchen*, 151.

27   Laura Relyea, "No Man Left Behind: The Recovery of Glacier Girl," *Medium*, September 28, 2015.

28   Balchen, *Come North*, 246.

29 "1943: Coast Guard Patrol Squadron VP-6CG Established," United State Coast Guard Aviation History.

30 Carlson, *Lifelines*, 70.

31 Ibid., 70–71

32 "Forlovelse" ["Engagement"], *Grønlandsposten*, no. 22 (November 16, 1943): 259.

33 Agerschou to Vibe (undated). Grønlands Styrelse 0030. 1942–1945. Grønlands radio og Grønlandsposten, redaktionelle papirer.

34 This was at least the case up until the end of 1944. "Begivenheder i Grønland under de første Krigsaar" ["Events in Greenland During the Early War Years," *Grønlandsposten* no. 25 (December 24, 1944): 303.

35 John B. Ocheltree, "Godthaab, Greenland," *The American Foreign Service Journal*, vol. 20, no. 9 (September 1943), 458.

36 "Greenlanders Send Musk-Ox to President," *The New York Times*, February 25, 1943: 23.

37 Agerschou to Vibe (undated). Grønlands Styrelse 0030. 1942–1945. Grønlands radio og Grønlandsposten, redaktionelle papirer.

38 Agerschou to Vibe (undated). Grønlands Styrelse 0030. 1942–1945. Grønlands radio og Grønlandsposten, redaktionelle papirer.

39 "Eske Brun og det moderne Grønlands tilblivelse," 100.

40 Quoted in Heinrich, *Eske Brun*, 127.

41 Quoted in Heinrich, *Eske Brun*, 127.

42 Smedal, *Patriotisme*, 75–76.

43 Ibid., 77.

44 Ibid., 47–48.

45 Ibid., 43.

46 Report by SS-*Obersturmführer* Georg Wolff on the situation in Norway in 1941 and early 1942, Stein Ugelvik Larsen, Beatrice Sandberg and Volker Dahm, *Meldungen aus Norwegen 1940–1945: Die geheimen Lageberichte des Befehlshabers der Sicherheitspolizei und des SD in Norwegen* [*Intelligence from Norway 1940–1945: The Secret Reports from the Commander of the Security Police and Security Service in Norway*], vol. 2, (Munich: Oldenbourg Wissenschaftsverlag, 2008), 568.

47 Lohne, "Grønlandssaken," 109–110; Stordalmo, "Grønlandssaken," 59–60.

48 Stordalmo, "Grønlandssaken," 61–62.

49 Smedal, *Patriotisme*, 59.

50 Ibid., 61.

51 Ibid., 70.

52 Ibid., 71.

53 Ibid., 85–86.

Chapter 17: "Bassgeiger"

1 Franz Fliri, "In memoriam em. O. Univ.-Prof. Dr. phil. Heinrich Schatz (1901–1982)," *Berichte des naturwissenschaftlichen-medizinischen Vereins in Innsbruck*, vol. 70 (October 1983): 291.

2 Janusz Piekalkiewicz, *Secret Agents, Spies & Saboteurs* (London: David & Charles, 1974), 480.

3 Selinger, *Von 'Nanok,'* 151.

4 Ibid., 153.

5 Piekalkiewicz, *Secret Agents*, 480.

6 *Kriegstagebuch der Seekriegsleitung 1939–1945* [*War Diary of the Naval Command 1939–1945*], Part A, vol. 47 (Herford and Bonn: Verlag E. S. Mittler & Sohn, 1994), 63 and 339–340.

7   Günter Triloff, "Unternehmen Bassgeiger" ["Operation Bassgeiger"], unpublished manuscript, Selinger archive, 1–2.
8   Triloff, "Unternehmen Bassgeiger," 1–3.
9   Heinrich Schatz, "Das Unternehmen 'Bassgeiger,' Vortrag beim Treffen des MWD im Flottenkommando in Glücksburg am 3. Mai 1977" ["Operation 'Bassgeiger,' Presentation at Meeting of Naval Weather Service at Naval Command in Glücksburg on May 3, 1977"]. Selinger archive.
10   Selinger, Von 'Nanok,' 203; Triloff, "Unternehmen Bassgeiger," 4–1.
11   Triloff, "Unternehmen Bassgeiger," 1–1.
12   Johann Zima, "Rekonstruktion des Tagebuches von Johann Zima aus der Zeit seiner Einsätze im hohen Norden bei den Unternehmen Knospe und Bassgeiger in den Jahren 1942 bis 1944" ["Reconstruction of Johann Zima's diary from the period of his deployment in the far North with the operations Knospe and Bassgeiger"], 53. Selinger archive.
13   "Unternehmen 'Bassgeiger,' Ostgrönland 1943/44," Selinger archive.
14   Selinger, Von 'Nanok,' 204.
15   Ibid., 204.
16   Adolf Mlodoch, "BV 222 der E-Stelle fliegt nach Grönland (Unternehmen 'Bassgeige')" ["BV-222 of the test area flies to Greenland (Operation Bassgeige)"], 8–14. Selinger archive; Selinger, Von 'Nanok,' 205.
17   Zima, "Rekonstruktion," 108.
18   Selinger, Von 'Nanok,' 207.
19   Blyth, "German Meterological Activities," 209.
20   Quoted from Blyth, "German Meterological Activities," 210.
21   Zima, "Rekonstruktion," 57.
22   Ibid., 147.
23   Brun, Grønlandsliv, 99.
24   Brun, "Nordøstgrønlands," 134.
25   Peter Nielsen, "Der konstateres ny tysk aktivitet paa Shannon-øen" ["New German Activity Is Discovered On Shannon Island"], Grønlandsposten, December 31, 1945, 297.
26   Olsen, Et hundeliv, 86.
27   Carlos Ziebell, "Nye rekognosceringer til Kap Sussi i februar 1944 ["Renewed reconnaissance of Cape Sussi in February 1944], Grønlandsposten, December 31, 1945: 297–298.
28   Zima, "Rekonstruktion," 171–172.
29   Triloff, "Unternehmen Bassgeiger," 13–3.
30   N. O. Jensen, "Aktionen mod Kap Sussie, april 1944" ["The Operation Against Cape Sussi, April 1944"], Grønlandsposten, December 31, 1945: 298–301.
31   Jensen, "Aktionen," 300.
32   Ibid., 300–301.
33   Zima, "Rekonstruktion," 187.
34   Triloff, "Unternehmen Bassgeiger," 23–1.
35   Jensen, "Aktionen," 300–301; Eugen Müller diary, April 22, 1944. Selinger archive.
36   Kurt Koos, "Eine Erinnerung," 93–94. Selinger archive.
37   Selinger, 246–247.
38   Olsen, Hundeliv, 141.
39   Koos, "Erinnerung," 96.
40   Selinger, Von 'Nanok,' 247.
41   Zima, "Rekonstruktion," 127.
42   Kurt Koos, "Eine Erinnerung," 109.

43 Zima, "Rekonstruktion," 198.

44 Selinger, *Von 'Nanok,'* 249.

45 Ibid.

46 Koos, "Erinnerung," 113.

Chapter 18: "Meteorology's Finest Hour"

1 Karl R. Johannessen, "Sverre Pettersen 1898–1974," *Bulletin of the American Meteorological Society*, vol. 56, no. 8 (August 1975): 893.

2 Winston S. Churchill, *The Second World War*, vol. 6, *Triumph and Tragedy* (New York NY: Houghton Mifflin, 1953), 18.

3 Robert C. Bundgaard, "Forecasts Leading to the Postponement of D-Day," in *Some Meteorological Aspects of the D-Day Invasion of Europe 6 June 1944*, eds. Roger H. Shaw and William Innes (Massachusetts MA: American Meteorological Society, 1984), 20.

4 James Martin Stagg, *Forecast for Overlord, June 6, 1944* (New York NY: W. W. Norton & Co., 1971), 51.

5 Irving P. Krick, "Role of Caltech Meteorology in the D-Day Forecast," in *Some Meteorological Aspects of the D-Day Invasion of Europe 6 June 1944*, eds. Roger H. Shaw and William Innes (Massachusetts MA: American Meteorological Society, 1984), 26.

6 "Letters from Participants in D-Day Forecasts," in *Some Meteorological Aspects of the D-Day Invasion of Europe 6 June 1944*, eds. Roger H. Shaw and William Innes (Massachusetts MA: American Meteorological Society, 1984), 94.

7 Selinger, *Von 'Nanok,'* 267–269.

8 Hans-Jürgen Alleweldt, "Bericht über die Unternehmung 'Edelweiss I'" ["Account of Operation 'Edelweiss I'"], Selinger archive, 2.

9 Weiss, "Bericht," 32.

10 Alleweldt, "Bericht," 2.

11 *U-703* war diary, August 30, 1944. Selinger archive.

12 *U-703* war diary, September 1, 1944. Selinger archive.

13 Ibid.

14 Alleweldt, "Bericht," 3.

15 *The Coast Guard at War: Greenland Patrol*, 182.

16 Alleweldt, "Bericht," 3.

17 *U-703* war diary, September 1, 1944. Selinger archive.

18 Alleweldt, "Bericht," 3–4.

19 Ibid., 4.

20 Ibid.

21 *The Coast Guard at War: Greenland Patrol*, 184.

22 Ibid.

23 Wilhelm Gockel, "Gockels Bericht über die Expeditionen von Weiss und Schmid" ["Gockel's Account of Weiss' and Schmid's Expeditions"], Selinger archive, 1.

24 Weiss, "Bericht," 32.

25 Untitled manuscript about "Edelweiss II" in Selinger archive, 30.

26 Selinger, *Von 'Nanok,'* 275.

27 Ibid., 277.

28 Letter from Karl Schmid to Franz Nusser, November 21, 1946. Seliger archive.

29 Letter from Schmid to Nusser, November 21, 1946.

30 Untitled manuscript about "Edelweiss II" in Selinger archive, 61.

31　Letter from Schmid to Nusser, November 21, 1946.

32　Blyth, "German Meteorological Activities," 216–218.

33　Letter from Schmid to Nusser, November 21, 1946.

34　Charles W. Thomas, *Ice Is Where You Find It*, (Indianapolis IN: Bobbs-Merrill Company, 1951), 179.

35　Letter from Schmid to Nusser, November 21, 1946.

36　*The Coast Guard at War: Greenland Patrol*, 196.

37　A German submarine, *U-505*, was also captured by the US Navy off the coast of Africa in June 1944.

38　*The Coast Guard at War: Greenland Patrol*, 194.

39　Letter from Karl Schmid to Franz Nusser, November 21, 1946. Seliger archive.

40　Stephen Bach, *Marlene Dietrich: Life and Legend* (Minneapolis MN: University of Minnesota Press, 2011), 290; Alexander Walker, *Dietrich* (New York NY: Harper & Row, 1984), 163.

41　Bach, *Marlene Dietrich*, 290 and 295.

42　Paul E. Ancker, "Narsarsuaq Air Base (B.W.-1), 1941–1958," *Tidsskriftet Grønland*, vol. 41 no. 4–5 (August 1993): 185.

43　Walker, *Dietrich*, 163.

44　Arthur Daley, "Letter From Greenland," *The New York Times*, December 21, 1944: 24.

45　Eske Brun to the Danish mission, August 29, 1944, quoted from Heinrich, "Eske Brun," 127.

46　Quoted from Horni, "British and U.S. post-neutrality policy," 275.

47　"Vaadeskud" ["Accidental Discharge"], *Grønlandsposten*, October 1, 1944: 221–222.

48　Ejnar Mikkelsen, *Svundne Tider*, 209–214; Ejnar Mikkelsen, "Østgrønlandskolonierne" ["The Colonies of East Greenland"], *Det Grønlandske Selskabs Aarsskrift* (1946): 160.

Chapter 19: The End

1　Albert Speer, *Erinnerungen* [*Memoirs*] (Frankfurt am Main: Verlag Ullstein, 1969), 496.

2　P. W. Stahl, *Geheimgeschwader* [*Secret Wing KG 200*] (Stuttgart: Motorbuch Verlag, 1984), 259.

3　Blyth, "German Meteorological Activities," 218; Selinger, *Von 'Nanok,'* 344–345.

4　Gerhard Schreiber, "Zur Kontinuität des Groß- und Weltmachtstrebens der deutschen Marineführung (Dokumentation)" ["On Continuity in the German Naval Command's Quest for Great and Global Power (Documentation)"], *Militärgeschichtliche Mitteilungen*, vol. 26 (1979): 149.

5　Saalwächter writes, among other things, that Germany must possess a numerically strong naval force "at the outbreak of war," strengthening the argument that he is either thinking counter-factually about what might have been, or about what might happen in a future war. Schreiber, "Zur Kontinuität," 151.

6　Ibid.

7　Ibid.

8　Gam, *Een gang*, 148–149.

9　"Godthaab i festens tegn" ["Festivities in Godthaab"], *Grønlandsposten*, May 16, 1945: 111.

10　"Danmark befriet: De tyske Tropper kapitulerer betingelsesløst" ["Denmark Liberated: German Troops Surrender Unconditionally"], *Grønlandsposten*, May 16, 1945: 110.

11　"Sejrens dag—krigen i Europa endt" ["V-Day—War in Europe is Over"], *Grønlandsposten*, May 16, 1945: 115.

12　"Godthaab i festens tegn," *Grønlandsposten*, May 16, 1945: 111.

13 Eske Brun, "Grønland under den anden verdenskrig" ["Greenland during World War Two"] in *Grønlandsbogen* [*The Greenland Book*], ed. Kaj Birket-Smith, Ernst Mentze and M. Friis Møller (Copenhagen: J. H. Schultz Forlag, 1950), 306.

14 Jørgen Fleischer, "Grønland under krigen," *Sermitsiak*, no. 19 (2005): 22.

15 Agerschou to Vibe (undated). Grønlands Styrelse 0030. 1942–1945. Grønlands radio og Grønlandsposten, redaktionelle papirer.

16 Dathan, *Reindeer Botanist*, 536.

17 Account by Knud Oldendow, December 13, 1961. Finn Løkkegaard papers, Håndskriftssamlingen, Danish National Archives.

18 Ejnar Mikkelsen, *Svundne*, 197.

19 Jane McBaine, "Post Profile—James Penfield," *American Foreign Service Journal*, vol. 20, no. 3 (March 1943): 147.

20 Philip E. Mosely, "Iceland and Greenland: An American Problem," in *Foreign Affairs*, vol. 18, no. 4 (July 1940): 746.

21 Vibe, *Ene ligger Grønland*, 10.

Postscript

1 Keenleyside, *Memoirs*, vol. 2, 191.

2 Not until December 1943 did the German naval command allow "Bassgeiger" to transmit regular reports to Tromsø. See Selinger, *Von 'Nanok,'* 207.

3 Berle and Jacobs (eds.), *Navigating the Rapids*, 331.

Bibliography

Abbazia, Patrick. *Mr. Roosevelt's Navy: The Private War of the U.S. Atlantic Fleet, 1939–1942*. Annapolis MD: Naval Institute Press, 1975.

Abel, James F. and Norman J. Bond. *Literacy in the Several Countries of the World*. Washington DC: United States Government Printing Office, 1929.

Ancker, Paul E. "Narsarsuaq Air Base (B.W.-1), 1941–1958." *Tidsskriftet Grønland*, vol. 41 no. 4–5 (August 1993): 125–252.

Bach, Stephen. *Marlene Dietrich: Life and Legend*. Minneapolis MN: University of Minnesota Press, 2011.

Baime, Albert J. *The Arsenal of Democracy: FDR, Detroit, and an Epic Quest to Arm an America at War*. Boston MA and New York NY: Houghton Mifflin Harcourt, 2014.

Balchen, Bernt. *War Below Zero: The Battle for Greenland*. London: George Allen & Unwin, 1945.

Balchen, Bernt. *Come North With Me*. London: Hodder and Stoughton, 1958.

Barlow, L. K., J. P. Sadler, A. E. J. Ogilvie, P. C. Buckland, T. Amorosi, J. H. Ingimundarson, P. Skidmore, A. J. Dugmore and T. H. McGovern. "Interdisciplinary investigations of the end of the Norse Western Settlement in Greenland," *The Holocene*, vol. 7, no. 4 (December 1997): 375–505.

Barr, Susan. *Norway—A Consistent Polar Nation? Analysis of an image seen through the history of the Norwegian Polar Institute*. Oslo: Kolofon, 2003.

Barr, William. "Gyrfalcons to Germany: Herdemerten's expedition to west Greenland, 1938." *Polar Record*, vol. 48, no. 2 (April 2012): 113–122.

Baumann, Gerhard Heinz. "Grönland-Flug von Gronau 1931" ["Gronau's Greenland Flight in 1931"]. *Aus dem Archiv der deutschen Seewarte*, vol. 52, no. 4 (1933): 33–48.

Becker, Richard. "Das Flugklima Grönlands" ["Flying Weather in Greenland"]. *Aus dem Archiv der deutschen Seewarte*, vol. 52, no. 4 (1933): 3–32.

Berle, Beatrice Bishop and Travis Beal Jacobs (eds.). *Navigating the Rapids 1918–1971: From the Papers of Adolf A. Berle*. New York NY: Harcourt Brace Jovanovich, 1973.

Blair, Clay. *Hitler's U-boat War: The Hunted, 1942–1945*. New York NY: Random House, 1996.

Blom, Ida. *Kampen om Erik Raudes Land [The Struggle for Erik the Red's Land]*. Oslo: Gyldendal Norsk Forlag, 1973.

Blyth, J. D. M. "German Meteorological Activities in the Arctic, 1940–45." *Polar Record*, vol. 6, no. 42 (July 1951): 185–226.

Bobé, Louis (ed.). *Diplomatarium Groenlandicum 1492–1814*. Copenhagen: C. A. Reitzels Forlag, 1936.

Bobé, Louis (ed.). *Peder Olsen Walløes Dagbøger fra hans Rejser i Grønland [Peder Olsen Walløe's Diaries From His Travels in Greenland]*. Copenhagen: G. E. C. Gad, 1927.

Brandt, Troels. *Dagbog fra Grønland 1938–1945 [Diary from Greenland 1938–1945]*. Nuuk: Forlaget Atuagkat, 1999.

Brun, Eske. "Grønland under den anden verdenskrig" ["Greenland during World War II"]. In *Grønlandsbogen [The Greenland Book]*, edited by Kaj Birket-Smith, Ernst Mentze and M. Friis Møller, 305–318. Copenhagen: J. H. Schultz Forlag, 1950.

Brun, Eske. *Mit Grønlandsliv [My Life in Greenland]*. Copenhagen: Gyldendal, 1985.

Bundgaard, Robert C. "Forecasts Leading to the Postponement of D-Day." In *Some Meteorological Aspects of the D-Day Invasion of Europe 6 June 1944*, edited by Roger H. Shaw and William Innes, 13–22 (Massachusetts MA: American Meteorological Society, 1984.

Burchardt, Lothar. *Amerikas langer Arm: Kontroversen um die Nutzung von Grönland in Zweiten Weltkrieg [America's Long Arm: Controversies over the Exploitation of Greenland in World War Two]*. Frankfurt am Main: Peter Lang, 2017.

Burkert, Paul. *Weisser Kampf [White Struggle]*. Berlin: Gustav Weise Verlag, 1938.

Bykofsky, Joseph and Harold Larsen. *The Transportation Corps: Operations Overseas [United States Army in World War II: The Technical Services]*. Washington DC: US Government Printing Office, 1957.

Carlson, William S. *Lifelines Through the Arctic*. New York NY: Duell, Sloan and Pearce, 1962.

Carter, John D. "The Early Development of Air Transport and Ferrying," in *The Army Air Forces in World War II*, vol. 1, *Plans and Early Operations: January 1939 to August 1942*, edited by Wesley Frank Craven and James Lea Cate, 310–265. Chicago IL: University of Chicago Press, 1948.

Chemnitz, Guldborg. "Kvinden i Grønland" ["The Woman in Greenland"]. In *Kvinderne og valgretten [The Women and Suffrage]*, edited by Ellen Strange Petersen, 265–275. Copenhagen: Schultz, 1965.

Chester, Edward W. *The United States and Six Atlantic Outposts: The Military and Economic Considerations*. Port Washington NY: Kennikat Press, 1980.

Christensen, Claus Bundgård, Joachim Lund, Niels Wium Olesen and Jakob Sørensen. *Danmark besat: Krig og hverdag [Denmark During the Occupation: War and Everyday Life]*. Copenhagen: Informations Forlag, 2015.

Churchill, Winston S. *The Second World War*, vol. 3, *The Grand Alliance*. New York NY: Houghton Mifflin, 1950.

Churchill, Winston S. *The Second World War*, vol. 6, *Triumph and Tragedy*. New York NY: Houghton Mifflin, 1953.

Clines, Carroll V. *Bernt Balchen: Polar Aviator*. Washington DC and London: Smithsonian Institution Press, 1999.

The Coast Guard at War: Greenland Patrol. US Coast Guard Headquarters, 1945.

The Coast Guard at War: Transports and Escorts, vol. 5, part 1, *Escorts*. Washington, DC: US Coast Guard Headquarters, 1949.

Congressional Record: Proceedings and Debates of the 76th Congress, Third Session, vol. 86, part 5 (April 18, 1940 to May 8, 1940). Washington DC: United States Government Printing Office, 1940.

Congressional Record: Proceedings and Debates of the 76th Congress, Third Session, vol. 86, part 7 (May 26, 1940 to June 12, 1940). Washington DC: United States Government Printing Office, 1940.

Conn, Stetson, Rose C. Engelman and Byron Fairchild. *Guarding the United States and Its Outposts [United States Army in World War II: The Western Hemisphere]*. Washington DC: Center of Military History, 1964.

Dahl, Hans Fredrik. *Vidkun Quisling: En fører for fall [Vidkun Quisling: A Leader Destined to Fall]*. Oslo: Aschehoug, 1992.

Dathan, Wendy. *The Reindeer Botanist: Alf Erling Porsild, 1901–1977*. Calgary: University of Calgary Press, 2012.

Desh, Bob. "The North-East Greenland Sledge Patrol." Foundation for Coast Guard History.

Dienel, Hans-Liudger and Martin Schiefelbusch. "German Commercial Air Transport until 1945." *Revue belge de Philologie et d'Histoire*, vol. 78, no. 3–4 (2000): 945–967.

Drivenes, Einar Arne. "Ishavsimperialisme" ["Arctic Ocean Imperialism"]. In *Norsk Polarhistorie [Norwegian Polar History]*, vol. 2, edited by Einar Arne Drivenes and Harald Dag Jølle, 175–257. Oslo: Gyldendal Norsk Forlag, 2004.

Dunbar, Max. "Grønlandsårene" ["The Years in Greenland"]. *Tidsskriftet Grønland*, vol. 40, no. 9–10 (December 1992): 267–275.

Dunbar, Max. *Essays from a Life: Scotland, Canada, Greenland, Denmark*. Montreal: McGill University Libraries, 1995.

Egede, Hans. *Det gamle Grønlands nye Perlustration eller Naturel-Historie [A New Survey or Natural History of Old Greenland]*. Copenhagen: Johan Christoph Groth, 1741.

Eirik the Red's Saga: A Translation. Translated by John Sephton. Liverpool: D. Marples & Co., 1880.

Elsässer, Christian. *Die Forschungsanstalt Graf Zeppelin 1937–1945: Ein Überblick [The Graf Zeppelin Research Institute 1937–1945: An Overview]*. Berlin: Logos Verlag, 2022.

Ernsted, Knud. "Hermann Ritter sagaen" ["The Hermann Ritter Saga"]. In *Polarboken 2011–2012 [The Polar Book 2011–2012]*, edited by Susan Barr, Ian Gjertz and Fridtjof Mehlum, 121–135. Oslo: Norsk Polarklubb, 2012.

Evenden, Matthew. "Aluminum, Commodity Chains, and the Environmental History of the Second World War." *Environmental History*, vol. 16, no. 1 (January 2011): 69–93.

Feith, Herbert. The Decline of Constitutional Democracy in Indonesia. Ithaca NY: Cornell University Press, 1962.

Fink, Troels. "Det danske gesandtskab i Washington 1940–42" ["The Danish Mission in Washington 1940–42"]. *Historie*, vol. 8, no. 3 (1970): 316–337.

Fleischer, Jørgen. *Forvandlingens år: Grønland fra koloni til landsdel [Years of Change: Greenland from Colony to Part of the Country]*. Nuuk: Atuakkiorfik, 1996.

Fliri, Franz. "In memoriam em. O. Univ.-Prof. Dr. phil. Heinrich Schatz (1901–1982)." Berichte des naturwissenschaftlichen-medizinischen Vereins in Innsbruck, vol. 70 (October 1983): 291–295.

Foreign relations of the United States. Diplomatic Papers, 1939, vol. 5: *The American Republics*. Washington DC: The United States Government Printing Office, 1957.

Foreign relations of the United States. Diplomatic Papers, 1940, vol. 2: *General and Europe*. Washington DC: Government Printing Office, 1957.

Foreign Relations of the United States. Diplomatic Papers, 1941, vol. 2, *Europe*. Washington DC: United States Government Printing Office, 1959.

Freuchen, Peter. *The Vagrant Viking: My Life and Adventures*. New York NY: Julian Messner Inc., 1953.

Gad, Finn. *Grønland under Krigen [Greenland During the War]*. Copenhagen. G. E. C. Gads Forlag, 1945.

Gad, Finn. "'La Grönlande, les Isles de Ferröe et l'Islande non comprises': A new look at the origins of the addition to Article IV of the Treaty of Kiel of 1814." *Scandinavian Journal of History*, vol. 4 (1979): 187–205.

Gad, Finn. "Tasiussaq-affæren af 1811" ["The Tasiussaq Affair of 1811"]. *Tidsskriftet Grønland*, vol. 28, no. 6 (August 1980): 175–184.

Gam, Mikael. *Een gang Grønland—altid Grønland [Greenland Stays With You]*. Copenhagen: Fremad, 1972.

Giæver, John. *Fra 'Little Norway' til Karasjok [From 'Little Norway' to Karasjok]*. Oslo: Tiden Norsk Forlag, 1975.

Grant, Shelagh D. "Why the *St. Roch*? Why the Northwest Passage? Why 1940? New Answers to Old Questions." *Arctic*, vol. 46, no. 1 (March 1993): 82–87.

Gronau, Wolfgang von. *Im Grönland-Wal: Dreimal über den Atlantik und einmal um die Welt [In the Grönland-Wal: Three Times Across the Atlantic and Once Around the World]*. Berlin: Verlag Reimar Hobbing, 1933.

Guldager, Ole. "Træk af Narsarsuaqs historie" ["Features of Narsarsuaq History"]. *Tidsskriftet Grønland*, vol. 47, no. 4–5 (August 1999): 151–171.

Gulløv, Hans Christian (ed.). *Grønlands forhistorie [The Prehistory of Greenland]*. Copenhagen: Gyldendal, 2004.

Hansen, Wallace. *Greenland's Icy Fury*. College Station, TX: Texas A&M University Press, 1994.

Hardarson, Solrun B. Jensdottir. "The 'Republic of Iceland' 1940–44: Anglo-American Attitudes and Influences." *Journal of Contemporary History*, vol. 9, no. 4 (October 1974): 27–56.

Haugan, Jørgen. *Solgudens fall: Knut Hamsun—en litterær biografi [Fall of the Sun God: Knut Hamsun, a Literary Biography]*. Oslo: Aschehoug, 2004.

Hearings Before the Committee on Naval Affairs of the House of Representatives on Sundry Legislation Affecting the Naval Establishment 1923–1924. Washington DC: Government Printing Office, 1924.

Heidbrink, Ingo. "'No One Thinks of Greenland': US-Greenland Relations and Perceptions of Greenland in the US from the Early Modern Period to the 20th Century." *American Studies in Scandinavia*, vol. 54, no. 2 (December 2022): 8–34.

Helms, Sara. "Signe Vest." In *Tasiilaq. Angmagssalik*, edited by Jørgen Fisker, 236–241. Umanak: Nordiske Landes Bogforlag, 1984.

Hennings, Poul. "Ikateq-basen under 2. verdenskrig" ["The Ikateq Base During World War Two"]. In *Tasiilaq. Angmagssalik*, edited by Jørgen Fisker, 257–258d. Umanak: Nordiske Landes Bogforlag, 1984.

Hinsley, F. H. *British Intelligence in the Second World War: Its Influence on Strategy and Operations*. London: Her Majesty's Stationery Office, 1979.

Holmes, Harry N. "National Survival through Science." *Science*, vol. 96, no. 2498 (November 13, 1942): 433–439.

Hoel, Adolf. "Norges Svalbard- og Ishavsundersøkelsers ekspedisjioner til Svalbard og Grønland under de to verdenskriger" ["The Expeditions of the Norwegian Svalbard and Arctic Ocean Survey to Svalbard and Greenland During the Two World Wars"]. In *Polarboken 1956 [The Polar Book 1956]*, edited by Helge Ingstad and Søren Richter, 178–190. Oslo: Norsk Polarklubb, 1956.

Hoidal, Oddvar K. *Quisling: A Study in Treason*. Oslo: Norwegian University Press, 1989.

Holzapfel, Rupert. "Deutsche Polarforschung 1940/45" ["German Polar Exploration 1940–1945"]. *Polarforschung*, vol 21, no. 2 (1951): 85–97.

Hudson's Bay Company History Foundation. "R. M. S. Nascopie." https://www.hbcheritage.ca/things/technology/rms-nascopie. Accessed June 19, 2024.

Hull, Cordell. *The Memoirs of Cordell Hull*. New York NY: The Macmillan Company, 1948.

Jackson, Sophie. *British Interrogation Techniques in the Second World War*. Cheltenham: The History Press, 2012.

Jansen, Henrik M. *A Critical Examination of the Written and Archaeological Sources' Evidence Concerning the Norse Settlements in Greenland*. Copenhagen: C. A. Reitzel, 1972.

Jensen, Frank Esmann. *Da fornuften sejrede. Det britiske udenrigsministeriums politik overfor Danmark under 2. Verdenskrig [When Common Sense Prevailed: The Policy of the British Foreign Office Toward Denmark During World War II]*. Copenhagen: Fremad, 1972.

Jensen, Jens Fog and Tilo Krause. *Slagmarksarkæologi i Nordøstgrønland: En arkæologisk-historisk undersøgelse af allierede og tyske vejrstationer fra Anden Verdenskrig [Battlefield Archeology in Northeast Greenland: An Archeological and Historical Investigation of Allied and German Weather Stations from World War II]*. Copenhagen: The Arctic Centre at the Ethnographic Collections, The National Museum of Denmark, 2009.

Johannessen, Karl R. "Sverre Petterssen 1898–1974." *Bulletin of the American Meteorological Society*, vol. 56, no. 8 (August 1975): 892–894.

Johansen, Johan. "Med amerikanske soldater på Grønlands innlandsis" ["With American Soldiers on Greenland's Ice Cap"]. In *Polarboken 1949: Liv og virke ved polene [The Polar Book 1949: Life and Work at the Poles]*, edited by Søren Richter, 53–57. Oslo: Norsk Polarklubb, 1949.

Jonassen, Jonas A. "Weather and Communications." In *The Army Air Forces in World War II*, vol. 7, *Services Around the World*, edited by Wesley Frank Craven and James Lea Cate, 311–374. Chicago IL: University of Chicago Press, 1958.

Karlsson, Gunnar. *The History of Iceland*. Minneapolis MN: University of Minnesota Press, 2000.

Keenleyside, Hugh L. *Memoirs of Hugh L. Keenleyside*, vol. 2: *On the Bridge of Time*. Toronto: McClelland and Stewart, 1982.

Kjær, Kjell-G. and Magnus Sefland, "The Arctic ship *Veslekari*." *Polar Record*, vol. 41, no. 1 (2005): 57–65.

Kjærgaard, Thorkild. "Freden i Kiel, Grønland og Nordatlanten 1814–2014" ["The Peace of Kiel, Greenland and the North Atlantic 1814–2014"]. *Fund og Forskning*, vol. 54 (2015): 379–398.

Kleivan, Inge. "Grønlandske sagn om nordboerne" ["Greenlandic Legends About the Norsemen"]. *Tidsskriftet Grønland*, vol. 30, no. 8–9 (September 1982): 314–329.

Knuth, Eigil. "Grønland under Krigen." In *De Fem Lange Aar. Danmark under Besættelsen 1940–1945 [The Five Long Years: Denmark During the Occupation 1940–1945]*. Edited by Johannes Brøndsted and Knud Gedde, 1413–1435. Copenhagen: Gyldendalske Boghandel, 1945.

Knutsen, Willie and Will C. Knutsen. *Arctic Sun on My Path: The True Story of America's Last Great Polar Explorer*. Guilford CT: The Lyons Press, 2005.

Kornfeld, Phoebe. *Passionate Publishers: The Founders of the Black Star Photo Agency*. Bloomington IN: Archway Publishing, 2021.

Krause, Tilo. "Tyskernes Grønlandsplaner under 2. Verdenskrig" ["German Plans for Greenland during World War Two"]. *Tidsskriftet Grønland*, vol. 55, no. 5–6 (December 2007): 200–210.

Krick, Irving P. "Role of Caltech Meteorology in the D-Day Forecast." In *Some Meteorological Aspects of the D-Day Invasion of Europe 6 June 1944*, edited by Roger H. Shaw and William Innes, 24–26 (Massachusetts MA: American Meteorological Society, 1984.

Kriegstagebuch der Seekriegsleitung 1939–1945 [War Diary of the Naval Command 1939–1945], Part A. Herford and Bonn: Verlag E. S. Mittler & Sohn, 1988—.

Kurzman, Dan. *No Greater Glory: The Four Immortal Chaplains and the Sinking of the Dorchester in World War II*. New York NY: Random House, 2004.

Langer, William L. and S. Everett Gleason. *The Challenge to Isolation: The World Crisis of 1937–1940 and American Foreign Policy*. New York NY: Harper & Row, 1952.

Langer, William L. and S. Everett Gleason. *The Undeclared War 1940–1941*. New York NY: Harper & Brothers, 1953.

Larsen, Stein Ugelvik, Beatrice Sandberg and Volker Dahm. *Meldungen aus Norwegen 1940–1945: Die geheimen Lageberichte des Befehlshabers der Sicherheitspolizei und des SD in Norwegen [Intelligence from Norway 1940–1945: The Secret Reports from the Commander of the Security Police and Security Service in Norway]*, vol. 1–2. Munich: Oldenbourg Wissenschaftsverlag, 2008.

Larsen, Troels Riis. "Grønland på vej—adskilt fra Danmark 1940–1945" ["Greenland on its Way: Separated from Denmark 1940–1945"]. In *Tro og samfund i Grønland i 300-året for Hans Egedes ankomst [Faith and Society in Greenland at the 300th Anniversary of Hans Egede's Arrival]*, edited by Aage Rydstrøm-Poulsen, Gitte Adler Reimer and Annemette Nyborg Lauritsen, 301–314. Aarhus: Aarhus Universitetsforlag, 2021.

Lash, Joseph P. *Roosevelt and Churchill 1939–1941: The Partnership That Saved the West*. New York NY: W. W. Norton & Co, 1976.

Lauridsen, John T. "'… et uhyre vindende væsen …' Nazisten som gik sine egne veje—Curt Carlis Hansen" ["'… An Extremely Likable Character …' The Nazi Who Chose His Own Path—Curt Carlis Hansen"]. In *Over stregen—under bevægelsen [Crossing the Line During the Occupation]*, edited by John T. Lauridsen, 178–209. Copenhagen: Gyldendal, 2007.

Lehmann, Ernst A. and Howard Mingos. *The Zeppelins: The Development of the Airship, with the Story of the Zeppelin Air Raids in the World War*. New York, NY: J. H. Sears & Company, 1927.

Leighton Richard M. and Robert W. Coakley. *Global Logistics and Strategy [United States Army in World War II: The War Department]*. Washington DC: US Government Printing Office, 1955.

"Letters from Participants in D-Day Forecasts." In *Some Meteorological Aspects of the D-Day Invasion of Europe 6 June 1944*, edited by Roger H. Shaw and William Innes, 93–114 (Massachusetts MA: American Meteorological Society, 1984.

Lidegaard, Bo. *I Kongens Navn [In the Name of the King]*. Copenhagen: Samleren, 1996.

Lie, Trygve. *Med England i ildlinjen 1940–42 [With England in the Firing Line 1940–42]*. Oslo: Tiden, 1956.

Lindboe, Asbjørn. *Fra de urolige trediveårene [From the Turbulent Thirties]*. Oslo: Johan Grundt Tanum Forlag, 1965.

Lynnerup, Niels. "Life and Death in Norse Greenland." In *Vikings: The North Atlantic Saga*, edited by William W. Fitzhugh and Elisabeth I. Ward, 285–294. Washington DC and London: Smithsonian Institution Press, 2000.

Løkkegaard, Finn. *Det danske gesandtskab i Washington 1940–1942 [The Danish Mission in Washington 1940–1942]*. Copenhagen: Gyldendal, 1968.

Magic Background of Pearl Harbor, The, vol. 2, Appendix. Washington DC: United States Government Printing Office, 1978.

Matthäus, Jürgen and Frank Bajohr. *The Political Diary of Alfred Rosenberg and the Onset of the Holocaust*. Lanham MD: Rowman & Littlefield Publishers 2015.

McBaine, Jane. "Post Profile—James Penfield." *American Foreign Service Journal*, vol. 20, no. 3 (March 1943): 147.

McCulloch, Tony. "Mackenzie King and the North Atlantic Triangle in the Era of Munich, 1938–1939." *London Journal of Canadian Studies*, vol. 36, no. 1 (2021): 1–23.

Mikkelsen, Ejnar. "Østgrønlandskolonierne" ["The Colonies of East Greenland"]. *Det Grønlandske Selskabs Aarsskrift* (1946): 155–167.

Mikkelsen, Ejnar. *Svundne Tider i Østgrønland: Fra Stenalder til Atomtid [Times Long Gone in Eastern Greenland: From the Stone Age to the Nuclear Age]*. Copenhagen: Gyldendal, 1960.

Mikkelsen, Peter Schmidt. *Nordøstgrønland 1908–60: Fangstmandsperioden [Northeast Greenland 1908–60: The Trapper Era]*. Copenhagen: Aschehoug, 2001.

Milner, Marc. *North Atlantic Run: The Royal Canadian Navy and the Battle for the Convoys*. Toronto: University of Toronto Press 1985.

Milner, Marc. "The Atlantic War." In *The Cambridge History of the Second World War*, vol. 1, *Fighting the War*, edited by John Ferris and Evan Mawdsley, 455–484. Cambridge: Cambridge University Press, 2015.

Morison, Samuel Eliot. *History of United States Naval Operations in World War II*, vol. 1, *The Battle of the Atlantic September 1939–May 1943*. Boston MA: Little, Brown and Company, 1947.

Morris, George Sculthorpe. *Convicts and Colonies: Thoughts on Transportation & Colonization, with Reference to the Islands and Mainland of Northern Australia*. London: Hope and Company, 1853.

Mosely, Philip E. "Iceland and Greenland: An American Problem." *Foreign Affairs*, vol. 18, no. 4 (July 1940): 742–746.

Munck, Ebbe. *Døren til den frie verden [The Door to the Free World]*. Copenhagen: Det Schønbergske Forlag, 1967.

Murray, David R. (ed.). *Documents on Canadian External Affairs*, vol. 7. Ottawa: Department of External Affairs, 1974.

Nagelstutz, Daniel. "'I dette sataniske Evangelium'" ["'In This Satanic Gospel'"]. *European Journal of Scandinavian Studies*, vol 51, no. 2 (2021): 298–318.

Norges Svaldbard- og Ishavs-Undersøkelser. *Report on the Activities of Norges Svalbard- og Ishavs-Undersøkelser 1936–1944*. Oslo: Jacob Dybwad, 1945.

Novak, Thaddeus D. *Life and Death on the Greenland Patrol*. Gainesville FL: University Press of Florida, 2005.

Næss, Harald S. (ed.), *Knut Hamsuns Brev [Knut Hamsun's Letters]*, vol. 6, *1934–1950*. Oslo: Gyldendal, 2000.

Odsbjerg, Anders. *Nordøstgrønlands slædepatrulje 1941–45 [The Northeast Greenland Sledge Patrol 1941–45]*. Copenhagen: Forlaget Komma, 1990.

Olsen, Kurt. *Et hundeliv [A Dog's Life]*. Copenhagen: Gyldendal, 1965.

Ostermann, H. "Et engelsk overfald paa et dansk etablissement i Grønland under krigen 1807–14" ["An English Attack on a Danish Establishment in Greenland During the War of 1807–14"]. *Det Grønlandske Selskabs Aarsskrift* (1931–32): 39–51.

Overbye, E. J. "Flyvning på Grønland" ["Aviation in Greenland"]. In *Grønlandsbogen [The Greenland Book]*, *vol. 2*, edited by Kaj Birket-Smith, Ernst Mentze and M. Friis Møller, 147–160. Copenhagen: J. H. Schultz Forlag, 1950.

Papers of George Catlett Marshall, vol. 2, *"We Cannot Delay," July 1, 1939–December 6, 1941*. Baltimore and London: The Johns Hopkins University Press, 1986.

Papers of George Catlett Marshall, vol. 3, *"The Right Man for the Job," December 7, 1941–May 31, 1943*. Baltimore and London: The Johns Hopkins University Press, 1991.

Papers of George Catlett Marshall, vol. 4, *"Aggressive and Determined Leadership," June 1, 1943–December 31, 1944*. Baltimore and London: The Johns Hopkins University Press, 1996.

Papers relating to the foreign relations of the United States with the address of the president to Congress December 4, 1917. Washington DC: Government Printing Office, 1926.

Papers relating to the foreign relations of the United States, 1922, vol. 2. Washington DC: Government Printing Office, 1938.

Papers relating to the foreign relations of the United States, 1929, vol. 1. Washington DC: Government Printing Office, 1943.

Papers relating to the foreign relations of the United States, Japan: 1931–1941, vol. 2. Washington DC: United States Government Printing Office, 1943.

Park, Robert W. "Stories of arctic colonization." *Science*, vol. 345, no. 6200 (August 29, 2014): 1004–1005.

Parlamentariske Kommissions Beretning [Report of the Parliament Commission]. Copenhagen: J. H. Schultz, 1945–1956.

Peary, Robert E. *Northward over the 'Great Ice'*. New York NY: Frederick A. Stokes Co., 1898.

Peirce, Benjamin Mills. *A Report on the Resources of Iceland and Greenland*. Washington DC: Government Printing Office, 1868.

Penfield, James K. "Northward Ho!" *American Foreign Service Journal*, vol. 18, no. 2 (February 1941): 65–68 and 96.

Piekalkiewicz, Janusz. *Secret Agents, Spies & Saboteurs*. London: David & Charles, 1974.

Pingel, C. "Antiquariske Efterretninger fra Grønland" ["Antiquarian Information from Greenland"]. *Annaler for Nordisk Oldkyndighed* (1838–1839): 219–261.

Pope, Maurice A. *Soldiers and Politicians*. Toronto: University of Toronto Press, 1962.

Public Papers and Addresses of Franklin D. Roosevelt, The. 1938 volume. Edited by Samuel I. Rosenman. New York NY: The Macmillan Company, 1941.

Public Papers and Addresses of Franklin D. Roosevelt, The. 1939 volume, ed. Samuel I. Rosenman. New York NY: The Macmillan Company, 1941.

Public Papers and Addresses of Franklin D. Roosevelt, The. 1940 volume, ed. Samuel I. Rosenman. New York NY: The Macmillan Company, 1941.

Raghavan, Maanasa et al. "The genetic prehistory of the New World Arctic." *Science*, vol. 345, no. 6200 (August 29, 2014): 1020.

Rasmussen, Bjarne (ed.). *Tilbageblik—2. bog: Tidligere telegrafister fortæller erindringer fra Grønland [Looking Back, vol. 2: Former Telegraphers Describe Memories from Greenland]* E-book, 2019.

Rem, Tore. *Knut Hamsun: Rejsen til Hitler [Knut Hamsun: Journey to Hitler].* Vordingborg: Vild Maskine, 2015.

Reynolds, David. "The Ultra Secret and Churchill's War Memoirs." *Intelligence and National Security,* vol. 20, no. 2 (June 2005): 209–224.

Riste, Olav. *'London-regjeringa': Norge i krigsalliansen 1940–1945 ['The London Government': Norway in the War Alliance 1940–1945],* vol. 1, *1940–1942: Prøvetid [Period of Trial].* Oslo: Det Norske Samlaget, 1973.

Riste, Olav. "Solidarity at Home and Abroad: The Norwegian Experience of World War Two." In *The Second World War as a National Experience,* edited by Sidney Aster, 91–104. Ottawa: The Canadian Committee for the History of the Second World War, 1981.

Rix, Robert W. *The Vanished Settlers of Greenland: In Search of a Legend and Its Legacy.* Cambridge: Cambridge University Press, 2023.

Robinson, Douglas H. *Giants in the Sky. A History of the Rigid Airship.* Henley-on-Thames: Foulis & Co., 1973.

Rodahl, Kåre. "Med 'Polarbjørn' til Grønland og med fallskjerm til Norge" ["With *Polarbjørnen* to Greenland and by Parachute into Norway"]. In *Polar-Årboken [The Polar Yearbook],* edited by Odd Arnesen, 52–66. Oslo: Gyldendal Norsk Forlag, 1945.

Rohwer, Jürgen. *Die U-Boot-Erfolge der Achsenmächte: 1939–1945 [U-Boat Successes of the Axis Powers, 1939–1945].* Munich: J. F. Lehmanns Verlag, 1968.

Roskill, S. W. *The War at Sea,* vol. 1, *The Defensive.* London: Her Majesty's Stationery Office, 1954.

Roskill, S. W. *The War at Sea,* vol. 2: *The Period of Balance.* London: Her Majesty's Stationery Office, 1956.

Rudi, Henry with Lars Normann Sørensen. *Isbjørnkongen [The Polar Bear King].* Oslo: Gyldendal Norsk Forlag, 1961.

Rudolph, M. "Geopolitische Überseeprobleme des dänischen Staates II" ["Geopolitical Problems for the Danish State Overseas II"]. *Zeitschrift für Geopolitik,* vol. 7, no. 5 (1930): 387–392.

Saxtorph, Sylv. M. "Sundhedsforhold" ["Health Conditions"]. In *Grønlandsbogen,* vol. 2, edited by Kaj Birket-Smith, Ernst Mentze and M. Friis Møller, 161–178. Copenhagen: J. H. Schultz Forlag, 1950.

Scheuer, Michael F. "On the Possibility that There May Be More To It Than That." *The American Review of Canadian Studies,* Vol. 12, No. 3 (Fall 1982): 72–83.

Schmider, Klaus H. *Hitler's Fatal Miscalculation Why Germany Declared War on the United States.* Cambridge: Cambridge University Press, 2021.

Schreiber, Gerhard. "Zur Kontinuität des Groß- und Weltmachtstrebens der deutschen Marineführung (Dokumentation)" ["On Continuity in the German Naval Command's Quest for Great and Global Power (Documentation)"]. *Militärgeschichtliche Mitteilungen,* vol. 26 (1979): 101–171.

Schultz, Jens Erik. *Krigen i Nordøstgrønland [The War in Northeast Greenland].* Rønde: XSirius Book, 2020.

Schwerdtfeger, Werner and Franz Selinger. *Wetterflieger in der Arktis 1940–1944 [Weather Pilot in the Arctic Region 1940–1944].* Stuttgart: Motorbuch Verlag, 1982.

Sefland, Magnus "Runne-familien frå Brandal: Nokre hendingar i krig og fred" ["The Runne Family from Brandal: Some Events in War and Peace"]. *Isflaket: Polarmagasin frå Ishavsmuseet,* vol. 23, no. 4 (2021): 4–9.

Selinger, Franz. *Von 'Nanok' bis 'Eismitte': Meteorologische Unternehmungen in der Arktis 1940–1945 [From 'Nanok' to 'Eismitte': Meteorological Undertakings in the Arctic].* Hamburg: Convent, 2001.

Skodvin, Magne (ed.). *Norge i krig: Fremmedåk og frihetskamp 1940–1945 [Norway at War: Foreign Yoke and Freedom Fight],* vol. 3, Tim Greve, *Verdenkrig [World War].* Oslo: Aschehoug, 1985.

Smedal, Gustav. *Patriotisme og Landssvik [Patriotism and Treason].* Oslo: Self-published, 1949.

Smith, Gordon. "'This was not the time for this type of 1890 imperialism': Cryolite, Control, and Canada-US Relations over Greenland, 1940." *The Northern Mariner/Le marin du nord*, vol. 31, no. 3 (Autumn 2021): 241–284.

Speer, Albert. *Erinnerungen [Memoirs]*. Frankfurt am Main: Verlag Ullstein, 1969.

Stagg, James Martin. *Forecast for Overlord, June 6, 1944*. New York NY: W. W. Norton & Co., 1971.

Stahl, P. W. *Geheimgeschwader KG 200 [Secret Wing KG 2000]*. Stuttgart: Motorbuch Verlag, 1984.

Stahr, Walter. *Seward: Lincoln's Indispensable Man*. New York NY: Simon & Schuster, 2012.

Steen, E. A. *Norges Sjøkrig 1940–1945 [Norway's War at Sea 1940–1945]*, vol. 7, *Marinens operasjoner i arktiske farvann og i Island, på Grønland, Jan Mayen og Svalbard [Naval Operations in Arctic Waters and at Iceland, Greenland, Jan Mayen and Svalbard]*. Oslo: Forsvarets krigshistoriske avdeling and Gyldendal Norsk Forlag, 1960.

Stefansson, Vilhjalmur. "The American Far North." *Foreign Affairs*, vol. 17, no. 3 (April 1939): 508–523.

Stefansson, Vilhjalmur. *Greenland*. Garden City NY: Doubleday, Doran & Co., 1942.

Sundt, Eilert (ed.). *Egedes Dagbog i Uddrag [Excerpts of Egede's Diary]*. Christiania (Oslo): P. T. Mallings Bogtrykkeri, 1860.

Svane, Aksel. "En 'uafhængig' gesandt" ["An 'Independent' Envoy"]. *Historisk tidsskrift*, 12, vol. 4, no. 3 (1970): 524–564.

Svensson, Sven. *Kristian den Andres planer på en arktisk ekspedition och deras förutsättningar [Christian II's Plans for an Arctic Expedition and Their Preconditions]*. Lund: C.W.K. Gleerup, 1960.

Thomas, Charles W. *Ice Is Where You Find It*. Indianapolis IN: Bobbs-Merrill Company, 1951.

Trial of the Major War Criminals Before the International Military Tribunal. Nuremberg 14 November 1945–1 October 1946, vol. 10, *Proceedings 25 March 1946–6 April 1946*. Nuremberg: International Military Tribunal, 1947.

Ulvensøen, Jon. *Brennpunkt Nord: Værtjenestekrigen 1940–45 [Flashpoint North: The Weather War 1940–45]*. Oslo: Forsvarsmuseet, 1991.

Vibe, Christian. *Ene ligger Grønland [Greenland Alone]*. Copenhagen: Gyldendal, 1946.

Vinding, Ole. *Grønland 1945 [Greenland 1945]*. Copenhagen: Gyldendal, 1946.

Weeks, William Earl. *The New Cambridge History of American Foreign Relations*, vol. 1: *Dimensions of the Early American Empire, 1754–1865* (Cambridge: Cambridge University Press, 2013.

Wagner, Gerhard (ed.). *Lagevorträge des Oberbefehlshabers der Kriegsmarine vor Hitler 1939–1945 [Briefings of Hitler by the Supreme Commander of the Navy, 1939–1945]*. Munich: J. F. Lehmanns Verlag, 1972.

Walker, Alexander. *Dietrich*. New York NY: Harper & Row, 1984.

Weiss, Gottfried. *Das arktische Jahr: Eine Überwinterung in Nordostgrönland [The Arctic Year: Spending the Winter in Northeast Greenland]*. Braunschweig: Georg Westermann Verlag, 1949.

West, Nigel. *Hitler's Nest of Vipers: The Rise of the Abwehr*. Barnsley: Pen and Sword Books, 2022.

Willoughby, Malcolm. *The U.S. Coast Guard in World War II*. Annapolis MD: United States Naval Institute, 1957.

Wiltse, Charles M. *The Medical Department: Medical Service in the Mediterranean and Minor Theaters [United States Army in World War II: The Technical Services]*. Washington DC: US Government Printing Office, 1965.

Wood, Edward P. *Per Ardua at Arcticum: The Royal Canadian Air Force in the Arctic and Sub-Arctic*. Antigonish: Mulroney Institute, 2007.

Unpublished sources

Berry, Dawn Alexandrea. "The North Atlantic Triangle and the Genesis and Legacy of the American Occupation of Greenland During the Second World War." PhD diss., University of Oxford, 2013.

Heinrich, Jens. "Eske Brun og det modern Grønlands tilblivelse 1932–64" ["Eske Brun and the Emergence of Modern Greenland 1932–64"]. PhD diss., University of Greenland, 2010.

Horni, Hanna i. "British and U.S. post-neutrality policy in the North Atlantic area 09.04.1940–1945: The role of Danish representatives." PhD diss., Swansea University, 2010.

Lohne, Ivar. "Grønlandssaken 1919–1945: Fra borgerlig nasjonalt samlingsmerke til nasjonalsosialistisk symbolsak" ["The Greenland Issue 1919–1945: From Conservative National Rallying Point to Symbolic Cause of National Socialism"]. Master thesis, University of Tromsø, 2000.

Peck, Caroline Patrice. "Maurice Francis Egan: Writer, Teacher, Diplomat." Master's diss., College of William & Mary, 1969.

Stordalmo, Ketil Edgar. "Grønlandssakens utvikling under den andre verdenskrig" ["The Evolution of the Greenland Issue During World War Two"]. Master thesis, University of Tromsø, 2006.

Archival sources

Bundeswehr Military History Museum, Dresden

Franz Selinger archive.

Bundesarchiv. Militärachiv, Freiburg

Archives of the Generalluftzeugmeister.

Danish National Archives

Grønlands Styrelse Hovedkontoret. 1942–1945.
Finn Løkkegaard papers, Håndskriftssamlingen.
Washington DC Diplomatic Representation. 1930–1946.

Danish National Library

Carlis Hansen papers.

Norwegian Polar Institute

Dagbok for Myggbukta fangststasjon N.Ø. Grønland: begynt den 1 august 1939 ført av Johan Johansen [Diary for Mosquito Bay Trapper Station, Northeast Greenland, Commenced on August 1939 by Johan Johansen].

Franklin D. Roosevelt Presidential Library and Museum

Press Conferences of President Franklin D. Roosevelt, 1933–1945.
Diaries of Henry Morgenthau, Jr.

United States Holocaust Memorial Museum

Alfred Rosenberg's Diary, Accession Number: 2001.62.14. RG Number: RG-71.

Foreign Affairs Oral History Collection, Association for Diplomatic Studies and Training

George L. West, oral history, interviewed by Charles Stuart Kennedy.
C. Gray Bream, oral history, interviewed by Charles Stuart Kennedy.

National Archives

General Records of the Department of State.

Library and Archives Canada

Diaries of William Lyon Mackenzie King, 1893 to 1950.

Newspapers, magazines

The American Foreign Service Journal.
Atuagagdliutit.
Berlingske Tidende.
Grønlandsposten.
Nationaltidende.
The New York Times.
Politiken.
Sermitsiak.
Der Spiegel.
United Brethren's Missionary Intelligencer.

Index

Abwehr, 60, 64, 66, 70, 98, 166, 199n6,
206n47
Africa, 3, 14, 18, 30, 75–76, 85, 109, 119,
171, 174, 219n37
Agerschou, Inge, Danish teacher, 148–149
air raid, 14, 35, 106, 115, 136, 138–141, 170
Alabama Hut, East Greenland, 159, 162
Alaska, vi, 10, 109, 171
Alcan, see Aluminum Company of Canada
Ålesund, city in Norway, 61, 64, 97–98
Alleweldt, Hans-Jürgen, German officer, 166,
168
Altona, German city, 114
aluminum, xi, 10, 25–26, 41, 88, 106–107
Aluminum Company of Canada, 25–26,
41–42, 46, 52, 54, 88, 194n2
American Civil War, 10
"Amerika-Bomber," 105
Angmagssalik, settlement in Greenland, 22, 29,
58, 108, 112, 146
Arctic Ocean, 9, 63, 173
Arke, William, member of Northeast Greenland
Sledge Patrol, 123
Arnold, Henry H., commander of US Army Air
Force, 102–103
Arnold, Milton W., American officer, 147
Aruba, 51
Atlantic Fleet, 86
Atlantic Ocean, vii, 2, 8, 10–11, 13–15, 17–18,
24, 26, 28–29, 43–44, 52, 55, 63–64, 67,
73, 75–76, 84, 86–87, 95–96, 98, 109,
114–115, 140–142, 144–145, 149, 155,
157, 165, 167, 180,
Australia, 6, 109
Austro-Hungary, 113–114, 153
aviation, xi, 11, 13–14, 16–17, 51, 57, 66, 75,
80, 93, 103, 105, 147, 166, 177, 181
Azores, 76, 171, 174, 180

Balchen, Bernt, Norwegian aviator, 102–103,
108, 138–140, 142, 147
Baldwin, Melvin A., American sailor, 143–144
Baltimore, 109
Bang-Jensen, Povl, Danish diplomat, 36
"Bassgeiger," German operation, 153–163, 166,
174, 180
Baumann, German meteorologist, 16
Becker, Richard, German officer, 140–141
Bering Straits, 2–3
Berle, Adolf A., US assistant secretary of state,
36–37, 39–40, 43, 45, 52–53, 75, 78–80,
82–83, 180
Berlin, 25, 27–28, 58–59, 71–73, 75–76, 85,
96, 105, 151–152, 154, 171
Bermuda, 24
Black Death, 4
"Black Star Publishing Co.," 75–76
Blechingberg, Einar, Danish diplomat, 75–76
Blohm & Voss BV 222 Wiking, German
airplane, 157, 162, 173
Bluie East 2 (Ikateq), 101, 108, 112, 172
Bluie West 1 (Narsarssuak), 87, 101–103,
108–110, 143, 148–149, 171
Bluie West 5 (Egedesminde), 101, 148
Bluie West 8 (Sondrestromfjord), 101–103, 108
"Bluies," US bases in Greenland, 87, 101–103,
108–110, 112, 143, 148–149, 171–172
Boehm, Hermann, German officer, 97–98, 150
Boeing B-17 Flying Fortress, American airplane,
138–139, 147
Boeing B-24 Liberator, American airplane, 25,
139–140
Book of Isaiah, 6
Borcherdt, Ulrich, German officer, 107
Bowdoin, American ship, 102
Bradley, Iacob, Norwegian intelligence
operative, 98–100

Brandt, Troels, Danish artist, 21–22, 33
Brazil, 13, 24
Bream, C. Gray, American diplomat, 108, 110
Breivik Hut, East Greenland, 127
British Navy, *see* Royal Navy
Bruce, Fraser, Aluminum Company of Canada executive, 41
Brun, Eske, Danish official, 23, 30, 33–34, 39, 54, 79–80, 87–88, 90, 93–94, 100, 103, 111, 125, 127, 129–130, 149, 158, 171, 175
Brünner, Joachim, German officer, 167, 169
Bullitt, William, US diplomat, 24
Burgess, Arthur, American soldier, 148–149
Burkert, Paul, German ethnologist and SS member, 1–2, 16, 25
Bürklen, Reinhold, German officer, 140–141
Burma, xii, 109
Buskø, Norwegian ship, 97–100, 150–151, 180
Butcher, R. W., American officer, 168–169

Cadogan, Alexander, British official, 96
Campbell, John, Lord Chief Justice, 9
Camp Crossville, Tennessee, 142
Canada, viii, xii, 2–3, 11–13, 23–24, 26, 40–47, 49–50, 52–54, 64, 75, 77–79, 81–82, 86–89, 94, 96, 103, 106, 110–111, 143, 154, 176, 179, 194n2
Cape Biot, East Greenland, 67–69
Cape Herschell, East Greenland, 124
Cape Hope, East Greenland, 137
Cape Sussi, East Greenland, 157, 159–162
Cape Wynn, East Greenland, 124–125, 127
Caribbean, 10, 12
Carlis Hansen, Curt, Danish Nazi, 59–61, 67–70
Carls, Rolf, German officer, 76–77
Carlson, William S., Arctic expert, 147
Charleston, 36
Chemnitz, Jørgen, Greenland politician, 175
China, v
Christian II, Danish king, 5
Christian X, Danish king, 175–176
Christianshaab, trading station in Greenland, 6
Churchill, Winston S., 85, 165, 203n23
Clausen, Frits, Danish Nazi leader, 27
Clavering Straits, East Greenland, 117, 123–124
Coast Guard, *see* United States Coast Guard

Coburg, German ship, 113, 154–158, 161–163
Coll, Axel, Norwegian agent for Abwehr, 64, 66
Columbus, Christopher, 3, 5
Compiègne, 55
Congress, United States, 10, 26, 39, 43, 51
Copenhagen, 5–8, 12–13, 22–23, 28, 33–34, 36–37, 42, 58–61, 63, 69, 75, 83, 151, 175–176
Corp, Oscar, Swedish engineer, 54, 110
cryolite, vi, xi–xii, 10, 25–26, 41–42, 44–45, 49, 51–52, 78, 80, 88, 106–108, 110, 143, 179
culture clash, 87–88, 149, 171–172
Cumming, Hugh, US official, 75–76, 81, 84
Curaçao, 51
Curtiss SOC-4, American airplane, 77
Curzon, Lord, British foreign secretary, 12
Czechoslovakia, 17, 114, 153, 166, 171

Dahl, Jonas, assumed name, 18
Danish Broadcasting Corporation, 176
Danish West Indies, *see* Virgin Islands
Daugaard-Jensen, Jens, Danish official, 23
Davidsen, Jehu, Greenland resident, 110, 112
Davis, Norman, head of American Red Cross, 44–45
Dead Man's Bay, East Greenland, 159–160
Dege, Wilhelm, German meteorologist, 153–154
Denmark, Danes, xi–xii, 6–10, 12–13, 18, 21–23, 25, 27–31, 33–44, 46, 49–50, 52–54, 57–61, 63–64, 66–73, 78–80, 83–85, 87–90, 94–96, 100, 107, 110–113, 121, 126, 129, 131, 133–135, 137, 145, 148–149, 151–152, 160–163, 171, 175–177
Deutsche Seewarte, German center for maritime meteorology, 61
Devold, Hallvard, Norwegian explorer, 18, 97–98, 100
Dietrich, Marlene, German-American actress, 171
Dönitz, Karl, German admiral, 133
Dorchester, American ship, 144–146
Dormer, Sir Cecil, British envoy to Norway, 95
Dornier Do 26, German airplane, 140–141
Dorset, ancient Greenland people, 2–3
Douglas C-53, American airplane, 147
Dove Bay, East Greenland, 100, 167–168
dum-dum bullets, 129–130, 162

Dunbar, Maxwell John, Canadian consul, 23, 94, 143–144, 176

Dutch East Indies, 22, 43–44, 46

Edelweiss I, German operation, 166–169, 173, 180

Edelweiss II, German operation, 169–171, 173, 180

education, 21, 30, 34–35, 79, 109, 153

Egan, Maurice Francis, US ambassador to Denmark, 12

Egede, Gerhard, vicar, 35

Egede, Hans, Norwegian vicar, 4–6, 8

Egedesminde, town in Greenland, 21, 148

Eisenhower, Dwight D., 165

Ella Island, East Greenland, 69, 78, 91, 93, 100, 135–137

Enigma, *see* Ultra

Erik the Red, *see* Thorvaldsson, Erik

"Erik the Red's Land," 18

Eskimo, *see* Inuit

Eskimoness, East Greenland, 91, 93, 100, 115, 120–121, 124–130, 133–135, 138–140, 159

Europe, vii, xi, 2–10, 13, 16–18, 21–22, 24–25, 34–39, 41–43, 51, 55, 61, 66, 69–71, 73, 75, 77, 81, 86, 90, 96, 109, 119, 141, 147, 154–155, 160, 165, 171, 173–174

Externsteine, German ship, 169–171

Falkland Islands, 9

Faroe Islands, 18, 26–27, 35, 42, 77, 95–96, 151–152

Federal Bureau of Investigation, 43, 76

Finkenstein, Ulrich Graf von, German intelligence officer, 60

Finland, 22,

Finse, town in Norway, 57, 106, 153–154

Fischer, Albrecht, Danish official, 50

Fiskeness, settlement in Greenland, 34, 175

Flohn, Hermann, German meteorologist, 165

Focke-Wulf, German aircraft manufacturer, 105, 115, 155

Focke-Wulf Fw 200 Condor, German airplane, 115, 155

Force X, 42, 44, 46–47

Foreign Affairs, 13–14

Forster, Thomas, British captain, 7–8

Fox, George L., American chaplain, 144

France, French, 7, 21, 24, 26, 29, 41–42, 44, 51, 55, 171

Frankfurt, 37

Franz Josef Land, archipelago north of Russia, 169

fraternization, viii, 110, 148, 172

Frederick IV, Danish king, 6, 9

Frederick V, Danish king, 7

Frederiksdal, settlement in Greenland, 9

Frederiksen, Erik, Greenland resident, 110

Freuchen, Peter, Danish explorer, 16

Fridtjof Nansen, Norwegian Coast Guard ship, 65–67, 69–71, 100

Friebel, Walter, German aviation engineer, 105

Furenak, Norwegian ship, 61, 63, 67–71, 91, 180

Gam, Mikael, Danish educator, 175

General Trade Company, 7

Georgi, Johannes, German explorer, 173–174

German Traffic Pilot School, 16

German Air Force, 15, 17, 57–58, 60, 84, 98, 105–106, 113, 139, 153, 155, 157, 162, 165–167, 173, 179–180

German Air Force units
5th Air Fleet, 57

German Army, 25, 34, 71, 150

German Army units
170th division, 34
198th division, 34

German Navy, xi, 26, 43, 58, 76, 97–98, 113–114, 117, 119, 123, 125, 127, 133, 138, 140, 150, 153–155, 166, 170, 174, 179

German Navy units
Naval Group Command North, 117, 123, 125, 127, 138
Seekriegsleitung H, 119

German Navy ships
Deutschland, 26
M-251, 115
Westerwald, 26

Germania Harbor, East Greenland, 120, 123, 131, 133–135

Germanialand, East Greenland, 155

Germany, Germans, xi–xii, 1, 12, 14–17, 21, 24–28, 36–38, 40–41, 43, 45, 53, 58, 72–73, 76–77, 85, 89–90, 93–97, 103, 105,

107, 113, 118–119, 126, 134, 136, 138, 140, 150, 152–155, 157, 160, 162, 166, 171, 173–175, 179–180

Gestapo, 100, 114, 134, 142

Giæver, John, Norwegian captain, 63–64, 66–67

Gockel, Wilhelm, German meteorologist, 169

Godhavn, city in Greenland, 21, 23, 33

Godthaab, Greenland capital, vii–ix, 5, 16, 23, 28–29, 35, 51–52, 54, 77–80, 83–85, 89–90, 94, 103, 108, 110, 112, 125, 130, 143, 148, 172, 175–176

Goldhöhe, German training facility, 153–154, 166

"Goldschmied," German operation, 169

Goose Bay, air base in Canada, 87, 110, 143

Göring, Hermann, commander of German air force, 15, 57, 60

Gothenburg, Swedish city, 18

Great Britain, vii, 7, 9–10, 13, 17, 21, 24, 26–27, 35, 41–44, 46–47, 54, 57, 66, 69–70, 75–76, 81, 84, 87, 95–96, 102, 106–108, 146, 174, 179–180

Great Circle Route, 14, 188n21

Great Koldewey, East Greenland, 168–169

"Greenland air gap," 145

Greenland Board, 23, 58–59, 176

Greenlanders, see Inuit

Gronau, Wolfgang von, German aviator, 16

Grønlandsposten, Greenland newspaper, 107

Grünewald, Max, German army officer, 25

GS-24, convoy, 143

Haabet, Danish ship, 4–5

Haabets Koloni, Danish colony in Greenland, 5

Haakon VII, Norwegian king, 18, 150

Hagelin, Albert Viljam, Norwegian minister, 152

Hagensen, Leif Regnar, Danish official, 90

Hague, the, 18, 28, 52, 71–73

Hague Convention, 53

Hamburg, 61, 114, 119

Hamburger Walfang-Kontor, German company, 114

Hamburgischer Correspondent, German newspaper, 18

Hamsun, Arild, Knuth Hamsun's son, 73

Hamsun, Knut, Norwegian author, 71–73, 96, 152

Hamsun, Tore, Knut Hamsun's son, 73

Hans Egede, Danish ship, 107

Hansa Bay, East Greenland, 117–121, 123, 125, 127, 130, 133–137, 139–142, 154–155, 158, 167

Hansen, Alice, Greenland resident, 148–149

Hazen, John Douglas, Canadian minister of the naval service, 11

health, 29–30, 112, 172

Hedin, Sven, Swedish explorer, 150

Heinrich Freese, German ship, 70

Hendra, H. J., Aluminum Company of Canada executive, 52, 54

Hensley, William N., US Army colonel, 14–15

Hermann, German ship, 114–115, 117–120, 133, 139–141, 150

Herschellhus, East Greenland, 138

Highland, town in upstate New York, 37

Hitler, Adolf, xi, 1, 17, 25–28, 71–73, 76, 78, 85, 89–90, 97, 113–114, 146, 150, 152, 160, 179–180

Hochstetter Forland, East Greenland, 126, 130, 135

Hoel, Adolf, Norwegian geologist, 96–98

Holmes, Harry N., American scientist, 107

Holsteinsborg, Town in Greenland, 14, 90

Holten-Møller, Hugo, Danish telegraph operator, 13

Holzapfel, Rupert, German officer, 58–59, 113, 153, 197 n7

"Holzauge," German operation, 113–114, 116, 118–119, 123, 133, 138, 140–141, 154, 158–159, 166, 173, 180

Horinouchi Kensuke, Japanese ambassador to Washington, 43

House of Representatives, 14, 39

Howarth, David, British author, viii–ix

Hull, Cordell, US secretary of state, 37–38, 43–46, 51, 55, 70–71, 82–84, 89, 95, 102–103, 172

"Hump," 147

Iceland, 2, 4, 10–11, 13–14, 17–18, 27, 38–39, 42, 52, 57, 60, 65–66, 69, 77–78, 85, 87, 95–96, 100, 109, 138–139, 142, 151, 171, 174

Independence I, ancient Greenland people, 2

Inuit, 3–5, 7–8, 25, 30, 34, 76, 111, 123, 126–128, 148, 153, 172

Ivigtut, 25–26, 41–42, 46, 49–55, 78, 80, 85–86, 88, 102, 106–108, 110, 143, 145, 179

Jakobshavn, town in Greenland, 112, 176

Jan Mayen, island in North Atlantic, 70

Japan, Japanese, xii, 43–44, 46, 103, 194–195n17, 195n26

Jensen, Marius, member of Northeast Greenland Sledge Patrol, 123–126, 130–131, 133–137

Jensen, Niels Ove, member of Northeast Greenland Sledge Patrol, 94, 160–161

Johansen, Johan, Norwegian trapper, 146

Johnston, Archibald, British poet, 9

Jonge, B. C. de, Dutch official, 22

Jonsson, Agnar Klemens, Danish diplomat, 36

Jope, Bernhard, German pilot, 84

Joyce, William ("Lord Haw-Haw"), 103

Juhl, Erik, Danish engineer, 88

Julianehaab, town in Greenland, 28, 94, 149

Julius Thomsen, Danish ship, 49, 52–54, 77, 175

Junkers Ju 290, German airplane, 105, 162

Junkers Ju 390, German airplane, 105

Kaiser, Karl, German sailor, 127, 135–136

Kampfgeschwader 200, 173

Kasper, Rudolf, German officer, 117–118, 120, 141

Kauffmann, Henrik, Danish envoy to Washington, 36–39, 44–46, 75–76, 78, 80, 82–85, 96, 102, 149

kayak, vii, 1

Keenleyside, Hugh, Canadian official, 41–42, 45, 49, 179

Keflavik, Iceland, 138–139

Kehdingen, German ship, 166–169

Kellogg, Frank B., US secretary of state, 13

Kerr, Philip, British ambassador to Washington, 43

Kiel, German port city, 8, 18, 72, 115, 150

King Oscar's Fjord, East Greenland, 66

King, Ernest J., US admiral, 86

Kirkwall, town in Orkney, 49, 52, 66

Kirkwood, Kenneth P., Canadian consul, 52, 89, 111

Kleinschmidt, Johan Conrad, 9

Knox, Frank, US secretary of navy, 93

Knudsen, Eli, member of Northeast Greenland Sledge Patrol, 126, 130–131, 133–135, 175

Knudsen, Knud, survivor of *Dorchester*, 145

Knutsen, Willie, American polar explorer, 77, 114

Koch, Fritz, German officer, 118

Koht, Halvdan, Norwegian foreign minister, 71

Konstanz, city in Germany, 169

Krause, Werner, German intelligence officer, 97–98

Kriegsmarine, *see* German Navy

Kuhn Island, East Greenland, 130

Kunak, Mikael, member of Northeast Greenland Sledge Patrol, 123

Kutdligssat, town in Greenland, 35

Labrador, 49, 78, 87, 109–110, 143

Lacey, Julius, American officer, 77

Latin America, 9, 13, 24, 75

"Laubfrosch," German operation, 166, 180

Lemos, Aage de, Danish police officer, 69–70, 91, 93

Lie, Trygve, Norwegian foreign minister, 95–96

Lindbergh, Charles, American aviator, 13

literacy, 30

Little Koldewey, East Greenland, 169–170

Little Pendulum, East Greenland, 117

Littmann, Friedrich, German sailor, 123, 127, 136, 211n6

Lockheed P-38 Lightning, American airplane, 147

Logan, R. A., Canadian officer, 103

London, 8, 12–13, 46, 49, 66, 69–71, 73, 84, 87, 95,

Lord Haw-Haw, *see* Joyce, William

Lovett, Robert A., US assistant secretary of war, 86

Lufthansa, 17

Luftwaffe, *see* German Air Force

Lund, Madz Thomsen, Danish official, 7–8

Lynge, Frederik, merchant, 35

MacDonald, G. L. W., Canadian officer, 50

MacDougall, William D., US rear admiral, 37

Mackenzie King, William Lyon, Canadian prime minister, 41–42, 44–46, 87, 194–195n7

Madelung, Georg, German aeronautical engineer, 57, 197n3

Magnusson, Magnus, US officer, 107

Marshall, George C., US Army chief of staff, 77–78, 87, 109, 138, 145

Marstrander, Carl, Norwegian professor, 18

Massey, Vincent, Canadian envoy to London, 46–47, 49

Mediterranean, 5, 14, 119, 171

Meersburg, city in Germany, 169

Messerschmitt, German aircraft manufacturer, 76, 105

Messerschmitt Me 264, German airplane, 105

meteorology, viii, xi, 16–17, 24–26, 57–58, 60–61, 65, 67–69, 77, 81–83, 91, 98, 113, 115, 119, 138, 151, 153–155, 158, 161, 165–166, 169, 173–174, 180, 188n23

MI5, 61

Milch, Erhard, German field marshal, 105–106

Mlodoch, Adolf, German pilot, 157

Moffat, Jay Pierrepont, US official, 37

Moffett, William A., American admiral, 14

Monroe, James, US president, 9

Monroe Doctrine, 9, 13, 38–40, 42–43, 46, 72–73, 82, 166

Montgomery, Bernard Law, British field marshal, 175

Moos, Siegfried, German-Jewish economist, 25

Morgenstierne, Wilhelm, Norwegian envoy to Washington, 70, 95, 150, 206n26

Morgenthau, Henry, US Treasury secretary, 39, 89, 103

Morison, Samuel Eliot, American historian, 85

Mørkefjord, East Greenland, 64

Mosely, Philip E., American political scientist, 14, 177

Mosquito Bay, East Greenland, 18, 63, 65–67, 98–100, 136–140, 146, 180

Munck, Ebbe, Danish journalist, 59–61, 68

N. B. McLean, Canadian ship, 42, 46, 49–50

Nanortalik, town in Greenland, 35

Napoleon, French emperor, 7

Napoleonic Wars, 7–8

Narvik, port city in Norway, 154–155

Nascopie, Canadian ship, 49–50, 52–55, 194n2

Nasjonal Samling, Norwegian Nazi party, 27

Nationaltidende, Danish newspaper, 85

Naval War Plans, 14

Navy Department, US, 14

Nazi ideology, party, viii, 1, 27–28, 52, 59–61, 63, 67, 69, 73, 89–90, 96–98, 100, 113–114, 118, 131, 142, 149, 172

Netherlands, Dutch, 6–7, 22, 43–44, 46, 51–52, 175

Nevada, American ship, 146

New Brunswick, 51

New Guinea, 1

New York, upstate, 37

New York City, 14–15, 39, 44, 75, 80, 88, 172

New York Giants, 171

New York Times, 79, 100

Newfoundland, 24, 51, 107, 143–144

Nielsen, Otto, Danish captain, 52

Nielsen, Peter, member of Northeast Greenland Sledge Patrol, 126, 130–131, 133–135, 137, 159

Nietzsche, Friedrich, German philosopher, 1

Noassen, Apollus, Inuit official, 34, 175

Norsemen, 3–5

North Atlantic, see Atlantic Ocean

Northeast Greenland Sledge Patrol, ix, 91–94, 99, 102, 115, 121, 123–131, 134, 136–138, 158–163, 175

Northwest Passage, 9

Norway, xii, 8, 18–19, 27–28, 33–34, 40–41, 43, 49, 57–58, 61, 63–67, 70–73, 77, 84, 93–99, 106, 115, 125, 139–141, 146, 149–152, 154–155, 163, 169–170, 174

Norwegian Arctic Seas Committee, 96, 151–152

Norwegian Coast Guard, 65, 69

Nova Scotia, 51–52

Novak, Thaddeus D., American sailor, 108, 111

Novotny, Wenzel, Czech–German sailor, 118, 127, 130, 135–136, 138, 213n45

Nusser, Franz, German meteorologist, 173–174

Oldendow, Knud Honoré, Danish official, 15–16, 58–59

Olsen, Kurt, member of Northeast Greenland Sledge Patrol, 126–130, 159

O'Malley, Raymond F., American sailor, 143–144

O'Reilly, Bernard, Irish author, 9

Orkney Islands, 49, 66, 96

Oslo, 18, 28, 57, 61, 71, 95–96, 98, 150–151
Ottawa, 41, 49, 86, 111, 143

Pacific Ocean, xii, 9–10, 12, 43–44, 46, 102, 109
Pan American Airways, 13
Pan-American Safety Zone, 24
Panama Canal, 12, 106
Panama City, 24
Panama Conference, 24, 86
Paul, apostle, 5
Paulsen, Carl Christian von, American officer, 142
PBY Catalina, American airplane, 93, 142, 148
Pearl Harbor, 24, 103, 113
Peary, Robert E., American explorer, 11–13
Penfield, James K., US consul, 50–54, 78–80, 82–83, 87–89, 94, 103, 111, 177
Pennsylvania Salt Manufacturing Company, 26, 45–46, 52
Perkins, Frances, US secretary of labor, 86
Permanent Court of International Justice, The Hague, 18, 71
Peter's Bay, East Greenland, 98–99
Petersen, Niels Oluf, Danish captain, 107
Peterson, Carl U., American officer, 143
Petterssen, Sverre, Norwegian meteorologist, 165
Philadelphia, 107, 109
Poland, 21–22, 24, 26, 34, 146
polar bears, 29, 123, 129, 134, 159, 162–163, 179, 205n61
Polar Circle, vii
Politiken, Danish newspaper, 60
Pope, Maurice, Canadian officer, 42, 46
Porsild, Alf Erling, Canadian official, 52
Pötzl, Robert, German soldier, 57
Poulsen, Ib, head of Northeast Greenland Sledge Patrol, 64, 66, 125–130, 137
Povlak, Anthony J., American sailor, 144
Power, Charles Gavan, Canadian official, 42, 46
Pritsch, Kurt, German meteorologist, 161
prostitution, 149, 171–172
psychological problems, 109–110

Qaqortok, town in Greenland, 4
Quebec, 49, 51
Quisling, Vidkun, Norwegian Nazi leader, 27–28, 73, 96–97, 151–152

Raeder, Erich, German admiral, 76
Read, J. E., Canadian official, 46
Rechlin, German test base, 105
Redfield, John, American pilot, 148
Reich Security Main Office, 166
Renthe-Fink, Cecil von, German official, 59, 85, 151
Revet, East Greenland, 130
Reykjavik, Iceland capital, 17, 65–66, 87, 142
Rhodes, Cecil, 53
Ribbentrop, Joachim von, German foreign minister, 71–73, 85, 152
Ringsel, Norwegian ship, 67, 71, 77
Rio Grande, 13
Ritter, Christiane, German author, 114
Ritter, Hermann, German officer, 113–115, 117–121, 123–125, 127–131, 133–142, 159
Robertson, Norman, Canadian official, 41
Rodebrügger, Johann, German officer, 154–155, 157, 161–163
Rogers, Edith, US Congresswoman, 39, 43, 51
Rome, 5
Roosevelt, Elliott, American officer, 108
Roosevelt, Franklin D., 14–15, 24, 37–39, 44, 51–52, 67, 70, 77, 79, 81–82, 85–87, 93, 109, 149, 175, 180
Rosenberg, Alfred, Nazi ideologue, 27
Rostock, port city in Germany, 154
Rothman, Hyman, American photographer, 142
Röttger, Hans, German officer, 120, 123, 134, 141, 211n6
Royal Air Force, 165
Royal Canadian Air Force, 103, 143
Royal Canadian Mounted Police, 42–43, 50, 53, 196n8
Royal Greenland Trading Department, 7
Royal Marines, 65–67, 70, 136
Royal Navy, 26, 43, 60, 63, 70, 107
Rudi, Henry, member of Northeast Greenland Sledge Patrol, 99–100, 102, 114, 121, 125, 127, 128–130, 134
Russia, Russian, v, xi, 9–10, 16, 22, 29, 37, 73, 85, 106, 114, 150–151, 169, 177, 179, 181

Saalwächter, Alfred, German officer, 174, 181
Sabine Island, East Greenland, 117, 120, 123–125, 133

Sachsen, see Hermann, German ship,
Saga of Erik the Red, The, 3
Sandodden, East Greenland, 130–131, 133, 135, 138, 175
Saqqaq, ancient Greenland people, 2
Sæther, Carl, British consul in Tromsø, Norway, 63
SC-121, convoy, 145
Scandinavia, 27, 36, 63, 151, 177
Schatz, Heinrich, German officer, 153–154, 156–157, 161–162
Scherer, Helmuth, German sailor, 115, 117–120, 140
Schiedermair, Rudolf, German official, 152
Schleswig-Holstein, 12, 18
Schmid, Karl, German officer, 169–171
Schmidt, Heinz, German sailor, xi–xii, 161
Schulte, Paul, German priest, 76
Schultz, Danish official, 90
Schultz, Carl Henrik, member of Northeast Greenland Sledge Patrol, 159
Schütze, Rudolf, German pilot, 84
Schutzstaffel, SS, 1, 16, 25, 166
Schwenke, Dietrich, German officer, 106
Scoresby Sound, settlement in Greenland, 58, 84, 93, 99–100, 136–137, 142, 148
Sears Roebuck, American company, 79
Selinger, Franz, German historian, viii
Sensse, Rudolf, German officer, 118, 120, 127, 130–131, 134, 136, 138, 140–142, 213n45
Seward, William H., US secretary of state, 10
Shannon Island, East Greenland, 141, 156–157, 159–160, 162, 170, 174
Shetland Islands, 96
Siberia, 2–3
Skancke, Ragnar, Norwegian official, 97
Skelton, Oscar D., Canadian official, 42, 49
Skinner, Carlton, US officer, 99–100
Skrælings (derogatory term for Inuit), 4
Sledge Patrol, *see* Northeast Greenland Sledge Patrol
Smedal, Gustav, Norwegian activist, 72–73, 96, 149–152, 201n60
Smith, Edward Hanson "Iceberg," American Coast Guard officer, 66–67, 77, 91, 94, 99, 102
Soar, Albert Henry, American soldier, 171
Sondrestrom Air Base, vii

Sondrestromfjord, 102–103
Sonora, town in the United States, 148
Sørensen, Christian, Danish sailor, 78, 88
South Carolina, 36
Soviet Union, *see* Russia,
Spaatz, Carl, American officer, 165
Spitsbergen, Norwegian-controlled island, 64, 77, 114
SS, *see Schutzstaffel*
Stagg, James Martin, British meteorologist, 165
Stahl, Peter Wilhelm, German pilot, 173
State Department, US, 10, 37–38, 43–44, 46, 50, 67, 70, 75–76, 78, 81–85, 87
Stefansson, Vilhjalmur, American explorer, 13
Stettinius, Edward, US secretary of state, 175
Stimson, Henry L., US secretary of war, 85, 93
Stockholm, 61, 69, 81, 95, 150
Stosstrupp Ella Insel, 135–138
Stumpff, Hans-Jürgen, German general, 57, 60
Sukkertoppen, town in Greenland, 28
Svalbard, Norwegian-controlled archipelago, 64, 77, 96
Svane, Aksel, Danish official, 23, 35–36, 39, 51–54, 77–80, 82–84, 88
Svenningsen, Nils, Danish official, 58
Sweden, Swedes, 8, 18, 114, 150, 152

Tasiussaq, trading station in Greenland, 7
Tau, Max, German publisher, 72
Terboven, Josef, German official, 71–72, 152
Thomas, Charles W., American officer, 170
Thomas, Edward, British intelligence officer, 60
Thorvaldsson, Erik, Icelandic Viking, 2–3, 87
Time magazine, 100
Tokyo, xii, 43–44
Torgilsbu, East Greenland, 67
Treaty of Kiel (1814), 8, 18, 72, 150
Triloff, Günter, German meteorologist, 154, 158, 160–161
Trinidad, 24
Tromsø, city in Norway, 63–64, 98, 114–115, 119, 123, 133, 157, 166, 168
Trondheim, city in Norway, 84, 115, 163
Trulove, British whaling ship, 7
Tvermose, Jørgen, Danish expedition member, 60–61, 67, 69–71

U-boats, 85, 107, 120, 143–146, 155,
167–169, 179
U-boats, individual
U-223, 144
U-355, 155
U-587, 107
U-703, 167–168
U-965, 169
Ullring, Ernst, Norwegian officer, 65–66, 69,
71
Ultra, viii, 60–61, 68, 138, 203n23
Ungertok, Norseman, 4
United Brethren's Missionary Intelligencer, The, 9
United States, vii, ix, xii, 9–15, 17, 24, 26,
28, 36, 38–40, 42–47, 50–51, 53, 57, 59,
66–67, 70–73, 75–86, 88–89, 95–96, 100,
102–103, 105–108, 110–111, 113–114,
142, 148, 150, 166, 174, 176–177, 179,
United States Air Force, vii
United States Army Air Force, 13, 77, 102,
109, 139, 147–148
United States Coast Guard, vi, 39–40, 50–51,
53–54, 66–67, 77–78, 82–83, 86, 88–91,
94, 99–100, 102, 111, 142–147, 149,
168–171
United States Coast Guard ships,
Campbell, 51–55
Cayuga, 83
Comanche, 50–54, 78, 102, 146
Duane, 77
Eastwind, 170–171
Escanaba, 143–146
Modoc, 102
Nanok, 107–108, 111
North Star, 86, 99, 102, 142, 145–146
Northland, 66–67, 77, 86, 90–91, 99, 102,
168–169
Raritan, 102, 144
Southwind, 170
Storis, 169
United States Coast Guard units,
Greenland Patrol, 102, 107, 143
Northeast Greenland Patrol (Task Force 11),
86, 91, 102
South Greenland Patrol, 102
VP-6 (air squadron), 147–148
United States Navy, 11, 14, 85–86, 93, 142
United States Navy ships,

Bear, 86, 100, 102
Chateau Thierry, 86
Munargo, 86

V-2 rocket, 174
Versailles Treaty, 16
Veslekari, Norwegian ship, 63–67, 71, 75–76,
94, 97, 136, 180, 199n6
Vest, Signe, Danish nurse, 112
Vibe, Christian, Danish biologist and journalist,
21, 34, 103, 110–111, 177
Vile, Robert C., American sailor, 146
Virgin Islands, 10, 12

Wagner, Hans, German sailor, 169
War Plans Division, 13–14
Ward, James A., American sailor, 144
Walker, Robert J., US Treasury secretary, 10
War and Peace, 110
Washington, George, 24
Washington DC, 14, 24, 26, 36–38, 44–46,
51, 53, 75, 79–81, 83–84, 86, 88, 93, 95,
138, 147, 150, 152, 172
weather, weather forecasts, *see* meteorology
Wegener, Alfred, German climatologist, 16, 58
Weiss, Gottfried, German meteorologist,
115, 117–120, 123–125, 134, 136–137,
140–141, 166–169, 171
Wenglorz, Heribert, German officer, 120,
211n52
West, George L., American diplomat, 50,
79–80, 87
Western Hemisphere, 9, 11, 13, 15, 24, 38–40,
42, 51, 59, 66, 70, 75, 86–87, 106, 108,
188n23, 194–195n17
Wikinger, German ship, 114
Wilhelmshaven, port city in Germany, 117,
123, 125
Wille, Moses, Inuit student, 172
Wolff, Georg, German officer, 151
World War I, 14, 16, 21–22, 24, 42, 57, 93,
114, 153, 174, 188n23

Yoshizawa Seijiro, Japanese ambassador to
Canada, 194–195n7

Zacher, Gerhard, German officer, 154,
158–159, 161–162

Zenith, German ship, 113
Zeppelin, ix, 14–15, 188n2 and n23
Zeppelins, individual
  L-59, 14

L-72, 14–15, 188n23
Ziebell, Carlos, member of Northeast
  Greenland Sledge Patrol, 159
Zima, Johann, German sailor, 155, 158, 162